The Way We Lived

Volume II
1865–Present

The Way We Lived

Essays and Documents
in American Social History
Seventh Edition

Frederick M. Binder
City University of New York, College of Staten Island

David M. Reimers
New York University

WADSWORTH
CENGAGE Learning·

Australia • Brazil • Japan • Korea • Mexico • Singapore • Spain • United Kingdom • United States

The Way We Lived: Essays and Documents in American Social History, Volume II: 1865–Present, Seventh Edition
Frederick M. Binder and David M. Reimers

Senior Publisher: Suzanne Jeans

Senior Sponsoring Editor: Ann West

Assistant Editor: Megan Chrisman

Editorial Assistant: Patrick Roach

Managing Media Editor: Lisa Ciccolo

Marketing Coordinator: Lorreen Towle

Marketing Communications Manager: Glenn McGibbon

Design Direction, Production Management, and Composition: PreMediaGlobal

Manufacturing Planner: Sandee Milewski

Rights Acquisition Specialist: Jennifer Meyer Dare

Cover Image: Smithsonian American Art Museum, Washington, DC/Art Resource, NY

For product information and technology assistance, contact us at **Cengage Learning Customer & Sales Support, 1-800-354-9706**

For permission to use material from this text or product, submit all requests online at **www.cengage.com/permissions**
Further permissions questions can be emailed to **permissionrequest@cengage.com**

Library of Congress Control Number: 2011942006

ISBN-13: 978-0-8400-2951-5

ISBN-10: 0-8400-2951-9

Wadsworth
20 Channel Center Street,
Boston, MA 02210
USA

Cengage Learning is a leading provider of customized learning solutions with office locations around the globe, including Singapore, the United Kingdom, Australia, Mexico, Brazil, and Japan. Locate your local office at **international.cengage.com/region**

Cengage Learning products are represented in Canada by Nelson Education, Ltd.

For your course and learning solutions, visit **www.cengage.com**

Purchase any of our products at your local college store or at our preferred online store **www.cengagebrain.com**

Instructors: Please visit **login.cengage.com** and log in to access instructor-specific resources.

Printed in the United States of America
1 2 3 4 5 6 7 16 15 14 13 12

Contents

Preface

History courses have traditionally emphasized the momentous events of our past. Wars and laws, technological advances and economic crises, ideas and ideologies, and the roles of famous heroes and infamous villains have been central to these studies. Yet what made events momentous is the impact they had on society at large, on people from all walks of life. Modern scholars' growing attention to social history is in part a recognition that knowledge of the experiences, values, and attitudes of these people is crucial to gaining an understanding of our past.

America's history as reflected in the everyday lives of its people provides the focus of these volumes. In preparing a work of selected readings, we have had to make choices about which episodes from our past to highlight. Each of those included, we believe, was significant in the shaping of our society. Every essay is followed by original documents that serve several purposes. They provide examples of the kinds of source materials used by social historians in their research; they help to illuminate and expand upon the subject dealt with in the essays; and they bring the reader into direct contact with the people of the past—people who helped shape, and people who were affected by, the "momentous events."

Our introduction to each essay and its accompanying documents is designed to set the historical scene and to call attention to particular points in the selections, raising questions for students to ponder as they read. A list of suggested readings follows after each of the major divisions of the text. We trust that these volumes will prove to be what written history at its best can be—interesting and enlightening.

We are pleased to note that favorable comments by faculty and students as well as the large number of course adoptions attest to the success of our first six editions. Quite naturally, we thus have no desire in our seventh edition to alter the basic focus, style, and organization of *The Way We Lived*. Many of those essays that our readers and we consider to have been the earlier editions' best remain intact. However, it is our belief that the new selections, reflecting recent scholarship, will identify and clarify significant issues in American social history even more effectively than those they replaced. In choosing new essays and documents for inclusion, we have sought to present a broader view of historical events and to illustrate the impact these events had on the lives of people.

Thus, in Volume I we include an essay relating the tribulations of victims of the slave trade, their capture in Africa, their forced march to the sea, and their brutal treatment aboard the slave ships carrying them to America. Another of our new essays focuses on the excitement resulting from the discovery of gold in California and the experiences of the 49ers who left their homes to seek golden fortunes. Yet another example of popular excitement is the new essay describing the religious enthusiasm of the Second Great Awakening.

In Volume II, as in Volume I, we have provided essays and documents revealing the experiences of people from a variety of American regions and walks of life. One of the essays added to this edition tells the story of a Norwegian immigrant who settled in the Midwest. Another describes the events leading up to a strike by women garment workers in Philadelphia. An idea of what was roaring about the "Roaring Twenties" can be gained by reading the new essay dealing with Prohibition, as well as the accompanying documents describing other aspects of that era. Readers will discover that, in addition to the eight new essays included in the two volumes of the seventh edition, there are a goodly number of new documents to be found in *The Way We Lived.*

We would like to thank the following reviewers for their excellent and helpful comments:

Ginette Aley, University of Southern Indiana;
John S. Baick, Western New England College;
Garna L. Christian, University of Houston—Downtown;
Michael B. Dougan, Arkansas State University;
Darryl C. Mace, Cabrini College;
Martin R. Menke, Rivier College;
Patrick D. Reagan, Tennessee Tech University;
Stephen Rockenbach, Northern Kentucky University; and
Michael Schaller, University of Arizona.

It is our hope that students will find as much pleasure in reading this new edition as we have had in creating it.

F. M. B.

D. M. R.

PART I

The Emergence of an Urban, Industrial Society, 1865–1920

Chapter 1

Reconstruction: Triumphs and Tragedies

Photri Images/Alamy

Freedmen, children as well as adults, laboring in the cotton fields of the South.

In the past, depictions of the era of Reconstruction have often portrayed the African Americans of the South as, on the one hand, recipients of assistance from federal government agencies and Northern missionary societies and, on the other hand, victims of legislative and extralegal measures to deny them their rights as citizens. Recognition that blacks themselves took an active role in shaping their own destiny has occurred relatively recently. Mark Andrew

3

Huddle's essay "To Educate a Race" tells the story of the African-American residents of the textile-manufacturing center of Fayetteville, North Carolina, and their largely successful efforts to establish elementary and secondary schools as well as teacher training institutions. What characteristics of Fayetteville's black community and its leaders were of particular significance in contributing to its successes? In what ways did the actions of both Southern and Northern whites lead Fayetteville's African Americans to look "to themselves for their own elevation?"

Although even the most tenacious Southerners recognized that slavery was finished and that the South needed a new system of labor, few white Southerners could accept the freedmen as social and political equals. From 1865 to 1866, Southern politicians established Black Codes to ensure white supremacy. Huddle's essay reveals that Fayetteville's African Americans did not passively sit back and submit to efforts by the white community to restrict their freedom and efforts at self-improvement. The first document provides evidence that such assertiveness was not limited to the North Carolina town. It is a letter from a freed slave to his former master. It speaks eloquently of the conditions and humiliations that he had endured in the past and also of the better life that he had built for himself. How would you describe the general tone of the letter?

Black Codes represented efforts to maintain white dominance through legislative acts. The onset of Radical Reconstruction brought an end to this tactic. In its place, to serve the same purpose, there arose secret societies, most notably the Ku Klux Klan, which employed terror and intimidation to achieve the goal of keeping the freedmen down. The second document is an excerpt from the initiation ritual of the Knights of the White Camelia, a secret society founded in New Orleans in 1867, and very much a clone of the Ku Klux Klan. You will note that the candidate for membership is required to take an oath "to cherish" the society's "grand principles." From your reading, what do you perceive these "principles" to have been?

Several members to Congress suggested that the newly emancipated slaves be given land to enable them to become self-sufficient, but such proposals were quickly rejected. Instead, sharecropping emerged during Reconstruction, and thus only a few freedmen succeeded in attaining the status of independent farmers. What of other opportunities? A clue to the answer may be found in the final document, written as late as forty-seven years after the Civil War's conclusion, in which a black woman describes her life as a servant and the conditions of other women of her race engaged in the same or similar occupations. Does the author's description warrant the assertion that black women servants were virtual slaves? State the reasons for your answer.

ESSAY

To Educate a Race

Mark Andrew Huddle

In 1877 Gov. Zebulon Vance urged an education reform program upon a skeptical North Carolina legislature. Central to Vance's plan was the establishment of state-funded normal schools for the training of teachers. The first normal school for the training of white teachers was to be overseen at a special summer course to be operated at the University of North Carolina at Chapel Hill. Scholars were to be trained in a variety of disciplines and indoctrinated in the latest educational theories and practices. Interestingly, at a time when only the rudiments of public instruction existed for white North Carolinians, Governor Vance also included a call for the creation of a "state colored normal school."

In consideration of the poor condition of African American education in the immediate aftermath of the Civil War and the need for state control of any such ventures, Governor Vance called on the representatives to fund not just a summer session, but a "long-term school" in which prospective black teachers might be instructed in "appropriate" educational techniques and philosophies as well as the subjects that they would teach. The act that eventually passed the legislature in 1877 set aside $2,000 for the funding of such an institution, and a special committee of the state board of education met in June of that year to act on the governor's personal recommendation that the school be located at Fayetteville, North Carolina.

The choice of Fayetteville as the site for the school was in no way random. Soon after the passage of Governor Vance's bill, the state board of education was besieged with offers from municipalities from across the state that were interested in providing a home for the first state normal school for African Americans. A meeting of the board of education on April 10, 1877, drew more than thirty African American representatives from fifteen counties. Fayetteville sent the formidable African Methodist Episcopal Zion (AMEZ) bishop James Walker Hood to that meeting, and his efforts on behalf of the town resulted in a visit to Fayetteville by Governor Vance and state superintendent of public instruction John C. Scarborough in June 1877. Both Vance and Scarborough were favorably impressed with what they saw and recommended to the board that Fayetteville serve as the site for the school.

SOURCE: "To Educate a Race," from Mark Andrew Huddle, "To Educate a Race: The Making of the First State Colored Normal School, Fayetteville, NC 1865–1877," *North Carolina Historical Review*, 74 (April, 1997): 135–160. Reprinted with permission of the North Carolina Office of Archives and History.

In actuality, historical precedent worked in Fayetteville's favor in the competition for the normal school. A sophisticated education effort in the town's black community had been under way since 1865. Noted African American educators Cicero and Robert Harris administered respectively the elementary Phillips School and the secondary Sumner School from 1866 until 1869, when the two schools were consolidated to form the Howard School. During the late 1860s, Fayetteville's African American schools owed much of their financial support to the northern-based American Missionary Association (AMA) and to the federal Freedmen's Bureau. It is distinctive that these schools were controlled by the African American community of Fayetteville, a community that had emerged from the war organized and with an agenda that emphasized the importance of education. In this tumultuous period, these blacks were able to maintain a remarkable independence of action in achieving their community goals. African American agency was the determining factor in the success of the Fayetteville experiment and its eventual designation as the State Colored Normal School....

[L]ong before the American Missionary Association (AMA) and Freedmen's Bureau began their work to establish a school among the freed people, Fayetteville had a large, organized African American community. There is significant evidence that a portion of this community was literate and that a number of free blacks actively engaged in the clandestine education of elements within the slave population. Historian John Hope Franklin has argued that among free blacks the apprenticeship system offered opportunities for the attainment of basic literacy. This desire for education certainly played a role in the urban setting of Fayetteville. From 1822 to 1824 the noted black educator and Presbyterian minister, John Chavis, whose academy in Raleigh was responsible for educating both whites and free blacks, taught at Fayetteville. There is also evidence that in 1850 a number of white elites established a short-lived day school for the training of free blacks. Finally, 1860 census data shows that approximately 11 percent of the adult (age twenty-one years and above) free black and mulatto population could read and/or write.

It is certain that a number of free blacks at Fayetteville secretly labored to teach basic reading and writing skills to slaves. When Robert Harris, a man most responsible for the success of the Howard School and the establishment of the State Colored Normal School, applied to the AMA for a teaching commission in 1864, the only experience of which he could boast was the work that he and his brother had done among the slave population at Fayetteville in the 1840s. Wrote Harris: "I have had no experience in [t]eaching except in privately teaching slaves in the south where I lived in my youth." Harris's older brother, William, also reported having taught for two years among the slaves of Fayetteville. In sum, the educational impulse was well established in Fayetteville's African American community by the end of the Civil War, when that community began a systematic effort to establish a school, train teachers, and reach out to freed people in the vicinity. All of these efforts preceded the establishment of the State Colored Normal School in 1877.

The Civil War proved particularly destructive for Fayetteville.... General Sherman and his troops occupied Fayetteville on March 11[, 1865]. On that same day, the general issued Special Field Order No. 28, which ordered the destruction of "all railroad property, all shops, factories, tanneries, &c., and all mills save one water-mill of sufficient capacity to grind meal for the people of Fayetteville." The demolition of the railroad was not limited to the town limits but was directed to take place "as far up as the lower Little River." The cavalry was also ordered to demolish the armory and everything pertaining to it. In addition to this destruction, there was considerable pillaging: livestock was seized, and Sherman's "bummers" were said to have visited every home in the city. One wealthy Fayetteville citizen reported property losses of nearly $100,000.

Fayetteville's black community was not spared in the ensuing turmoil. In October 1865, a local African American reported to newspaper correspondent John Dennett that every black home had been ransacked during Sherman's occupation. A black man seen on the streets "with a good suit of clothes, or a new pair of shoes, was halted at once and made to exchange" with a Union soldier. As a result, Dennett reported, Fayetteville's African Americans "no longer believed that every man of Northern birth must be their friends and they more clearly [looked] to themselves for their own elevation."

Union soldiers were not the only threat to Fayetteville blacks. According to Dennett's informant, soon after Sherman's withdrawal from the city, whites moved quickly to reestablish control of the town and reinstitute elements of the antebellum slave code. Public whipping was reinstated as punishment for blacks who broke the law. Blacks were banned from meeting together for worship; they were even barred from carrying walking sticks within the city limits. Fayetteville's African-American population did not simply submit to these indignities: black leaders let it be known that, if members of the white community did not desist from their attacks, they would request that a garrison of black soldiers be stationed in the town. The freed people were obviously aware of the chastening effect that such a contingent would have on the unreconstructed element in Fayetteville. In any case, the town's white leaders decided to make an accommodation with local blacks and requested that a representative of the Freedmen's Bureau be stationed in the town to serve as an arbiter for any disputes that might arise between the two groups.

In this uncertain environment, Fayetteville blacks struggled to build a community, and the center for this organizing process was Evans Chapel. One of the first of many thorny issues that had to be resolved concerned the question of denominational affiliation. The post-emancipation South witnessed the dual phenomena of northern missionaries flooding into the section to work among the freed people and the black disengagement from white southern churches. In the black mind, freedom was commensurate with independent institutions; and, along with schools, the churches had been and would continue to be the focal point of the African American community. With all of these African-American souls available for salvation, northern and southern denominations engaged in an intense competition to bring the former slaves into their respective organizations.

Among the several denominations leading the first wave into the South were the African Methodist Episcopal (AME) and African Methodist Episcopal Zion (AMEZ) Churches. These northern black missionaries saw themselves as uniquely suited to work among the freed people. Both denominations were united by race and common experience with their charges; what these smaller churches lacked in resources they made up for in missionary zeal. While the AME held the organizational upper hand among blacks throughout much of the South, in North Carolina the AMEZ was supreme.

The AMEZ and other black denominations resisted white charity, arguing that such largess perpetuated perceptions of white superiority among the former slaves. The church became the focus of African American life and culture as the freed people came to have their children christened, their marriages sanctified, and their funerals officiated. Black churches sponsored outings—both religious and secular—and provided necessary social services that contributed to an evolving sense of community. In a more abstract sense, these institutions provided a sense of belonging that was so important as the social organization of the slave system disappeared.

The missionary impulse had its most profound effect in the area of education. Emancipation brought opportunity to the freed people; however, without education—particularly the ability to read and write—the former slaves were unprepared to take advantage of all that could be available to them. For the missionaries, the most important part of education was teaching the freed people to read, which gave each individual personal access to the stories and lessons of the Bible. The AMEZ and other black churches took an active role in planning and implementing education programs: church buildings were used as schoolhouses, and congregations raised money to support teachers and students alike. The churches were not alone in their efforts to assist the former slaves.

Along with northern denominations that came to work among the freed people came northern benevolent societies.... One of the most prominent of these benevolent societies was the American Missionary Association, an abolitionist missionary organization founded in 1846 and headquartered in New York City.

The first AMA support at Fayetteville was for the educational efforts of a white Congregationalist minister, the Reverend David Dickson. In

December 1865, shortly after the failure of an attempt by Fayetteville's African American community to establish a school at Evans Chapel, the AMA dispatched Dickson and his wife, Mary, to North Carolina. Although Dickson was quite active in Fayetteville for a mere five months, his correspondence records the complex environment that fostered the founding and growth of the African American school there. The missionary's first official act was to meet with the Freedmen's Bureau agent, Major H. C. Lawrence, who, in turn, introduced him to Fayetteville's mayor and white elite. Dickson reported that he received considerable encouragement from the town's white leaders, and he later commented that the "better class of people here are in favor of having the Negro instructed." Fayetteville's white elite generally supported the combined efforts of the Freedmen's Bureau and the AMA to educate blacks. This is not to argue that the town's white populace was somehow more enlightened than the inhabitants of the rest of the Cape Fear region, where racial conflicts were severe. Early in the postwar period Fayetteville's white and black communities seem to have reached an uneasy accommodation that acknowledged a tenuous white acceptance of a literate work force in the process of economic reconstruction. Much of the AMA correspondence from the period confirms the general acceptance by local whites of black schooling. The local press periodically published articles that extolled the virtues of African American education and emphasized the need for southern white control of that process. Although occasionally Dickson lamented his treatment at the hand of those he characterized as lower-class whites, the level of white-against-black violence appears to have been lower than in other parts of North Carolina and throughout the South.

David Dickson's letters also reveal Fayetteville's African American community to be proud and well organized. In one letter the missionary vividly describes the 1866 Emancipation Day celebrations, during which blacks throughout the region met at Evans Chapel to march past the former slave market in remembrance of circumstances not long past.

More significantly, the Reverend Mr. Dickson's correspondence illustrates the explosive growth of the Fayetteville school. In the "Report of Freemen's Schools for the Southern District of North Carolina, January, 1866," the clergyman reported that in the one month in which he had served at Fayetteville, the student population had jumped from seventy-five "scholars" to 245. Although the number of students fluctuated from season to season, especially at planting and harvest times, the African-American school exhibited steady growth. By the middle of February, Dickson was forced to hire two black assistants and expand the school's offerings to include two day-sessions and one night-school. His report to the AMA for February 1866 noted 272 students enrolled in these classes.

David Dickson's tenure among Fayetteville's freed people was cut short in April 1866. After suffering a "bilious attack," the clergyman was forced to undergo a period of convalescence. Mary Dickson attempted to carry on her husband's work. But when an attack of dysentery further weakened the AMA missionary, a local physician recommended that the Dicksons leave Fayetteville immediately. Rev. David Dickson died while in transit to Philadelphia.

The AMA moved quickly to replace David Dickson. Local blacks took an active role in this process and lobbied for a black replacement. The ideal choice was Robert W. Harris, who had been born in 1840 to free black parents in Fayetteville....

In Virginia, Robert Harris [had] quickly established himself not only as a talented teacher but also as an advocate for the rights of the former slaves. In March 1866, he boldly offered the readers of the *American Missionary* his prescription for racial uplift in the South, calling on "northern capitalists" to purchase large tracts of land, which could be divided into small plots and sold to the freed people at cost. He also declared that the condition of black southerners was dependent upon the continued activism of a victorious North. Yet, he demonstrated a great deal of tact when dealing with local whites, a talent learned through hard experience. He was especially respected by AMA officials for his zealous temperance activities. All of these factors played a role in the decision by the AMA to consider Harris for the Fayetteville vacancy in the autumn of 1866.

Another important element in the decision to send Robert Harris to North Carolina was the active participation of Fayetteville's African-American community in the process. The AMA queried local black leader John S. Leary about conditions in the town. He assured officials that a school would flourish there and went on to stress the importance of a "native teacher" in the success of any such venture. Leary then took an active role both in arranging for the leasing of two buildings for the school and in securing a commitment from the Freedmen's Bureau for financial assistance.

Robert Harris arrived in Fayetteville in late November 1866. His first act as AMA superintendent of schools was to name his younger brother, Cicero, as his assistant. Next, he divided his students into primary and intermediate grade levels based on their educational attainments. Cicero Harris was given responsibility for the primary grades, which were designated as the "Phillips School"; Robert Harris assumed control of the intermediate levels, which were called the "Sumner School." In his first report from the North Carolina field, Harris declared a total enrollment of 321 students in the school.

Despite the uncertainties of these years, the African-American school at Fayetteville exhibited tremendous growth well into the 1870s. Although enrollment tended to fluctuate wildly depending on the season, the institution boasted as many as six hundred students....

Initially, the school was in session from September to May. However, by 1869 the Harris brothers were seeking financial support to keep the school open throughout the summer months. Citing the "urgings of the people" and the need to prepare a group of young people to fill teaching responsibilities in the small, rural schools of the region, Robert Harris felt compelled to keep the doors open. According to the educator, his school was so inextricably "connected with the educational, religious, social and industrial affairs of the people that we cannot be spared."

The curriculum at Fayetteville emphasized practicality. The majority of instruction in the school focused on reading and writing. Students were also taught arithmetic with an emphasis on the types of problem-solving skills that would be useful when negotiating for one's labor. As the educational apparatus became more sophisticated, the curriculum boasted geography and science classes, the latter of which revolved around the school's acquisition of a telescope in 1869.

The Harrises' school provided special attention to the moral development of its students. This aspect of the curriculum reflected the close ties of the school to the AMEZ Church. Not only were classes often held in the church—the only structure large enough to house the student body—but the Harris brothers also taught the Sunday school at Evans Chapel. They used their ties to the Congregationalist-based American Missionary Association to procure religious tracts for distribution among their pupils....

Another facet of this moral education was temperance. One of the first primers used by Robert Harris was entitled *The Temperance Almanac,* which contained stories concerning the evils of overindulgence and the glories of overcoming the "demon rum." In December 1868, Harris announced the organization of a "Band of Hope." Members pledged themselves to abstain from alcohol, tobacco, and profane language. Children, in particular, were singled out for membership; and a periodical titled the *Youth's Temperance Banner* was the reading material of choice in the Fayetteville Band of Hope. Members' rules also included a prohibition against marble-playing "for keeps," a practice that Robert Harris equated with gambling. Between December 1868 and January 1872, the Harrises' Band of Hope had as many as 136 members.

The success of black education efforts at Fayetteville stemmed in part from the willingness of the white community to countenance those efforts. An integral element in this tenuous accommodation was the unusually high esteem accorded to both the local Freedmen's Bureau agent and the contingent of federal troops stationed in the town. The local newspaper often expressed the appreciation of white Fayetteville to bureau officials who "labored in ... responsible and gentlemanly fashion." According to the Fayetteville *News,* "No negro felt any injustice, and no white man felt annoyed or troubled with the officious interference which has occasioned elsewhere so much complaint." On one notable occasion, the *News* rose to the defense of the federals when they were accused by the Raleigh *Progress* of using an altercation at a local house of prostitution to foment a "war of the races." The *News* blasted the *Progress* for its "bad taste and lack of dignity" and further remarked that "the best feelings prevail between the citizens and soldiers here."

It would be inaccurate to portray postbellum Fayetteville as some sort of racial Shangri-La.* There were bitter, sometimes violent, conflicts. In May 1866, the *News* reported that a mob "got up by mullattoe scamps" had attempted to free a black male from the town jail. Local whites, especially "all returned soldiers," were admonished to arm themselves. The news story concluded with the warning that "[p]repared we have nothing to fear; unprepared we might lose some of our best citizens." In February 1867, a black man, Archie Beebe, was arrested for attacking a white woman, Mrs. Elvina Massey. While being transported to jail after an arraignment, Beebe and the sheriff's deputies protecting him were attacked by an angry white mob. In the ensuing melee, Beebe was murdered. The *News* commented on the event: "It is one of those instances where awful justice speaks from the mouth of the people and the bloody mark of vengeance is stamped by man's hand."

With the onset of radical Reconstruction in the spring of 1867, the community became increasingly politicized, and black-white relations were placed under increasing strain. The center for black political activity, not surprisingly, was the Evans Chapel AMEZ Church, which was also flourishing under the adroit leadership of the Reverend James Walker Hood. The Republican Party held its first organizational meeting in Cumberland County at the chapel on April 4, 1867. Addressing the gathering were Rev. J. W. Hood and John S. Leary; Cicero Harris also took an active role in the proceedings. Noticeably absent from that meeting (and all subsequent political gatherings) was Robert Harris. Although the educator often commented on local politics in his private correspondence, his public pronouncements on political issues were exceedingly rare.

As a native of Fayetteville, Harris no doubt recognized the political and social complexities in the town. The success of his school was contingent upon the goodwill of local whites and his own personal standing among them. The local white elite generally favored the educational work among the freed people—if the efforts were controlled by the "Southern states." While Harris's ties to the northern-based AMA and the federal Freedmen's Bureau were public knowledge, he was quick to downplay these affiliations by shifting the focus of any query toward his North Carolina upbringing. It is testimony to Robert Harris's diplomatic skills that his school never fell into disfavor with the white community. His studious avoidance of politics was matched only by his strenuous efforts to bring stability and self-sufficiency to the school....

---

*An imaginary land of beauty, peace, and harmony described in James Hilton's novel *Lost Horizon*. (Eds.)

The most important accomplishment in Robert Harris's bid for independence and institutional stability was the construction of a new building to permanently house the Phillips and Sumner Schools under one roof. Soon after arriving in Fayetteville, the educator began soliciting assistance from the Freedmen's Bureau and the AMA to build a new structure for the school. In September 1867, he queried the bureau's superintendent of education, F. A. Fiske, as to whether there was "any hope for a school-house in Fayetteville?" Fiske replied in the affirmative; and, in November, Harris informed AMA officials that members of the community had purchased two lots for the school and that a deed for the property had been forwarded to the Freedmen's Bureau offices for approval. In March 1868, Cicero Harris was able to report that a contract to build a "large and commodious school-building" had been awarded and that construction would soon commence.... The building was dedicated in early April 1869; and the Howard School, named after Freedmen's Bureau chief Gen. O. O. Howard, opened for its first official session the following September.

Robert Harris's most enduring legacy to North Carolina education was in the training of teachers.... In the beginning, it was necessity that forced Harris beyond providing basic literacy to Fayetteville's freed people. The crush of students descending on the school placed great strains on the teachers, and Harris's repeated requests for northern teachers went unheeded by AMA officials. In one of his first reports, the educator acknowledged that he had employed two local blacks as temporary instructors. While both of these women, Mary Payne and Caroline Bryant, were literate, neither met with his complete approval. Still, the large number of scholars at the Phillips and Sumner Schools forced Harris to continue the practice of hiring locals. In December 1867, he announced that he had hired two of his most promising students as assistants in the primary school. Interestingly, these teachers did not receive commissions, and their salaries were to be paid by local subscription. The success of this system was soon readily apparent, and Harris's regular requests for northern teachers ceased.

The impact of training the most talented students for the classroom was felt most in the small rural schools in Cumberland and surrounding counties. In the immediate postwar period, the records of the Freedmen's Bureau include numerous requests for teachers and material support throughout the region. There were so many requests, in fact, that many outlying schools began using Robert Harris as an intermediary between themselves and the bureau. A great source of anxiety for rural teachers was the insecurity caused by the rapid turnover of the Freedmen's Bureau agents. A remedy for this uncertainty was to give Harris the responsibility for placing teachers in appropriate schools and seeing to their needs. In June 1868, he reported that there was a great demand for teachers in rural Cumberland and Moore Counties. Harris was soon placing his most promising students in teaching positions at Beaver Creek, Lower Rockfish, Black River, and Manchester in

Cumberland County and at Jonesboro in Moore County. By January, his operation had spread to Harnett and Bladen Counties, and as many as fifteen schools fell under his purview. Thus, by supplying teachers to black schools in neighboring towns and counties, Robert Harris's Fayetteville institution was functioning as a normal school a full decade before the State of North Carolina officially established it as the South's first "state colored normal school."

By the end of 1870, the Freedmen's Bureau ceased providing educational assistance to the former slaves. The last trickle of aid to the Howard School from the American Missionary Association ended in 1872. By then the school had established its independence and a well-defined sense of mission. Robert Harris continued to train young black men and women as educators until his death in 1879....

The State Colored Normal School has had a lasting legacy in North Carolina history.... In 1939 the State Colored Normal School was renamed as Fayetteville State Teachers College, and in 1963 as Fayetteville State College. Since 1969, when it joined the University of North Carolina system, the school has operated as Fayetteville State University. The institution has come a long way from the anxious days of Reconstruction. The long-term vision of Fayetteville's African American community—in both slavery and in freedom, passed down through the generations—continues to have a profound influence on that city, North Carolina, and the nation.

DOCUMENTS

A Letter
"To My Old Master," c. 1865

TO MY OLD MASTER, COLONEL P. H. ANDERSON,
BIG SPRING, TENNESSEE

Sir: I got your letter, and was glad to find that you had not forgotten Jourdon, and that you wanted me to come back and live with you again, promising to do better for me than anybody else can. I have often felt uneasy about you. I thought the Yankees would have hung you long before this, for harboring Rebs they found at your house. I suppose they never heard about your going to Colonel Martin's to kill the Union soldier that was left by his company in their stable. Although you shot at me twice before I left you, I did not want to hear of your being hurt, and am glad you are still living. It would do me good to go back to the dear old home again, and

SOURCE: L. Maria Child, *The Freedmen's Book* (1865).

see Miss Mary and Miss Martha and Allen, Esther, Green, and Lee. Give my love to them all, and tell them I hope we will meet in the better world, if not in this. I would have gone back to see you all when I was working in the Nashville Hospital, but one of the neighbors told me that Henry intended to shoot me if he ever got a chance.

I want to know particularly what the good chance is you propose to give me. I am doing tolerably well here. I get twenty-five dollars a month, with victuals and clothing; have a comfortable home for Mandy—the folks call her Mrs. Anderson—and the children—Milly, Jane, and Grundy—go to school and are learning well. The teacher says Grundy has a head for a preacher. They go to Sunday school, and Mandy and me attend church regularly. We are kindly treated. Sometimes we overhear others saying, "Them colored people were slaves" down in Tennessee. The children feel hurt when they hear such remarks; but I tell them it was no disgrace in Tennessee to belong to Colonel Anderson. Many darkeys would have been proud, as I used to be, to call you master. Now if you will write and say what wages you will give me, I will be better able to decide whether it would be to my advantage to move back again.

As to my freedom, which you say I can have, there is nothing to be gained on that score, as I got my free papers in 1864 from the Provost-Marshal-General of the Department of Nashville. Mandy says she would be afraid to go back without some proof that you were disposed to treat us justly and kindly; and we have concluded to test your sincerity by asking you to send us our wages for the time we served you. This will make us forget and forgive old scores, and rely on your justice and friendship in the future. I served you faithfully for thirty-two years, and Mandy twenty years. At twenty-five dollars a month for me, and two dollars a week for Mandy, our earnings would amount to eleven thousand six hundred and eighty dollars. Add to this the interest for the time our wages have been kept back, and deduct what you paid for our clothing, and three doctor's visits to me, and pulling a tooth for Mandy, and the balance will show what we are in justice entitled to. Please send the money by Adam's Express, in care of V. Winters, Esq., Dayton, Ohio. If you fail to pay us for faithful labors in the past, we can have little faith in your promises in the future. We trust the good Maker has opened your eyes to the wrongs which you and your fathers have done to me and my fathers, in making us toil for you for generations without recompense. Here I draw my wages every Saturday night; but in Tennessee there was never any payday for the Negroes any more than for the horses and cows. Surely there will be a day of reckoning for those who defraud the laborer of his hire.

In answering this letter, please state if there would be any safety for my Milly and Jane, who are now grown up, and both good-looking girls. You know how it was with poor Matilda and Catherine. I would rather stay here and starve—and die, if it come to that—than have my girls brought to shame by the violence and wickedness of their young masters. You will also please state if there has been any schools opened for the colored children in your neighborhood. The great desire of my life now is to give my children an education, and have them form virtuous habits.

Say howdy to George Carter, and thank him for taking the pistol from you when you were shooting at me.

FROM YOUR OLD SERVANT,

JOURDON ANDERSON

The Knights of the White Camelia, 1868

Questions

1. Do you belong to the white race? *Answer.*—I do.
2. Did you ever marry any woman who did not, or does not, belong to the white race? *Ans.*—No.
3. Do you promise never to marry any woman but one who belongs to the white race? *Ans.*—I do.
4. Do you believe in the superiority of your race? *Ans.*—I do.
5. Will you promise never to vote for anyone for any office of honor, profit, or trust who does not belong to your race? *Ans.*—I do.
6. Will you take a solemn oath never to abstain from casting your vote at any election in which a candidate of the Negro race shall be opposed to a white man attached to your principles, unless or prevented by severe illness or any other physical disability?*Ans.*—I will.
7. Are you opposed to allowing the control of the political affairs of this country to go in whole or in part into the hands of the African race, and will you do everything in your power to prevent it? *Ans.*—Yes.
8. Will you devote your intelligence, energy, and influence to the furtherance and propagation of the principles of our Order?*Ans.*—I will.
9. Will you, under all circumstances, defend and protect persons of the white race in their lives, rights, and property against all encroachments or invasions from any inferior race, and especially the African? *Ans.*—Yes.
10. Are you willing to take an oath forever to cherish these grand principles and to unite yourself with others who, like you, believing in their truth, have firmly bound themselves to stand by and defend them against all? *Ans.*—I am.

SOURCE: Walter L. Fleming, ed., *Documents Relating to Reconstruction* (Morgantown, W. Va.: 1904), No. 1.

The commander shall then say: If you consent to join our Association, raise your right hand and I will administer to you the oath which we have all taken:

Oath

I do solemnly swear, in the presence of these witnesses, never to reveal, without authority, the existence of this Order, its objects, its acts, and signs of recognition; never to reveal or publish, in any manner whatsoever, what I shall see or hear in this Council; never to divulge the names of the members of the Order or their acts done in connection therewith. I swear to maintain and defend the social and political superiority of the white race on this continent; always and in all places to observe a marked distinction between the white and African races; to vote for none but white men for any office of honor, profit, or trust; to devote my intelligence, energy, and influence to instill these principles in the minds and hearts of others; and to protect and defend persons of the white race in their lives, rights, and property against the encroachments and aggressions of an inferior race.

I swear, moreover, to unite myself in heart, soul, and body with those who compose this Order; to aid, protect, and defend them in all places; to obey the orders of those who, by our statutes, will have the right of giving those orders; to respond at the peril of my life to a call, sign, or cry coming from a fellow member whose rights are violated; and to do everything in my power to assist him through life. And to the faithful performance of this oath, I pledge my life and sacred honor....

"We Are Literally Slaves," 1912

I am a negro woman, and I was born and reared in the South. I am now past forty years of age and am the mother of three children. My husband died nearly fifteen years ago, after we had been married about five years. For more than thirty years—or since I was ten years old—I have been a servant in one capacity or another in white families in a thriving Southern city, which has at present a population of more than 50,000. In my early years I was at first what might be called a "house-girl," or, better, a "house-boy." I used to answer the doorbell, sweep the yard, go on errands and do odd jobs. Later on I became a chambermaid and performed the usual duties of such a servant in a home. Still later I was graduated into a cook, in which position I served at different times for nearly eight years in all. During the last ten years I have been a nurse. I have worked for only four different families during all these thirty years. But, belonging to the servant class,

SOURCE: "More Slavery at the South," by a Negro Nurse, *Independent*, 25 January 1912, 196–200.

which is the majority class among my race at the South, and associating only with servants, I have been able to become intimately acquainted not only with the lives of hundreds of household servants, but also with the lives of their employers....

To begin with, then, I should say that more than two-thirds of the negroes of the town where I live are menial servants of one kind or another, and besides that more than two-thirds of the negro women here, whether married or single, are compelled to work for a living,—as nurses, cooks, washerwomen, chambermaids, seamstresses, hucksters, janitresses, and the like. I will say, also, that the condition of this vast host of poor colored people is just as bad as, if not worse than, it was during the days of slavery. Tho today we are enjoying nominal freedom, we are literally slaves. And, not to generalize, I will give you a sketch of the work I have to do—and I'm only one of many.

I frequently work from fourteen to sixteen hours a day. I am compelled by my contract, which is oral only, to sleep in the house. I am allowed to go home to my own children, the oldest of whom is a girl of 18 years, only once in two weeks, every other Sunday afternoon—even then I'm not permitted to stay all night. I not only have to nurse a little white child, now eleven months old, but I have to act as playmate or "handy-andy," not to say governess, to three other children in the home, the oldest of whom is only nine years of age. I wash and dress the baby two or three times each day, I give it its meals, mainly from a bottle; I have to put it to bed each night; and, in addition, I have to get up and attend to its every call between midnight and morning. If the baby falls to sleep during the day, as it has been trained to do every day about eleven o'clock, I am not permitted to rest. It's "Mammy, do this," or "Mammy, do that," or "Mammy, do the other," from my mistress, all the time. So it is not strange to see "Mammy" watering the lawn in front with the garden hose, sweeping the sidewalk, mopping the porch and halls, dusting around the house, helping the cook, or darning stockings. Not only so, but I have to put the other three children to bed each night as well as the baby, and I have to wash them and dress them each morning. I don't know what it is to go to church; I don't know what it is to go to a lecture or entertainment or anything of the kind. I live a treadmill life; and I see my own children only when they happen to see me on the streets when I am out with the children, or when my children come to the "yard" to see me, which isn't often, because my white folks don't like to see their servants' children hanging around their premises. You might as well say that I'm on duty all the time—from sunrise to sunrise, every day in the week I am the slave, body and soul, of this family. And what do I get for this work—this lifetime bondage? The pitiful sum of ten dollars a month! And what am I expected to do with these ten dollars? With this money I'm expected to pay my house rent, which is four dollars per month, for a little house of two rooms, just big enough to turn round in; and I'm expected, also, to feed and clothe myself and three children. For two years my oldest child, it is true, has helped a little toward our support by taking in a little washing at home. She does the washing and ironing of two white families, with a total of five persons; one of these families pays her $1.00 per week, and the other 75 cents per week, and my daughter has to furnish her own soap and starch and wood For six months my youngest child, a girl about thirteen years old, has been nursing, and she receives $1.50 per week but has no night work. When I think of the low rate of wages we poor colored people receive, and when I hear so much said about our unreliability, our untrustworthiness, and even our vices, I recall the story of the private soldier in a certain army who, once upon a time, being upbraided by the commanding officer because the heels of his shoes were not polished, is said to have replied "Captain, do you expect all the virtues for $13 per month?"...

Ah, we poor colored women wage earners in the South are fighting a terrible battle, and because of our weakness, our ignorance, our poverty, and our temptations we deserve the sympathies of mankind. Perhaps a million of us are introduced daily to the privacy of a million chambers throughout the South, and hold in our arms a million white children, thousands of whom, as infants, are suckled at our breasts—during my lifetime I myself have served as "wet nurse" to more than a dozen white children. On the one hand, we are assailed by white men, and on the other hand, we are assailed by black men, who should be our natural protectors; and, whether in the cook kitchen, at the washtub, over the sewing machine, behind the baby carriage, or at the ironing board, we are but little more than pack horses, beasts of burden, slaves! In the distant future, it may be, centuries and centuries hence, a monument of brass or stone will be erected to the Old Black Mammies of the South, but what we need is present help, present sympathy, better wages, better hours, more protection, and a chance to breathe for once while alive as free women. If none others will help us, it would seem that the Southern white women themselves might do so in their own defense, because we are rearing their children—we feed them, we bathe them, we teach them to speak the English language, and in numberless instances we sleep with them—and it is inevitable that the lives of their children will in some measure be pure or impure according as they are affected by contact with their colored nurses.

Chapter 2

The Last Frontier

Chinese workers building the transcontinental railroad.

From eastern North Dakota south to the Texas panhandle and west to the Rocky Mountains lay the Great Plains, a region at one time considered so bleak and uninhabitable that travelers referred to it as the "Great American Desert." In time, however, it would prove a source of immense wealth in minerals, grains, and livestock. This last American frontier—the land of the miner, the farmer, and the cowboy—by the late 1800s underwent a dramatic transformation paralleling change in the large cities and smoking factories of the urban, industrial East.

American literature and folklore have immortalized those who settled and tamed the Great Plains—the miners and their wide-open towns; the sod-house farmers; and, above all, the cowboys. But we all too often overlook the racial and ethnic diversity of those who built the West. Moreover, we forget what a critical role technology played in developing this region. The railroad, for example, was among the most important factors propelling the westward movement. In the essay "Linking a Continent and a Nation," Jack Chen highlights the role of Chinese immigrants in building the transcontinental railroad. How does Chen's description compare to popular depictions in western novels, in the movies, and on television?

While Jack Chen's essay notes that the business leaders responsible for the construction of the transcontinental railroad eagerly employed thousands of Chinese laborers, not everyone viewed their arrival so favorably. The first document is by Dennis Kearney, an Irish-born California labor leader. Kearney emerged in the 1870 as the spokesman for a new political party, the Workingmen's Party, which attacked the what he called "aristocrats," those enjoying immense profits because of workingmen's low wages. What was the basis of Kearney's attack of Chinese workers? Was it simply economics and a question of wages for white workers? Given the relatively small Chinese population at the time, do you think Kearney's fears regarding the racial makeup of California were realistic?

Farmers also benefited from technology—steel plows to cut rough sod, windmills to pump water from deep in the ground, and barbed wire to fence off land on the treeless plains. There was also the lure of cheap or free land, thanks to the Homestead Act of 1862. This incentive pulled Americans from the East and immigrants from Europe. Farmers could tolerate the loneliness of rural life, but there were some hardships that they could not overcome. The second document, a memoir of a German woman who farmed in South Dakota in the 1880s, tells of her life there and her eventual decision to give up farming. Why did her family make this decision?

The last document, by Theodore Roosevelt, tells about a typical "cow town," Miles City, Montana. A romantic view of cowboys, it also reveals much about the ethnic diversity of the new Westerners. How does Roosevelt's picture complement the essay by Jack Chen?

ESSAY

Linking a Continent and a Nation

Jack Chen

Without the "Chinamen's" knowledge and respect for explosive powders, ability to work on the side of near vertical cliffs at dizzying heights and survive hardships which white men could not

SOURCE: Chapter 6: "Linking a Continent and a Nation" (pp. 65–77) from *The Chinese of America: From the Beginning to the Present* by Jack Chen. Copyright © 1980 by Jack Chen. Reprinted by permission of HarperCollins Publishers.

endure, the Central Pacific would never have been completed when it was but much later.

R. W. HOWARD, *The Great Iron Trail*

The Chinese filled swamps, cut into mountains, dug tunnels, built bridges. As one historian notes, "The work was so obviously needed and all groups and areas vied with each other to build a railroad in their area, so that they would have welcomed the devil himself had he built a road. The lack of white laborers was too evident to cause even the most ardent anti-Chinese to resent their employment on such work.

ROBERT E. WYNNE, *Reaction to the Chinese in the*
Pacific Northwest and British Columbia

The expansion of the railroad system in the United States was astonishingly swift. England had pioneered the building of railways and for a time was the acknowledged leader in the field, but from the moment the first locomotive was imported into the United States in 1829 the farsighted saw railways as the obvious solution for transport across the vast spaces of the American continent. By 1850, 9,000 miles of rails had been laid in the eastern states and up to the Mississippi. The California Gold Rush and the opening of the American West made talk about a transcontinental line more urgent. As too often happens, war spurred the realization of this project.

The West was won. California was a rich and influential state, but a wide unsettled belt of desert, plain, and mountains, separated it and Oregon from the rest of the states. As the economic separation of North and South showed, this situation was fraught with danger. It could lead to a political rift. In 1860, it was cheaper and quicker to reach San Francisco from Canton in China—a sixty-day voyage by sea—than from the Missouri River, six months away by wagon train. The urgent need was to link California firmly with the industrialized eastern states and their 30,000 miles of railways. A railway would cut the journey to a week. The threat of civil war loomed larger between North and South over the slavery issue. Abraham Lincoln's Republican administration saw a northern transcontinental railway as a means to outflank the South by drawing the western states closer to the North. In 1862, Congress voted funds to build the 2,500-mile-long railway. It required enormous resourcefulness and determination to get this giant project off the drawing boards. Not much imagination was required to see its necessity, but the actual building presented daunting difficulties. It was calculated that its cost would mount to $100 million, double the federal budget of 1861.

It was Theodore Judah, described by his contemporaries as "Pacific Railroad Crazy," who began to give substance to the dream. An eastern engineer who had come west to build the short Sacramento Valley Railroad, he undertook a preliminary survey and reported that he had found a feasible route crossing the Sierra by way of Dutch Flat. But the mainly small investors who supported his efforts could not carry through the whole immense undertaking. With rumors of civil war between North and South, San Francisco capitalists, mostly Southerners, boycotted the scheme as a northern plot, and pressed for a southern route. Then the "Big Four," Sacramento merchants, took up the challenge: Leland Stanford as president, C. P. Huntington as vice-president, Mark Hopkins as treasurer, and Charles Crocker, in charge of construction, formed the Central Pacific Railway Company. Judah was elbowed out.

The Big Four came as gold seekers in 1849 or soon after but found that there was more money to be made in storekeeping than in scrabbling in the rocks in the mountains. As Republicans, they held the state for the Union against the secessionists. Leland Stanford, the first president of the Central Pacific, was also the first Republican governor of California.

The beginnings were not auspicious. The Union Pacific [UP] was building from Omaha in the East over the plains to the Rockies, but supplies had to come in by water or wagon because the railways had not yet reached Omaha. The Civil War now raged and manpower, materials and funds were hard to get. The Indians were still contesting invasion of their lands. By 1864, however, with the Civil War ending, these problems were solved. The UP hired Civil War veterans, Irish immigrants fleeing famine and even Indian women, and the line began to move westward.

The Central Pacific, building eastward from Sacramento, had broken ground on January 8, 1863, but in 1864, beset by money and labor problems, it had built only thirty-one miles of track. It had an even more intractable manpower problem than the UP. California was sparsely populated, and the gold mines, homesteading, and other lucrative employments offered stiff competition for labor. Brought to the railhead, three out of every five men quit immediately and took off for the better prospects of the new Nevada silver strikes. Even Charles Crocker, boss of construction and raging like a mad bull in the railway camps, could not control them. In the winter of 1864, the company had only 600 men working on the line when it had advertised for 5,000. Up to then, only white labor had been recruited and California white labor was still motivated by the Gold Rush syndrome. They wanted quick wealth, not hard, regimented railway work. After two years only fifty miles of track had been laid.

James Strobridge, superintendent of construction, testified to the 1876 Joint Congressional Committee on Chinese Immigration: "[These] were unsteady men, unreliable. Some would not go to work at all.... Some would stay until pay day, get a little money, get drunk and clear out." Something drastic had to be done.

In 1858, fifty Chinese had helped to build the California Central Railroad from Sacramento to Marysville. In 1860, Chinese were working on the San Jose Railway and giving a good account of themselves, so it is surprising that there was so much hesitation about employing them on the Central Pacific's western end of the first transcontinental railway. Faced with a growing crisis of no work done and mounting costs, Crocker suggested hiring Chinese. Strobridge strongly objected: "I will not boss Chinese. I don't think they could build a railroad." Leland Stanford was also reluctant. He had advocated exclusion of the Chinese from California and was embarrassed to reverse himself. Crocker, Huntington, Hopkins, and Stanford, the Big Four of the Central Pacific, were all merchants in hardware, dried goods, and groceries in the little town of Sacramento. Originally, they knew nothing about railroad building, but they were astute and hard-headed businessmen. Crocker was insistent. Wasted time was wasted money. The CP's need for labor was critical. The men they already had were threatening a strike. Finally fifty Chinese were hired for a trial.

Building the Transcontinental Railroad

In February 1865, they marched up in self-formed gangs of twelve to twenty men with their own supplies and cooks for each mess. They ate a meal of rice and dried cuttlefish, washed and slept, and early next morning were ready for work filling dump carts. Their discipline and grading—preparing the ground for track laying—delighted Strobridge. Soon fifty more were hired, and finally some 15,000 had been put on the payroll. Crocker was enthusiastic: "They prove nearly equal to white men in the amount of labor they perform, and are much more reliable. No danger of strikes among them. We are training them to all kinds of labor: blasting, driving horses, handling rock as well as pick and shovel." Countering Strobridge's argument that the Chinese were "not masons," Crocker pointed out that the race that built the Great Wall could certainly build a railroad culvert. Up on the Donner Pass today the fine stonework embankments built by the Chinese are serving well after a hundred years.

Charles Nordhoff, an acute observer, reports Stobridge telling him "[The Chinese] learn all parts of the work easily." Nordhoff says he saw them "employed on every kind of work.... They do not drink, fight or strike; they do gamble, if it is not prevented; and it is always said of them that they are very cleanly in their habits. It is the custom, among them, after they have had their suppers every evening, to bathe with the help of small tubs. I doubt if the white laborers do as much." As well he might. Well-run boardinghouses in California in those days proudly advertised that they provided guests with a weekly bath.

Their wages at the start were $28 a month (twenty-six working days), and they furnished all their own food, cooking utensils, and tents. The headman of each gang, or sometimes an American employed as clerk by them, received all the wages and handed them out to the members of the work gang according to what had been earned. "Competent and wonderfully effective because tireless and unremitting in their industry," they worked from sun-up to sundown.

All observers remarked on the frugality of the Chinese. This was not surprising in view of the fact that, with a strong sense of filial duty, they came to America in order to save money and return as soon as possible to their homes and families in China. So they usually dressed poorly, and their dwellings were of the simplest [construction]. However, they ate well: rice and vermicelli (noodles) garnished with meats and vegetables, fish, dried oysters, cuttlefish, bacon and pork, and chicken on holidays, abalone meat, five kinds of dried vegetables, bamboo shoots, seaweed, salted cabbage, and mushrooms, four kinds of dried fruit, and peanut oil and tea. This diet shows a considerable degree of sophistication and balance compared to the beef, beans, potatoes, bread, and butter of the white laborers. Other supplies were purchased from the shop maintained by a Chinese merchant contractor in one of the railway cars that followed them as they carried the railway line forward. Here they could buy pipes, tobacco, bowls, chopsticks, lamps, Chinese-style shoes of cotton with soft cotton soles, and ready-made clothing imported from China.

On Sundays, they rested, did their washing, and gambled. They were prone to argue noisily, but did not become besotted with whiskey and make themselves unfit for work on Monday. Their sobriety was much appreciated by their employers.

Curtis, the engineer in charge, described them as "the best roadbuilders in the world." The once skeptical Strobridge, a smart, pushing Irishman, also now pronounced them "the best in the world." Leland Stanford described them in a report on October 10, 1865, to [President] Andrew Johnson:

> As a class, they are quiet, peaceable, patient, industrious, and economical. More prudent and economical [than white laborers] they are contented with less wages. We find them organized for mutual aid and assistance. Without them, it would be impossible to complete the western portion of this great national enterprise within the time required by the Act of Congress.

Crocker testified before the congressional committee that "if we found that we were in a hurry for a job of work, it was better to put on Chinese at once." All these men had originally resisted the employment of Chinese on the railway.

Four-fifths of the grading labor from Sacramento to Ogden was done by Chinese. In a couple of years more, of 13,500 workers on the payroll 12,000 were Chinese. They were nicknamed "Crocker's Pets."

Appreciating Chinese Skills

The Chinese crews won their reputation the hard way. They outperformed Cornish men brought in at extra wages to cut rock. Crocker testified,

> They would cut more rock in a week than the Cornish miners, and it was hard work, bone labor. [They] were skilled in using the hammer and drill, and they proved themselves equal to the very best

Cornish miners in that work. They were very trusty, they were intelligent, and they lived up to their contracts.

Stanford held the Chinese workers in such high esteem that he provided in his will for the permanent employment of a large number on his estates. In the 1930s, some of their descendants were still living and working lands now owned by Stanford University.

The Chinese saved the day for Crocker and his colleagues. The terms of agreement with the government were that the railway companies would be paid from $16,000 to $48,000 for each mile of track laid. But there were only so many miles between the two terminal points of the projected line. The Union Pacific Company, working with 10,000 mainly Irish immigrants and Civil War veterans, had the advantage of building the line through Nebraska over the plains and made steady progress. The Central Pacific, after the first easy twenty-three miles between Newcastle and Colfax, had to conquer the granite mountains and gorges of the Sierra Nevada and Rockies before it could emerge onto the Nevada-Utah plains and make real speed and money. The line had to rise 7,000 feet in 100 miles over daunting terrain. Crocker and the Chinese proved up to the challenge. After reaching Cisco, there was no easy going. The line had to be literally carved out of the Sierra granite, through tunnels and on rock ledges cut on the sides of precipices.

Using techniques from China, they attacked one of the most difficult parts of the work: carrying the line over Cape Horn [promontory], with its sheer granite buttresses and steep shale embankments, 2,000 feet above the American River canyon. There was no foothold on its flanks. The indomitable Chinese, using age-old ways, were lowered from above in rope- held baskets, and there, suspended between earth and sky, they began to chip away with hammer and crowbar to form the narrow ledge that was later laboriously deepened to a shelf wide enough for the railway roadbed, 1,400 feet above the river.

Behind the advancing crews of Chinese builders came the money and supplies to keep the work going. This was an awesome exercise in logistics. The Big Four, unscrupulous, dishonest, and ruthless on a grand scale, were the geniuses of this effort. The marvel of engineering skill being created by Strobridge and his Chinese and Irish workers up in the Sierra was fed by a stream of iron rails, spikes, tools, blasting powder, locomotives, cars, and machinery. These materials arrived after an expensive and hazardous eight-month, 15,000-mile voyage from East Coast ports around Cape Horn to San Francisco, thence by river boat to Sacramento, and so to the railhead by road.

The weather, as well as the terrain, was harsh. The winter of 1865–1866 was one of the severest on record. Snow fell early, and storm after storm blanketed the Sierra Nevada. The ground froze solid. Sixty-foot drifts of snow had to be shoveled away before the graders could even reach the roadbed. Nearly half the work force of 9,000 men were set to clearing snow.

In these conditions, construction crews tackled the most formidable obstacle in their path: building the ten Summit Tunnels on the twenty-mile stretch between Cisco, ninety-two miles from Sacramento and Lake Ridge just west of Cold Stream Valley on the eastern slope of the summit. Work went on at all the tunnels simultaneously. Three shifts of eight hours each worked day and night.

The builders lived an eerie existence. In *The Big Four*, Oscar Lewis writes,

> Tunnels were dug beneath forty-foot drifts and for months, 3,000 workmen lived curious mole-like lives, passing from work to living quarters in dim passages far beneath the snow's surface…. [There] was constant danger, for as snows accumulated on the upper ridges, avalanches grew frequent, their approach heralded only by a brief thunderous roar. A second later, a work crew, a bunkhouse, an entire camp would go hurtling at a dizzy speed down miles of frozen canyon. Not until months later were the bodies recovered; sometimes groups were found with shovels or picks still clutched in their frozen hands.

On Christmas Day, 1866, the papers reported that "a gang of Chinamen employed by the railroad were covered up by a snow slide and four or five [note the imprecision] died before they could be exhumed." A whole camp of Chinese railway workers was enveloped during one night and had to be rescued by shovelers the next day.

No one has recorded the names of those who gave their lives in this stupendous undertaking. It is known that the bones of 1,200 men were shipped back to China to be buried in the land of their forefathers, but that was by no means the total score. The engineer John Gills recalled that "at Tunnel No. 10, some 15–20 Chinese [again, note the imprecision] were killed by a slide that winter. The year before, in the winter of 1864–65, two wagon road repairers had been buried and killed by a slide at the same location."

A. P. Partridge, who worked on the line, describes how 3,000 Chinese builders were driven out of the mountains by the early snow. "Most … came to Truckee and filled up all the old buildings and sheds. An old barn collapsed and killed four Chinese. A good many were frozen to death." One is astonished at the fortitude, discipline and dedication of the Chinese railroad workers.

Many years later, looking at the Union Pacific section of the line, an old railwayman remarked, "There's an Irishman buried under every tie of that road." Brawling, drink, cholera, and malaria took a heavy toll. The construction crew towns on the Union Pacific part of the track, with their saloons, gambling dens, and bordellos, were nicknamed "hells on wheels." Jack Casement, in charge of construction there, had been a general in the

Civil War and prided himself on the discipline of his fighting forces. His work crews worked with military precision, but off the job they let themselves go. One day, after gambling in the streets on payday (instigated by professional gamblers) had gotten too much out of hand, a visitor, finding the street suddenly very quiet, asked him where the gamblers had gone. Casement pointed to a nearby cemetery and replied, "They all died with their boots on." It was still the Wild West.

It is characteristic that only one single case of violent brawling was reported among the Chinese from the time they started work until they completed the job.

The Central Pacific's Chinese became expert at all kinds of work: grading, drilling, masonry, and demolition. Using black powder, they could average 1.18 feet daily through granite so hard that an incautiously placed charge could blow out backward. The Summit Tunnel work force was entirely composed of Chinese, with mainly Irish foremen. Thirty to forty worked on each face, with twelve to fifteen on the heading and the rest on the bottom removing material.

The Donner tunnels, totaling 1,695 feet, had to be bored through solid rock, and 9,000 Chinese worked on them. To speed the work, a new and untried explosive, nitroglycerin, was used. The tunnels were completed in November 1867, after thirteen months. But winter began before the way could be opened and the tracks laid. That winter was worse than the preceding one, but to save time it was necessary to send crews ahead to continue building the line even while the tunnels were being cut. Therefore, 3,000 men were sent with 400 carts and horses to Palisade Canyon, 300 miles in advance of the railhead. "Hay, grain and all supplies for men and horses had to be hauled by teams over the deserts for that great distance," writes Strobridge. "Water for men and animals was hauled at times 40 miles." Trees were felled and the logs laid side by side to form a "corduroy" roadway. On log sleds greased with lard, hundreds of Chinese manhandled three locomotives and forty wagons over the mountains. Strobridge later testified that it "cost nearly three times what it would have cost to have done it in the summertime when it should have been done. But we shortened the time seven years from what Congress expected when the act was passed."

Between 10,000 and 11,000 men were kept working on the line from 1866 to 1869. The Sisson and Wallace Company (in which Crocker's brother was a leading member) and the Dutch merchant Cornelius Koopmanschap of San Francisco procured these men for the line. Through the summer of 1866, Crocker's Pets—6,000 strong—swarmed over the upper canyons of the Sierra, methodically slicing cuttings and pouring rock and debris to make landfills and strengthen the foundations of trestle bridges. Unlike the Caucasian laborers, who drank unboiled stream water, the Chinese slaked their thirst with weak tea and boiled water kept in old whiskey kegs filled

28

by their mess cooks. They kept themselves clean and healthy by daily sponge baths in tubs of hot water prepared by their cooks, and the work went steadily forward.

Crocker has been described as a "hulking, relentless driver of men." But his Chinese crews responded to his leadership and drive and were caught up in the spirit of the epic work on which they were engaged. They cheered and waved their cartwheel hats as the first through train swept down the eastern slopes of the Sierra to the meeting of the lines. They worked with devotion and self-sacrifice to lay that twenty-odd miles of track for the Central Pacific Company in 1866 over the most difficult terrain. The cost of those miles was enormous—$280,000 a mile—but it brought the builders in sight of the easier terrain beyond the Sierra and the Rockies. Here costs of construction by veteran crews were only half the estimated amount of federal pay.

By summer 1868, an army of 14,000 railway builders was passing over the mountains into the great interior plain. Nine-tenths of that work force was Chinese. More than a quarter of all Chinese in the country were building the railway.

When every available Chinese in California had been recruited for the work, the Central Pacific arranged with Chinese labor contractors in San Francisco to get men direct from China and send them up to the railhead. It was evidently some of these newcomers who fell for the Piute Indian's tall tales of snakes in the desert "big enough to swallow a man easily." Thereupon "four or five hundred Chinese took their belongings and struck out to return directly to Sacramento," reports the *Alta California,* "Crocker and Company had spent quite a little money to secure them and they sent men on horseback after them. Most of them came back again kind of quieted down, and after nothing happened and they never saw any of the snakes, they forgot about them." At least one Chinese quit the job for a similar reason. His daughter, married to a professor of Chinese art, told me that her father had worked on the railway but quit because "he was scared of the bears." He later went into domestic service.

By September 1868, the track was completed for 307 miles from Sacramento, and the crews were laying rails across the plain east of the Sierra. Parallel with the track layers went the telegraph installers, stringing their wires on the poles and keeping the planners back at headquarters precisely apprised of where the end of the track was.

The Great Railway Competition

On the plains, the Chinese worked in tandem with all the Indians Crocker could entice to work on the iron rails. They began to hear of the exploits of the Union Pacific's "Irish terriers" building from the east. One day, the Irish laid six miles of track, they were told. The Chinese of the Central Pacific topped this with seven. "No Chinaman is going to beat us," growled the

Irish, and the next day, they laid seven and a half miles of track. They swore that they would outperform the competition no matter what it did.

Crocker taunted the Union Pacific that his men could lay ten miles of track a day. Durant, president of the rival line, laid a $10,000 wager that it could not be done. Crocker took no chances. He waited until the day before the last sixteen miles of track had to be laid and brought up all needed supplies for instant use. Then he unleashed his crews. On April 28, 1869, while Union Pacific checkers and newspaper reporters looked on, a combined gang of Chinese and eight picked Irish rail handlers laid ten miles and 1,800 feet more of track in twelve hours. This record was never surpassed until the advent of mechanized track laying. Each Irishman that day walked a total distance of ten miles, and their combined muscle handled sixty tons of rail.

So keen was the competition that when the two lines approached each other, instead of changing direction to link up, their builders careered on and on for 100 miles, building lines that would never meet. Finally, the government prescribed that the linkage point should be Promontory [Point], Utah.

Competition was keen, but there seems to be no truth in the story that the Chinese and Irish in this phase of work were trying to blow each other up with explosives. It is a fact, however, that when the two lines were very near each other, the Union Pacific blasters did not give the Central Pacific men timely warning when setting off a charge, and several Chinese were hurt. Then a Central Pacific charge went off unannounced and several Irishmen found themselves buried in dirt. This forced the foremen to take up the matter and an amicable settlement was arranged. There was no further trouble.

On May 10, 1869, the two lines were officially joined at Promontory [Point], north of Ogden in Utah. A great crowd gathered. A band played. An Irish crew and a Chinese crew were chosen to lay the last two rails side by side. The last tie was made of polished California laurel with a silver plate in its center proclaiming it "The last tie laid on the completion of the Pacific Railroad, May 10, 1869." But when the time came it was nowhere to be found. As consternation mounted, four Chinese approached with it on their shoulders and they laid it beneath the rails. A photographer stepped up and someone shouted to him "Shoot!" The Chinese only knew one meaning for that word. They fled. But order was restored and the famous ceremony began; Stanford drove a golden spike into the last tie with a silver hammer. The news flashed by telegraph to a waiting nation. But no Chinese appears in that famous picture of the toast celebrating the joining of the rails.

Crocker was one of the few who paid tribute to the Chinese that day: "I wish to call to your minds that the early completion of this railroad we have built has been in large measure due to the poor, despised class of laborers called the Chinese, to the fidelity and industry they have shown." No one even mentioned the name of Judah.

The building of the first transcontinental railway stands as a monument to the union of Yankee and Chinese-Irish drive and know-how. This was a formidable combination. They all complemented each other. Together they did in seven years what was expected to take at least fourteen.

In his book on the building of the railway, John Galloway, the noted transportation engineer, described this as "without doubt the greatest engineering feat of the nineteenth century," and that has never been disputed. David D. Colton, then vice-president of the Southern Pacific, was similarly generous in his praise of the Chinese contribution. He was asked, while giving evidence before the 1876 congressional committee, "Could you have constructed that road without Chinese labor?" He replied, "I do not think it could have been constructed so quickly, and with anything like the same amount of certainty as to what we were going to accomplish in the same length of time."

And, in answer to the question, "Do you think the Chinese have been a benefit to the State?" West Evans, a railway contractor, testified, "I do not see how we could do the work we have done, here, without them; at least I have done work that would not have been done if it had not been for the Chinamen, work that could not have been done without them."

It was heroic work. The Central Pacific crews had carried their railway 1,800 miles through the Sierra and Rocky mountains, over sagebrush desert and plain. The Union Pacific built only 689 miles, over much easier terrain. It had 500 miles in which to carry its part of the line to a height of 5,000 feet, with another fifty more miles in which to reach the high passes of the Black Hills. With newly recruited crews, the Central Pacific had to gain an altitude of 7,000 feet from the plain in just over 100 miles and make a climb of 2,000 feet in just 20 miles.

All this monumental work was done before the age of mechanization. It was pick and shovel, hammer and crowbar work, with baskets for earth carried slung from shoulder poles and put on one-horse carts.

For their heroic work, the Chinese workmen began with a wage of $26 a month, providing their own food and shelter. This was gradually raised to $30 to $35 a month. Caucasians were paid the same amount of money, but their food and shelter were provided. Because it cost $0.75 to $1.00 a day to feed a white unskilled worker, each Chinese saved the Central Pacific, at a minimum, two-thirds the price of a white laborer (1865 rates). Chinese worked as masons, dynamiters, and blacksmiths and at other skilled jobs that paid white workers from $3 to $5 a day. So, at a minimum, the company saved about $5 million by hiring Chinese workers.

Did this really "deprive white workers of jobs" as anti-Chinese agitators claimed? Certainly not. In the first place, experience had proved that white workers simply did not want the jobs the Chinese took on the railroad. In fact, the Chinese created jobs for white workers as straw bosses, foremen, railhandlers, teamsters, and supervisors.

The wages paid to the Chinese were, in fact, comparable to those paid unskilled or semiskilled labor in the East (where labor was relatively plentiful), and the Chinese were at first satisfied. Charles Nordhoff estimated that the frugal Chinese could save about $13 a month out of those wages. The *Alta California* estimated their savings at $20 a month and later, perhaps, as wages increased, they could lay aside even more. With a bit of luck, a year and a half to two years of work would enable them to return to China with $400 to buy a bit of land and be well-to-do farmers.

But the Chinese began to learn the American way of life. On one occasion in June 1867, 2,000 tunnelers went on strike, asking for $40 a month, an eight-hour day in the tunnels, and an end to beating by foremen. "Eight hours a day good for white man, all same good for Chinese," said their spokesman in the pidgin English common in the construction camps. But solidarity with the other workers was lacking, and after a week the strike was called off when the Chinese heard that Crocker was recruiting strikebreakers from the eastern states.

When the task was done, most of the Chinese railwaymen were paid off. Some returned to China with their hard-earned savings, and the epic story of building the Iron Horse's pathway across the continent must have regaled many a family gathering there. Some returned with souvenirs of the great work, chips of one of the last ties, which had been dug up and split up among them. Some settled in the little towns that had grown up along the line of the railway. Others took the railway to seek adventure further east and south. Most made their way back to California and took what jobs they could find in that state's growing industries, trades, and other occupations. Many used their traditional and newly acquired skills on the other transcontinental lines and railways that were being swiftly built in the West and Midwest. This was the start of the diaspora of the Chinese immigrants in America.

The Union and Central Pacific tycoons had done well out of the building of the line. Congressional investigation committees later calculated that, of $73 million poured into the Union Pacific coffers, no more than $50 million could be justified as true costs. The Big Four and their associates in the Central Pacific had done even better. They had made at least $63 million and owned most of the CP stock worth around $100 million and 9 million acres of land grants to boot.

Ironically, the great railway soon had disastrous results for the Chinese themselves. It now cost only $40 for an immigrant to cross the continent by rail and a flood of immigrants took advantage of the ease and cheapness of travel on the line the Chinese had helped to build. The labor shortage (and resulting high wages) in California turned into a glut. When the tangled affairs of the Northern Pacific line led to the stock market crash of Black Friday, September 19, 1873, and to financial panic, California experienced its first real economic depression. There was devastating unemployment, and the Chinese were made the scapegoats.

Building Other Lines

The expansion of the railroads was even faster in the following decade. In 1850, the United States had 9,000 miles of track. In 1860, it had 30,000. In 1890, it had over 70,000 miles. Three years later, it had five transcontinental lines.

The first transcontinental railway was soon followed by four more links: (1) the Southern Pacific–Texas and Pacific, completed in 1883 from San Francisco to Texas by way of Yuma, Tucson, and El Paso; (2) the Atcheson, Topeka, and Santa Fe, completed in 1885 from Kansas City to Los Angeles via Santa Fe and Albuquerque; (3) the Northern Pacific, completed in 1883 from Duluth, Minnesota, to Portland, Oregon; and (4) the Great Northern (1893). The skill of the Chinese as railroad builders was much sought after, and Chinese worked on all these lines. Some 15,000 worked on the Northern Pacific, laying tracks in Washington, Idaho, and Montana; 250 on the Houston and Texas line; 600 on the Alabama and Chattanooga line; 70 on the New Orleans line. Nearly 500 Chinese were recruited for the Union Pacific even after the lines were joined. Many worked in the Wyoming coal mines and during the summer months doubled as track laborers. They carried the Southern Pacific lines over the burning Mojave Desert. They helped link San Francisco with Portland in 1887.

The Canadian Pacific seized the chance to enlist veteran Chinese railwaymen from the Southern Pacific and Northern Pacific railroads and also brought Chinese workers direct from China. In 1880, some 1,500 were working on that line, increasing to 6,500 two years later. Casualties were heavy on this line. Hundreds lost their lives while working on it.

Chinese railwaymen helped on the Central and Southern Pacific's main line down the San Joaquin Valley in 1870 and 1871. They worked on the hookup to Los Angeles and the loop with seventeen tunnels over the Tehachapi Pass completed in 1876. On this line, 1,000 Chinese worked on the 6,975-foot San Fernando Tunnel, the longest in the West. This rail link between San Francisco and Los Angeles, tapping the rich Central Valley, played a major role in the development of California's agriculture, later its biggest industry. They worked on the line north from Sacramento along the Shasta route to Portland, which was reached in 1887. In 1869, the Virginia and Truckee line employed 450 Chinese, veterans of the Central Pacific, to grade its track. When the Virginia and Truckee's Carson and Colorado branch line was planned from Mound House to Benton, its tough manager Yerington arranged with the unions for the grading to be done by white labor to Dayton and by Chinese from Dayton on south. "If the entire line had to be graded by white labor, I would not think of driving a pick into the ground, but would abandon the undertaking entirely," he said.

Chinese laborers worked on the trans-Panamanian railway, which linked the Pacific and the Atlantic before the Panama Canal was completed. This railway played a major role in speeding up the economic development of the United States, but it was not built without sacrifice: hundreds of the Chinese builders died of fever and other causes during its construction.

This by no means completes the list of contributions of the Chinese railway workers. The transcontinental lines on which they worked "more than any other factor helped make the United States a united nation," writes the *Encyclopedia Britannica* ["Railways"]. They played a major role in building the communications network of iron roads that was the transport base of American industrial might in the twentieth century.

Speaking eloquently in favor of the Chinese immigrants, Oswald Garrison Villard said,

> I want to remind you of the things that Chinese labor did in opening up the Western portion of this country.... [They] stormed the forest fastnesses, endured cold and heat and the risk of death at hands of hostile Indians to aid in the opening up of our northwestern empire. I have a dispatch from the chief engineer of the Northwestern Pacific telling how Chinese laborers went out into eight feet of snow with the temperature far below zero to carry on the work when no American dared face the conditions.

And these men were from China's sun-drenched south, where it never snows.

In certain circles, there has been a conspiracy of silence about the Chinese railroadmen and what they did. When U.S. Secretary of Transportation John Volpe spoke at the "Golden Spike" centenary, not a single Chinese American was invited, and he made no mention in his speech of the Chinese railroad builders.

DOCUMENTS

California Must Be All American, *1878*

... To add to our misery and despair, a bloated aristocracy [business leadership] has sent to China—the greatest and oldest despotism in the world—for a cheap working slave. It rakes the slums of Asia to find the meanest slave on earth—the Chinese coolie—and imports him here to meet the free American in the Labor market, and still further widen the breach between the rich and the poor, still further to degrade white Labor. These cheap

SOURCE: Dennis Kearney, "Appeal from California," *Indianapolis Times*, February 18, 1878.

slaves fill every place. Their dress is scant and cheap. Their food is rice from China. They hedge twenty in a room, ten by ten. They are wipped curs, abject in docility, mean, contemptible and obedient in all things. They have no wives, children or dependents.

They are imported by companies, controlled as serfs, worked like slaves, and at last go back to China with all their earnings. They are in every place, they seem to have no sex. Boys work, girls work; it is all alike to them. The father of a family is met by them at every turn. Would he get work for himself? Ah! A stout Chinaman does it cheaper. Will he get a place for his oldest boy? He can not. His girl? Why, the Chinaman is in her place too! Every door is closed. He can only go to crime or suicide, his wife and daughter to prostitution, and his boys to hoodlumism and the penitentiary.

Do not believe those who call us savages, rioters, incendiaries, and outlaws. We seek our ends calmly, rationally, at the ballot box. So far good order has marked all our proceedings. But, we know how false, how inhuman, our adversaries are. We know that if gold, if fraud, if force can defeat us, they will all be used. And we have resolved that they shall not defeat us. We shall arm. We shall meet fraud and falsehood with defiance, and force with force, if need be. We are men, and propose to live like men in this free land, without the contamination of slave labor, or die like men, if need be, in asserting the rights of our race, our country, and our families.

California must be all American or all Chinese. We are resolved that it shall be American, and are prepared to make it so. May we not rely upon your sympathy and assistance?

Homesteading in South Dakota in the 1880s, 1930

On May 6, 1881, I left my beloved Fatherland and came to America. I still do not know why I left, for I was working for some very fine people with whom I had been for three years. They always said, "Stay here." I would have liked very much to go back once more but that did not come to pass. I was often homesick.

I already knew my husband in the old country. On May 26, 1881, I arrived at my sister's near Bloomington, Illinois. I worked for an English Methodist family. They were very fine people, and I often think of them. They have gone to "The Eternal Home" long ago.

October 20th, 1881, we were married in Bloomington, Illinois, at the parsonage of the Lutheran minister. My husband was working for $20.00 per month and free house rent. We lived in a little log cabin with one room and a small kitchen attached. Those were very beautiful times. We

SOURCE: Family history of Caroline Reimers, author's possession, 1930.

had two cows, hogs and chickens. But my husband was always desirous to have land of his own, and land in Illinois was too high in price for us to buy.

So when reservations were offered in South Dakota in 1883, my husband and his three brothers went to South Dakota and each staked a claim for 160 acres of land. It (South Dakota) has a very beautiful climate but lacks rain. We were there for 12 years....

In 1888 we had the great snowstorm in South Dakota where so many school children lost their lives because the roofs were blown from the schoolhouses. The wind blew from 70 to 80 miles per hour and it was a dreadful storm.

In 1889 we had the great prairie-fire in which we lost everything, by fire, except our house and horses and cows. Everything else was burnt. That almost frightened us into leaving, for our children started to go to school a distance of two miles out in the prairie.

So we traded our land for two horses. There were no good years. We sold our best cows for $15.00, wheat for 35¢, corn for 15¢. We raised two bushels per acre. Those were hard years. But we always had enough to eat to satisfy our hunger.

We had no money, so we hitched our three horses to a moving wagon and started to Missouri, to my husband's brother in Marceline. It took us three weeks and a few days....

A Montana Cowtown, 1899

A true "cow town" is worth seeing,—such a one as Miles City, for instance, especially at the time of the annual meeting of the great Montana Stockraisers' Association. Then the whole place is full to overflowing, the importance of the meeting and the fun of the attendant frolics, especially the horse-races, drawing from the surrounding ranch country many hundreds of men of every degree, from the rich stock-owner worth his millions to the ordinary cowboy who works for forty dollars a month. It would be impossible to imagine a more typically American assemblage, for although there are always a certain number of foreigners, usually English, Irish, or German, yet they have become completely Americanized; and on the whole it would be difficult to gather a finer body of men, in spite of their numerous shortcomings. The ranch-owners differ more from each other than do the cowboys; and the former certainly compare very favorably with similar classes of capitalists in the East. Anything more foolish than the demagogic outcry against "cattle kings" it would be difficult to imagine.

SOURCE: Theodore Roosevelt, *Ranch Life and the Hunting-Trail* (New York: Century Co., 1899), 7, 10–11. Reprinted University Microfilms, Ann Arbor, Michigan, 1966.

Indeed, there are very few businesses so absolutely legitimate as stock-raising and so beneficial to the nation at large; and a successful stock-grower must not only be shrewd, thrifty, patient, and enterprising, but he must also possess qualities of personal bravery, hardihood, and self-reliance to a degree not demanded in the least by any mercantile occupation in a community long settled. Stockmen are in the West the pioneers of civilization, and their daring and adventurousness make the after settlement of the region possible. The whole country owes them a great debt....

The bulk of the cowboys themselves are South-westerners; but there are also many from the Eastern and the Northern States, who, if they begin young, do quite as well as the Southerners. The best hands are fairly bred to the work and follow it from their youth up. Nothing can be more foolish than for an Easterner to think he can become a cowboy in a few months' time. Many a young fellow comes out hot with enthusiasm for life on the plains, only to learn that his clumsiness is greater than he could have believed possible; that the cowboy business is like any other and has to be learned by serving a painful apprenticeship; and that this apprenticeship implies the endurance of rough fare, hard living, dirt, exposure of every kind, no little toil, and month after month of the dullest monotony. For cowboy work there is need of special traits and special training, and young Easterners should be sure of themselves before trying it. The struggle for existence is very keen in the far West, and it is no place for men who lack the ruder, coarser virtues and physical qualities, no matter how intellectual or how refined and delicate their sensibilities. Such are more likely to fail there than in older communities. Probably during the past few years more than half of the young Easterners who have come West with a little money to learn the cattle business have failed signally and lost what they had in the beginning. The West, especially the far West, needs men who have been bred on the farm or in the workshop far more than it does clerks or college graduates.

Some of the cowboys are Mexicans, who generally do the actual work well enough, but are not trustworthy; moreover, they are always regarded with extreme disfavor by the Texans in an outfit, among whom the intolerant caste spirit is very strong. Southern-born whites will never work under them, and look down upon all colored or half-caste races. One spring I had with my wagon a Pueblo Indian, an excellent rider and roper, but a drunken, worthless, lazy devil; and in the summer of 1886 there were with us a Sioux half-breed, a quiet, hard-working, faithful fellow, and a mulatto, who was one of the best cow-hands in the whole round-up.

Chapter 3

Indian Schools: "Americanizing" the Native American

Bettmann/Corbis

Native American girls at the Carlisle School for Indians, Carlisle, Pa.

The white settlers' movement onto the Great Plains devastated Native American tribes who had roamed the area for centuries. As on previous frontiers farther east, the Indians resisted the encroachment with some initial success, their most notable victory the defeat of General George Custer at the Little Bighorn River in 1876. However, the whites' superior manpower and technology, fueled by their desire to fulfill a "manifest destiny" to develop the entire continent, overcame the Native Americans, and in the end the whites removed virtually all of them to reservations.

During the 1870s and 1880s, even while the last Indian wars raged, the federal government passed legislation and instituted policies designed to solve the "Indian problem" by "Americanizing" them—assimilating them into American society. The federal government encouraged them, sometimes forcefully, to exchange their lands, held by the tribe as a whole, for individual holdings that they were expected to farm. Equally important, the government sought to educate their children away from their traditional cultures and provide them with the skills, knowledge, and attitudes deemed necessary for the new way of life that the dominant white culture dictated.

By 1881 the federal government operated 106 Indian day and boarding schools to accomplish these objectives. Although most of the schools were on or adjacent to reservation land, white educators placed their greatest faith in nonreservation boarding schools far removed from parental and tribal influences. Robert A. Trennert's essay, "Educating Indian Girls at Nonreservation Boarding Schools, 1878–1920," provides a detailed view of this policy in action. What do you think the advocates of Indian education meant by "assimilation"? To what does the author attribute the failure of the government's Indian-school policies during this period?

The first document consists of excerpts from the "Rules for Indian Schools" set forth by the Bureau of Indian Affairs (1890). What attitudes toward their mission and toward Native American youth would these instructions likely engender in the minds of the teachers who read them? In what ways does each of the rules cited contribute to the broad objectives of the government's Indian-education policies? What can you conclude about the immediate and long-term objectives of Indian education?

Although the government expressed its land and educational policies in positive terms, these principles in fact reflected the prevailing belief that the Native American culture was inferior. At the turn of the century, many social scientists had adapted Darwin's biological theories of evolution to explain social development, drawing conclusions totally rejected by their counterparts today. Specifically, they developed a theoretical hierarchy of superior and inferior races that placed northern Europeans at the top and Indians, blacks, and southern and eastern Europeans, among others, at the bottom. The second document, a 1905 report of the Board of Indian Commissioners, typifies the attitudes underlying governmental policies until the 1930s. This report sheds light on the basis for Indian policy and reveals much of the rationale for the immigration-restriction and racial-segregation laws of the era. In the final document, a Native American recalls her first days as a student in a government boarding school. How effective do you believe the treatment she received was in achieving the goal of weaning her away from her Indian culture, of "Americanizing" her? What evidence can you provide to demonstrate that educational policies and practices regarding Native American and other minority cultures have changed since the nineteenth and early twentieth centuries?

ESSAY

Educating Indian Girls
at Nonreservation Boarding Schools, 1878–1920

Robert A. Trennert

During the latter part of the nineteenth century the Bureau of Indian Affairs made an intensive effort to assimilate the Indian into American society. One important aspect of the government's acculturation program was Indian education. By means of reservation day schools, reservation boarding schools, and off-reservation industrial schools, the federal government attempted to obliterate the cultural heritage of Indian youths and replace it with the values of Anglo-American society. One of the more notable aspects of this program was the removal of young Indian women from their tribal homes to government schools in an effort to transform them into a government version of the ideal American woman. This program of assimilationist education, despite some accomplishments, generally failed to attain its goals. This study is a review of the education of Indian women at the institutions that best typified the government program—the off-reservation industrial training schools. An understanding of this educational system provides some insight into the impact of the acculturation effort on the native population. Simultaneously, it illustrates some of the prevalent national images regarding both Indians and women.

The concept of educating native women first gained momentum among eighteenth-century New England missionaries who recommended that Indian girls might benefit from formal training in housekeeping. This idea matured to the point that, by the 1840s, the federal government had committed itself to educating Indian girls in the hope that women trained as good housewives would help their mates assimilate. A basic premise of this educational effort rested on the necessary elimination of Indian culture. Although recent scholarship has suggested that the division of labor between the sexes within Indian societies was rather equitable, mid-nineteenth-century Americans accepted a vision of Native American women as slaves toiling endlessly for their selfish, slovenly husbands and fathers in an atmosphere of immorality, degradation, and lust. Any cursory glance at contemporary literature provides striking evidence of this belief. Joel D. Steele, for example, in his 1876 history of the American nation described Indian society in the following terms: "The Indian was a barbarian.... Labor he considered degrading, and fit only for women. His squaw, therefore, built his wigwam,

SOURCE: Robert A Trennert, "Educating Indian Girls at Nonreservation Boarding Schools, 1878–1920," *Western Historical Quarterly* 13 (July 1982): 169–90. Copyright by the Western History Association. Reprinted by permission.

cut his wood, and carried his burdens when he journeyed. While he hunted or fished, she cleared the land ... and dressed skins."

Government officials and humanitarian reformers shared Steele's opinion. Secretary of the Interior Carl Schurz, a noted reformer, stated in 1881 that "the Indian woman has so far been only a beast of burden. The girl, when arrived at maturity, was disposed of like an article of trade. The Indian wife was treated by her husband alternately with animal fondness, and with the cruel brutality of the slave driver." Neither Steele nor Schurz was unique in his day; both expressed the general opinion of American society. From this perspective, if women were to be incorporated into American society, their sexual role and social standing stood in need of change.

The movement to educate Indian girls reflected new trends in women's education. Radical changes in the economic and social life of late nineteenth-century America set up a movement away from the traditional academy education of young women. Economic opportunity created by the industrial revolution combined with the decline of the family as a significant economic unit produced a demand for vocational preparation for women. The new school discipline of "domestic science," a modern homemaking technique, developed as a means to bring stability and scientific management to the American family and provide skills to the increasing number of women entering the work force. In the years following the Civil War, increased emphasis was placed on domestic and vocational education as schools incorporated the new discipline into their curriculum. Similar emphasis appeared in government planning for the education of Indian women as a means of their forced acculturation. However, educators skirted the question of whether native women should be trained for industry or homemaking.

During the 1870s, with the tribes being confined to reservations, the government intensified its efforts to provide education for Indian youth of both sexes. The establishment of the industrial training schools at the end of the decade accelerated the commitment to educate Indian women. These schools got their start in 1878 when Captain Richard Henry Pratt, in charge of a group of Indian prisoners at Fort Marion, Florida, persuaded the government to educate eighteen of the younger male inmates at Hampton Normal Institute, an all-black school in Virginia, run by General Samuel C. Armstrong. Within six months Pratt and Armstrong were pleased enough with the results of their experiment to request more students. Both men strongly believed that girls should be added to the program, and Armstrong even went so far as to stipulate that Hampton would take more Indian students only on condition that half be women. At first Indian Commissioner Ezra A. Hayt rejected the proposal, primarily because he questioned the morality of allowing Indian women to mix with black men, but Armstrong's argument that "without educated women there is no civilization" finally prevailed. Thus, when Pratt journeyed west in the fall of 1878 to recruit more students, he fully expected half to be women.

Pratt was permitted to enlist fifty Indian students on his trip up the Missouri River. Mrs. Pratt went along to aid with the enlistment of girls. Although they found very little problem in recruiting a group of boys, they had numerous difficulties locating girls. At Fort Berthold, for instance, the Indians objected to having their young women taken away from home. Pratt interpreted this objection in terms of his own ethnocentric beliefs, maintaining that Indian tribes made their "squaws" do all the work. "They are too valuable in the capacity of drudge during the years they should be at school to be spared to go," he reported. Ultimately it required the help of local missionaries to secure four female students. Even then there were unexpected problems. As Pratt noted, "One of the girls [age ten] was especially bright and there was a general desire to save her from the degradation of her Indian surroundings. The mother [age twenty-six] said that education and civilization would make her child look upon her as a savage, and that unless she could go with her child and learn too, the child could not come." Pratt included both mother and daughter. Not all the missionaries and government agents, however, shared Pratt's enthusiasm. At Cheyenne River and other agencies a number of officials echoed the sentiments of Commissioner Hayt regarding the morality of admitting girls to a black school, and they succeeded in blocking recruitment. As a result, only nine girls were sent to Hampton.

Although the educational experiences of the first Indian girls to attend Hampton have not been well documented, a few things are evident. The girls were kept under strict supervision and were separated from the boys except during times of classroom instruction. In addition, the girls were kept apart from black pupils. Most of the academic work was focused on learning the English language, and the girls also received instruction in household skills. The small number of girls, of course, made it difficult to implement a general educational plan. Moreover, considerable opposition remained to educating Indian women at Hampton. Many prominent reformers expected confrontations, or even worse, love affairs, between black and red. Others expressed concern that Indian students in an all-black setting would not receive sufficient incentive and demanded they have the benefit of direct contact with white citizens.

Captain Pratt himself wanted to separate the Indians and blacks, and despite the fact that no racial trouble surfaced at Hampton, he pressured the government to create a school solely for Indians. Indian contact with blacks did not fit in with his plans for native education, and he reminded Secretary Schurz that Indians could become useful citizens only "through living among our people." The government consented, and in the summer of 1879 Pratt was authorized to open a school at Carlisle Barracks, Pennsylvania, "provided both boys and girls are educated in said school." Thus, while Hampton continued to develop its own Indian program, it was soon accompanied by Carlisle and other all-Indian schools.

Under the guidance of General Armstrong at Hampton and Captain Pratt at Carlisle, a program for Indian women developed over a period of several years. Although these men differed on the question of racial mixing, they agreed on what Indian girls should be learning. By 1880, with fifty-seven Indian girls at Carlisle and about twenty at Hampton, the outlines of the program began to emerge. As rapidly as possible the girls were placed in a system that put maximum emphasis on domestic chores. Academic learning clearly played a subordinate role. The girls spent no more than half a day in the classroom and devoted the rest of their time to domestic work. At Carlisle the first arrivals were instructed in "the manufacture and mending of garments, the use of the sewing machine, laundry work, cooking, and the routine of household duties pertaining to their sex."

Discipline went hand in hand with work experience. Both Pratt and Armstrong possessed military backgrounds and insisted that girls be taught strict obedience. General Armstrong believed that obedience was completely foreign to the native mind and that discipline was a corollary to civilization. Girls, he thought, were more unmanageable than boys because of their "inherited spirit of independence." To instill the necessary discipline, the entire school routine was organized in martial fashion, and every facet of student life followed a strict timetable. Students who violated the rules were punished, sometimes by corporal means, but more commonly by ridicule. Although this discipline was perhaps no more severe than that in many non-Indian schools of the day, it contrasted dramatically with tribal educational patterns that often mixed learning with play. Thus, when Armstrong offered assurances that children accepted "the penalty gratefully as part of his [her] education in the good road," it might be viewed with a bit of skepticism.

Another integral part of the program centered on the idea of placing girls among white families to learn by association. The "outing" system, as it was soon called, began almost as quickly as the schools received students. Through this system Pratt expected to take Indian girls directly from their traditional homes and in three years make them acceptable for placement in public schools and private homes. By 1881 both Carlisle and Hampton were placing girls in white homes, most of which were located in rural Pennsylvania or New England. Here the girls were expected to become independent, secure a working knowledge of the English language, and acquire useful domestic skills. Students were usually sent to a family on an individual basis, although in a few cases several young women were placed in the same home. Emily Bowen, an outing program sponsor in Woodstock, Connecticut, reveals something of white motives for participation in the service. Miss Bowen, a former teacher, heard of Pratt's school in 1880 and became convinced that God had called upon her to "lift up the lowly." Hesitating to endure the dangers of the frontier, she volunteered instead to take eight Indian girls into her home to "educate them to return and be a blessing to their people." Bowen proposed to teach the girls "practical things, such as housework, sewing, and all that is necessary to make home comfortable and pleasant." In this manner, she hoped, the girls under her charge would take the "true missionary spirit" with them on their return to their people.

Having set the women's education program in motion, Pratt and his colleagues took time to reflect on just what result they anticipated from the training. In his 1881 report to Commissioner Hiram Price, Pratt charted out his expectations. Essentially he viewed the education of native girls as a supportive factor in the more important work of training boys. To enter American society, the Indian male needed a mate who would encourage his success and prevent any backsliding. "Of what avail is it," Pratt asked, "that the man be hard-working and industrious, providing by his labor, food and clothing for his household, if the wife, unskilled in cookery, unused to the needle, with no habits of order or neatness, makes what might be a cheerful, happy home only a wretched abode of filth and squalor?" Pratt charged Indian women with clinging to "heathen rites and superstitions" and passing them on to their children. They were, in effect, unfit as mothers and wives. Thus, a woman's education was supremely important, not so much for her own benefit as for that of her husband. Pratt did acknowledge that girls were required to learn more than boys. An Indian male needed only to learn a single trade; the woman, on the other hand, "must learn to sew and to cook, to wash and iron, she must learn lessons of neatness, order, and economy, for without a practical knowledge of all these she cannot make a home."

The size of the girls' program increased dramatically during the 1880s. The government was so taken with the apparent success of Carlisle and Hampton that it began to open similar schools in the West. As the industrial schools expanded, however, the women's program became institutionalized, causing a substantial deviation from the original concept. One reason for this change involved economic factors. The Indian schools, which for decades received $167 a year per student, suffered a chronic lack of funds; thus, to remain self-sufficient, they found themselves relying upon student labor whenever possible. Because they already believed in the educational value of manual labor, it was not a large step for school officials to begin relying upon student labor to keep the schools operating. By the mid-1880s, with hundreds of women attending the industrial schools, student labor had assumed a significant role in school operations. Thus, girls, originally expected to receive a useful education, found themselves becoming more important as an economic factor in the survival of the schools.

The girls' work program that developed at Hampton is typical of the increasing reliance on Indian labor. By 1883 the women's training section was divided into such departments as sewing, housekeeping, and laundry, each in the charge of a white matron or a black graduate. The forty-one girls assigned to the sewing department made the school's bedding, wardrobe, and curtains. At Winona Lodge, the dormitory for Indian girls that also supported the housework division, the matron described the work routine as follows: "All of the Indian girls, from eight to twenty-four years old, make their own clothes, wash and iron them, care for their rooms, and a great many of them take care of the teachers' rooms. Besides this they have extra work, such as sweeping, dusting, and scrubbing the corridors, stairs, hall, sewing-room, chapel, and cleaning other parts of the building." In addition, a large group of Indian girls worked in the school laundry doing the institution's wash.

Conditions were even more rigorous at western schools where a lack of labor put additional demands on female students. At Genoa, Nebraska, the superintendent reported that the few girls enrolled in that school were kept busy doing housework. With the exception of the laundry, which was detailed to the boys, girls were responsible for the sewing and repair of garments, including their own clothes, the small boys' wear, underwear for the large boys, and table linen. The kitchen, dining room, and dormitories were also maintained by women students. Similar circumstances prevailed at Albuquerque, where Superintendent P. F. Burke complained of having to use boys for domestic chores. He was much relieved when enough girls enrolled to allow "the making of the beds, sweeping, and cleaning both the boys' and girls' sleeping apartments." Because of inadequate facilities there were no girls enrolled when the Phoenix school opened in 1891; but as soon as a permanent building was constructed, Superintendent Wellington Rich requested twenty girls "to take the places now filled by boys in the several domestic departments of the school." Such uses of student labor were justified as a method of preparing girls for the duties of home life.

Some employees of the Indian Service recognized that assembly line chores alone were not guaranteed to accomplish the goals of the program. Josephine Mayo, the girls' matron at Genoa, reported in 1886 that the work program was too "wholesale" to produce effective housewives. "Making a dozen beds and cleaning a dormitory does not teach them to make a room attractive and homelike," she remarked. Nor did cooking large quantities of a single item "supply a family with a pleasant and healthy variety of food, nicely cooked." The matron believed that Indian girls needed to be taught in circumstances similar to those they were expected to occupy. She therefore suggested that small cottages be utilized in which girls could be instructed in the care of younger students and perform all the duties of a housewife. Although Mayo expressed a perceptive concern for the inherent problems of the system, her remarks had little impact on federal school officials. In the meantime, schools were expected to run effectively, and women continued to perform much of the required labor.

Not all the girls' programs, of course, were as routine or chore oriented as the ones cited above. Several of the larger institutions made sincere efforts to train young Indian women as efficient householders. Girls were taught to care for children, to set tables, prepare meals, and make domestic repairs. After 1896 Haskell Institute in Kansas provided women with basic commercial skills in stenography, typing, and bookkeeping. Nursing, too, received attention at some schools. A number of teachers, though conventional in their views of Indian women's role, succeeded in relaxing the rigid school atmosphere. Teachers at Hampton, for instance, regularly invited small groups of girls to their rooms for informal discussions. Here girls, freed from the restraints of the classroom, could express their feelings and receive some personal encouragement. Many institutions permitted their girls to have a dress "with at least some imitation of prevailing style" and urged them to take pride in their appearance.

The industrial schools reached their peak between 1890 and 1910. During this period as many as twenty-five nonreservation schools were in operation. The number of Indian women enrolled may have reached three thousand per annum during this period and females composed between 40 and 50 percent of the student body of most schools. The large number of young women can be attributed to several factors: girls were easier to recruit, they presented fewer disciplinary problems and could be more readily placed in the "outing" system, and after 1892 they could be sent to school without parental consent.

Women's education also became more efficient and standardized during the 1890s. This was due in large part to the activities of Thomas J. Morgan, who served as Indian commissioner from 1889 to 1893. Morgan advocated the education of Indian women as an important part of the acculturation process, believing that properly run schools could remove girls from the "degradation" of camp life and place them on a level with "their more favored white sisters." The commissioner hoped to accomplish this feat by completely systematizing the government's educational program. "So far as possible," he urged, "there should be a uniform course of study, similar methods of instruction, the same textbooks, and a carefully organized and well understood system of industrial training." His suggestions received considerable support, and by 1890, when he issued his "Rules for Indian Schools," the standardization of the Indian schools had begun. Morgan, like Pratt before him, fully expected his concept of education to rapidly produce American citizens. The results were not what the commissioner expected. While standardization proved more efficient, it also exacerbated some of the problems of the women's educational program.

Under the direction of Morgan and his successors, the Indian schools of the era became monuments to regimentation from which there was no escape. This development is obvious in the increasing emphasis on military organization. By the mid-nineties most girls were fully incorporated into the soldierly routine. As one superintendent noted, all students were organized into companies on the first day of school. Like the boys, the girls wore uniforms and were led by student officers who followed army drill regulations. Every aspect of student life was regulated. Anna Moore, a Pima girl attending the Phoenix Indian School, remembered life in the girls' battalion as one of marching "to a military tune" and having to drill at five in the morning. Most school officials were united in their praise of military organization. Regimentation served to develop a work ethic; it broke the students' sense of "Indian time" and ordered their life. The merits of military organization, drill, and routine in connection with discipline were explained by one official who stated that "it teaches patriotism, obedience, courage, courtesy, promptness, and constancy."

Domestic science continued to dominate the women's program. Academic preparation for women never received much emphasis by industrial school administrators despite Morgan's promise that "literary" training would occupy half the students' time…. One reason for the lack of emphasis on academics was that by 1900 many school administrators had come to feel that Indians were incapable of learning more. One school superintendent did not consider his "literary" graduates capable of accomplishing much in white society, while another educator described the natives as a "child race."

The extent to which every feature of the girls' program was directed toward the making of proper middle-class housewives can be seen in the numerous directives handed down by the government. By the early twentieth century every detail of school life was regulated. In 1904 Superintendent of Indian Schools Estelle Reel issued a three-page circular on the proper method of making a bed. Much of this training bore little relationship to the reservation environment to which students would return. A few programs were entirely divorced from reality. The cooking course at Sherman Institute in California, for instance, taught girls to prepare formal meals including the serving of raw oysters, shrimp cocktails, and croquettes. In another instance, Hampton teachers devoted some of their energies to discussing attractive flower arrangements and the proper selection of decorative pictures.

Another popular program was the "industrial" cottage. These originated in 1883 at Hampton when the school enrolled several married Indian couples to serve as examples for the students. The couples were quartered in small frame houses while learning to maintain attractive and happy homes. Although the married students did not long remain at Hampton, school officials began to use the cottages as model homes where squads of Indian girls might practice living in white-style homes. By 1900 similar cottages were in use at western schools. The industrial cottage at Phoenix, for example, operated a "well-regulated household" run by nine girls under a matron's supervision. The "family" (with no males present) cleaned and decorated the cottage, did the regular routine of cooking, washing, and sewing, and tended to the poultry and livestock in an effort "to train them to the practical and social enjoyment of the higher life of a real home."

The outing system also continued to be an integral part of the girls' program. As time went on, however, and the system was adopted at western locations, the original purposes of the outings faded. Initially designed as a vehicle for acculturation, the program at many locations became a means of providing servants to white householders. At Phoenix, for example, female pupils formed a pool of cheap labor available to perform domestic services for local families. From the opening of the school in 1891, demands for student labor always exceeded the pool's capacity. One superintendent estimated that he could easily put two hundred girls to work. Moreover, not all employers were interested in the welfare of the student. As the Phoenix superintendent stated in 1894, "The hiring of Indian youth is not looked upon by the people of this valley from a philanthropic standpoint. It is simply a matter of business." In theory, school authorities could return pupils to school at any time it appeared they were not receiving educational benefits; but as one newspaper reported, "What a howl would go up from residents of this valley if the superintendent would exercise this authority."

Even social and religious activities served an educational purpose. When Mrs. Merial Dorchester, wife of the superintendent of Indian schools, made a tour of western school facilities in the early 1890s, she recommended that school girls organize chapters of the King's Daughters, a Christian service organization. Several institutions implemented the program. At these locations girls were organized by age into "circles" to spend spare time producing handcrafted goods for charity. School officials supported such activity because the necessity of raising their own funds to pay dues instilled in the girls a spirit of Christian industry. The manufacture of goods for charity also enhanced their sense of service to others. Said one school superintendent, the organization is "effective in furnishing a spur to individual effort and makes the school routine more bearable by breaking the monotony of it." Although maintaining a nonsectarian stance, the schools encouraged all types of religious activity as an effective method of teaching Christian values and removing the girls from the home influence.

An important factor in understanding the women's program at the industrial schools is the reaction of the girls themselves. This presents some problems, however, since most school girls left no record of their experiences. Moreover, many of the observations that have survived were published in closely controlled school magazines that omitted any unfavorable remarks. Only a few reliable reminiscences have been produced, and even these are not very informative. Despite such limitations, however, several points are evident. The reaction of Indian girls to their education varied greatly. Some came willingly and with the approval of their parents. Once enrolled in school, many of these individuals took a keen interest in their education, accepted discipline as good for them, and worked hard to learn the ways of white society. An undetermined number may have come to school to escape intolerable conditions at home. Some evidence suggests that schools offered safe havens from overbearing parents who threatened to harm their children. For other girls the decision to attend a nonreservation school was made at considerable emotional expense, requiring a break with conservative parents, relatives, and tribesmen. In a few cases young women even lost their opportunity to marry men of their own tribe as they became dedicated to an outside lifestyle.

Many girls disliked school and longed to return home. The reasons are not hard to find. The hard work, discipline, and punishment were often oppressive. One Hopi girl recalled having to get down on her knees each Saturday and scrub the floor of the huge dining hall. "A patch of floor was scrubbed, then rinsed and wiped, and another section was attacked. The work was slow and hard on the knees," she remembered. Pima schoolgirl [Anna] Moore experienced similar conditions working in the dining hall at Phoenix: "My little helpers and I hadn't even reached our teen-aged years yet, and this work seemed so hard! If we were not finished when the 8:00 a.m. whistle sounded, the dining room matron would go around strapping us while we were still on our hands and knees.... We just dreaded the sore bottoms." In a number of instances, teachers and matrons added to the trauma by their dictatorial and unsympathetic attitudes. A few girls ran away from school. Those who were caught received humiliating punishment. Runaway girls might be put to work in the school yard cutting grass with scissors or doing some other meaningless drudgery. In a few cases recalcitrant young ladies had their hair cut off. Such experiences left many girls bitter and anxious to return to the old way of life.

The experiences of Indian girls when they returned home after years of schooling illustrate some of the problems in evaluating the success of the government program. For many years school officials reported great success for returned students. Accounts in articles and official documents maintained that numbers of girls had returned home, married, and established good homes. The Indian Bureau itself made occasional surveys purporting to show that returned students were doing well, keeping neat homes, and speaking English. These accounts contained a certain amount of truth. Some graduates adapted their education to the reservation environment and succeeded quite well. Many of these success stories were well publicized. There is considerable evidence to suggest, however, that the reports were overly optimistic and that most returning girls encountered problems.

A disturbingly large number of girls returned to traditional life upon returning home. The reasons are rather obvious. As early as 1882, the principal of Hampton's Indian Division reported that "there is absolutely no position of dignity to which an Indian girl after three years' training can look forward to with any reasonable confidence." Although conditions improved somewhat as time went on, work opportunities remained minimal. Girls were usually trained in only one specialty. As the superintendent of the Albuquerque school reported, girls usually returned home with no relevant skills. Some spent their entire school stay working in a laundry or sewing room, and though they became expert in one field, they had nothing to help them on the reservation. As the Meriam Report* later noted, some Indian girls spent so much time in school laundries that the institutions were in violation of state child labor laws. In another instance, one teacher noted how girls were taught to cook on gas ranges, while back on the reservation they had only campfires.

Moreover, the girls' educational achievements were not always appreciated at home. Elizabeth White tells the story of returning to her Hopi home an accomplished cook only to find that her family shunned the cakes and pies she made in place of traditional food, called her "as foolish as a white woman," and treated her as an outcast. As she later lamented, her school-taught domestic skills were inappropriate for the Hopis. Girls who refused to wear traditional dress at home were treated in like manner. Under these circumstances, many chose to cast off their learning, to marry, and return to traditional living. Those young women who dedicated themselves to living in the white man's style often found that reservations were intolerable, and unable to live in the manner to which they had become accustomed, they preferred to return to the cities. Once there the former students tended to become maids, although an undetermined number ended up as prostitutes and dance hall girls.

Employment opportunities for educated Indian women also pointed up some of the difficulties with the industrial schools. In fairness, it must be admitted that trained women probably had more opportunities than their male counterparts. Most of those who chose to work could do so; however, all positions were at the most menial level. If a girl elected to live within the white community, her employment choices were severely limited. About the only job available was that of domestic service, a carryover from the outing system. In this regard, the Indian schools did operate as employment agencies, finding jobs for their former students with local families. Despite the fact that some Indian women may have later come to feel that their work, despite its demeaning nature, provided some benefits for use in later life, many of their jobs proved unbearably hard. After being verbally abused, one former student wrote that "I never had any Lady say things like that to me." Another reported on her job, "I had been working so hard ever since I came here cleaning house and lots of ironing. I just got

---

* The 1928 Meriam Report was an intense study of the conditions of American Indians and the operations of the Bureau of Indian Affairs, conducted by the Institute for Government Research under the auspices of the Department of the Interior. (Eds.)

through ironing now I'm very tired my feet get so tired standing all morning." Unfortunately, few respectable jobs beyond domestic labor were available. Occasionally girls were trained as nurses or secretaries only to discover that they could find no work in Anglo society.

The largest employer of Indian girls proved to be the Indian Bureau. Many former students were able to secure positions at Indian agencies and schools; in fact, had it not been for the employment of former students by the paternalistic Indian service, few would have found any use for their training. The nature of the government positions available to Indian girls is revealing. Almost all jobs were menial in nature; only a few Indian girls were able to become teachers, and none worked as administrators. They were, rather, hired as laundresses, cooks, seamstresses, nurses' helpers, and assistant matrons. Often these employees received little more than room, board, and government rations, and even those who managed to be hired as teachers and nurses received less pay than their white counterparts.... Indian girls could find work, but only in the artificial environment of Indian agencies and schools located at remote western points and protected by a paternalistic government. Here they continued to perform tasks of domestic nature without promise of advancement. Nor were they assimilated into the dominant society as had been the original intent of their education.

School administrators were reluctant to admit the failings of the system. As early as the 1880s some criticism began to surface, but for the most part it was lost in the enthusiasm for training in a nonreservation environment. After 1900, however, critics became more vocal and persistent, arguing that the Indian community did not approve of this type of education, that most students gained little, and that employment opportunities were limited at best. More important, this type of education contributed little to the acculturation effort. As one opponent wrote, "To educate the Indian out of his [or her] home surroundings is to fill him with false ideas and to endow him with habits which are destructive to his peace of mind and usefulness to his community when the educational work is completed." Commissioner Leupp (1905–1909) was even more vocal. He generally accepted the increasingly prevalent theory that Indians were childlike in nature and incapable of assimilating into white society on an equal basis. Leupp suggested that the system failed to produce self-reliant Indians and, instead of giving Indian children a useful education, protected them in an artificial environment. Other school officials echoed the same sentiments. In this particular respect it was suggested that boarding school students were provided with all the comforts of civilization at no cost and thus failed to develop the proper attitude toward work. Upon returning to the reservations, therefore, they did not exert themselves and lapsed into traditionalism.

Despite increasing criticism, the women's educational program at the nonreservation schools operated without much change until after 1920.

Girls were still taught skills of doubtful value, were hired out as maids through the outing system, did most of the domestic labor at the schools, and returned to the reservation either to assume traditional life or accept some menial government job. By the late twenties, however, the movement to reform Indian education began to have some impact. Relying upon such studies as the 1928 Meriam Report, reformers began to demand a complete change in the Indian educational system. Among their suggestions were that industrial boarding schools be phased out and the emphasis on work training be reduced. Critics like [future Commissioner of Indian Affairs] John Collier argued that the policy of removing girls from their homes to educate them for a life among whites had failed. Instead, girls were discouraged from returning to the reservation and had received little to prepare them for a home life. Collier's arguments eventually won out, especially after he became Indian commissioner in 1933. Thus ended this particular attempt to convert Native American women into middle-class American housewives....

DOCUMENTS

Rules for Indian Schools, 1890

General Rules

39. The Sabbath must be properly observed. There shall be a Sabbath school or some other suitable service every Sunday, which pupils shall be required to attend. The superintendent may require employés to attend and participate in all the above exercises; but any employé declining as a matter of conscience shall be excused from attending and participating in any or all religious exercises....

41. All instruction must be in the English language. Pupils must be compelled to converse with each other in English, and should be properly rebuked or punished for persistent violation of this rule. Every effort should be made to encourage them to abandon their tribal language. To facilitate this work it is essential that all school employés be able to speak English fluently, and that they speak English exclusively to the pupils, and also to each other in the presence of pupils.

42. Instruction in music must be given at all schools. Singing should be a part of the exercises of each school session, and wherever practicable instruction in instrumental music should be given.

SOURCE: U.S. Bureau of Indian Affairs, "Rules for Indian Schools" *Annual Report of the Commissioner of Indian Affairs, 1890* (Washington, D.C., 1890), cxvi, cl–clii.

43. Except in cases of emergency, pupils shall not be removed from school either by their parents or others, nor shall they be transferred from a Government to a private school without special authority from the Indian Office.

44. The school buildings should be furnished throughout with plain, inexpensive, but substantial furniture. Dormitories or lavatories should be so supplied with necessary toilet articles, such as soap, towels, mirrors, combs, hair, shoe, nail, and tooth brushes, and wisp brooms, as to enable the pupils to form exact habits of personal neatness.

45. Good and healthful provisions must be supplied in abundance; and they must be well cooked and properly placed on the table. A regular bill of fare for each day of the week should be prepared and followed. Meals must be served regularly and neatly. Pains should be taken not only to have the food healthful and the table attractive, but to have the bill of fare varied. The school farm and dairy should furnish an ample supply of vegetables, fruits, milk, butter, cottage cheese, curds, eggs, and poultry. Coffee and tea should be furnished sparingly; milk is preferable to either, and children can be taught to use it. Pupils must be required to attend meals promptly after proper attention to toilet, and at least one employé must be in the dining room during each meal to supervise the table manners of the pupils and to see that all leave the table at the same time and in good order....

47. So far as practicable, a uniform style of clothing for the school should be adopted. Two plain, substantial suits, with extra pair of trousers for each boy, and three neat, well-made dresses for each girl, if kept mended, ought to suffice for week-day wear for one year. For Sunday wear each pupil should be furnished a better suit. The pupils should also be supplied with underwear adapted to the climate, with night clothes, and with handkerchiefs, and, if the climate requires it, with overcoats and cloaks and with overshoes.

48. The buildings, outhouses, fences, and walks should at all times be kept in thorough repair. Where practicable, the grounds should be ornamented with trees, grass, and flowers.

49. There should be a flag staff at every school, and the American flag should be hoisted, in suitable weather, in the morning and lowered at sunset daily.

50. Special hours should be allotted for recreation. Provision should be made for outdoor sports, and the pupils should be encouraged in daily healthful exercise under the eye of a school employé; simple games should also be devised for indoor amusement. They should be taught the sports and games enjoyed by white youth, such as baseball, hopscotch, croquet, marbles, bean bags, dominoes, checkers, logomachy, and other word and letter games, and the use

of dissected maps, etc. The girls should be instructed in simple fancy work, knitting, netting, crocheting, different kinds of embroidery, etc.

51. Separate play grounds, as well as sitting rooms, must be assigned the boys and the girls. In play and in work, as far as possible, and in all places except the school room and at meals, they must be kept entirely apart. It should be so arranged, however, that at stated times, under suitable supervision, they may enjoy each other's society; and such occasions should be used to teach them to show each other due respect and consideration, to behave without restraint, but without familiarity, and to acquire habits of politeness, refinement, and self-possession....

53. Corporal punishment must be resorted to only in cases of grave violations of rules, and in no instances shall any person inflict it except under the direction of the superintendent to whom all serious questions of discipline must be referred.* Employés may correct pupils for slight misdemeanors only.

54. Any pupil twelve years of age or over, guilty of persistently using profane or obscene language; of lewd conduct; stubborn insubordination; lying; fighting; wanton destruction of property; theft; or similar misbehavior, may be punished by the superintendent either by inflicting corporal punishment or imprisonment in the guardhouse; but in no case shall any unusual or cruel or degrading punishment be permitted....

Industrial Work

56. A regular and efficient system of industrial training must be a part of the work of each school. At least half of the time of each boy and girl should be devoted thereto—the work to be of such character that they may be able to apply the knowledge and experience gained, in the locality where they may be expected to reside after leaving school. In pushing forward the school-room training of these boys and girls, teachers, and especially superintendents, must not lose sight of the great necessity for fitting their charges for the every-day life of their after years.

---

* In some of the more advanced schools it will be practicable and advisable to have material offenses arbitrated by a school court composed of the advanced students, with school employés added to such court in very aggravated cases. After due investigation, the amount of guilt should be determined and the quantity of punishment fixed by the court, but the approval of the superintendent shall be necessary before the punishment is inflicted, and the superintendent may modify or remit but may not increase the sentence.

57. A farm and garden, if practicable an orchard also, must be connected with each school, and especial attention must be given to instruction in farming, gardening, dairying, and fruit growing.
58. Every school should have horses, cattle, swine, and poultry, and when practicable, sheep and bees, which the pupils should be taught to care for properly. The boys should look after the stock and milk the cows, and the girls should see to the poultry and the milk.
59. The farm, garden, stock, dairy, kitchen, and shops should be so managed as to make the school as nearly self-sustaining as practicable, not only because Government resources should be as wisely and carefully utilized as private resources would be, but also because thrift and economy are among the most valuable lessons which can be taught Indians. Waste in any department must not be tolerated.
60. The blacksmith, wheelwright, carpenter, shoemaker, and harness maker trades, being of the most general application, should be taught to a few pupils at every school. Where such mechanics are not provided for[,] the school pupils should, so far as practicable, receive instruction from the agency mechanics.
61. The girls must be systematically trained in every branch of housekeeping and in dairy work; be taught to cut, make, and mend garments for both men and women; and also be taught to nurse and care for the sick. They must be regularly detailed to assist the cook in preparing the food and the laundress in washing and ironing.
62. Special effort must be made to instruct Indian youth in the use and care of tools and implements. They must learn to keep them in order, protect them properly, and use them carefully.

A Government Official Describes Indian Race and Culture, 1905

We believe that the strength of our American life is due in no small part to the fact that various and different race elements have entered into the making of the American the citizen of the United States in the twentieth century. No one racial stock is exclusively in control in our land. The typical modern American is a fine "composite," with race elements drawn from many sources. We do not believe that the Government of the United States in dealing with its Indian wards would act righteously or wisely if it were to attempt to crush out from those who are of Indian descent all the racial traits which differentiate the North American Indian from the other race stocks of the world. Certain conceptions of physical courage, a certain

SOURCE: U.S. Department of Interior, "Board of Indian Commissioners' Reports," in *Annual Reports* (June 30, 1905), H. Doc. 20: 59th Cong., 1st sess., 17–18.

heroic stoicism in enduring physical pain, an inherited tendency to respect one's self, even if that tendency shows itself at times in unwarrantable conceit, are race traits which have value, if the people who have them become civilized and subject themselves to the laws of social morality and to the obligation of industrial efficiency, which are essential if any race stock or any group of families is to hold its own in the modern civilized world.

But the facts seem to us to be that good results are to be hoped for not by keeping the North American Indians peculiar in dress or in customs. We think that the wisest friends of the Indian recognize with great delight and value highly the art impulse in certain Indian tribes, which has shown itself in Indian music, in Indian art forms—such as the birchbark canoe, in Indian basketry, and more rarely in Indian pottery. But we firmly believe that the way to preserve the best of what is distinctively characteristic in the North American Indians is to civilize and educate them, that they may be fit for the life of the twentieth century under our American system of self-government. Because we value the elements for good which may come into our American life through the stock of North American Indians, we wish to see children of Indian descent educated in the industrial and practical arts and trained to habits of personal cleanliness, social purity, and industrious family life. We do not believe that it is right to keep the Indians out of civilization in order that certain picturesque aspects of savagery and barbarism may continue to be within reach of the traveler and the curious, or even of the scientific observer. In the objectionable "Indian dances" which are breaking out afresh at many points we see not a desirable maintenance of racial traits, but a distinct reversion toward barbarism and superstition. We believe that while the effort should never be made to "make a white man out of an Indian," in the sense of seeking to do violence to respect to parents or a proper or intelligent regard for what is fine in the traits and the history of one's ancestors, it is still most desirable that all the Indians on our territory should come as speedily as possible to the white man's habits of home-making, industry, cleanliness, social purity, and family integrity.

Precisely as all intelligent American patriots have seen danger to our national life in the attempt, wherever it has been made, to perpetuate in the United States large groups of foreign-born immigrants who try to keep their children from learning English and seek to perpetuate upon our territory (at the cost of true Americanism for their children) what was characteristic in the life of their own people on other continents and in past generations, precisely as in such cases we feel that the hope of our American system lies in the public schools and such educational institutions as shall maintain standards of public living that inevitably bring the children of foreign-born immigrants into the great body of English-speaking, home-loving, industrious, and pure-minded Americans—precisely so does it seem to us that all the efforts of the Government, and far more of distinctive missionary effort on the part of the Christian people of this country than has ever yet been used with this end in view, should be steadily employed in the effort to make out of the Indian children of this country intelligent, English-speaking, industrious, law-abiding Americans. We believe that the breaking up of tribal funds as rapidly as practicable will help toward this end. Even if many of the Indians do for a time misuse money while they are learning how to use it properly, even if some of them squander it utterly, we believe that there is hope for the Indians in the future only as by education, faith in work, and obedience to Christian principles of morality and clean living, their children shall come to have the social standards and the social habits of our better American life throughout the land.

Our task is to hasten the slow work of race evolution. Inevitably, but often grimly and harshly by the outworking of natural forces, the national life of the stronger and more highly civilized race stock dominates in time the life of the less civilized, when races like the Anglo-Saxon and the Indian are brought into close contact. In our work for the Indians we want to discern clearly those influences and habits of life which are of the greatest advantage in leading races upward into Christian civilization; and these influences and habits we wish to make as strongly influential as possible, and as speedily as possible influential upon the life of all these American tribes. It is not unreasonable to hope that through governmental agencies and through the altruistic missionary spirit of one of the foremost Christian races and governments of the world much can be done to hasten that process of civilization which natural law, left to itself, works out too slowly and at too great a loss to the less-favored race. We want to make the conditions for our less-favored brethren of the red race so favorable that the social forces which have developed themselves slowly and at great expense of time and life in our American race and our American system of government shall be made to help in the uplifting of the Indians and to shorten that interval of time which of necessity must elapse between savagery and Christian civilization.

The Cutting of My Long Hair, c. 1885

The first day in the land of apples was a bitter-cold one; for the snow still covered the ground, and the trees were bare. A large bell rang for breakfast, its loud metallic voice crashing through the belfry overhead and into our sensitive ears. The annoying clatter of shoes on bare floors gave us no peace. The constant clash of harsh noises, with an undercurrent of many voices murmuring an unknown tongue, made a bedlam within which

SOURCE: Zitkala-Sa (Gertrude Simmons Bonnin), "The School Days of an Indian Girl," *Atlantic Monthly* (January–March, 1900), 45–47.

I was securely tied. And though my spirit tore itself in struggling for its lost freedom, all was useless.

A paleface woman, with white hair, came up after us. We were placed in a line of girls who were marching into the dining room. These were Indian girls, in stiff shoes and closely clinging dresses. The small girls wore sleeved aprons and shingled hair. As I walked noiselessly in my soft moccasins, I felt like sinking to the floor, for my blanket had been stripped from my shoulders. I looked hard at the Indian girls, who seemed not to care that they were even more immodestly dressed than I, in their tightly fitting clothes. While we marched in, the boys entered at an opposite door. I watched for the three young braves who came in our party. I spied them in the rear ranks, looking as uncomfortable as I felt.

A small bell was tapped, and each of the pupils drew a chair from under the table. Supposing this act meant they were to be seated, I pulled out mine and at once slipped into it from one side. But when I turned my head, I saw that I was the only one seated, and all the rest at our table remained standing. Just as I began to rise, looking shyly around to see how chairs were to be used, a second bell was sounded. All were seated at last, and I had to crawl back into my chair again. I heard a man's voice at one end of the hall, and I looked around to see him. But all the others hung their heads over their plates. As I glanced at the long chain of tables, I caught the eyes of a paleface woman upon me. Immediately I dropped my eyes, wondering why I was so keenly watched by the strange woman. The man ceased his mutterings, and then a third bell was tapped. Every one picked up his knife and fork and began eating. I began crying instead, for by this time I was afraid to venture anything more.

But this eating by formula was not the hardest trial in that first day. Late in the morning, my friend Judéwin gave me a terrible warning. Judéwin knew a few words of English; and she had overheard the paleface woman talk about cutting our long, heavy hair. Our mothers had taught us that only unskilled warriors who were captured had their hair shingled by the enemy. Among our people, short hair was worn by mourners, and shingled hair by cowards!

We discussed our fate some moments, and when Judéwin said, "We have to submit, because they are strong," I rebelled.

"No, I will not submit! I will struggle first!" I answered.

I watched my chance, and when no one noticed I disappeared. I crept up the stairs as quietly as I could in my squeaking shoes,—my moccasins had been exchanged for shoes. Along the hall I passed, without knowing whither I was going. Turning aside to an open door, I found a large room with three white beds in it. The windows were covered with dark green curtains, which made the room very dim. Thankful that no one was there, I directed my steps toward the corner farthest from the door. On my hands and knees I crawled under the bed, and cuddled myself in the dark corner.

From my hiding place I peered out, shuddering with fear whenever I heard footsteps near by. Though in the hall loud voices were calling my name, and I knew that even Judéwin was searching for me, I did not open my mouth to answer. Then the steps were quickened and the voices became excited. The sounds came nearer and nearer. Women and girls entered the room. I held my breath and watched them open closet doors and peep behind large trunks. Some one threw up the curtains, and the room was filled with sudden light. What caused them to stoop and look under the bed I do not know. I remember being dragged out, though I resisted by kicking and scratching wildly. In spite of myself, I was carried downstairs and tied fast in a chair.

I cried aloud, shaking my head all the while until I felt the cold blades of the scissors against my neck, and heard them gnaw off one of my thick braids. Then I lost my spirit. Since the day I was taken from my mother I had suffered extreme indignities. People had stared at me. I had been tossed about in the air like a wooden puppet. And now my long hair was shingled like a coward's! In my anguish I moaned for my mother, but no one came to comfort me. Not a soul reasoned quietly with me, as my own mother used to do; for now I was only one of many little animals driven by a herder.

Chapter 4

Immigrant Life and Labor in an Expanding Economy

Minnesota Historical Society/CORBIS

A Minnesota sod house, home of Norwegian immigrant
Beret Olesdater Hagebak, c. 1896.

Between 1870 and 1924, over 25 million immigrants, overwhelmingly of European origin, poured into the United States. During the initial years, Ireland and Germany were the leading sending nations. By 1900, however, their numbers were overtaken by immigrants from southern and eastern Europe, including large waves of Italians, Jews, Poles, Hungarians, and Slovaks. Whether they were driven by economic, religious, or political necessity, they viewed America as the great land of opportunity.

Most of the immigrants settled in the major cities of America, where an expanding manufacturing economy, growing networks of urban transportation, and ever-increasing construction of new factories, housing, and office buildings offered job opportunities that required few entry level skills. In an era when coal provided the major source of energy, mining towns attracted a considerable number of immigrants whose muscles were the main requirement for employment. As the nation's population grew, so too did the demand for food to feed the urban masses. Some immigrants, particularly those who had been peasants in their lands of origin, abandoned the American cities in which they had originally settled and headed for the nation's farmlands.

Yet even the lives of northern and western Europeans could be difficult, as demonstrated in the essay and the final document. In the essay "An Immigrant's Anguish: The Americanization of Johanes Johansen," Robert F. Zeidel tells the story of Johanes Johansen, a Norwegian immigrant who left his native land in 1869, to seek a better life in the United States. Several themes stand out. One was his longing to return to his native land. What does the essay say about his failure to go home until very late in his life? Why did he eventually change his name and become an American? How was he affected by the fact that his family was transnational, with some members settling in New Zealand?

The first document is from a report of an interview with Irish immigrant Sam Gray conducted by P. A. Speck as part of a study of foreign-born unemployed floating laborers. What factors do you think might account for the failures of Sam Gray?

If urban working conditions were so bad here, why did so many immigrants come to America from Europe? We might find the answer in the second document, the story of Rocco Corresca, a poor Italian immigrant. What does his description of his first days in the United States indicate about the hardships experienced by the newcomers? In the end, what was the consequence of Rocco's success in America?

The final document is taken from the column "The Bintel Brief," in the Yiddish newspaper the *Daily Forward*, which offered help to immigrants coping with American society. What does it tell of the life of a working class immigrant young women? And what support did the "Bintel Brief" offer?

ESSAY

An Immigrant's Anguish: The Americanization of Johanes Johansen

Robert Zeidel

After nearly twenty years, John Holt poignantly remembered the day in 1869 when his younger self, then known as Johanes Johansen, left his native Norway on a journey that would take him to a new home in the timberlands of west-central Wisconsin. In an 1887 journal entry, but penned to "Dearest Mother," Holt wrote as an anguished son asking for

SOURCE: Robert F. Zeidel, "An Immigrant's Anguish: The Americanization of Johanes Johansen", *Wisconsin Magazine of History* (Winter 2003–2004), pp. 2–13. Reprinted with permission.

parental absolution: "Yes, dear Mother, if I could only reach you, I would hug you with tears of regret. You must excuse and forgive your 'son of pain' who so proudly left you to such sorrow on my departure." He had not cried when they parted, but as he had passed through the nearby countryside, tears had streamed from his eyes. As he remembered it, he "nearly regretted having left," and only the fear of cowardly shame kept him from turning back. The young traveler steadied himself with the thought that he would soon return, never thinking that after his departure, he would never see his family again. Had he known his fate, and that of his family, he "would probably not have left." As it was, he kept his childhood home, "those happy times with you and father," in his thoughts, dreams, and prayers.

John Holt's story, specifically his moments of despair, disappointment, and anger, within the context of a generally bountiful and rewarding life, helps to elucidate the difficult, and often painful, side of American immigration. Although he enjoyed considerable economic and personal success, he simultaneously struggled with disconnection from his childhood family and homeland. Consistently—in letters, a diary, and a brief autobiography—he revealed his anguish, emotionally describing how deeply he missed "the blessed time" of his Norwegian youth. Even in his eighty-ninth year, when he could look back on fifty-five years of marriage, hold great-grandchildren in his arms, and contemplate the memories of a productive life, the feelings remained.

No one individual embodies the "universal immigrant," and indeed, among the millions of migrants, arriving at different times under varied circumstances, there has been a decided lack of commonality. Oscar Handlin, in his seminal book *The Uprooted*, interpreted the immigrant experience as being much like John Holt's, one of "broken homes, interruptions of a familiar life, separation from known surroundings, the becoming a foreigner and ceasing to belong." Other studies, especially those which emphasized community migration and an accompanying transplantation of cultures, have demonstrated less traumatic transitions. Both depictions are important in understanding the full-spectrum of the American immigrant experience, but Holt's transformation from Norwegian exile to established American exemplifies the uprooted type, reminding us that immigration is a matter of anxious separation, even as it offers the prospect for a new and better life.

The writings which Holt used to convey his often painful metamorphosis typify a Norwegian-American tendency to use such prose for self-revelation, as "an element of confession," thereby providing an intimate portrait of the migration experience. Unfortunately, Holt gives less insight than others into his motivations for recording his thoughts and memories, but similar immigrant authors have indicated almost a compulsion to verbalize their immigration and assimilation stories, to put the details of their lives down on paper so as to share them with others. This act of preservation and dissemination itself became part of the immigrant experience. In Holt's case, his literary efforts seem to be an exercise in introspection, an effort to try to understand the meaning of the events in his life, and also to share his story, and whatever lessons it may hold, with others. In one instance, he apologized for saying too much, as he "only intended to give a short biographical sketch of myself," yet the more detailed account indicates an importance for the author and presumed interest on the part of reader. In some instances, his recollection of factual details seems confused, but not his accompanying emotions. Whether in his first letter home or his last biographical at sketch. Holt emphasized his feelings of separation from his Norwegian roots.

On January 2, 1850, John Holt began life as Johanes Johansen, the first of nine children born to Johanes and Sedsil [Olsdatter] Johansen. His birth, an Upper Riset Farm, at Furries. Hedmark Fylkc county, Norway, coincided with the country's demographic revolution. Between 1815 and 1865, Norway's population almost doubled. A rising birthrate and dramatically declining death rate resulted in one of the highest growth rates in Europe. For a country that remained overwhelmingly rural 81 percent but with only 3 percent of its land tillable, and that lacked significant industrialization, the burgeoning population began to put a strain on resources and economic opportunity. While true mass emigration did not begin until the 1860s, demographic changes did provide a classic push factor for those pondering their future.

The elder Johansen's frequent moves and identification as a furrier, a pre-industrial artisan, indicates that the family belonged to the growing number of *husmenner,* or cotters, "an intermediate rural class," of agricultural workers without their own land. Other evidence indicates that the Johansens were tenant farmers, a more independent class that occupied and worked land belonging to others. The 1865 Norwegian Census lists the family an *inrusmand med jord*—tenant with land, meaning that the family members were tenants to whom the owner granted a small allotment which they worked for their own profit. In any case, it is doubtful that the family owned its longtime home, later described by Holt as a small farm in llechmark County, a largely forested area of east-central Norway. Since it was the child's third home in his first two years, it is unlikely that the Johansens were *bonder,* or small landholders. There is no indication that the younger Johanes expected to inherit family land, through the practice of *acir,* or lineal descent to the oldest son. Instead, following his confirmation at about age fifteen, Johanes briefly practiced his father's profession, before the elder sent him to Vang, so that he could learn the more profitable trade of farming.

Uncertainty characterized the life of the Johansens and other mid-nineteenth century Norwegian cotters. Despite the country's population growth and land use limitations, it still could provide all of its inhabitants with some manner of economic opportunity, although more people did strain the social and cultural fabric. Division increased between the elite landed *bonder* and landless cotters. In the early nineteenth century, ample work opportunities for the cotters resulted in earlier marriage, and with longer periods of marital fertility, family size also rose. So too did the practice of "night courting," or premarital sex, but not all of those which resulted in conception led to nupitals. Cotters, then had more children, both legitimate and illegitimate, creating complications concerning their economic future. By mid-century, prudence suggested that they put off marriage and family until they had achieved some degree of economic success but why if that day never came.

Other forces also shook the cotter world. The growing numbers of those born out of wedlock produced a pietistic backlash, in the form of moral condemnation, which pressured young men and women to follow socially acceptable behaviour. Young Johanes for example, saw "the importance which a good and well-run society had on out lives," and though he made this observation in comparison to the "coarse raw" life of an American lumber camp, he elsewhere emphasized the importance of Christian teachings during his Norwegian youth. He stopped short of condemning those who engaged in unruly behavior, but clearly their lifestyle would have had no appeal to young Johanes. If his own prospects for traditional marriage and family seemed questionable, this may have influenced his decision to emigrate. Additionally, he and his family adhered to the teaching of Hans Nielsen Hauge, who emphasized the role of lay leadership within the official Norwegian Lutheran Church. This break from theological orthodoxy created men and women more willing and better able to contemplate such a radical choice as immigration. Johanes, for instance, apparently did not seek permission from the official Lutheran church to emigrate, as did some of his traveling companions.

When coupled with the fact that few of the landless could ever hope to own land, these social developments created a climate ripe for making such a fateful determination. Surviving accounts do not provide a thorough explanation of why young Johanes chose to emigrate, but given the implied connection to "his future" career opportunities, Norway's socioeconomic tensions almost certainly contributed to his emotionally arduous decision to leave for America. Also, in a first letter home, he notes that "I don't think that I will like it here in America, but the money is good." His intentions to return relatively soon, perhaps "in a couple of years," suggest that he hoped his American sojourn would provide a type of quick economic gain not readily available in his homeland. At this still early phase in Norwegian-American immigration, this was a common practice. An off-hand comment about his sister Oline not knowing that he was leaving suggests that it was an impulsive decision; when presented with an opportunity to go to America and see what it had to offer, he took it.

Johansen's journey followed a typical immigrant path. He left Christiania (now Oslo) on September 14, 1869, in the company of a friend, Ole Guldbransen, and his family from Vang, and after a brief stop in Kristiansand, sailed to Scotland. After traversing that country by train, he boarded the Anchor Line's *Iowa*, one of the largest immigrant steamers, for the trip to the United States. An interesting hybrid, which in itself gives a sense of the changing times, the ship had both coal-fired engines and four masts. The Atlantic crossing took nineteen storm-filled days, the most that it had ever taken the *Iowa*, and a relieved lot of seasick passengers disembarked at New York City. Johanes's traveling party stayed at Castle Garden Immigration Station for one night and then boarded a train for Chicago. There, they waited three days for their luggage, during which time Johanes unsuccessfully looked for work at a tanning factory. Finding none, he continued his journey via train and then river boat, eventually arriving at Eau Claire, Wisconsin.

The trip included a bizarre example of the hardships of immigrant travel. Although everyone survived the mid-Atlantic storms, Ole Guldbransen's "old mother Tsuit Stokket" died on route from New York to Chicago. The elderly matriarch got off of the train at a station and sat down between cars on an adjoining track. Since that train had no engine, no one worried about her safety, but when one did attach unexpectedly, it moved the cars and crushed her. Johanes appreciated the journey's dangers, writing to his family, "I think that you will thank God, along with me, who has protected me from all danger and spared my life during such a long and dangerous trip."

If that journey had taken Johanes from a land of uncertainty, he entered one of optimism and opportunity. Wisconsin had been a state for only twenty-one years, since 1848, but at the time of his arrival it was on the verge of an industrial and agricultural boom. Natural resources, especially timber, abounded. Key to unlocking the state's economic potential was improvement of transportation, especially the construction of railroads. Both the cutting of trees and the laying of track, along with the ubiquitous growth of farming, would require labor, such as that offered by newly arrived immigrants.

Johanes was one of many who chose Wisconsin as a destination. According to the 1870 federal census, Wisconsin had 364, 499 foreign-born residents (35 percent of the total population), including 40,046 Norwegians, the largest number for any state. The earliest groups of Norwegians in the United States had settled in upstate New York and northeastern Illinois' Fox River Valley, but by the 1850s, Wisconsin had become their most popular destination. One early sojourner called it "the best and most healthful place for the Norwegians." Here, in this potential land of plenty, Johanes would make his new home.

When Johanes noted that the money "was good" in the United States, he may have been a little optimistic. He had not been able to find a work as a tanner in Chicago in 1869, and he did not find steady employment in Wisconsin until the spring of 1870, when he found a job as a brick layer. Whatever his remuneration, it was not "wages," and he soon took a job with Chapman, Thorp & Company, which owned farms and a sawmill near Eau Claire. Johanes worked five weeks on a farm and then through the summer at the mill. Employment for Chapman, Thorp had an unexpected benefit. Thorp was the father-in-law of Ole Bull, a well-known Norwegian-American violinist, and in the fall of 1870, Johanes got tickets to hear him play.

Arrival of Eau Claire's first railroad, the Omaha Rail in 1870, provided Johanes's next employment. That fall and winter, he worked on a construction crew which was cutting right-of-way through the Knapp Hills, located about thirty-five miles west of Eau Claire. At the vanguard of settlement, in the midst of what was then still wilderness, Johanes and the other laborers, an ethnically diverse crew, lived rough and tumble lives. An oak log shanty, chinked with clay, provided shelter from the Wisconsin winter. "Evenings," he remembered, "were spent playing cards, making music, sometimes dancing, and other wild goings on." Such frivolity troubled the young Norwegian immigrant, giving him pause to think about the more orderly world of his departed homeland. After working on the railroad for about a year, Johanes and three other immigrants from Norway's Guldbrandsdalen region set out for the farming community of Erin Prairie, a predominantly Irish-American community in St. Croix County, where completely different concerns would cut short Johanes's stay.

In August 1871 he found work with farmer William Hennesy, which brought with it two significant opportunities: education and potential marriage. While Johanes had learned some English, Hennesy encouraged him to pursue more instruction, so that he could increase his chances of succeeding in business. Hennesy also had two teenage daughters, and Johanes reminded himself of the tale of a similarly situated immigrant who had been tricked into matrimony, by a farm lass who exploited his limited use of English. In that tale, the man only knew how to say "yes, yes," which he unsuspectingly replied to a magistrate's conjoining questions. Johanes promised himself that he would not be so tricked, but also told himself that he must be careful, for once a woman got "a slight hold," it would not be "easy to tear oneself away." He left Hennesy's employment, returned to Eau Claire, and then made his way west to the nearby small town of Cedar Falls, near Menomonie, Wisconsin. The reasons for Johanes's relocation suggests a negative attitude towards women, but more likely he did not want to make any commitment that might encumber his anticipated return to Norway. Or, given his eventual choice of bride, he may have wanted to save himself for a woman of Norwegian descent.

Johanes's financial situation quickly improved. Railroad work had allowed him to pay all his debts and, in typical immigrant fashion, even send a little money back to his Norwegian family. Now, he was about to embark upon his principal occupation. Johanes intended to work a mill in Cedar Falls owned by Jewett and Company, but after a week, the foreman offered him a position helping the cook at the company boarding house. He remembered that the offer was for "'a quick, smart, young man.'" Johanes took the job, and thereby learned the cooking trade which he would ply for the next twenty-five years. By the summer of 1873 he had worked his way up to head cook, providing meals for up to 150 men. Given that the lumberjacks were not above "running out" cooks whose fare did not meet their gastronomic standards, Johanes's long tenure attests to his culinary success.

The young immigrant may have left the job at Erin Prairie for fear of marital entrapment, but by 1873, he had developed a serious romantic interest in Norwegian immigrant Martine Hansen. Born in 1850 on the Barstad farm, Sokndalen, in what is now Rogaland Fylke, she had come to the United States at the age of seven. In an appropriate admixture of cultures, Johanes and Martine married in 1873, in a traditional Norwegian Lutheran church, the First Lutheran Church of Eau Claire, at a ceremony officiated by Pastor Amund Johnsen, on the quintessential American holiday, the Fourth of July. Records do not indicate those in attendance, but Johanes no doubt dwelt on the obvious omissions, his Norwegian friends and family. Unfortunately, there are no known sources that give Martine historical voice, which would be insightful given the developments that she and Johanes soon would confront.

Shortly after his joyous nuptials, it became apparent that marriage and economic success had effectively changed his plans to return to Norway in five years' time from his departure. Although he now contemplated a visit to Norway, he increasingly entertained thoughts of "how wonderful it would be if he could get his parents and siblings to come to America." Immigrants frequently engaged in this type of "chain migration," where by an initial immigrant or group paved the way for family or villagers to join them. Nothing seemed to preclude this happening with the Johansens, particularly in light of their son's success, but then, "as lightening from a clear sky," came un expected news; the entire family was moving to New Zealand!

Johanes's oldest sister, Oline, had married clergyman Edward Neilsen, who, while performing a funeral, "had been called by the spirit to emigrate" and be "a servant of the Lord in the Methodist faith," in New Zealand. Neilsen's conviction affected not only him and his wife, but also the rest of the Johansens. Johanes's two younger sisters (other sources say only one at that time) would accompany the couple, and his parents and other siblings would come later.

The connection with Methodism was in itself was unusual. There were only about three thousand such adherents amongst an overwhelmingly and officially Lutheran population of 1.8 million Norwegians. One source, however, did identify Neilsen as some sort of hybrid "Methodist Lutheran," but the exact nature of his faith, both before and after the defining spiritual call, remains unclear. Johanes' writings indicate his family's connection to Hauge's teaching, dissenting from the official Lutheran creed, but they also make several references to his attending American Lutheran churches, although this simply may have been because Johanes could not find what he called "haugianer" congregations. Unfortunately, there is almost no other information about the Johansen family's religious beliefs. Therefore, one can only speculate as to whether the entire family had embraced Methodism, and whether broader religious matters, as well as the family's specific plans to leave for New Zealand, also troubled Johanes.

There was no such uncertainty as to how he felt about the emigration decision itself. "To go back to Norway would be easy enough," he mused, at leased to see his kinfolk, "but to join them in New Zealand. (Ufda!)" They never would be joining him in America, nor would he be able to reunite with them in Norway. He had gone far enough, and was not going to go any further. Unstated, but obvious, he truly had become an American, a Norwegian-American, but still an American. His work and his marriage attested to his success. A return letter, which explained all of this to Neilsen, implored him to instead come to America. Such epistles worked in the case of myriad other immigrant letters, but not this time. "The Spirit" had moved Neilsen to leave for New Zealand, and nothing could change his mind.

Johanes's response, although recorded some years later, reveals both his profound disappointment and the extent of his new immigrant identity. He had been "led astray," he reasoned, in going to a new land with the false trust that he soon would be reunited with family. Now, "the cold and cruel whip of fate," had "turn[ed] away its mighty hand," and what he had envisioned as a temporary separation would be permanent. He could see his "dearly beloved mother," feel the "burn" of her tears, but what, he asked rhetorically, revealing the sense of betrayal which had remained throughout the years, could he have done? He could not have gone to New Zealand, nor had it been the plan at the time of his departure. "We will be spread in all directions and made strangers in this world," he angrily proclaimed, "and therefore my name shall no longer be Johanes Johnson, but John J. Holt—because I have been lost and will not be found again."

The choice of names is interesting. His *Autobiography* indicates that his childhood home was located on Holtsveen, or "Holt's Road," but in Norwegian, one of the meanings of *holdt* is "to endure or last." Descendants attribute Johanes's new name to the Norwegian location, but his use of "because" in the sentence explaining the name change suggests a causal effect. Perhaps, his new name was meant to convey both the end of his old-world identity, and the affirmation of the emergence of a new, yet connected one in the United States. Despite a sense of the forlorn, the essence of the child Johanes, in metamorphic form, would survive, as the American John Holt. The sources do not provide a definitive answer, but Holt suggests this notion of preservation, writing and referring to himself in the third person, immediately after announcing the name change, "Thus Johanes wept in his heart, while the small home that he had left, with all of its dear memories, became alive in his mind." The Norwegian immigrant had become the American John Holt, but a part of Johanes, son of Johanes and Sedsil Johansen, and of Norway, would endure.

Separation would continue to trouble the man now known as John Holt. In 1878, five years after his marriage and news of his family's emigration decisions, he began a short-lived, intermittent diary, including summaries of letters to friends and family members, with numerous entries revealing his continued inner turmoil. He was "well and in good shape," but nonetheless troubled. In addition to references of twenty below zero temperatures and the isolation of the lumber camps, one of the first entries described the fate of a little bird who had sought shelter from the cold in Johanes's cook shack. It flew in through the open door and eventually settled on a window sill, where the resident cat discovered and killed it. It reminded Johanes "of all souls that are lost." Perhaps, despite a good job and growing family, including daughter Junietta (later called Nettie, one of his five children) who had started to say "dada," he considered himself one of the unfortunates.

America had been good to Holt, but all of his success and accomplishments were not enough to alleviate the pain that he felt from being away from his birth family and the friends of his youth. The diary indicates that Holt's parents had not left for New Zealand until 1877, and news of a shipwreck led him to worry that it had been their vessel. Finally, he received a letter which, to his relief, let him know that the family had arrived safely. Still, even this happy news could do only so much to assuage an obviously aching heart. When he tried to convey thanks to his brother-in-law Edward Nielsen for all that he had done for his parents, it brought tears to his eyes. Later, he described the contents of a letter to cousin Gunor Haave, who still lived in Norway, in similarly melancholy terms: "Looked back to childhood where we often played together. How uncertain one's life is and how full of changes, dear memories, and deep losses."

Holt allowed himself to think about following his family to New Zealand, but he realized that it would never happen. "It would be my greatest happiness in life," he wrote his cousin Gunor, "if I could see my dear and precious parents and siblings here in the land of the living on earth. I love them all dear and think about them often." He similarly wrote to his sister, lamenting the fact that they had not written since her departure for New Zealand and expressing his love for her. He also conveyed both his continued sense of loss and thoughts of joining her and the other family members. Yet, the very things which had made his life in America successful prevented him from fulfilling this wish. He had put down roots in his new country, established a career, built a home, and started a family. These, he acknowledged in a subsequent letter to his sister, effectively prevented him from leaving. All that he could do was regret the tears that he had caused his faraway family and friends and ask God to bless them.

The now permanently American Holt balanced overall success with occasional strife. During the years after his marriage and awareness of his parents' emigration plans, a chain of events took him to his long-time home of Menomonie, Wisconsin. He quit Jewett and Company, after working three years without a break, and in 1875 went into a short-lived partnership with John C. Storm running the Central House hotel and saloon at Baldwin, in west-central Wisconsin. Holt ran the hotel and Storm the saloon. Unfortunately, Storm imbibed too much of his own product, and when Holt realized that this was ruining the business, running up several hundred dollars in virtually uncollectible debt, he determined either to sell his share or buy out his too-often inebriated partner. Storm bought his partner's share, with the payment including a lot in Menomonie. Holt thereafter started building a home on his recently acquired property, and went to work cooking for Knapp, Stout & Company in 1875.

For the next fourteen years, Holt labored at Knapp, Stout and lived in Menomonie. He and his wife Martine soon moved into their new home, where most of their children would be born. Work for Knapp, Stout followed a seasonal round. Holt cooked for the men at the sawmill during the summer, and then in fall went into the woods for several months to cook at one of the camps. In the years when he took part in the spring "drive," floating the logs down river to a mill, he did not return home until June. It was hard work, but Holt prided himself on having developed a good reputation as both a cook and a colleague, and also as a musician. His musical prowess included the ability to play several instruments and to compose popular songs.

Ditties about camp life particularly appealed to Holt's coworkers, but so too did a popular waltz that Holt named *Seterwaltz*, a tale of the Norwegian summer farm. Touching on familiar themes of detachment and remembrance, it described how milkmaids took cattle to graze at higher elevations during the summer months. The maids lived in small cabins, called *seter*, and spent their days watching the herds and making butter and other dairy products. Young men would visit the young ladies on Saturday nights. In his *Autobiography*, Holt described his waltz as having "a deep and sorrowful melody that the old Norwegians in the camp, who had left the 'old country' and now remembered, could not hear enough." They often requested it before they went to bed, "because then they would sleep so well afterwards." Like similar ballads, it was not anti-emigration, but a sentimental statement of loss due to migration.

Realities of being away at camp re-emphasized family separation in July 1880. Holt was cooking for a summer haying crew when he received word that his daughter Tomasine was gravely ill. She had been a sickly child, unable to walk or stand at fifteen months, but the family hoped that she would improve. Upon hearing that her condition had worsened precipitously, Holt raced home to the ailing child. Arriving too late, he "did not get to see my little one again"; nor had he been at home when she was born. Descriptions of her funeral, found in Holt's last diary entry, nonetheless speak of his faith in an ultimate, spiritual reunion, "up there where we never will be parted. Give us this O God in Jesus name." His convictions come across clearly, but his life story suggests that the "we" may have meant more than his present nuclear family mourning the death of a child.

In 1889 the Holts moved to an eighty-acre farm near Colfax, about twenty-five miles north of Menomonie. John had little experience with farming, and wanting to minimize economic risk, he continued to spend winters cooking at logging camps. After two years, he sold the Menomonie house, which allowed him to buy a team of horses, a wagon, and other farm implements. Only fifteen acres had originally been tilled, but now he could expand the operation. He also bought more land, bringing his total holdings to about 200 acres, some of which supported a dairy herd. In 1891 he quit cooking and devoted his full attention to agriculture.

The move to Colfax also allowed Holt to live in an area "where the majority of people are Norwegian." Until this time, he had felt a sense of isolation, living as part of an ethnically mixed work force—which Holt once describe as "a very tough crew" consisting of "Norwegians, Swedes, Germans, Irishmen and a Frenchman!"—in a Yankee-dominated World. He had traveled to America with the Norwegian Guldbransen family, but they soon had left the Eau Claire area. He did marry a fellow Norwegian immigrant, but almost immediately after beginning married life, learned that he would never again see his own family. In Colfax his situation began to resemble a more typical immigrant experience, in that he was living in an ethnic enclave or community. Holt, however, also stressed his Americanization, noting that he had twice been elected "to the English school board in the area, and has twice been both treasurer and secretary of same." Johanes Johansen Gallos (following Norwegian custom the final name referred to the farm in Norway where he had last worked) had filed the initial petition for naturalization in 1873, but it was John Holt who became a naturalized citizen in 1906.

In 1914, on the cusp of the Great War, sixty-four year-old Holt finally made his long awaited trip to Norway, but it was more of a visit than a return. His 1903 *Autobiography* conveyed his wish to see his childhood home, to look upon the fir trees that he climbed as a youth, and that in his mind "seem to still sway, and to wait for him yet." He also feared that he never again would actually see them. Other than a brief mention, nothing survives to convey Holt's feelings when he actually got to Norway, but they must have been bittersweet. His father, and perhaps also his mother, had died in faraway New Zealand, where the rest of the family now lived.

His youngest brother, Ludvig, who took over their father's New Zealand farm, was twenty years younger, meaning that the two had never laid eyes on each other. So, while the great fir trees may have swayed still, the voices of the Johansen family were nothing more than fading echoes in the Norwegian mist.

Other than this emotionally charged trip to Norway, Holt's later years attest to his American success. He and his wife Martine lived happily on their Colfax farm until she died in 1928, after a short illness. Speaking of her death, and providing one of the few insights into her personality and character, in his diary Holt described Martine as having lived the life of a quiet homemaker, who faced death "happily in the faith of her Savior." He thereafter left the farm and went to live with his oldest daughter, widow Nettie Stalson, and her children. Surviving family photographs from his final years show him holding some of his many grand- and great-grand-children. Holt lived to the age of ninety-four. He died in 1944 and was buried in the Norton Lutheran Church cemetery near his rural Colfax farm.

At the end of his 1903 *Autobiography*, Holt provides a fitting assessment of his life and immigrant experience. In so doing, he delineates a familiar theme; considerable personal achievement against a backdrop of underlying sadness. His words convey pride in his family and in his professional success, "What can be said of Johanes, is that he always has been a dependable and sober man and a true and hardworking employee." He avoided disagreements, had never been in a fight, nor had he contracted a serious illness, remarkable feats for one "traveling so far in a world where the adjectives 'mean' and 'dangerous' are common." Although his part had been relatively small, he had contributed to a great American epic, the harvesting of the Midwestern pinery. Yet, he coupled this positive self-assessment with the memories of his long-lost Norwegian home and family. When their "memories returned," anguish and disappointment moderated his pride in his successful immigrant odyssey.

DOCUMENTS

Struggles of an Irish Immigrant, *c. 1913*

SAM GRAY

35 years, pretty husky man, although his face is rather thin and worn out looking. Irish. 12 years in the United States. A shipyard painter in

SOURCE: Melvyn Dubofsky and Joseph A. McCartin, eds., *American Labor: A Documentary Collection* (New York: Palgrave Macmillan, 2004), 97–99.

England. Clerks in the shipping offices were agitating the people to go to America; they said that America was a better country with much higher wages than in England. He thinks that the clerks did this in the interest of the shipping companies. He believed at that time in the clerks' agitation, and he read the same in the newspapers. This is the reason he came to America.

He left his painting trade for the following reason: He felt its bad influence upon his health in England. When he came over he tried to continue the same trade here, but very soon he noticed the danger of white lead poison—"painter's colic." He quit the trade never to return again to it. He became a casual laborer, earning at first good wages on different jobs. He wrote to his parents in Ireland once every two months sending some money with each letter. But in the later years he fell down and it became more difficult to get jobs....

His home is in Ireland. His mother and sister are living there.... He has no home, no relatives, and no friends in America. Other people call him a hobo, but he calls himself just a common laborer belonging to the ranks which are roaming over the country. He earns his living by laboring.

A year ago he was in Milwaukee. He came here [Chicago] on Nov. 1, having $35.00. Two weeks he "rested," drank with other "floaters" in the saloons—both whiskey and beer; went to shows, and courted the girls. After two weeks the money was gone. He started to look for work, during which time he was helped out by his temporary friends—other laborers, whom he knew, and who continued to come in from work with money. Once he went to the Catholic Sisters who gave him [food] to eat, and once he was three days having nothing to eat whatever.

The first night he came to Milwaukee he slept in the Rescue Mission; paid $0.10 for a night, had a hot bath and had his clothes fumed which is a necessity when coming in from construction and all other camps. He looked for work all over the city; wanted a job in a factory ... but could not get anything.... The Free Employment Office then shipped him out to an ice camp in Salem, Wis., 10 hours a day, pay $1.50 a day if he worked less than a month and $1.75 if he worked a month or over. He paid $4.00 for camp and board; 2 men slept in a bunk; bunks were two story high. They lived in an old house. The bedding was very dirty and lousy; 38 men slept in one room and the air was foul. Every morning the men complained of headaches and bad tastes in their mouths. The room was swept only once a week by "bullcooks," but never mopped; no cuspidors, no washing or bathing facilities. The board was good and the foreman was fair. Worked five weeks—the icehouse was filled. He had $20 and paid his way to Milwaukee where he "rested" one week. The Free Employment Office then shipped him to a railway construction camp in Medford, Wis., 10 hours a day; $1.75 per day; board was $4.00; two men in a bunk and bunks were two stories high; 22 men slept in a car....

He could only stand to be with the foreman three weeks. In order to get his pay he was compelled to go to Stevens Point, 60 miles. He jumped a freight train and from there he jumped another freight to Minneapolis. He spent three days there for having a "little time." He then walked to Hudson, 16 miles from Minneapolis. He got work with a railway "steel gang;" 10 hours a day; $2 per day; $4.50 for board.... After six weeks he quit because he could not eat the grub. He "beat" his way back to Minneapolis. There he "rested" two weeks. After this his money was all gone. He jumped a freight to Milwaukee. He was here 3 days without work; his "friends" helped him out.... The State Free Employment Office then shipped him to a telephone gang in Mecqon, 14 miles from Milwaukee; 9 hours a day, pay $30 a month with sleeping place and board.

An Italian Bootblack's Story, 1902

We came to Brooklyn to a wooden house in Adams Street that was full of Italians from Naples. [A man named] Bartolo had a room on the third floor and there were fifteen men in the room, all boarding with Bartolo. He did the cooking on a stove in the middle of the room and there were beds all around the sides, one bed above another. It was very hot in the room, but we were soon asleep, for we were very tired.

The next morning, early, Bartolo told us to go out and pick rags and get bottles. He gave us bags and hooks and showed us the ash barrels. On the streets where the fine houses are the people are very careless and put out good things, like mattresses and umbrellas, clothes, hats and boots. We brought all these to Bartolo and he made them new again and sold them on the sidewalk; but mostly we brought rags and bones. The rags we had to wash in the backyard and then we hung them to dry on lines under the ceiling in our room. The bones we kept under the beds till Bartolo could find a man to buy them.

Most of the men in our room worked at digging the sewer. Bartolo got them the work and they paid him about one quarter of their wages. Then he charged them for board and he bought the clothes for them, too. So they got little money after all.

Bartolo was always saying that the rent of the room was so high that he could not make anything, but he was really making plenty. He was what they call a padrone* and is now a very rich man. The men that were living with him had just come to the country and could not speak English. They had all been sent by the young man we met in Italy. Bartolo told us all that

*A padrone is a labor boss who secured employment for immigrants. (Eds.)

SOURCE: *Independent* 54 (December 4, 1902): 2865–67.

we must work for him and that if we did not the police would come and put us in prison.

He gave us very little money, and our clothes were some of those that were found on the street. Still we had enough to eat and we had meat quite often, which we never had in Italy. Bartolo got it from the butcher—the meat that he could not sell to other people—but it was quite good meat. Bartolo cooked it in the pan while we all sat on our beds in the evening. Then he cut it into small bits and passed the pan around, saying:

"See what I do for you and yet you are not glad. I am too kind a man, that is why I am so poor."

We were with Bartolo nearly a year, but some of our countrymen who had been in the place a long time said that Bartolo had no right to us and we could get work for a dollar and a half a day, which, when you make it *lire* (reckoned in the Italian currency) is very much. So we went away one day to Newark and got work on the street. Bartolo came after us and made a great noise, but the boss said that if he did not go away soon the police would have him. Then he went, saying that there was no justice in this country.

We paid a man five dollars each for getting us the work and we were with that boss for six months. He was Irish, but a good man and he gave us our money every Saturday night. We lived much better than with Bartolo, and when the work was done we each had nearly $200 saved. Plenty of the men spoke English and they taught us, and we taught them to read and write. That was at night, for we had a lamp in our room, and there were only five other men who lived in that room with us.

We got up at half-past five o'clock every morning and made coffee on the stove and had a breakfast of bread and cheese, onions, garlic and red herrings. We went to work at seven o'clock and in the middle of the day we had soup and bread in a place where we got it for two cents a plate. In the evenings we had a good dinner with meat of some kind and potatoes. We got from the butcher the meat that other people would not buy because they said it was old, but they don't know what is good. We paid four or five cents a pound for it and it was the best, tho I have heard of people paying sixteen cents a pound.

When the Newark boss told us that there was no more work Francisco and I talked about what we would do and we went back to Brooklyn to a saloon near Hamilton Ferry, where we got a job cleaning it out and slept in a little room upstairs. There was a bootblack named Michael on the corner and when I had time I helped him and learned the business. Francisco cooked the lunch in the saloon and he, too, worked for the bootblack and we were soon able to make the best polish.

Then we thought we would go into business and we got a basement on Hamilton Avenue, near the Ferry, and put four chairs in it. We paid $75 for the chairs and all the other things. We had tables and looking glasses there and curtains. We took the papers that have the pictures in and made the place high toned. Outside we had a big sign that said:

THE BEST SHINE FOR TEN CENTS

Men that did not want to pay ten cents could get a good shine for five cents, but it was not an oil shine. We had two boys helping us and paid each of them fifty cents a day. The rent of the place was $20 a month, so the expenses were very great, but we made money from the beginning. We slept in the basement, but got our meals in the saloon till we could put a stove in our place, and then Francisco cooked for us all. That would not do, tho, because some of our customers said that they did not like to smell garlic and onions and red herrings. I thought that was strange, but we had to do what the customers said. So we got the woman who lived upstairs to give us our meals and paid her $1.50 a week each. She gave the boys soup in the middle of the day—five cents for two plates....

We had said that when we saved $1,000 each we would go back to Italy and buy a farm, but now that the time is coming we are so busy and making so much money that we think we will stay. We have opened another parlor near South Ferry, in New York. We have to pay $30 a month rent, but the business is very good. The boys in the place charge sixty cents a day because there is so much work.

A Bintel Brief, 1907

Dear Editor,

I am one of those unfortunate girls thrown by fate into a dark and dismal shop, and I need your counsel.

Along with my parents, sisters and brothers, I came from Russian Poland where I had been well educated. But because of the terrible things going on in Russia we were forced to emigrate to America. I am now seventeen years old, but I look younger and they say I am attractive.

A relative talked us into moving to Vineland, New Jersey, and here in this small town I went to work in a shop. In this shop there is a foreman who is an exploiter, and he sets prices on the work. He figures it out so that the wages are very low, he insults and reviles the workers, he fires them and then takes them back. And worse than all of this, in spite of the fact that he has a wife and several children, he often allows himself to "have fun" with some of the working girls. It was my bad luck to be one of the girls that he tried to make advances to. And woe to any girl who doesn't willingly accept them.

SOURCE: Isaac Metzker, *A Bintel Brief: Sixty Years of Letters from the Lower East Side to the Daily Jewish Forward* (Garden City, NJ: Doubleday and Co., 1971), 72–73.

Though my few hard-earned dollars mean a lot to my family of eight souls, I didn't want to accept the foreman's vulgar advances. He started to pick on me, said my work was no good, and when I proved to him he was wrong, he started to shout at me in the vilest language. He insulted me in Yiddish and then in English, so the American workers could understand too. Then, as if the Devil were after me, I ran home.

I am left without a job. Can you imagine my circumstances and that of my parents who depend on my earnings? The girls in the shop were very upset over the foreman's vulgarity but they don't want him to throw them out, so they are afraid to be witnesses against him. What can be done about this? I beg you to answer me.

Respectfully,
A Shopgirl

ANSWER:

Such a scoundrel should be taught a lesson that could be an example to others. The girl is advised to bring out into the open the whole story about the foreman, because there in the small town it shouldn't be difficult to have him thrown out of the shop and for her to get her job back.

Chapter 5

Women's Sphere: Women's Work

Women factory workers. c, 1910.

During most of the nineteenth century and into the early years of the twentieth the notion predominated that, when it came to work, men and women occupied separate spheres. Married women's work centered in the home; for unmarried women there were few female occupations open. Elementary school teaching and nursing were deemed respectable for middle-class women. For the poor, domestic service and the in-home production of such items as clothing and artificial flowers were available.

During the final decades of the nineteenth century, American urban growth and an expanding industrial economy opened innumerable jobs for men. For urban women there were some gains in opportunity, notably as factory workers in the garment industry, as secretaries and typists in business offices, and as sales clerks in department stores.

For city women, employment opportunities often carried with them low pay, long hours, and dangerous working conditions. This was particularly true of the burgeoning garment industry of New York and Philadelphia, which attracted thousands of young immigrant women to its shops. In his essay

"The 'Girl Army' and the Philadelphia Shirtwaist Strike, 1904-1910," Daniel Sidorick paints a vivid picture of the rise of this industry, of the owners who ran it, and particularly of the workers who labored in it. The author describes the "abysmal wages and working conditions" suffered by the young working girls, but what is his explanation of why they flocked to these jobs? As the essay moves toward a description of the great shirtwaist strike, be aware of how gender and ethnicity played a role in the struggle between management and labor. Also take note of the responses to the strike and the strikers by the police, on the one hand, and socially prominent women on the other. Finally, can you point to examples of working conditions today that approach those against which the young Philadelphia garment workers rose up in protest?

Women attempting to enter prestigious, traditionally male occupations often met with considerable resistance and drew on huge stores of courage in their perseverance. The first document is a 1916 newspaper account of the recollections of Dr. Anna Manning Comfort, who graduated in the first class of the New York Medical College and Hospital for Women in 1865. In what ways did the perception of a separate place for women within the medical profession shift between 1865 and 1916?

Although popular beliefs about women's natural capacities supported their entry into teaching, clerical jobs, nursing, factory work, librarianship, social work, and even medicine, they were also used to exclude women from positions of leadership in those fields, to deny them the right to vote, and to bar their entry into other professions. In 1872 the U.S. Supreme Court upheld a decision of the Illinois courts denying Myra Bradwell a license to practice law on the grounds of her sex. The second document presents Supreme Court Justice Bradley's majority opinion in support of the Court's decision. Notice that his argument rested heavily on traditional perceptions of women's natures.

The Court's decision in *Bradwell v. Illinois* set back women's rights, yet the era did see victories as well. That same year (1872), the Illinois legislature removed all restrictions to women's entry into the professions. Similar actions were taken in other states. In 1869 Arabella Mansfield of Iowa became the first woman to practice law.

By 1891 the nation boasted two hundred licensed women lawyers. (Of course, the figure represented less than one percent of the nation's attorneys.) As the final document reveals, the struggle was far from over. In a 1901 article in the *Independent* magazine, Henry T. Finck took a strong stance against women in the work force. Though, as you will note, he did recognize that for some needy women work outside the home was necessary, he insisted, "Men still prefer, and always will prefer, the home girl to any other kind." Is there evidence of similar views still being expressed today? If so, state examples.

ESSAY

The "Girl Army" and the Philadelphia Shirtwaist Srike, 1909–1910 (2004)

Daniel Sidorick

The women's clothing industry in the United States in 1860 consisted of fewer than two hundred shops employing less than six thousand workers, mostly women. As the industry grew (to 84,000 workers in 1900) and as some facets of the trade became more mechanized, the proportion of male workers rose rapidly, jumping from under one-tenth of the workforce in 1880 to one-third in 1890. In the last decade of the century men continued to work in significant numbers in the older sectors of the industry, but around the turn of the century a new branch of the industry grew rapidly, the waist and dress trade. The shirtwaist industry took advantage of favorable aspects of the existing clothing trade while emphasizing some newer trends and technologies: unlike older sectors it contained several large factories that dominated the business, but utilized one of the distinguishing features of the old garment industry, a proliferation of small subcontractors. The new shirtwaist manufacturers hired mostly women. A characteristic that the new segment of the industry shared with the old was the predominance of Jewish immigrants as both manufacturers and workers although the former were typically German-Jewish earlier immigrants, while the latter were usually more recent Russian-Jewish immigrants. An aspect of the shirtwaist industry that had been of little consequence previously but was to become a central tenet of the apparel industry was its dependence on "fashion." Because of the rapidly changing demands of retailers, manufactures were reluctant to maintain large inventories and instead alternated between rush periods when orders arrived and slack periods when there was little work; reductions in workforce during slack seasons averaged 42 percent.

The subcontracting system was especially notorious for its role in perpetuating the poor working conditions and abysmal wages characteristic of the industry. This system had many advantages for the large manufactures and retailers.

It allowed them to offload some of the fixed capital costs onto contractors, who provided sewing machines and the physical location for the work, often in warehouses converted into numerous small manufacturing establishments crowded together and separated from one another with flimsy (and fire-prone) partitions. The system shielded the large manufactures

SOURCE: From Daniel Sidorick, "'The Girl Army': The Philadelphia Shirtwaist Strike of 1909-1910." Pennsylvania History. Vol. 71, No. 3 (Summer 2004), 323–324, 327–330, 330–339. Published by the Pennsylvania Historical Association. Used by permission.

from the volatility of the industry—they could maintain a moderate manufacturing capability in their factories and distribute additional work to as many contractors was as were needed during the busy seasons. The number of small contractors substantial, but their position was decidedly subservient in an industry increasingly dominated by several large manu- factures, like M. Haber & Company, which employed some nine hundred women and men in a single factory.

The early twentieth century was a time of expansion and change for wage-earning women in the United States and in Philadelphia. The number of women nationally who worked outside the home soared from one million in 1890 to eight million in 1910. Many worked in the garment industry, and the proportion of Philadelphia wage-earners employed in the women's cloth- ing industry grew from 7.4 percent in 1899 to 9.0 percent in 1914. The flood of women entering the labor market helped the owners to keep wages and con- ditions depressed. While it was estimated that a family of five needed $900 per year for a minimal standard of living, working women in Pennsylvania in 1909 averaged $299. The forty-five female shirtwaist workers in Philadel- phia interviewed by government investigators in 1905 had weekly earnings ranging from $1.92 to $12.00, with an average of $6.69. Concerned investiga- tors noted that "the average wage ... will barely cover the actual cost of main- tenance of a very economical, prudent woman." The effect of the low wages on the shirtwaist workers was compounded by the severe seasonality of their work as well as the petty exactions of their employers, who made them pay for needles, water, and sometimes power to run the sewing machines. The already abysmal wages and working conditions worsened after 1905. In the relentless drive to minimize costs employers hired increasingly younger women in the shirtwaist shops—the median age in Philadelphia dropped from 23 in 1905 to 20 in 1910. The financial crisis after the panic of 1907 encouraged the ongoing movement for efficiency typified by Taylorism, and many shirtwaist workers reported drops in their pay between 1905 and 1909.

Despite these hardships, factory work also provided an arena for expanded social interactions. Young women who went to work in the factories—especially the larger factories—found not only oppressive working conditions but also some measure of independence and opportunities to build friendships and create social networks with their peers. Outside the control of family members, many enthusiastically sought out and embraced features of American culture that would identify them as modern Americans. These included such lofty goals as education as well as an intense interest in fashionable clothing, dancing, and men. As in many of the dime novels aimed at working women, marriage was viewed as an escape, for most women left factory work after marriage. Yet this interest in consumer culture and the opposite sex did not preclude simultaneous participation in defiant strikes, for, as Susan Glenn notes, "[w]omen's dreams ... were broad and varied enough to embrace romantic images of marriage and equally romantic visions of class struggle." The independence and self-assertiveness displayed by these young women developed in struggles with family tradition, their employers, and even the union that represented them.

While the Philadelphia garment industry had seen sporadic strikes, only a small number of women were organized into unions. This resulted both from the disorganization inherent in the industry itself, spread among large factories, small shops, and hundreds of contractors, and from the ambivalence or indifference of many male union leaders toward organizing women. Their union, the International Ladies' Germent Workers Union (ILGWU), was a member of the craft-oriented American Federation of Labor, although it contained both craft locals and locals organized along industrial lines. The best paid and most skilled garment workers—the cutters—were organized into all-male craft locals. The union leadership also consisted mostly of men. The cutters played a crucial role in the industry: to begin with, they were better paid and they had a distinct path toward upward mobility. They were usually the workers hired to be inside contractors and they were the ones who, after saving about $50, could open their own small shops and join the competition in bidding for work from the manufactures. The successful ones could hope to move up one day to the ranks of the manufacturers. Other men moved into union staff jobs, some out of commitment to socialist or anarchist ideals, but some as just another business opportunity. Interestingly, a number of men listed in the early history of the union, written in 1924, had even moved from being organizers and union officials into becoming businessmen themselves. Thus A. Axelrod had been an "active member of Local 1 in 1910 [and] chairman of the New York Joint Board," but was a "dress sub-manufacture" in 1924; similarly, B. Witashkin was a former waistmaker, then a vice-president of the International from 1910 to 1912, but was "in business" in 1924. Daniel Soyer has shown that, for male Jewish immigrants in the early twentieth century, class was often an ambiguous notion, resulting from the clash of Jewish radical traditions with the desire and possibilities for upward mobility. For the unmarried women working in the large shirtwaist factories in Philadelphia, however, class was a far more clear-cut concept.

All elements of the shirtwaist industry in Philadelphia as in New York—the union, most of the workers, and the manufactures—were part of the Jewish immigrant community. A small percentage of the workforce was made up of Italian immigrants and white native-born Americans, with just a few African Americans. Forty percent of Jews in Philadelphia worked in the garment industry in the first decade of the twentieth century, and the immigrants lived in tightly clustered neighborhoods in close proximity to their jobs. Virtually all Jewish shirtwaist makers lived in two small neighborhoods: one in South Philadelphia, between Second and Eighth streets from Spruce to Mifflin streets, and one in Northern Liberties, around Fourth and Fairmount streets.

In these neighborhoods a large number of institutions, formal and informal, comprised a vibrant and evolving community. Synagogues representing every home region in Europe were located throughout the neighborhoods; Jewish retail stores lined South Street and stood on most street corners. Out-of-work immigrants clustered at the informal labor market, dubbed the "pig market," at Fifth and South streets. Immigrants who had joined socialist and anarchist movements in Europe continued their political activity at the dozens of workers' associations and unions in South Philadelphia. As early as 1889 anarchists had established a Jewish Federation of Labor there and left-wing unions became a part of Philadelphia's Jewish life. Radical activities extended beyond workplace concerns: in 1907 a large number of Jewish women met in Forward Hall on Pine Street to declare a strike over the price of kosher beef, led by a strike committee of over thirty women. More established members of the community took a different approach to integrating the new immigrants into the American way of life. German-Jewish immigrants who had arrived a generation earlier set up organizations to ease the transition for new immigrants. One of these was the Young Women's Union, which started a kindergarten at 238 Pine Street in 1885, then branched into other work similar to that of Christian settlement houses in Philadelphia. Among numerous other charitable institutions was the Hebrew Orphans' Home; Morris Haber, owner of the largest shirtwaist company in the city, was its president.

Streets where the shirtwaist makers lived were overwhelmingly populated by other Russian Jewish immigrants. Although the few large manufacturers lived out of the neighborhoods, often in mansions along Fairmount Park, the two clustered communities housed shirtwaist operators, contractors, and small manufactures next door to one another (as well as butchers, liquor salesmen, musicians, and many other workers in the garment industry). For example, a garment manufacturer lived at 232 Catharine Street with his wife, eight children, and servant, while next door at 230 four young women (three of them shirtwaist makers) boarded with a Hebrew teacher and his family.

On the boundaries of their neighborhoods lived other immigrants and occasionally African Americans. The older, established immigrants, especially the Irish, sometimes battled the newcomers, but the Jews got on fairly well with the Italians who were arriving during the same period. The headworker at College Settlement at 433 Christian Street reported ongoing "racial animosities" in 1907 among "Slavs, Celts [and] Hebrews." While relations between Jews and Italians were, on the whole, amicable, there was some antagonism among Jews toward what the *Jewish Exponent* characterized as "the influx of Italian immigrants prepared to work for incredibly low wages.' Although Italians comprised only a small proportion of shirtwaist workers, their numbers could conceivably be sufficient to depress the wages of all. The same could not be said about African Americans: before 1910 they were largely excluded from the industry. Although they made up 5.5 percent of Philadelphia's population in 1910, no records were found of any working in the shirtwaist industry before the strike. The ILGWU was later among the most progressive unions in Philadelphia in supporting integrated workplaces and unity of workers across ethnic and racial lines, but the initial entry of African Americans into the Philadelphia women's clothing industry was "by the route which so often occurred in other industries—importation as strikebreakers." Once they were working in the industry (after the strike) the union made attempts to organize them, but one black woman in Philadelphia reported that "they never ask us to join except when they want to strike." In any case, on the eve of the strike of 1909, about 85 percent of Philadelphia shirtwaist makers were Jewish immigrants. About the same proportion were women, and thus these two factors, gender and ethnicity, were to affect profoundly the development of the class battle between capitalists and workers in the great Philadelphia shirtwaist strike of 1909.

The Strike: December 20, 1909–February 6, 1910

New York's shirtwaist industry had erupted in a general strike on November 22, 1909, after months of smaller strikes and a dramatic meeting in Cooper Union, where thousands of workers swore an oath to shut down the industry. Between 15,000 and 40,000 answered the call, and the manufacturers responded with strikebreakers and vicious attacks on the young pickets, aided by a city government and police who seemed interested only in protecting the property of the owners. One of the tactics of the manufactures was to shift orders to non-striking areas outside the city, and especially to Philadelphia. Union officials led by special organizer Ben Frischwasser hurried to Philadelphia to ascertain the potential strength of the union there. Local 15 leaders reported a treasury of only $200 but claimed three thousand members out of fifteen thousand shirtwaist workers in Philadelphia, and a poll of twenty-five organized shops found sympathy for joining New York in a general strike. The president of Philadelphia's Central Labor Union (CLU), John J. Murphy, promised the support of the labor movement in the city, and a CLU meeting appointed five members to take charge of the strike. Official support appeared ready for a strike, but many doubted that the "girls and men" in the shops would respond.

As it turned out, the Philadelphia workers were more than ready to strike, and not only to support their New York sisters. True, "it was considered emphatically inconsistent with union principles for union operators to produce waists for firms which had been repudiated by their sisters in New York," but most workers in Philadelphia were not "union operators" and the loyalty of those who were was largely untested. The previous four years, however, had seen bad circumstances turn to worse as the number of small contractors proliferated and the large retailers and manufacturers consolidated control of the industry and used their favorable position to squeeze ever more profit from the manufacture of shirtwaists.

On the final Sunday afternoon before Christmas of 1909, Philadelphia's newspaper readers found an article in the *Public Ledger* about a puzzling new phenomenon taking place in New York. Society women and college girls were joining the picket lines of the immigrant girls on strike against New York's shirtwaist manufacturers. Readers were accustomed to stories about the activities of suffragettes, but this attempt at sisterhood across the great divide of class was unprecedented, for it went beyond traditional concern for the poor to actual support for a strike, on the picket lines and in the courts. Meanwhile, that same Sunday afternoon, workers from Philadelphia's shirtwaist shops were streaming into the Labor Lyceum at Sixth and Brown streets. Director Clay of Philadelphia's Department of Public Safety had tried to prevent the meeting, banning the use of the originally planned venue, the Arch Street Theater, because a Yiddish leaflet advertising the meeting was "revolutionary in nature," according to an interpretation by one of the director's aides. The speakers *were* uncompromising in their attacks on the greed of the manufacturers, if not quite revolutionary. Famed labor agitator Mary Harris, better known as Mother Jones, urged the girls to "[g]et the spirit of revolt and be a woman," and trolleymen's union head C. O. Pratt assured the workers they would not stand alone if they chose to strike: "the trolleymen would remember how they helped them during the [trolleymen's] strike and would gladly reciprocate." Abraham Rosenberg, the International President of the ILGWU who had just come from New York to chair the meeting, read a strike resolution in English and Yiddish to the six thousand workers who crowded the meeting hall. Demands included the fifty-hour week, an increase in wages, the end of the detested system of charging girls for needles and other supplies, and, to enforce the rest of the provisions, the union shop. The workers responded to the speakers with ceaseless applause and "[w]hen Chairman Rosenberg took the vote every girl in the place arose and voted to strike." Mother Jones encouraged them to rely on their own strength and avoid entanglements with the wealthy women who had begun supporting the New York strike: "It's not a Mrs. Belmont or an Anne Morgan that we want, but independent workers who will assert their rights.... We don't want charity brigades or temperance lecturers ... if they will leave us alone we will come out alright."

The next morning everyone went to work as usual, but at 9:00 a.m. thousands of young women, and some men, stopped their work, put on their coats, and walked out to join the first massive strike of women in Philadelphia's history. The spirit on the streets and in the union meeting places was exhilarating. Rosenberg estimated that 7,500 girls and 300 men had walked out, and crowds gathered on the streets to listen to Mother Jones's impassioned speeches and "jeered every policeman that they met." In the nine meeting halls music mixed with the hectic work of hastily convened committees: "several hundred of the girls waltzed and two-stepped to the music of the strained pianos.... It was a general labor festival, with a strong undercurrent of socialism."

Some manufacturers nervously offered to satisfy all the demands of the strikers except union recognition, but at the largest manufacturer in the city, M. Haber at 225 South Fifth Street, the city police ominously doubled the size of their force guarding the factory. Meanwhile, the most prominent representative of reform in the city, Florence Sanville of the Consumer's League, offered timid support for the strikers' demands and hinted that her group might be willing to play a mediating role: "We have brought about most of the reforms by co-operating with the employers, and that is our chief mission."

Over the first few days of the strike, the positions of the strikers and the large manufacturers hardened, while various groups in the middle, including the press, reformers, and some manufacturers, scrambled to find some compromise. The Haber company declared its resolve to abandon the city rather than deal with the union and used its leverage to pull together a meeting of thirty manufactures, extracting a pledge from each refusing to settle with the union; the *Public Ledger* noted that the larger plants were "assuming a sprit of aggressiveness." Haber's striking employees meanwhile bitterly told reporters of the degrading conditions they were forced to endure. The factory workers had to pay two cents a day for water from a hydrant while the "office girls drink sterilized bottled water" and in the "dull season" they were kept in the shop whether there was work or not on pain of dismissal, though they were paid by the piece. Most dangerous of all, the doors of the building were kept locked, "and should a fire occur we would all be trapped and burned alive." Hundreds of pickets spread throughout the factory districts downtown and in nearby neighborhoods, and arrests began the second day of the strike. The very first arrests were of a small manufacturer (who lived in the same neighborhood as the workers) and two strikers, but, significantly, this was also the last arrest reported in the *Public Leger* or the *Call* of anyone on the side of the owners; the several hundred arrests that followed were all of strikers and their supporters. A police sergeant even visited manufacturers to determine where additional police help might be needed. The owners again made overtures to the workers offering improvements if they would abandon their demand for union recognition, but at every one of "a chain of meetings ... the strikers declared that they would not surrender on this point." Some of the manufacturers, however, capitulated to the strikers' demands and reopened.

Early support for the strikers ranged all the way from the very qualified sympathy of a *Public Ledger* editorial (which, however, warned against the evils of the "thoroughly unjust and un-American" closed shop) to the strong support of the trolleymen, United Hebrew Trades, and Socialist party. Fifty trolleymen and mechanics joined the strikers at union headquarters, many acted as pickets when off-duty (as did the Milkmen's Union), and they began taking up collections at almost every car barn in the city. The United Hebrew Trades voted to levy a per capita tax on all its members for the strike fund, and Mary Charsky of the Socialist party spoke at a tumultuous meeting and helped resolve a simmering dispute between anarchist and socialist strikers.

On the fourth day of the strike Margaret Dreier Robins, president of the Women's Trade Union League (WTUL), and Agnes Nestor, head of the Glove Makers' Union, arrived from Chicago and began establishing some order in what was admittedly a chaotic uprising. Robins did picket duty herself, spoke at up to nine giant meetings a day in "meeting mad" Philadelphia, and promised to win support, especially financial, from the city's society women. Her efforts had only limited success initially: on January 4 (day 16 of the strike) she reported that contributions from clubwomen so far totaled less than $100. Two days later she opened the Philadelphia headquarters of the WTUL just down the street from the Haber factory; there she and workers from the College Settlement (which had already begun strike support work of its own) began serving lunch daily to the strikers. For Robins, the effect of sweatshop work on children was the greatest evil, and the sight of seventy girls and boys aged 11 to 14 among the pickets validated the importance of her efforts. A picture of four young pickets on the front pages of two newspapers also helped to win sympathy among the public. However, the plight of the "helpless girls" did not quite convince clubwomen to pry open their pocket-books until Robins demonstrated the connection between the rights of women workers and suffrage. Gradually members of several clubs and the Pennsylvania Women's Suffrage Association started joining the settlement workers and WTUL members in strike support work, and some even began providing bail for arrested strikers.

While they may have looked like "helpless girls" to their society benefactors, the strikers were acting more like committed activists in a movement that was changing their lives, the industry, and the city. Every day up to two thousand pickets fanned out across the factory districts, talking to the women still working and urging them to join their sisters. Often their activities became adventures worthy of dime-novel heroines, as when a fourteen-year-old leader of the Markers' and Cleaners' Union used subterfuge to get hired in a factory that was still in operation, tried to talk the workers into joining the strike, then was fired on the spot when her true intentions were discovered. Company managers and police became increasingly belligerent as bosses pointed out workers to be arrested and police followed their orders. Strikers were arrested for distributing leaflets, for "annoying" strikebreakers, and even for walking in front of a factory. By December 29 police began making wholesale arrests and, by January 7, some three hundred strikers had been taken into custody. When they were not picketing, they crowded into union halls, attended union dances and variety shows, and discussed and debated strike tactics. On Christmas day, despite one of the heaviest snows the city had ever seen, strikers crowded into a hall on South Third Street for a "grand dance" and into another at Seventh and Morris streets to listen to speeches by Mother Jones, Mary Charsky from the Socialist party, and Isaac Dornblum, the organizer of the "picker army." The next day, eight shirtwaist operators hosted a dinner for some seventy child workers at the College Settlement. The union at this point was still enthusiastically leading the battle against the manufactures, and its president Abe Rosenberg expected a quick settlement.

The actions and dedication of the strikers suggested that their jobs were more than merely a source of "pin money." Many contributed vital support to their families, some were living independently (usually as boarders) and needed every penny to make ends meet, and some were the sole support of invalid parents or younger siblings. Fifteen-year-old Bessie Ingeston's father was blind and her mother was an invalid; Bessie's income from her job supported that whole family. Seventeen-year-old Eva Goldenzweig provided the only income for herself and her father in the row house on Marshall Street that they shared with three other families. The sacrifices demanded by the strike were immense, and though some were forced to return to work, most of the strikers held out. Rose Schneiderman, a working-class leader of the WTUL, captured their feelings when she said, at yet another mass meeting, "We starve while we are working: what does it matter if we starve now?" At the same meeting, an organizer from the bakers' union reminded the workers of the essential position they held in their industry: "The bosses advertise for girls, not machines."

The bosses were advertising for girls daily, with dozens of want-ads appearing daily in the *Philadelphia Inquirer* and the *Public Ledger.* Some companies in desperation even advertised for phony housework and waitress jobs, then tried to convince the women who showed up to work in shirtwaist shops. The low inventories in this fashion-dependent industry left the companies especially vulnerable to any strike lasting more than a few days. Nonetheless the man who quickly became leader of the hard-line manufacturers, Leo Becker of the Haber Company, denied that the owners were suffering; on the contrary, "the manufacturers were in a position to dictate terms." On December 27 he declared, "We will bring the union to terms this week"; a week later he remarked that "manufacturers have been overwhelmed by applications for work." He was selected president of the hastily convened Manufacturers Association, and his company used its control of supplies and influence with lending institutions to compel most firms to fall into line. Becker's statements during the strike became increasingly strident. He demanded more police protection, claimed strikers were planning to bomb his house, and filed for an injunction against the union, claiming that the strike had cost his company alone over $50,000 (contradicting his own statements of a few days earlier)....

Four weeks into the bitter shirtwaist strike in the severest winter in recorded Philadelphia history (1909–1910), union leader Abraham Rosenberg had just about given up. Hundreds of strikers, mostly girls in their teens, had been arrested by a hostile city government, union funds were almost depleted, and the manufactures were maintaining a no-negotiation stance enforced by a few large companies who controlled access to materials. Meanwhile, the workers' "allies," society women who had joined the picker lines and raised money out of sympathy for the girls' plight, were urging "class harmony" and cooperation as the best method to improve working conditions.

After thousands of garment workers had crowded into New Royal Hall at Seventh and Morris streets in South Philadelphia for a mass meeting on Sunday afternoon, January 16, Rosenberg ascended the platform. He reviewed the state of the strike, then revealed the contents of the manufacturers' "final offer": if the strikers would return to work Monday, the manufactures would set up a committee to arbitrate all issues with the workers but one—union recognition. When Rosenberg recommended that the strikers accept this proposal as the best they could hope to win, the hall exploded in anger. As local reporter recorded:

> Whatever order there had been previously was instantly thrown to the winds. A wildly discordant chorus of jeers and hoots met Rosenberg's report, and all over the hall girls and men sprang to their chairs and cried: "No, no. We will never return unless we are recognized as a union...."

Rosenberg left the platform: "I'm through ... I've done the best I can and they will not listen." Other labor leaders tried to restore some order, but the rank-and-file chairwomen from each shop were quickly surrounded by garment workers who demanded that they "fight any attempt to arbitrate."

Contrary to observers' expectations of an imminent collapse of the strike, the workers returned to the picket lines more determined than ever. Rosenberg reluctantly resumed leadership of the strike, and the strike took on "new life.... The girls have once again shown their allegiance to their cause and its leaders ... with all their old vigor and determination." By early February the manufacturers granted *de facto* recognition to the union by signing an agreement with union delegates ending the strike. The settlement did not include the closed shop but did significantly improve wages and conditions. More importantly, the general strike of some seven thousand shirtwaist workers was, to borrow Nancy MacLean's words, an "unprecedented awakening in consciousness and collective activity" for the young women who confronted industrial capitalism and overcame odds previously thought insurmountable.

This incident was one of many that demonstrated the resolute determination of the Philadelphia shirtwaist strikers to see their struggle through to victory, even in defiance of their union leaders, when necessary, and to the amazement of almost all observers. Such militancy and solidarity of young working women were not unusual in this period, as historians have shown for the simultaneous New York strike and for many other groups and places.

DOCUMENTS

Only Heroic Women Were Doctors Then (1865), 1916

Changes in the position of women in the world in the last fifty years were emphasized by Dr. Anna Manning Comfort, graduate of the New York Medical College and Hospital for Women in its first class in 1865, at a luncheon in her honor, given by the Faculty and Trustees of the college at Delmonico's yesterday. Dr. Comfort was graduated at the age of 20, and she is only in the early seventies, alert and well preserved, though she has had a vigorous career, has been married, and is the mother of three children.

"Students of today have no idea of conditions as they were when I studied medicine," said Dr. Comfort. "It is difficult to realize the changes that have taken place. I attended the first meeting when this institution was proposed, and was graduated from the first class. We had to go to Bellevue Hospital for our practical work, and the indignities we were made to suffer are beyond belief. There were 500 young men students taking postgraduate courses, and we were jeered at and catcalled, and the 'old war horses,' the doctors, joined the younger men.

"We were considered aggressive. They said women did not have the same brains as men and were not trustworthy. All the work at the hospital was made as repulsively unpleasant for us as possible. There were originally six in the class, but all but two were unable to put up with the treatment to which we were subjected and dropped out. I trembled whenever I went to the hospital and I said once that I could not bear it. Finally the women went to the authorities, who said that if we were not respectfully treated they would take the charter from the hospital!

"As a physician there was nothing that I could do that satisfied people. If I wore square-toed shoes and swung my arms they said I was mannish, and if I carried a parasol and wore a ribbon in my hair they said I was too feminine. If I smiled they said I had too much levity, and if I sighed they said I had no sand.

"They tore down my sign when I began to practice, the drug stores did not like to fill my prescriptions, and the older doctors would not consult with me. But that little band of women made it possible for the other women who have come later into the field to do their work. When my first patients came and saw me they said I was too young, and they asked in horrified tones if I had studied dissecting just like the men. They were shocked at that, but they were more shocked when my bills were sent in to find that I charged as much as a man.

SOURCE: "Only Heroic Women Were Doctors Then," *New York Times*, April 9, 1916.

"I believe in women entering professions," said Dr. Comfort, "but I also believe in motherhood. For the normal woman it is no more of a tax to have a profession as well as family life than it is for a man to carry on the multitudinous duties he has outside the family. I had three sons of my own and two adopted ones, and I am as proud of my motherhood as of my medical career. I gave as much of my personality to my children in an hour as some mothers do in ten. My children honored me and have been worth while in the world."

There were many expressions of esteem for Dr. Comfort and she was overcome when it was announced that money had been raised for an Anna Manning Comfort scholarship in the hospital.

Letters of regret were read from John Burroughs and Colonel Theodore Roosevelt among others.

"I believe in women in the medical profession, and in politics, and in all worthy pursuits," said John Burroughs.

"I am amazed to learn that this is the only institution in this State, and one of two in the United States, exclusively for the woman medical student," said Colonel Roosevelt. "There should be others and women of refinement would be drawn into the profession who will not study medicine in a co-educational college, and more women doctors are needed."

Dr. Walter G. Crump, who spoke of the need for medical colleges exclusively for women, said:

"We learn from the [1910] Flexner report that there is an overproduction of doctors, but nine out of ten of the women doctors practice. There are demands continually for women physicians which cannot be filled. They are needed in many places where women and girls are to be under a physician's care."

Dr. Mary A. Brinkman, who was one of the early graduates of the college, spoke. She said she could corroborate many of the things told by Dr. Comfort....

Women's Separate Sphere, 1872

The claim of the plaintiff, who is a married woman, to be admitted to practice as an attorney and counsellor-at-law, is based upon the supposed right of every person, man or woman, to engage in any lawful employment for a livelihood. The Supreme Court of Illinois denied the application on the ground that, by the common law, which is the basis of the laws of Illinois, only men were admitted to the bar, and the legislature had not made any change in this respect, but had simply provided that no person should be admitted to practice as attorney or counsellor without having previously obtained a license for that purpose from two justices of the Supreme Court,

SOURCE: Justice Bradley's majority opinion in *Bradwell v. Illinois* (December 1872).

and that no person should receive a license without first obtaining a certificate from the court of some county of his good moral character. In other respects it was left to the discretion of the court to establish the rules by which admission to the profession should be determined. The court, however, regarded itself as bound by at least two limitations. One was that it should establish such terms of admission as would promote the proper administration of justice, and the other that it should not admit any persons, or class of persons, not intended by the legislature to be admitted, even though not expressly excluded by statute. In view of this latter limitation the court felt compelled to deny the application of females to be admitted as members of the bar. Being contrary to the rules of the common law and the usages of Westminster Hall* from time immemorial, it could not be supposed that the legislature had intended to adopt any different rule.

The claim that, under the fourteenth amendment of the Constitution, which declares that no State shall make or enforce any law which shall abridge the privileges and immunities of citizens of the United States, the statute law of Illinois, or the common law prevailing in that State, can no longer be set up as a barrier against the right of females to pursue any lawful employment for a livelihood (the practice of law included), assumes that it is one of the privileges and immunities of women as citizens to engage in any and every profession, occupation, or employment in civil life.

It certainly cannot be affirmed, as an historical fact, that this has ever been established as one of the fundamental privileges and immunities of the sex. On the contrary, the civil law, as well as nature herself, has always recognized a wide difference in the respective spheres and destinies of man and woman. Man is, or should be, woman's protector and defender. The natural and proper timidity and delicacy which belongs to the female sex evidently unfits it for many of the occupations of civil life. The constitution of the family organization, which is founded in the divine ordinance, as well as in the nature of things, indicates the domestic sphere as that which properly belongs to the domain and functions of womanhood. The harmony, not to say identity, of interests and views which belong, or should belong, to the family institution is repugnant to the idea of a woman adopting a distinct and independent career from that of her husband. So firmly fixed was this sentiment in the founders of the common law that it became a maxim of that system of jurisprudence that a woman had no legal existence separate from her husband, who was regarded as her head and representative in the social state; and, notwithstanding some recent modifications of this civil status, many of the special rules of law flowing from and dependent upon this cardinal principle still

---

*Westminster Hall was the ancient seat of English law, established in the twelfth century. (Eds.)

exist in full force in most States. One of these is, that a married woman is incapable, without her husband's consent of making contracts which shall be binding on her or him. This very incapacity was one circumstance which the Supreme Court of Illinois deemed important in rendering a married woman incompetent fully to perform the duties and trusts that belong to the office of an attorney and counsellor.

It is true that many women are unmarried and not affected by any of the duties, complications, and incapacities arising out of the married state, but these are exceptions to the general rule. The paramount destiny and mission of woman are to fulfil the noble and benign offices of wife and mother. This is the law of the Creator. And the rules of civil society must be adapted to the general constitution of things, and cannot be based upon exceptional cases.

The humane movements of modern society, which have for their object the multiplication of avenues for woman's advancement, and of occupations adapted to her condition and sex, have my heartiest concurrence. But I am not prepared to say that it is one of her fundamental rights and privileges to be admitted into every office and position, including those which require highly special qualifications and demanding special responsibilities. In the nature of things it is not every citizen of every age, sex, and condition that is qualified for every calling and position. It is the prerogative of the legislator to prescribe regulations founded on nature, reason, and experience for the due admission of qualified persons to professions and callings demanding special skill and confidence. This fairly belongs to the police power of the State; and, in my opinion, in view of the peculiar characteristics, destiny, and mission of woman, it is within the province of the legislature to ordain what offices, positions, and callings shall be filled and discharged by men, and shall receive the benefit of those energies and responsibilities, and that decision and firmness which are presumed to predominate in the sterner sex.

For these reasons I think that the laws of Illinois now complained of are not obnoxious to the charge of abridging any of the privileges and immunities of citizens of the United States.

Employments Unsuitable for Women, 1901

ONE OF THE MOST IMPORTANT PROBLEMS to be solved in the new century is this: shall women be flowers or vegetables, ornamental or useful? In other words, shall women work, and, if so, what shall their work be and where shall it be—in the garden attached to the home or in the field at large?

Every country is obliged to have its arsenals where rifles, cannon, and other implements of war are manufactured at an enormous cost; yet every

SOURCE: Henry T. Finck: "Employments Unsuitable for Women," *Independent*, April 11, May 16, 1901.

civilized person must hope and pray that all these things are made in vain and that the money spent on them is absolutely wasted. The same attitude should be observed by every person of culture toward the question of woman's work away from home. There always will be thousands of poor widows, orphans, and unmarried women who will be compelled to support themselves; and as fortunes are apt to be lost and no one can know whose turn is next, all parents, however wealthy, should have their daughters trained thoroughly in some employment which will enable them, in case of need, to make their own living. But here, again, all should hope and pray that the money thus expended was thrown away.

Instead of recognizing this important truth, a considerable number of agitators are trying hard to persuade women that it is their duty to make themselves independent and self-supporting, not only potentially but actually. Their incessant clamor has dazed and hypnotized many of our girls into the belief that they must not stay under the parental roof, but *must* go out into the world like their brothers to seek their fortunes. The epidemic delusion that home is no place for a girl—a delusion as dangerous to the soul as the plague is to the body—seems to be gaining ground daily. Not long ago a girl, whose father, though not rich is quite able and willing to take care of her, and, in fact, needs her to help with the housework, informed me that her friends were constantly telling her she ought to be ashamed to fall a burden to her father any longer. She had about made up her mind to become a shopgirl when I gave her a piece of my mind on the subject and induced her to stay at home.

An incalculable amount to harm is done by this foolish and criminal warfare on homelife. Instead of being encouraged in the tendency to leave the refining atmosphere of home, girls should be taught that, except under the stress of poverty, it is selfish as well as suicidal on their part to go out and work. Selfish because they take away the work which poor women and men absolutely need for their daily bread; suicidal because, by offering themselves so cheaply to employers, they either drive out the men or, by lowering their wages from family standard to the individual standard and make it impossible for them to marry; therefore these same girls who had hoped, thus going out to work to increase their marriage chances, are left to die as old maids, or "new women," as they now prefer to call themselves.

Had they remained at home and cultivated the graces and refined allurements of femininity, their chances for the good marriage and a happy life would have been much better. Men still prefer, and always will prefer, the home girl to any other kind.

They want a girl who has not marred her beauty and ruined her health by needless work, or rubbed off the peach bloom of innocence by exposure to a rough world—a girl who has been trained by a sensible mother to understand and, if necessary, perform all the various functions and details that make home a comfort and a joy.

Chapter 6

The Triumph of Racism

W.E.B. Du Bois, one of the Founders of the National Association for the Advancement of Colored People.

In the decades following the Civil War, while the northern and western states turned to industrialization with the aid of immigrant laborers, the South remained largely agricultural. Some white Southerners, like Henry Grady of the *Atlanta Constitution,* urged the former Confederate states to follow the example of the rest of the nation and build cities, factories, and railroads. Indeed, the South did experience a modicum of industrial and urban growth before World War I. But the region still lagged behind the rapid pace of change elsewhere in the United States.

In another way, too, the white South continued to look to the past. Once Congress admitted the ex-Confederate states back into the union and federal troops had withdrawn from the South, white Southerners were free to pursue a system of race relations more to their taste than that imposed by Radical Republicans during the Reconstruction era (1865–1876). This system stipulated that blacks be segregated in most areas of public life, be denied the right to vote, and generally be limited to working as landless farmers.

In his essay on the Supreme Court's *Plessy v. Ferguson* decision (1896), Keith Weldon Medley points out that among the Southern states, postwar Louisiana offered the brightest hope for easing racial inequality. African Americans participated in politics and benefited from the integration of many public facilities for a number of years after the removal of federal troops. But soon the rising tide of white racism destroyed their dreams; as in other states around the turn of the century, Louisiana ultimately established a rigid system of white supremacy.

It was one thing for white legislators to enact measures to disfranchise and segregate African Americans; it was another for these laws to receive the sanction of the United States Supreme Court. After all, the Fourteenth and Fifteenth Amendments to the Constitution seem to preclude such legislation. Medley's essay centers on the case of Homer Plessy's challenge to Louisiana's separate coach law. How did the Supreme Court manage to conclude that segregation did not violate the Fourteenth Amendment, which supposedly guarantees equal protection of the law? What implications did the Plessy decision hold for racial segregation in other areas of southern life?

Segregation was only one of the injustices suffered by African Americans in the age of Jim Crow. From the 1880s until World War I, there were approximately 100 lynchings yearly, mostly of blacks and mostly in the South. Not all mob executions were lynchings; some blacks were burned to death—this witnessed by hundreds of spectators who were known to fight over bones to take home as souvenirs. Only a small number of these acts of violence involved allegations of black men raping white women. In most cases, the mere accusation of rape was enough to trigger the gathering of a mob. The first document presents Senator Benjamin Tillman's defense of the disfranchisement of black voters in Mississippi. Tillman also excused the lynching of blacks in his speech on the floor of the United States Senate. On what grounds did he argue that lynching was justified? A sad low point of African-American political involvement came when the last black still in the House of Representatives, George White, lost his seat in 1900. His farewell speech, which is the second document, was given about the same time as Tillman's. There would not be another black Congressman until Illinois elected Oscar De Priest from the south side of Chicago in 1928.

Faced with the triumph of racism at the turn of the century, blacks protested through organizations such as the National Association for the Advancement of Colored People (NAACP). In the last document, W.E.B. Du Bois, a founder of the NAACP, issues a call for equality. In view of the conditions portrayed in the essay and Senator Tillman's racial outbursts, do you think that there was any real possibility for the realization of Du Bois's program in the first decade of the twentieth century?

ESSAY

The Birth of "Separate but Equal"
Keith Weldon Medley

On Tuesday evening, a Negro named [Homer] Plessy was arrested by Private Detective Cain on the East Louisiana train and locked up for violating Section 2 of Act 111 of 1890, relative to separate coaches.... He waived examination yesterday before Recorder Monlin and was sent before the criminal court under $500 bond.

This modest announcement appeared in the New Orleans *Daily Picayune* on June 9, 1892. Little noticed at the time, it recorded a moment of tragic significance for the people of America. For it marked not only the end of an era that had begun with Reconstruction, but the start of a half-century in which the rights and hopes of black people in the South, briefly raised up by Reconstruction, were all but extinguished.

In time it would make famous the names of a New Orleans shoemaker and a judge from Massachusetts, as the joint label on the landmark Supreme Court decision *Plessy* v. *Ferguson*. The issue was apparently resolved by the Court in 1896. But the running racial and judicial struggle involved did not have its most dramatic climax until a half-century later, with the decision known as *Brown* v. *Board of Education*.

Confrontation over a place in a public conveyance suggests a parallel with Rosa Parks. But her refusal to give up her bus seat to a white passenger in Montgomery, Alabama, was partly triggered by happenstance. Plessy's action on that warm New Orleans afternoon a century ago was an act of civil disobedience carefully planned and orchestrated by a group of black Republicans, lawyers and journalists known in the French-speaking areas of New Orleans as the Comité des Citoyens.

The story of their case and of their calculated yet desperate judicial fight is rooted not merely in the history of what happened in the South after the Civil War, but in the texture of life in New Orleans itself. Even before the Civil War, New Orleans had been a rich, cosmopolitan trading port and a place where people of color had accomplished a great deal.

Originally French, then Spanish, then French again before being bought by Thomas Jefferson in 1803 (along with what would become half of the United States), it was a city with a remarkable mix of colors and cultures, as well as a penchant for violence and vice. On the eve of the war in 1860,

SOURCE: The Birth of 'Separate but Equal' from "The Sad Story of How 'Separate but Equal' was Born," by Keith Weldon Medley, from *Smithsonian* (February 1994), 104-17. Copyright © by Keith Weldon Medley. Reprinted by permission of the author.

the population was pushing 170,000, including 25,000 Irish and 20,000 German immigrants, and 15,000 African-American slaves about to be freed. But New Orleans also had a greater concentration of free people of color than any other city in the Deep South, some 10,000 people who had gained their freedom well before the Civil War began.

Homer Plessy was born free in March 1862, only a month before Yankee gunboats overran the city's Mississippi River defenses, taking control of the port while the war lasted. Like Plessy's family, many black New Orleanians were French-speaking and Roman Catholic. Some had come from Haiti to escape the bloody revolution at the beginning of the 19th century, when Haitians won their independence from France. Some had fought in 1815 with Andrew Jackson against the British in the Battle of New Orleans. The majority were working class, but many were landowners, businessmen, [and] skilled artisans.

Full Inheritances and Paternal Surnames

Though interracial marriage had been officially banned and streetcars segregated, the city had fewer social restrictions about intermingling between whites and blacks than other areas in the South. Many de facto marriages between the races lasted a lifetime; the children produced often received full inheritances and paternal surnames. Some were sent to Europe for their education. Some became rich and prominent citizens.

So hopes ran high on June 11, 1864, as thousands joyfully gathered in Congo Square, the site of weekend slave gatherings, to celebrate a great event: on May 9 of that year, Louisiana had approved an emancipation ordinance. Ratification of the 13th Amendment to the Constitution would come in 1865, followed by the 14th in 1868, which said that if you were born in the United States you were a citizen, and that no state could deprive you of your rights, liberty or property without due process of law. By 1870 the 15th Amendment made clear that no citizen could be deprived of the right to vote on the basis of race, color or previous condition of servitude.

In 1867 New Orleans removed the black stars previously used to designate the city's segregated streetcars. That was the year of the Reconstruction Act, passed by still-powerful Radical Republicans in Washington, which sent U.S. armies of occupation into the South and gave military commanders in five areas there the right to protect life and property with federal force. They set up a procedure to register voters and see that lately freed slaves were allowed to vote, held elections, established black schools, and created machinery whereby Southern states were to ratify the 14th Amendment. In New Orleans and all over the South, Army commanders had the power to appoint and dismiss local officials.

By 1869 when Homer Plessy was 7, New Orleans began experimenting with integrated public schools—the only Southern city to do so. Blacks served with whites on juries and public boards. New Orleans had an integrated police department with a color-blind municipal pay scale. Thanks to Reconstruction, too, Plessy grew to manhood while blacks, who made up most of the Republican Party in the South, voted enthusiastically in large numbers and served in high office. Between the years 1868 and 1896, racial intermarriage was made legal, and Louisiana elected 32 black state senators and 95 state representatives. It had the only black governor in U.S. history before the late 1980s. (In the same period the South as a whole voted 600 black state representatives into office and sent 16 black congressmen to Washington.)

Apparently Plessy left no papers. City records, however, tell a good deal about him and about the racially mixed, middle-class faubourg, or suburb, where he lived. He began making shoes in 1879, married Louise Bordenave in 1888 and attended Mass at St. Augustine's Catholic Church on St. Claude Street. The church had been established by whites and free people of color before the war; services were conducted in French and Latin. The newlyweds could afford to rent a house near the corner of Ursulines Street on North Claiborne Avenue in the Faubourg Tremé.

Outside the Plessys' bedroom window was Congregation Hall, home of Saturday night "grand dancing festivals" where, for 15 cents, New Orleanians swayed to the sounds of Professor Moret's String Band. By the 1890s, Tremé had become an integrated enclave of several races, numbering among its residents many musicians and artists, who tended to be radical and egalitarian. There were also a number of dramatic clubs and benevolent religious societies that would contribute heavily to the Comité des Citoyens, among them the Société des Francs Amis (Homer Plessy became its vice president), which provided medical and funeral expenses for dues-paying members.

Following the Civil War, the full-scale occupation of the South as a defeated nation, along with Reconstruction programs, cost the American taxpayers considerable money, not including the pay and maintenance of the 6,000-odd federal soldiers. Yet for years the Republican Party, dominated by former abolitionists, maintained the political power and the will necessary to try remaking the former Confederate States.

There was no swift and easy way, however, for four million ex-slaves, just freed and without education, to be integrated into a racist, bitterly defeated and economically collapsing South. Race hatred, intimidation and riots flared. The Ku Klux Klan spread pamphlets and terror, which eventually included the murder of influential Reconstruction figures both black and white. It also embarked on the systematic intimidation of newly enfranchised black voters. The power of the Republican Party in Southern states, overwhelmingly based on those same black voters, began to wane, and Southern Democrats started to take back the South. The power of Republicans in Washington, especially after the Recession of 1873, was vulnerable to Democrats who could claim that Reconstruction cost money and had no hope of success.

In the North there had been optimistic expectations for economic recovery in a free-labor South and for the immediate effects of black suffrage. "We need no vast expenditures. We need no standing army," Senator Richard Yates, a Radical Republican, had once declared. "The ballot will finish the Negro question." By the early 1870s that was clearly not so, and just as clear was the fact that many states in the North and West, which as late as 1868 did not permit black suffrage or integration, would not long concern themselves with the rights of blacks in the South. After the ratification of the 15th Amendment, an Illinois newspaper expressed a prevalent Northern view: "The Negro is now a voter and a citizen. Let him hereafter take his chances in the battle of life."

The specific political event that brought an end to Reconstruction and the withdrawal of occupation troops from the South was the Presidential election of 1876. Republicans had dominated national politics since Lincoln. But in 1876 neither Republican Rutherford B. Hayes nor Democrat Samuel J. Tilden got enough undisputed electoral votes to win. A deal was made, known as the Hayes-Tilden Compromise. Hayes would become President by being ceded the electoral votes of a number of Southern states in return for recalling the armies of occupation (they departed in 1877) and yielding to Democrats the control of the last three Southern states—including Louisiana—still run by the Republican Party. For their part, Southern Democratic leaders in those states agreed to maintain civil rights policies.

Among them was Louisiana's Democratic gubernatorial candidate Francis T. Nicholls, an ex-Confederate general who lost an arm and a leg in the Civil War. Nicholls swore to uphold "equal rights and common interests" and to "obliterate the color line in politics." For a while he kept his word. But without the Reconstruction programs and the bayonets of the armies to support them, lately freed blacks were at a hopeless disadvantage. All over the South, the advances made in the 1870s began to be undone. The pace accelerated in 1883 when the Supreme Court, which was also changing its makeup, declared the civil rights enforcement act of 1875 unconstitutional. This meant that the federal government, lacking the means and will, pretty well got out of the business of making sure that the new civil rights laws were applied in the South.

The erosion of civil rights went more slowly in New Orleans than elsewhere. But the city began reestablishing segregated schools, and in 1890 Nicholls approved the Louisiana Legislature's passage of the Separate Car Act.

The act decreed "equal but separate accommodations for the white and colored races" on Louisiana railway cars. Under its terms any railway company that did not provide separate coaches for blacks and whites could be fined $500. Except for "nurses attending children of the other race," individual whites and blacks would be forbidden to ride together, or risk a $25 fine or 20 days in jail. It was the passage of this bill that finally launched Homer

Plessy into history. The fight involved a black newspaper, *The Crusader,* the six remaining black state senators and ultimately the Comité des Citoyens, which coalesced around *The Crusader.*

At the State Capitol, Senator Henry Demas thundered at his fellow legislators: "Like the Jews, we have been driven from our houses and firesides, from our churches and schoolhouses ... and from the elevated avenues of livelihood, and now, in order to reach the lowest depth of infamy ... you are willing to forget that you are men and vote for the passage of this bill." But the Separate Car Act passed the Louisiana Senate by a vote of 23 to 6.

The Crusader was a formidable enemy. A weekly founded in 1889 by attorney Louis Martinet to combat the increasingly virulent racism of other New Orleans papers, it called itself "spicy, progressive, liberal, stalwart, fearless," and stood for "A Free Vote and Fair Count, Free Schools, Fair Wages, Justice and Equal Rights." It cost a nickel and carried classified ads for everything from pianos, sails, cotton scales and first communion wreaths to ointments that claimed to "relax"—straighten—the hair. *The Crusader's* star contributor was Rodolphe Desdunes. The son of a Cuban mother and a Haitian father, Desdunes worked as a customs agent by day and, with smoking pen, scribbled polemical columns by night. Hundreds of his articles, still preserved in the archives of Xavier University in New Orleans, offer a window into the desperate fight to keep civil rights from slipping away.

"Colored people have largely patronized the railroads heretofore," Desdunes wrote on July 19, 1890. "They can withdraw the patronage from these corporations and travel only by necessity." He proposed a boycott not unlike the one launched in Montgomery, Alabama, 70 years later.

The 1890s were not a good time to exercise civil disobedience in the American South, or to get on the wrong side of a mob, whether you were black or not. The year 1892 alone produced 226 mob murders, mostly of black men, the highest number in the recorded history of lynchings. In New Orleans, on March 14, 1891, a newspaper editor and a prominent attorney led a crowd of several thousand to Parish Prison. Angry over the acquittal of Italian immigrants accused of the killing of police chief David Hennessy, they broke in, hunted down a group of 11 Italians, shot them, then hanged some from streetlamps and shot them again. Mournfully reflecting on the mood in New Orleans, a black woman told a reporter: "Thank God it wasn't a nigger who killed the Chief."

To combat what became known as the "Jim Crow car law," *The Crusader* and the Comité des Citoyens acquired a small but influential membership. It involved C. C. Antoine, a former officer in the Union Army, who had served four years (1873–77) as Louisiana's lieutenant governor, and wealthy philanthropist Aristide Mary, who had financed lawsuits against other resegregated establishments.

The Comité also included sail manufacturer Arthur Estéves, who became its president. To fight the Jim Crow car law, it was prepared to solicit funds not only from benevolent, social and religious societies in town but from former abolitionists in such faraway cities as Washington, D.C., Chicago and San Francisco. About $3,000 was quickly raised to launch two test cases: one to challenge legal segregation of trains on interstate routes and one to challenge segregation on conveyances within the state. The aim: to "seek redemption" from the Supreme Court of the United States. "We find this the only means left us," a Comité statement concluded. "We must have recourse to it, or sink into a state of helpless inferiority."

It was a forlorn hope, but not as forlorn as it would become in the slow process of going through the legal system. For one thing, on the face of it, if you gave any thought to the intent of the men who wrote the 14th Amendment, the Separate Car Act seemed a clear violation of the constitutional rights of the black citizens of Louisiana. But public opinion in the North had changed rapidly, and so, in the years after 1877, had the makeup of the Supreme Court, which lost its reasonable mix of justices sympathetic to the subject of civil rights.

Some railroad companies initially had been against the bill. It was going to cost money to build and run extra cars—for the bill implied that if a half empty "white" car was waiting, and even if only one black passenger showed up, he or she would have to have a whole separate-but-equal vehicle made available. In a city that had for so long seen so much racial mixing, railway conductors would now have to decide who was white and who was black—a touchy business, especially since some wives and husbands would not be allowed to ride together.

One of the reasons that Homer Plessy was picked for the job was that he had fair skin. Had it been left to chance, he probably could have ridden the train in the "whites only" section unnoticed. But by prearrangement between the Comité and the East Louisiana Railroad, everything was ready for him when he came.

On June 7, 1892, Plessy strolled to the Press Street depot, which included a restaurant and a combination waiting room and ticket office (both still open to him), bought a first-class ticket and, ignoring the new "Colored Only" sign, sat down in the coach reserved for whites. It was to depart at 4:15 P.M., cross a bridge spanning Lake Pontchartrain and pass through Abita Springs for a two-hour run to Covington.

Hardly had the train started moving when conductor J. J. Dowling approached Plessy. "Are you a colored man?" he asked. "Yes," answered Plessy. "Then you will have to retire to the colored car," said Dowling. Plessy stated that he had paid for his ticket and intended to ride to Covington. Dowling signaled the engineer to stop. A private detective, Captain Chris Cain, hired by the Comité, came aboard and warned Plessy:

"If you are colored you should go into the car set apart for your race. The law is plain and must be obeyed."

When Plessy again refused, he was taken a half-mile down to Elysian Fields Avenue for booking at the Fifth Precinct Station. Members of the Comité met him, and a judge released him on temporary bail. The next day a story in a New Orleans daily described Plessy as a "snuff-colored descendant of Ham." After a hearing, Comité member Paul Bonseigneur plunked down a $500 bond (raised by putting his own house in hock) to guarantee Plessy's appearance for trial. Plessy was 30 years old. The future of constitutional rights for blacks in America would ride on his day in court.

Enter John Howard Ferguson, 54, the judge whose name would forever be linked to Plessy's in American history. The lawyer son of a shipowner on the island of Martha's Vineyard, Massachusetts, Ferguson had come South after hearing of opportunities there from returning Civil War soldiers. He was what Southerners called a carpetbagger—meaning anybody who came South after the fighting to administer the remade South or to look for profit in the South's adversity. He married the daughter of a prominent local attorney, a Louisiana Unionist noted for his condemnations of slavery, and began practicing law. Ferguson served in Governor Nicholls' 1876 Legislature. Eventually he campaigned for Murphy Foster, the man who replaced Nicholls as governor and engineered passage of the Separate Car Act. Ferguson was made a judge and assigned the Plessy case a month after Plessy's arrest.

But only a short time after becoming a judge, in another Comité-generated case, he ruled that the Separate Car Act was unconstitutional on trains that traveled through several states—because of the federal government's predominant interest in interstate commerce. The Comité celebrated the decision, and Louis Martinet chortled in print: "Jim Crow is dead as a doornail."

He was wrong. At Plessy's arraignment, *Homer Adolph Plessy* v. *The State of Louisiana,* one of Plessy's lawyers, James Walker, argued that neither the state nor any railroad conductor representing it had the right to deny Plessy's liberty on the basis of race, since Plessy was a citizen, and the 14th Amendment clearly said that "no state shall make or enforce any law which shall abridge the privileges or immunities of any citizen of the United States." Judge Ferguson did not agree. The state, he claimed, had a legal right to regulate railroad companies operating solely within the state. Plessy had not been deprived of his liberty. "He was simply deprived of the liberty of doing as he pleased, and of violating a penal statute with impunity."

A swift appeal was presented to the State Supreme Court, which instantly agreed with Ferguson's decision. The 14th Amendment guaranteed black individuals "equality" but did not guarantee "identity or community" with white society. The glum Comité now could look only northward to the Supreme Court of the United States in Washington. As time passed, Plessy's prospects grew worse.

In the decade leading up to 1896, when the case at last was argued before the Court, seven Justices had been replaced—mostly by men who shared the increasingly prevalent belief that Reconstruction had largely failed and that blacks must fend for themselves. The only holdovers from Reconstruction times were John Marshall Harlan of Kentucky, a Hayes appointee, and the aging Stephen J. Field, who had been appointed in 1863 by Lincoln.

Attorney Albion Tourgée, who eventually argued the case for the Comité, estimated that only one Justice would firmly lean to Plessy's side, three would be uncertain and five, frankly opposed. In a letter to Louis Martinet he added a foreboding postscript: "It is of the utmost importance that we should not have a decision *against* us as the court has *never* reversed itself on a constitutional question."

Tourgée was not the only one to notice the changing temper of the Supreme Court. In 1894 Louisiana again placed racial restrictions on marriage and prohibited citizens of opposite races from using the same railroad depot waiting rooms.

The Comité's chances dwindled as the climate of opinion changed, even among people of color. Voices in some quarters argued that resisting white supremacy always evoked harsher responses, and that the struggle for decent conditions was what mattered most, not integration. In 1895 Booker T. Washington, head of Tuskegee Institute, publicly called for accommodation with segregation. Washington argued that in the face of white hatred, integration simply stirred up opposition. The main thing was to concentrate on making segregated schools work, on learning trades and on getting ahead in life.

But the Comité had pledged to see the case to the end. By late fall 1895 everything was in place. Albion Tourgée, with lawyers S. F. Phillips and F. D. McKenny, had filed final papers for the October 1895 term in *Homer A. Plessy* v. *J. H. Ferguson*. Tourgée went before the Supreme Court in April 1896. State arguments were made by Louisiana's Attorney General M. J. Cunningham and lawyers Lionel Adams and Alexander Porter Morse.

On May 18 the Court issued a ruling. With only one dissent it granted states the right to forcibly segregate people of different races. Writing for the majority, Justice Henry Billings Brown, appointed by Benjamin Harrison, dismissed Plessy's 14th Amendment claims and, as precedent, pointed to the existence of separate schools in the District of Columbia and the long-standing bans on interracial marriage. The only test of such segregation, he said, would be whether or not the regulations were reasonable. The Court also stated that "legislation is powerless to eradicate racial instincts or to abolish distinctions based upon physical differences." As for determining who was black or white, that was left to the discretion of each state.

The lone dissenter was Justice John Marshall Harlan. "The destinies of two races in this country," Harlan wrote, "are indissolubly linked together, and the interests of both require that the common government of all shall not permit the seeds of race hate to be planted under the sanction of law.... The thin disguise of 'equal' accommodations for passengers in railroad coaches will not mislead anyone, nor atone for the wrong this day done."

The decision was remanded to the Supreme Court of Louisiana on September 28, 1896. The Comité issued a final statement: "In passing laws which discriminate between its citizens," it declared, "the State was wrong.... Notwithstanding this decision ... we, as freemen, still believe that we were right, and our cause is sacred."

On January 11, 1897, Homer Plessy returned to court for sentencing. By then, times had changed dramatically. The Comité had disbanded; *The Crusader* had ceased publication. All over the South, white supremacists were firmly in control of the Legislatures. Judge Ferguson had stepped down in 1896, and Judge Joshua Baker was presiding. Plessy changed his plea to guilty, paid a $25 fine and walked out into the brave new world of a segregated Louisiana.

Those in the black community who thought racial separation would bring peace were in for a rude awakening. Emboldened by the Supreme Court's Plessy decision, in February 1898 Louisiana called a constitutional convention in New Orleans to lay down a blueprint for white supremacy. Endorsed by Governor Foster, the delegates made it illegal to run an integrated school, allocated state money as a "pension fund" for the relatives of Confederate soldiers, declared the Louisiana Democratic Party a "whites only" organization and used various devices, such as the "grandfather clause," to keep blacks and immigrants from voting. "Our mission was to establish the supremacy of the white race," the chairman of the judiciary committee bluntly declared. In the four years from 1896 to 1900, more than 120,000 black voters were removed from the rolls, their numbers dropping from 45 percent to 4 percent of eligible voters. By 1900 Louisiana did not have a single black representative in its Legislature. There would be none until 1967.

While legislation made things "separate," the "equal" treatment of the Supreme Court ruling seldom materialized. The greatest disaster would come in education. The South spent very little money on black schools. In New Orleans, the city school board did not open a public high school for blacks until 1917. Even then, black teachers were paid less than their white counterparts, and their pupils received second-hand books and supplies.

One by one the civil rights gains of Reconstruction vanished. So too did the principals in the *Plessy* v. *Ferguson* case. Judge Ferguson died in 1915 at age 77. In a front-page story, the *Times-Picayune* lauded him as one who "allied himself with the Democratic reform element" and "took part in the struggle for white supremacy." He was buried in the Lafayette Cemetery on

Washington Avenue. In August 1925, some 50,000 white-robed members of the Ku Klux Klan marched in Washington, D.C.

Homer Plessy had died a few months earlier that year. His obituary in the *Times-Picayune* was simple: "PLESSY—on Sunday, March 1, 1925, at 5:10 A.M., Homer A. Plessy, 63 years, beloved husband of Louise Bordenave." On the front page of the same paper was the headline "Supreme Court Puts Approval on Segregation," referring to a Louisiana Supreme Court ruling that upheld a segregated housing ordinance in New Orleans. Plessy lies with his mother's family in St. Louis Cemetery No. 1, a 200-year-old integrated Catholic grave-yard in the Tremé area. Fifteen years after his death there were only 886 regis-tered black voters in the state of Louisiana.

Nearly 15 more years would pass before NAACP attorney Thurgood Marshall obtained a rehearing of Plessy's cause in another landmark case, *Brown* v. *Board of Education*. In that instance, the Court overturned the 1896 ruling and declared "separate but equal" to be unconstitutional. That time, Homer Plessy won.

DOCUMENTS

Senator Benjamin Tillman Defends Disfranchisement and Lynching of African Americans, 1900

... And he [Senator John C. Spooner, of Wisconsin] said we had taken their rights away from them. He asked me was it right to murder them in order to carry the elections. I never saw one murdered. I never saw one shot at an election. It was the riots before the elections precipitated by their own hot-headedness in attempting to hold the government, that brought on conflicts between the races and caused the shotgun to be used. That is what I meant by saying we used the shotgun.

I want to call the Senator's attention to one fact. He said that the Republican party gave the negroes the ballot in order to protect them-selves against the indignities and wrongs that were attempted to be heaped upon them by the enactment of the black code. I say it was because the Republicans of that day, led by Thad Stevens, wanted to put white necks under black heels and to get revenge. There is a difference of opinion. You have your opinion about it, and I have mine, and we can never agree.

I want to ask the Senator this proposition in arithmetic: In my State there were 135,000 negro voters, or negroes of voting age, and some 90,000

SOURCE: "Speech of Senator Benjamin R. Tillman, March 23, 1900," *Congressional Record, 56th Congress, 1st Session*, 3223–3224.

or 95,000 white voters. General Canby set up a carpetbag government there and turned our State over to this majority. Now, I want to ask you, with a free vote and a fair count, how are you going to beat 135,000 by 95,000? How are you going to do it? You had set us an impossible task. You had handcuffed us and thrown away the key, and you propped your carpetbag negro government with bayonets. Whenever it was necessary to sustain the government you held it up by the Army.

Mr. President, I have not the facts and figures here, but I want the country to get the full view of the Southern side of this question and the justification for anything we did. We were sorry we had the necessity forced upon us, but we could not help it, and as white men we are not sorry for it, and we do not propose to apologize for anything we have done in connection with it. We took the government away from them in 1876. We did take it. If no other Senator has come here previous to this time who would acknowledge it, more is the pity. We have had no fraud in our elections in South Carolina since 1884. There has been no organized Republican party in the State.

We did not disfranchise the negroes until 1895. Then we had a constitutional convention convened which took the matter up calmly, deliberately, and avowedly with the purpose of disfranchising as many of them as we could under the fourteenth and fifteenth amendments. We adopted the educational qualification as the only means left to us, and the negro is as contented and as prosperous and as well protected in South Carolina to-day as in any State of the Union south of the Potomac. He is not meddling with politics, for he found that the more he meddled with them the worse off he got. As to his "rights"—I will not discuss them now. We of the South have never recognized the right of the negro to govern white men, and we never will. We have never believed him to be equal to the white man, and we will not submit to his gratifying his lust on our wives and daughters without lynching him. I would to God the last one of them was in Africa and that none of them had ever been brought to our shores. But I will not pursue the subject further.

I want to ask permission in this connection to print a speech which I made in the constitutional convention of South Carolina when it convened in 1895, in which the whole carpetbag regime and the indignities and wrongs heaped upon our people, the robberies which we suffered, and all the facts and figures there brought out are incorporated, and let the whole of the facts go to the country. I am not ashamed to have those facts go to the country. They are our justification for the present situation in our State. If I can get it, I should like that permission; otherwise I shall be forced to bring that speech here and read it when I can put my hand on it. I will then leave this matter and let the dead past bury its dead.

George H. White's Farewell Speech to Congress, 1901

[A few] ignorant men [of color] who chanced … to hold office are given as a reason why the black man should not be permitted to participate in the affairs of the government which he is forced to pay taxes to support. [Rep. Wilson] insists that they, the Southern whites, are the black man's best friend, and that they are taking him by the hand and trying to lift him up; that they are educating him. For all that he and all Southern people have done in this regard, I wish in behalf of the colored people of the South to extend our thanks. We are not ungrateful to friends, but feel that our toil has made our friends able to contribute the stinty pittance which we have received at their hands. I read in a Democratic paper a few days ago, The Washington Times, an extract [which] showed that the money for each white child in the State ranged from three to five times as much per-capita as was given to each colored child. This is helping us some, but not to the extent that one would infer from the gentleman's speech.

If the gentleman to whom I have referred will pardon me, I would like to advance the statement that the musty records of 1868, filed away in the archives of Southern capitols, as to what the Negro was thirty-two years ago, is not a proper standard by which the Negro living on the threshold of the twentieth century should be measured.

Since that time we have reduced the illiteracy of the race at least 45 percent. We have written and published nearly 500 books. We have nearly 800 newspapers, three of which are dailies. We have now in practice over 2,000 lawyers, and a corresponding number of doctors. We have accumulated over $12,000,000 worth of school property and about $40,000,000 worth of church property. We have about 140,000 farms and homes, valued in the neighborhood of $750,000,000, and personal property valued about $170,000,000. We have raised about $11,000,000 for educational purposes, and the property per-capita for every colored man, woman and child in the United States is estimated at $75. We are operating successfully several banks, commercial enterprises among our people in the South land, including one silk mill and one cotton factory. We have 32,000 teachers in the schools of the country; we have built, with the aid of our friends, about 20,000 churches, and support 7 colleges, 17 academies, 50 high schools, 5 law schools, 5 medical schools and 25 theological seminaries. We have over 600,000 acres of land in the South alone. The cotton produced, mainly by black labor, has increased from 4,669,770 bales in 1860 to 11,235,000 in 1899. All this was done under the most adverse circumstances.

We have done it in the face of lynching, burning at the stake, with the humiliation of "Jim Crow" laws, the disfranchisement of our male citizens, slander and degradation of our women, with the factories closed against us,

SOURCE: *Congressional Record*, 56th Congress, 2d Session, pp. 1635–1638.

no Negro permitted to be conductor on the railway cars, whether run through the streets of our cities or across the prairies of our great country, no Negro permitted to run as engineer on a locomotive, most of the mines closed against us. Labor unions—carpenters, painters, brick masons, machinists, hackmen and those supplying nearly every conceivable avocation for livelihood—have banded themselves together to better their condition, but, with few exceptions, the black face has been left out. The Negroes are seldom employed in our mercantile stores. At this we do not wonder. Some day we hope to have them employed in our own stores. With all these odds against us, we are forging our way ahead, slowly, perhaps, but surely. You may tie us and then taunt us for a lack of bravery, but one day we will break the bonds. You may use our labor for two and a half centuries and then taunt us for our poverty, but let me remind you we will not always remain poor! You may withhold even the knowledge of how to read God's word and learn the way from earth to glory and then taunt us for our ignorance, but we would remind you that there is plenty of room at the top, and we are climbing!

A Call for Equality, 1905

...We believe that [Negro] American citizens should protest emphatically and continually against the curtailment of their political rights. We believe in manhood suffrage: we believe that no man is so good, intelligent or wealthy as to be entrusted wholly with the welfare of his neighbor.

We believe also in protest against the curtailment of our civil rights. All American citizens have the right to equal treatment in places of public entertainment according to their behavior and deserts.

We especially complain against the denial of equal opportunities to us in economic life; in the rural districts of the south this amounts to peonage and virtual slavery; all over the south it tends to crush labor and small business enterprises: and everywhere American prejudice, helped often by iniquitous laws is making it more difficult for Negro-Americans to earn a decent living.

Common school education should be free to all American children and compulsory. High school training should be adequately provided for all, and college training should be the monopoly of no class or race in any section of our common country. We believe that in defense of its own institutions, the United States should aid common school education, particularly in the south, and we especially recommend concerted agitation to this end. We urge an increase in public high school facilities in the south, where the Negro-Americans are almost wholly without such provisions. We favor well-equipped trade and technical schools for the training of artisans, and the need of adequate and liberal endowment for a few institutions of higher education must be patent to sincere well-wishers of the race.

SOURCE: W.E.B. Du Bois, *Cleveland Gazette*, July 22, 1905.

We demand upright judges in courts, juries selected without discrimination on account of color and the same measure of punishment, and the same efforts at reformation for black as for white offenders. We need orphanages and farm schools for dependent children, juvenile reformatories for delinquents, and the abolition of the dehumanizing convict-lease system....

We hold up for public execration the conduct of two opposite classes of men; the practice among employers of importing ignorant Negro-American laborers in emergencies, and then affording them neither protection nor permanent employment; and the practice of labor unions of proscribing and boycotting and oppressing thousands of their fellow-toilers, simply because they are black. These methods have accentuated and will accentuate the war of labor and capital, and they are disgraceful to both sides....

We regret that this nation has never seen fit adequately to reward the black soldiers who in its five wars, have defended their country with their blood, and yet have been systematically denied the promotions which their abilities deserve. And we regard as unjust, the exclusion of black boys from the military and navy training schools....

The Negro race in America, stolen, ravished and degraded, struggling up through difficulties and oppression, needs sympathy and receives criticism; needs help and is given hindrance, needs protection and is given mob violence, needs justice and is given charity, needs leadership and is given cowardice and apology, needs bread and is given a stone. This nation will never stand justified before God until these things are changed.

Especially are we surprised and astonished at the recent attitude of the church of Christ—on the increase of a desire to bow to racial prejudice, to narrow the bounds of human brotherhood, and to segregate black men in some outer sanctuary. This is wrong, unchristian and disgraceful to twentieth century civilization....

And while we are demanding, and ought to demand, and will continue to demand the rights enumerated above, God forbid that we should ever forget to urge corresponding duties upon our people.

The duty to vote.
The duty to respect the rights of others.
The duty to work.
The duty to obey the laws.
The duty to be clean and orderly.
The duty to send our children to school,
The duty to respect ourselves, even as we respect others....

Chapter 7

America Goes to War

25026

An American doughboy awaits the attack order.

In April 1917, after months of debate and disagreement on whether to join the war in Europe, the United States declared war on Germany. Unlike the major European powers embroiled in the conflict since 1914, America's participation in the war was brief—only about a year and a half. Nevertheless, the war exerted a tremendous impact on Americans, soldiers and civilians alike. For the first time, Americans went off to fight on European soil, and they felt certain that their participation would play a crucial role in defeating the Germans and their allies.

The United States had to mobilize its economy in order to support its allies and build an army to fight in Europe. After some confusion, the nation's industrial and agricultural might was effectively organized and financed. The building of an army also required great effort. The immense problems encountered in creating a fighting force capable of assisting our allies on the battlefields are vividly described in an essay by Meirion and Susie Harries. Based on your reading of this piece, what appear to have been the most difficult challenges facing the civilian and military leaders in their efforts to create this force? How effectively, in your opinion, did they meet the challenges? Finally, what does the essay indicate were the most serious obstacles a new recruit had to overcome in making the transition from civilian to military life?

Throughout the war, the federal government used propaganda to convince the public that the cause was noble, a clash between the forces of good and evil. Victory required the absolute loyalty and support of all citizens; any hint of questionable patriotism prompted great concern. For German Americans particularly, the patriotic near-hysteria of these times proved a terrible burden. In restaurants sauerkraut was renamed "liberty cabbage," and hamburger emerged as "liberty steak." Cincinnati's German Street was renamed English Street, and Pittsburgh banned the playing of Ludwig van Beethoven's music. German Americans were harassed and threatened with physical harm if they failed to demonstrate their commitment to the American war effort. The pressure on German Americans to declare their loyalty is vividly reflected in the first document, a statement by a German American distributed by the Committee on Public Information, an agency created by the federal government to generate public support for the war. How did the author's assessment of the war enable him to embrace the American cause without cutting his emotional ties to his native land?

Although a large segment of the population opposed entry into the war right up until 1917, support for the war effort flourished once the United States joined the conflict. Nevertheless, not all Americans supported the war; those who did not and refused to serve in the armed forces on the grounds of religion or conscience suffered condemnation. The second document reveals the experiences and convictions of Mennonites, who, despite their profound religious objections to the war, were drafted into the army. What relationship, if any, can you discern between the patriotic fervor of wartime society and intensified intolerance?

As the essay reveals, conscientious objectors were not the only ones to suffer prejudice during the war. The final document is a directive issued by a French liaison office to French officers at the insistence of the American army. What does it reveal about white America's attitudes toward black troops and African Americans generally?

ESSAY

---•◦•---

Building a National Army
Meirion and Susie Harries

In the early fall of 1917, watchers by the rail tracks would have seen a remarkable display of young Americans riding to their appointed camps and cantonments, an unrehearsed pageant of America's ethnic diversity: Chocktaws and Cochin Chinese, "Hebrews" (the Army's classification) from everywhere in the Diaspora, Greeks, Italians, English, Irish, Scots, Slavs, Swedes, Germans, Austrians, Albanians, Poles, Armenians, Syrians, Finns, Hispanics, and Japanese. (In Hawaii, the National Guard gained its first Japanese company.) Blacks went on separate trains.

To this army of Babel came men of all shapes and sizes: lanky recruits of Scots blood from the mountains of North Carolina, short and stocky Mediterraneans from the Northeast, where recent immigration had been heaviest. The minimum size was five feet, one inch and 128 pounds; any smaller, and the man would have been unable to carry the regulation army pack (though occasionally lighter men were accepted if they had special skills). The maximum was six feet, six inches; any taller, and the man was likely to have poor circulation. The weight limits were 190 pounds for infantry, engineers, and artillery and 165 pounds for the cavalry.

The average recruit measured five feet, seven and a half inches and weighed 141½ pounds, a meaningless statistic in this miscellany of manhood—except at the unit level, where the average was crucial in determining the sizes of uniforms to be supplied and quantity of rations allocated. Divisions with a high proportion of immigrants from eastern Europe received a smaller average ration and smaller uniforms than midwestern divisions formed of strapping Scandinavians and Germans. Few were racially as mixed as New York's 77th Division, whose theme song ran: "The Jews and the Wops,/The Dutch and the Irish cops,/They're all in the Army now" and which boasted forty-two different languages or dialects spoken in its ranks.

During the war, some 400,000 first-generation immigrants were drafted, including some who were alien enemies and ineligible. This influx was too much for Major General George Bell of the 33rd Division, whose contingent of around 15,000 National Guard volunteers had been fleshed out with conscripts. He complained to the Adjutant General that "the local boards in

SOURCE: "Building a National Army," from *The Last Days of Innocence* by Meirion Harries and Susie Harries, Copyright © 1997 by Meirion and Susie Harries. Used by permission of Random House Inc.

Illinois had very evidently spared men of the draft age of American birth or stock at the expense of those of foreign birth or patronage."

Many who had known only the ghettos of the East Coast cities could not speak English or understand commands. Bombarded with unintelligible instructions and forced to eat such unfamiliar substances as boiled potatoes and stewed apricots, they created serious morale problems in their units. Recent German or Austrian immigrants had the additional anxiety, so military intelligence reported, of having been warned that "if it were known in their home countries that they were in the American army, their families would be hunted out and killed." This rumor was recognized as one of many deliberate propaganda attempts to disrupt recruitment and ruin morale in the camps. Army authorities believed the Lutheran Church Board to be one of Germany's instruments, noting "its efforts to place its pastors in as many camps, forts and other military establishments as possible."

The plight of these first-generation immigrants was compounded by prejudice. Anti-Semitism inevitably surfaced. One night, six weeks after his induction from the Bronx, Private Otto Gottschalk found himself dragged from his tent, stripped, and thrown into a ditch of black muck. He was forced to drink the filthy water and was then badly beaten.

In the early days of the draft, a high proportion of "unsuitable" immigrants appears to have been sent straight back to the ghetto. Later, attempts were made to fit them for service. Where there were enough of them, immigrants were banded together into "development battalions" under officers of their own. At one point, Camp Gordon, in Georgia, had two Slav companies and two Italian and one Russian-Jewish battalion. They quickly became well disciplined and proficient in drill, and when asked how many of them were ready and willing to go abroad immediately, 92 percent stepped forward.

This jumble of colors, cultures, and languages, European, Asian, and Latin, mercilessly underlined the isolation of the black Americans who formed a large section of the intake—larger, perhaps, than was just. No blacks were appointed to the draft boards, and local boards often used their powers to conscript a far higher proportion of blacks than whites relative to population. In part, this was to compensate for the higher number of whites enlisting voluntarily. (Blacks, after all, had very few units to volunteer for.) But draft boards also had a tendency to use selective service as a means of "cleaning up" the neighborhood. A General Staff report noted, "The physical condition of a large part of the colored draft is very poor. Many must be entirely eliminated and a large proportion of those left are not fit for combat duty. The Surgeon General reports that 50% are infected with venereal disease." There was no organized conspiracy to fill the Army with the poorest and "least socially desirable" blacks, but, judging from the results, that is often what happened.

Whatever damage the draft boards had inflicted by their "selection" techniques the Army compounded by its treatment of its black draftees. Few received more than six weeks' training, and their living conditions were often appalling. In October 1917, black stevedore and labor battalions were formed at Camp Hill, Virginia. Six thousand men arrived at the camp to find "no barracks, no mess halls, no clothing, no sanitary arrangements of any kind." In the coldest winter in Virginia for twenty-five years, those who could find room packed themselves into small, dirty tents pitched on the bare earth, while the less fortunate were obliged to stand in front of fires all night. Those who inevitably fell sick were taken to the crowded large tent that served as a hospital, where they lay on the frozen ground with neither cots nor thick blankets.

Camp Hill was an extreme case, but a War Department inspector criticized the white officers of all these black noncombatant units for their indifference to their men. The NCOs, he continued, had often been promoted to their positions "because of previous knowledge of negroes, usually gotten on plantations, public works, turpentine farms and the like." At Camp Hill, an NCO was often selected from the ranks "because he is a 'husky' and will beat and abuse the men. Two such sergeants are in the guard house now for killing other soldiers under their command." The seeds of hatred, inefficiency, and even mutiny were being sown.

The inevitable consequence was low morale and indifference among black labor units when they got to Europe. "We have experienced considerable difficulty in getting the proper amount of work out of the negro stevedores at the various ports," W. W. Atterbury, Pershing's Director General of Transportation, was later to complain. "Fining them and putting them in the guard-house is very little punishment for them and to be dishonorably discharged and sent home is just what they desire." From Liverpool, one of England's major ports, the commanding officer of a detachment of stevedores reported that police and local citizens had begged for them to be withdrawn. "They are without exception the most worthless aggregation of humanity that was ever collected in one unit."

As for the black combat troops, who had originally been intended to share facilities with white troops, they were eventually consigned to segregated units; worse, they were at no point allowed to assemble and train as complete divisions in the United States. While white divisions could seek to develop esprit and identity from the beginning of their training, the fragmented black divisions barely knew what their senior officers looked like, so infrequently could these officers visit the various units scattered among the cantonments in which the National Army was training.

Arriving at the railheads, the new recruits were marshaled into columns by newly commissioned lieutenants trying to summon up the principles of command. The officers at least had the advantage of being in uniform; the recruits were still in civilian clothes, many wearing their best suits as if they were going to a wedding and clutching a few belongings or the remains of the food they had been given for the journey by the send-off committees in their hometowns.

After a brisk march, they got their first sight of the camp or cantonment that was to be home for months to come: "a far-spreading city of wooden buildings," one remembered, "whose flat roofs extended one after another in exact order like the biscuits in a baker's pan." (He was describing one of the sixteen hutted cantonments built for the National Army; members of the National Guard, who were used to living in tents, were housed in sixteen canvas cities farther south.)

If the recruits still cherished any spark of chivalry or romance about their induction, the medical orderlies waiting inside the gates soon introduced a note of gritty realism. Inspections for vermin and venereal disease and a vicious schedule of inoculations against smallpox, typhoid, and other contagious diseases left the new arrivals with barely the strength to crawl to their barracks.

And what they found there was rarely inspiring. The basic design of the company barracks was sound. Each was to be a two-storied wooden building, the second floor a vast dormitory lined with iron cots, the first floor equipped with kitchen, storerooms, mess hall, and captain's office. Unfortunately, few of the buildings were ready. The delay in deciding on the precise size and structure of the infantry division had entailed constant alterations to the cantonment blueprint. Infirmary buildings, for example, were planned at a time when the Table of Organization prescribed thirty-three men for the medical detachment of an infantry regiment. This number was increased to forty-eight, and the building was too small before it was ever used.

The quality of the work that had been done left much to be desired. Far to the south, near a Houston still in shock after the summer massacre,* the officers and men of the Illinois National Guard—now designated the 33rd Division—found Camp Logan "in a decidedly unfinished state." The hospital had been built without heating or running water—the construction quartermaster had put in two faucets on his own initiative—and the engineers pronounced the storehouses to be so faulty that it was only a matter of time before they collapsed. At Camp MacArthur, Texas, the builders laid water mains made of wood that had been lying around for months, and when the water was turned on, typhoid ran through the camp.

All these camps were huge, and the numbers rose as the war progressed. Camp Dix, near Trenton, New Jersey, was built for 38,000 men but at one point housed 54,500. The sanitation demands of such concentrations of human life were immense, yet little thought had been given to

*Several black soldiers were killed in a race riot in 1917. (Eds.)

them. Camp Sherman, Ohio, produced without effort 982,500 pounds of garbage a month and its horses 120 tons of manure a day. The men of Camp Custer, Michigan, filled 1,200 garbage cans a day. None of the camps had waterproof surfaces where the trash cans could be kept, so the earth around the cans became a morass of mashed and rotting waste, magnificent breeding grounds for flies—but nothing compared to the lakes of sewage that loitered in the vicinity of most camps.

At Camp Lee, Virginia, home to the 80th Division, a single creek carried the daily consignment of effluent into a marsh nearby, where it settled. The division's engineers decided to clear the marsh by dredging a channel, but in damming the creek to permit dredging to begin, they created, in the words of a visiting entomologist, a "semi-solid mass of sewage 600 feet long and alive with fly larvae." The comfort levels of latrines matched their sanitary standards; the seats in most had a square hole—an easier shape to cut than an oval.

Among the new arrivals at the camps and cantonments were the conscientious objectors. The Selective Service Act had forced the draft boards to induct them for combatant or noncombatant duty, depending on the nature of their objection, but several months passed before the War Department laid down a policy as to their treatment.

Newton Baker's* intention was that the government's attitude to those who had "personal scruples" about the war should be reasonably liberal, especially in the case of those whose objections were religious: Mennonites (who had come from Russia specifically to avoid war), Quakers, Dukhobors, Seventy-Day Adventists, Plymouth Brethren, Christadelphians, and so on. He specifically ordered that Mennonites and the members of certain other sects should not be compelled to wear uniforms, as their raiment was a tenet of their faith. It was his express wish that conscientious objectors should be segregated from serving soldiers, given noncombatant duty if they had been deemed eligible for it, and treated with "tact and consideration."

The military authorities had far less sympathy. Going "soft on slackers," they felt, was unfair to ordinary conscripts. Many objectors, now that they had been inducted, flatly refused to perform even noncombatant duties, since these still served the purpose of the war, and declined to obey army discipline, wear uniforms, march, drill, or even, in extreme cases, keep clean. Most of the division commanders, like Leonard Wood at Camp Funston, Kansas, felt it their duty to convert them to the ways of war. The pressure they applied took various forms—verbal abuse, humiliation, courts-martial and exaggerated legal penalties, beating, and, in extreme cases, what amounted to torture.

---

*Newton Baker was Secretary of War from 1916 to 1921. (Eds.)

Hutterites, whose faith forbade them to cut their hair, had their beards shaved off by force. Dukhobors were forced into military dress or tormented if they refused. One who was ducked under a faucet on a freezing day subsequently died of pneumonia; his widow, upon receiving his body for burial, was appalled to find it in full uniform, a desecration of his faith.

The most brutal treatment was generally reserved for those whose scruples were ideological rather than religious—and this included not only socialists and others with political objections to the war but those whose objections were made in the name of humanity rather than that of any recognized creed. A great many were eventually "persuaded" to accept military discipline or noncombatant duties, but almost four thousand held out.

Sheldon W. Smith refused to sign the Army's clothing slip. "They put a pen in my hand and held it there to make a mark…. Next I was stripped in a violent manner and taken inside and dressed [in uniform] amidst arm twisting, thumping etc." Then he was taken to the bathhouse, where he was stripped again, held under the shower, and scrubbed with a broom. His captors whipped him with their belts, put a rope around his neck, and lashed it to a pipe, hauling on it until he could not breathe and all the while shouting at him to give in. "The bathing was continued until I was chilled and shook all over; part of the time they had me on my back with face under a faucet and held my mouth open. They got a little flag ordering me to kiss it and kneel down to it."

When the severity of the treatment being handed out in some camps was brought to Baker's attention at the end of 1917, he was horrified and ordered that, from the start of 1918, all "personal scruples," including nonreligious ones, should be classed as objections of conscience and his previous strictures observed. Baker would ultimately review all courtmartial sentences, disapproving a tenth of them altogether and mitigating a further 185 out of a total of 540. None of the seventeen death sentences was carried out.

But in the interim neither he nor the President would intervene any more closely to protect individual rights. The force of public opinion—from the press, the parents of serving soldiers, even the clergy—was against the objectors, and it was a factor neither Wilson nor Baker was prepared to ignore.

Far more worrisome to the Army than either immigrants or conscientious objectors were the draft boards' peculiar ideas as to what constituted physical suitability for service on the Western Front. Of the conscripts inducted during the war, an estimated 196,000 had venereal disease on arrival at camp. Of the 22,000 men examined at Camp Lewis, Washington, 5,000 had thyroid enlargement. Orthopedic problems, particularly foot defects, were commonplace; in one camp, 18 percent of the men had foot trouble, which drill soon revealed. The dentists at Camp Lee examined 38,963 draftees and found 10,596 suffering from infected root canals.

Problems varied with the conscripts' ethnic stock. According to Army Medical Department statistics, French Canadians had the poorest overall health in general: a high incidence of stunted growth, tuberculosis, and nervous and mental defects. Germans and Austrians were prone to alcoholism, varicose veins, and flat feet. "Sections of the black belt of the South," medical officers reported, showed higher-than-average arthritis, manic-depressive psychoses, and heart valve disease, lower-than-average obesity.

From an intake of 6,600 at one camp—and these were men who had passed through the mill of the draft boards—1,600 were immediately discharged as unfit and/or "unsuited, worthless, non-English-speaking, illiterate and venereally diseased." Where there was some hope of remedying the defects, the men were assigned to holding units. Camp Devens, Massachusetts, for example, had a battalion including 134 venereal, 151 neuropsychiatric, 368 cardiovascular, and 1,271 orthopedic cases.

Whatever their vital statistics or their moral standards, the raw levies all had one thing in common; they were in the camps and cantonments to be trained individually in the skills of the soldier and collectively, with their officers, molded into efficient units ready for war. The War Department's strategy had no frills. Besides instructors sent over from Europe by the English and French, they produced company-grade officers—captains and lieutenants—to train the men and then depended on the regular army (and, to a lesser extent, National Guard) officers—majors, colonels, and above—to weld the companies into battalions, regiments, and brigades. The objective was a division that was militarily efficient, a responsive organism of great power.

Many of the professional officers had theoretical knowledge of how to handle large units, but none had any practical experience of anything resembling a 28,000-man division; nevertheless, they rose to their task. The newly commissioned company-grade officers, in the Army for less than half a year, were even further at sea, each finding himself suddenly responsible for the welfare, discipline, and instruction of 250 men, with no protective shield of seasoned drill sergeants to cow the insubordinate.

Black company-grade officers of the 92nd Division struggled to create cohesion and maintain morale. Not only was the division never assembled in one place, but hanging over it was General Ballou's warning that "white men made the Division, and they can break it just as easily if it becomes a trouble-maker." The officers hardly advanced their own cause. "The vast majority of colored officers," remembered the regimental surgeon of the 349th Field Artillery, "held themselves distinctly aloof from the colored enlisted men ... [who] used to nickname their colored officers 'Monkey Chasers.'"

At first, not surprisingly, the key figures in the National Army cantonments were the eight hundred or so British and French instructors. They were all veterans, often with wound stripes on their sleeves, and they brought the callousness of the front with them. "We made an attack one day," one told his pupils.

> As our first wave carried the enemy trench, they heard shouts from a dugout: "Kamerad!" The Germans surrendered. The first wave rushed on, leaving it to the second wave to take the prisoners. As soon as the first wave had passed, the Germans emerged from their dugout with a hidden machine gun and broke it out on the backs of the men who had been white enough not to give them the cold steel. So now, men, when we hear "Kamerad" coming from the depths of a dugout in a captured trench we call down: "How many?" If the answer comes back "Six," we decide that one hand grenade ought to be enough to take care of six and toss it in.

It was impossible in these home camps for either men or units to be made fully ready for combat. Communications being what they were, the knowledge and experience accumulating daily in France was simply not crossing the Atlantic. After six months of war, the General Staff in Washington recognized that it was receiving information that was at best three weeks old. In France, Pershing created an elaborate system of schools to provide instruction for every branch and level of the service: staff officers, unit commanders, candidates for commissions, specialists from every staff and supply department, artillerymen, intelligence officers, pilots. Ideally, all the incomers should have achieved a basic level of competence before crossing to France, but the AEF* schools were equipped to improve on the training of any unit in any branch, with the benefit of having more immediate knowledge of field conditions.

At Langres, forty miles south of Chaumont, Pershing established the critically important Staff College, which, in a frenetic three-month course, attempted to turn out war managers. In addition, his Training Branch developed a three-month training cycle for divisions in France, covering small-unit training, staff work, and combined arms practice and ending with a period in the trenches brigaded with Allied units.

Infantry training was only one of the specializations that together created the complex mechanisms of a division. A man's occupation in civilian life would often dictate his role in the Army: typists were assigned to headquarters staff, garment workers to the quartermaster, construction workers to engineer battalions, pharmacists to medical units, cooks to the kitchens, backwoodsmen to sniper units. In theory, motorized transportation units should have been especially hard to staff. There were usually men who knew how to handle horses, but in 1917 truck and tractor drivers were few and far between. Nevertheless, the appeal of driving was irresistible

*American Expeditionary Force. (Eds.)

and men often lied about their experience with motor vehicles in order to get behind the wheel.

Native Americans made some of the U.S. Army's most awe-inspiring soldiers. Though Americanization was accelerating, and as many Indians were lawyers, doctors, and engineers by 1914 as were employed in hunting, trapping, or guiding, many still brought skills that adapted remarkably well to conditions on the Western Front. Possibly because of Chief of Staff Hugh Scott's deep interest in their culture, they were not discriminated against, provided there was "no colored admixture." In all, 6,509 were inducted and the same number volunteered, a total of almost 30 percent of all adult Indian males. The percentages varied from tribe to tribe: roughly 40 percent of the Oklahoma Osage and Quapaw served, while less than 1 percent of the Navajo did so. In the federal Indian schools where Americanization had free rein, almost 100 percent of males enlisted, many lying about their age. "I felt no American could or should be better than the first American," explained one Siletz volunteer.

In 1917–1918, young Indian males were still in touch with traditional hunting and fighting skills. In the cantonments, they provided an object lesson to the urban conscripts in techniques of concealment and stealth by slipping across "no-man's-land" to snatch a "German" from the trenches opposite. Their languages were regarded as excellent substitutes for code, though a new vocabulary had to be evolved to deal with the terminology of modern war: machine guns became "little guns shoot fast" and battalions were indicated by "one, two and three grains of corn."

Zane Grey,* touring Wild West shows, and other more authentic by-products of a culture so recently vibrant had all imprinted the Germans with stereotypical images of "Red Indians." They were terrified of the specter of the "red man" and drafted extra snipers into sectors where Indians were spotted, "specially to pick off these dangerous men." Recognizing an opportunity for psychological warfare, the War Department gave serious thought to "attempting a limited number of night raids with men camouflaged as Indians in full regalia."

In the early days of sorting and allocating men, the Army relied a good deal on personal impressions and the direct question "What can you do?" But this was the second decade of the twentieth century, when the psychologist had begun to make an impression, and when Pershing complained that "too many mental incompetents were being shipped abroad," it seemed time to try newer methods. Psychologist Robert M. Yerkes was able to persuade the War Department "to adopt a scientific basis for assessing the quality of the new recruits."

*A well-known author of the American West. (Eds.)

During the war, 3 million soldiers were given intelligence tests—one test for the literate, another for those considered illiterate. (The literacy test itself provided perhaps the biggest shock: throughout the Army, 24.9 percent of men could neither read the paper nor write a letter home—in English, at least—and this was the criterion employed.) Men who were rated "feebleminded" because they scored so low on the intelligence test were immediately discharged from the Army without review by a disability board—until the authorities realized that many college graduates were using this as an ingenious escape route from the Army.

By today's standards, the tests were obviously flawed, geared remorselessly to the middle-class native English speaker with questions on literature, tennis, and the like. Even so, a grading of "A" to "E" offered a simple, convenient reference tool to personnel officers struggling to allocate thousands of new recruits in a hurry. Once the men with relevant experience had been assigned, each company would receive a mixture of grades. Men who had scored lower than "C" would not be permitted to apply for commissions.

Life in the Army offered the clearest demonstration that the grip of the federal government was closing ever more tightly around the individual. It was a protective as well as coercive clasp. In the late 1890s, William Gibbs McAdoo (then a dealer in railway bonds) had helped the "penniless and starving" wives and families of servicemen in the Spanish-American War. Now, as Secretary of the Treasury, he urged that "the basis of the family's support ... should be an allotment of a fixed proportion of the soldier's pay." Enlisted married men were obliged to make over half their $33 monthly pay to their families, which the government then supplemented.

The allotment could not fully compensate for the induction of a husband or son. Draft boards seem to have applied the "genuine dependency" exemption very narrowly, and across the country division headquarters were inundated with applications for the release of enlisted men or for more money in lieu. Desperate letters told of starving children, sick and bedridden relatives. In their bemused incoherence and their combination of greed and optimism with genuine hardship, these were a constant source of amusement to headquarters staff, who circulated a list of the choicest pleas. "My boy has been put in charge of a spittoon. Will I get more money now?" "I didn't know my husband had a middle name, and if he did, I do not think it was 'None.'" "You ask for my allotment number: I have four boys and two girls." "I am writing to ask you why I have not received my elopement." "I have not received my husband's pay and will be forced to lead an immortal life." "Please return my marriage certificate. Baby has not eaten in three days."

Material support was only one aspect of the government's paternalism. McAdoo and Cabinet colleagues such as Daniels, Baker, and Wilson made the soldier's moral welfare in camp their concern as well. Baker, a reformer by inclination, remembered the public outrage in 1916 at the plague of brothels spreading along the Mexican border with the soldiers. He knew people were afraid of the effects of these huge new concentrations of troops, and he threw his weight behind a morality campaign; by the end of 1917, some 110 red-light districts near camps had been closed. At the level of private enterprise, the concerned citizens of the National Allied Relief Committee raised funds to bus vulnerable American servicemen through "the London danger zone" and save them "from the distressing and terrible dangers of the streets."

For help in finding something to take the place of the customary army pleasures, Baker turned to a friend, Raymond Fosdick, a thirty-three-year-old moralist and social reformer and the brother of the well-known clergyman Harry Emerson Fosdick. Baker asked him to provide the men with "wholesome recreation and enjoyment." This he was to achieve by coordinating the various voluntary organizations operating in the camps—bodies such as the YMCA, the Jewish Welfare Board, and the Knights of Columbus, up to thirty-six of them in some camps. Under Fosdick's Committee on Training Camp Activities, the men came to enjoy community songs, Liberty Theaters (occasionally graced by the singing of the President's daughter Margaret), YMCA huts (blacks usually excluded) where they could read magazines and write letters, Hostess Houses (separately provided for blacks) where they could meet female visitors in civilized surroundings, athletics, football and baseball, and educational programs aimed particularly at illiterates and the foreign-born. A small pamphlet published by the YMCA in 1917 offered the man about to go overseas a remarkable selection of handy French expressions: "I should like very much to see the periscope of a submarine"; "I have pawned my watch"; "A piece of shell hit me in the arm"; "Do not stick your head above the trench"; "Here I am, here I stay."

The young American male in those days was deemed by the War Department to be remarkably ignorant about sex; Fosdick's committee set out to put him straight. He was taught the facts of life and the risks of low life. "A German bullet is cleaner than a whore," announced one poster, showing a surprising lack of tact. "You wouldn't use another man's toothbrush. Why use his whore?" The potentially horrific results of normal intercourse seem so to have traumatized the youths of America that some of the young men moved swiftly from a state of ignorance to a widespread preference for alternatives, or so the Paris prostitutes claimed.

The motive of the military authorities for combating vice was military efficiency, not spiritual improvement. Where Fosdick's civilians concentrated on deterrence and moral suasion, the Army blandly provided prophylaxis at any hour of the day and night, somewhat undermining the credibility of the righteous. Contracting a venereal disease was a punishable offense, but this was because it was careless and unnecessary and detracted from the soldier's usefulness, not because it was wicked.

Neither military personnel nor civilians were entirely successful in combating venereal disease. At some camps the scale of the problem verged on the unmanageable. So many conscripts on leave from the camps in Kansas and Missouri headed for the prostitutes on Kansas City's Twelfth Avenue that it had been nicknamed "Woodrow Wilson Avenue—a piece at any price." Local authorities often refused to cooperate in the campaign against the local red-light district, which might be a useful factor of a community's economy. Seattle had to be declared off limits, New Orleans failed to see the point of the campaign, and Galveston, Texas, remained an open city. Where prostitutes were pushed out, they often took up residence in the black districts of town, beyond the reach of the authorities' interest, and into the vacuum stepped the amateurs, hero-worshiping girls, some as young as twelve, who were determined to give themselves to the uniform.

In France, Pershing was very much more draconian, certainly more so than the natives. The French provided licensed brothels for their troops, and in 1918 Premier Georges Clemenceau offered similar services to the AEF. When Baker saw the letter, he exclaimed to Fosdick, "For God's sake, Raymond, don't show this to the President or he'll stop the war." Pershing personally inspected the VD returns every day. He declared red-light districts off limits and had them patrolled; MPs were then found to have the highest incidence of VD in the AEF. Men returning to camp drunk were automatically assumed to be infected and were treated, by force if necessary.

The Army also fought a constant, if losing, battle at home against the temptations of alcohol. In the "dry" states, soldiers helped bootleggers make a killing; in "wet" ones, the authorities created "dry" zones around the camps, but the regulations proved nearly impossible to enforce. Men found lemon or ginger "extracts" with a 9 percent alcohol content perfectly satisfactory. The punishment for selling liquor to men in uniform was a year's imprisonment, so the soldiers took off their tunics or paid the proprietor in advance, whereupon the barman "treated" them to drinks.

In Pershing's domain, beyond the reach of the moral crusaders, military efficiency was again the only criterion. Spirits were forbidden, but the men were allowed to buy beer and wine, and "Major Van Rooge" and "Captain Van Blank" became constant companions. Pershing did curb the intake by supporting the move to retain half the pay even of men without dependants. The soldiers' spending power worried him because of the impact it was having on the morale of French and British soldiers, who were paid far less. "$10 a month," he remarked, "is more spending money than a man in the trenches ought to have."

Drugs, which were widely used in society, duly made their appearance in the Army. Military intelligence gave warning of the sale to troops in southern cantonments of "the Chihuahua or Marihuana weed. This is a plant smoked by Mexicans of the lower classes; its use produces insanity and homicidal mania." The death-dealing weed proved popular, and by the summer of 1918 it had spread as far as Seattle. At Camp Devens, Special Agent Kelleher surprised a narcotics dealer in barracks at six one evening "with a complete outfit of hypodermic syringes, a spoon for heating the concoction, and quite a lot of morphine." Waiting in line were three conscripts with their sleeves rolled up.

DOCUMENTS

German-American Loyalty, *1917*

My emotions tell me one thing at this awful time, but my reason tells me another. As a German by birth it is a horrible calamity that I may have to fight Germans. That is natural, is it not? But as an American by preference, I can see no other course open....

For 25 years Germany has shown dislike for the United States—the Samoan affair, the Hongkong contretemps, the Manila Bay incident, the unguarded words of the Kaiser himself, and, lastly, the Haitian controversy in 1914.... And it has not been from mere commercial or diplomatic friction. It is because their ideals of government are absolutely opposite. One or the other must go down. It is for us to say now which it shall be.

Because of my birth and feelings beyond my control I have no particular love for the French and less for the British. But by a strange irony of fate I see those nations giving their blood for principles which I hold dear, against the wrong principles of people I individually love. It is a very unhappy paradox, but one I can not escape. I do not want to see the allies triumph over the land of my birth. But I very much want to see the triumph of the ideas they fight for.

It sickens my soul to think of this Nation going forth to help destroy people many of whom are bound to me by ties of blood and friendship. But it must be so. It is like a dreadful surgical operation. The militaristic, undemocratic demon which rules Germany must be cast out. It is for us to do it—now. I have tried to tell myself that it is not our affair, that we should have contented ourselves with measures of defense and armed neutrality. But I know that is not so. The mailed fist has been shaken under our nose before. If Prussianism triumphs in this war the fist will continue to shake. We shall be in real peril, and those ideas for which so much of the world's best blood has been spilled through the centuries will be in danger of extinction. It seems to me common sense that we begin our defense by

SOURCE: C. Kotzenabe, "German-American Loyalty," in Committee on Public Information, War Information Series, *American Loyalty* (Washington, D.C.: Government Printing Office, 1917), 5–6.

immediate attack when the demon is occupied and when we can command assistance.

There is much talk of what people like me will do, and fear of the hyphen. No such thing exists. The German-American is as staunch as the American of adoption of any other land and perhaps more so. Let us make war upon Germany, not from revenge, not to uphold hairsplitting quibbles of international law, but let us make war with our whole heart and with all our strength, because Germany worships one god and we another and because the lion and the lamb can not lie down together. One or the other must perish.

Let us make war upon the Germany of the Junkerthum,* the Germany of frightfulness, the Germany of arrogance and selfishness, and let us swear not to make peace until the Imperial German Government is the sovereign German people.

Letters from Mennonite Draftees, 1918

DEAR BROTHER _____:

I went to Camp Cody, N. Mex., June 25, 1918. At first I drilled without a rifle, but later was asked to take one, explaining that the President's orders concerning the C.O.'s [conscientious objectors] required it, and I would get into noncombatant service in due time. I accepted it, and in two weeks was transferred to the infantry where, of course, I was asked again to take the rifle, and I saw that I had been deceived. I refused and explained why. Several nights after this, while I was in bed, some privates threw water into my bed, put a rope around my neck and jerked me out on the floor.

The next day two sergeants came to my tent and took me out, tied a gun on my shoulder and marched me down the street, one on each side of me, kicking me all the way. I was asked again whether I would take the rifle and drill. I refused and was taken to the bath-house, put under the shower bath where they turned on the water, alternating hot and cold, until I was so numb that I could scarcely rise. Just then one of the higher officers came in and asked what they were about. They explained that they were giving me a bath. The officer told me to dress and go to my tent, that he wanted to interview me himself. He asked if I would take a rifle and drill. I told him that I could not. He ordered my sergeant to put me on company street work until they got my transfer, and in three weeks I was given noncombatant service.

VERY TRULY YOURS, _____;

Junkerthum refers to the Prussian military aristocracy. (Eds.)

SOURCE: J. S. Hartzler, *Mennonites in the World War or Nonresistance Under Test* (Scottdale, Pa.: Mennonite Publishing House, 1922), 124–127.

DEAR BROTHER _____:

I came home Wednesday evening, Feb. 5. To get home, receive a hearty welcome and many expressions of joy for the effort made to maintain the faith, was alone worth the hardships which we endured.

I had been gone a few days more than ten months, of which I spent twenty-four days in our company, ten days in detention camp, seventy-eight days in the guard-house, one night in the Kansas City Police "lock-up," one hundred ninety-seven days in the disciplinary barracks (Fort Leavenworth, Kans.) and two days on the way home....

I do not approve of such practices as the world was engaged in, and will give them neither moral nor material support though it may mean imprisonment or even death for not doing so. If the army would never kill a man, I can not see how a person could become a part of it, giving moral and material support to its maintenance and still retain a Christian character. The standards it upholds and the injustices it practices are unbelievable to a man who never saw them.... The only part that I can have in the army is suffering its punishments. Its purposes and those of Christianity are as different as night and day. The aims of the army are coercion, terrorism, carnal force; the ideals of Christianity are love, meekness, gentleness, obedience to the will of God, etc. When these ideals are maintained to the best of our ability, by God's grace He will provide care and protection in ways not imagined by man.

As to noncombatant service: all branches of service have one purpose; viz., to make the whole system a stronger organization of terrorism, destruction, and death. While I would not have been directly killing any one, I would have been doing a man's part in helping another do the act, and lending encouragement to the same. To support a thing and refuse to do the thing supported is either ignorance or cowardice. To refuse to go to the trenches and still give individual assistance to another doing so, is either an improper knowledge of the issues at stake or downright fear to face the bullets. I have a greater conscientious objection against noncombatant than against combatant service. I feel that the principle is the same, and that both are equally wrong. I would feel guilty toward the other man to accept service where the danger was not so great....

To an observer it may have seemed ridiculous to refuse to even plant flowers at the base hospital. In the first place, that was the duty of the working gang under the quartermaster's department. Technically I would not have been doing military duty for I had not "signed up"; virtually I would have been rendering service because I was at work.... The farther one went with the military officers the farther they demanded him to go. I felt that the farther I went the less reason I could give for stopping, so I concluded that the best place to stop was in the beginning. It was on the charge of refusing to plant flowers that I received my court-martial sentence of ten years of hard labor in the disciplinary barracks at Fort Leavenworth, Kans.

FRATERNALLY YOURS, _____.

Racism and the Army, 1918

French Military Mission

STATIONED WITH THE AMERICAN ARMY
AUGUST 7, 1918

Secret Information Concerning Black American Troops

1. It is important for French officers who have been called upon to exercise command over black American troops, or to live in close contact with them, to have an exact idea of the position occupied by Negroes in the United States. The information set forth in the following communication ought to be given to these officers and it is to their interest to have these matters known and widely disseminated. It will devolve likewise on the French Military Authorities, through the medium of the Civil Authorities, to give information on this subject to the French population residing in the cantonments occupied by American colored troops.

2. The American attitude upon the Negro question may seem a matter for discussion to many French minds. But we French are not in our province if we undertake to discuss what some call "prejudice." American opinion is unanimous on the "color question" and does not admit of any discussion.

The increasing number of Negroes in the United States (about 15,000,000) would create for the white race in the Republic a menace of degeneracy were it not that an impassable gulf has been made between them.

As this danger does not exist for the French race, the French public has become accustomed to treating the Negro with familiarity and indulgence.

This indulgence and this familiarity are matters of grievous concern to the Americans. They consider them an affront to their national policy. They are afraid that contact with the French will inspire in black Americans aspirations which to them [the whites] appear intolerable. It is of the utmost importance that every effort be made to avoid profoundly estranging American opinion.

Although a citizen of the United States, the black man is regarded by the white American as an inferior being with whom relations of business or service only are possible. The black is constantly being censured for his

SOURCE: From BELLESILES. BIBLIOBASE #234, 1E. © 1998 Wadsworth, a part of Cengage Learning, Inc. Reproduced by permission. www.cengage.com/permissions

want of intelligence and discretion, his lack of civic and professional conscience and for his tendency toward undue familiarity.

The vices of the Negro are a constant menace to the American who has
to repress them sternly. For instance, the black American troops in France
have, by themselves, given rise to as many complaints for attempted rape
as all the rest of the army. And yet the [black American] soldiers sent us
have been the choicest with respect to physique and morals, for the number
disqualified at the time of mobilization was enormous.

Conclusion

1. We must prevent the rise of any pronounced degree of intimacy between
French officers and black officers. We may be courteous and amiable with
these last, but we cannot deal with them on the same plane as with the
white American officers without deeply wounding the latter. We must not
eat with them, must not shake hands or seek to talk or meet with them outside of the requirements of military service.

2. We must not commend too highly the black American troops, particularly in the presence of [white] Americans. It is all right to recognize their
good qualities and their services, but only in moderate terms, strictly in
keeping with the truth.

3. Make a point of keeping the native cantonment population from
"spoiling" the Negroes. [White] Americans become greatly incensed at any
public expression of intimacy between white women with black men. They
have recently uttered violent protests against a picture in the "Vie Parisi-
enne" entitled "The Child of the Desert" which shows a [white] woman in
a "cabinet particulier" with a Negro. Familiarity on the part of white
women with black men is furthermore a source of profound regret to our
experienced colonials who see in it an over-weening menace to the prestige
of the white race.

Military authority cannot intervene directly in this question, but it can
through the civil authorities exercise some influence on the population.

Suggestions for Further Reading

On Southern black Americans after the Civil War, consult Eric Foner, *Reconstruction: America's Unfinished Revolution, 1863–1967* (1988). See also John Hope Franklin, *Reconstruction After the Civil War* (1961). Leon Litwack, *Been in the Storm for So Long: The Aftermath of Slavery* (1979); Edward Ayers, *The Promise of the New South: Life After Reconstruction* (1992); Jacqueline Jones, *The Disposed: America's Underclass from the Civil War to the Present* (1992); Neil McMillen, *Dark Journey: Black Mississippi in the Age of Jim Crow* (1989); and Leon F. Litwack, *Trouble in Mind; Black Southerners in the Age of Jim Crow* (1998). For the convict lease system see Douglas A. Blackmon, *Slavery By Another Name: The Re-Enslavement of Black Americans from the Civil War to World War II* (2008). For culture, see Grace Elizabeth Hall, *Making Whiteness: The Culture of Segregation in the South, 1890–1940* (1998). A book dealing with memory is David W. Dwight, *Race and Reunion: The Civil War in American Memory* (2001). A book dealing with the courts and Africans Americans is Lawrence Goldstone, *Inherently Unequal: The Betrayal of the Equal Rights by The Supreme Court, 1865–1903* (2011).

For settlement of the frontier, general works are Donald Worster, *Under Western Skies: Nature and History in the American West* (1992) and Richard Bartell, *The New Country: A Social History of the American Frontier, 1776–1890* (1974). See also Joe B. Frantz and Julian E. Choate, Jr., *The American Cowboy: The Myth and the Reality* (1955). A controversial view is found in Patricia Nelson Limerick, *The Legacy of Conquest: The Unbroken Past of the American West* (1987). See also Walter Nugent, *Into the West: The Story of Its People* (1999). For immigrants in the West see Elliott Robert Barken, *From All Points: America's Immigrant West, 1870s–1952* (2007).

On American Indians, consult Francis Paul Prucha, *The Great White Father: The United States Government and the American Indians* (1984); and Vine Deloria, Jr., *Custer Died for Your Sins: An Indian Manifesto* (1969). On education, see Myriam Vuckovic, *Voices from Haskell: Indian Students Between Two Worlds* (2008) and Clyde Ellis, *To Change Them Forever: Indian Education at the Rain Mountain Boarding School, 1893–1920* (1996). On education see Margaret Szasz, *Education and the American Indians: The Road to Self-Determination, 1928–1973* (1974). Especially worthwhile is Rani-Henrik Aivdersson, *The Lakota Ghost Dance of 1890* (2008). On the New Deal see also Philip Kenneth, *John Collier's Crusade for Indian Reform, 1920–1954* (1977). See also Rex Smith, *Moon of the Popping Trees: The Tragedy at Wounded Knee and the End of the Indian Wars* (1975). For urbanization see Donald L. Fixico, *The Urban Indian Experience in America* (2000).

On women and education see Barbara Solomon, *In the Company of Educated Women: A History of Women and Higher Education in America* (1985). On reform, see Theda Skocpol, *Protecting Soldiers and Mothers: The Political Origins of Social Policy* (1992). On work see David Katzman, *Seven Days a*

Week: Women and Domestic Service in Industrializing America (1978). On birth control see Linda Gordon, *Woman's Body, Woman's Right: A Social History of Birth Control in America* (1979) and James Reed, *From Private Vice to Public Virtue: The Birth Control Movement in the United States Since 1830* (1977). On feminism, see Nancy Cott, *The Grounding of Modern Feminism* (1987). On immigrant women see Suzanne M. Sinke, *Dutch Immigrant Women in the United States, 1880–1920* (2002). On equity, see Alice Kessler-Harris, *In Pursuit of Equity: Women, Men, and the Quest for Economic Citizenship in Twentieth-Century America* (2001). Another good book is Linda Gordon, *The Great Arizona Orphan Abduction* (1999). On women in professions see Ellen S. More, *Restoring the Balance: Women Physicians and the Profession of Medicine, 1890–1995* (1999); Barbara Harris, *Beyond Her Sphere: Women and the Professions in American History* (1978); and Dee Garrison, *Apostles of Culture: The Public Libraries and American Society, 1876–1920* (1979).

On immigration see Stephan Themstrom, ed. *The Harvard Encyclopedia of American Ethnic Groups* (1980). Informative is Roger Daniels, *Guarding the Golden Door: American Immigration Policy and Immigrants Since 1882* (2004). A general work is John Bodnar, *The Transplanted: A History of Immigrants in Urban America* (1985). John Higham, *Strangers in the Land* (1968) is still worthwhile, but for nativism see Aristide R. Zolberg, *A Nation By Design: Immigration Policy in the Fashioning of America* (2006) and Gary Gerstle, *American Crucible: Race and Nation in the Twentieth Century* (2001). Another treatment of nativism is Mathew Fry Jacobson, *Whiteness of a Different Color: European Immigrants and the Alchemy of Race* (1998). There are many histories of groups and ethnicity in cities, but start with Nancy Foner, *From Ellis Island to JFK: New York's Two Great Waves of Immigration* (2001); Kathy Peiss, *Cheap Amusements: Leisure in Turn of the Century New York* (1985); Erika Lee, *At America's Gates: Chinese Immigrants, During the Exclusion Era, 1882–1943* (2003); Diane C. Vecchio, *Merchants, Midwives, and Laboring Women: Italian Women and Urban America* (2006); and Mae M. Ngai, *Impossible Subjects: Illegal Aliens and the Making of Modern America* (2004). Two books deal with America's main entry stations: Vincent J Cannato, *American Passage: The History of Ellis Island* (2009) and Erica Lee and Judy Yung, *Angel Island: Immigrant Gateway to America* (2010).

For industrialization and American workers, see Herbert Gutman, *Work, Culture and Society in Industrializing America* (1976). See also Stephan Thernstrom, *The Other Bostonians* (1973). For southern mill workers, see Jacqueline Dowd Hall et al., *Like a Family: The Making of a Southern Cotton Mill World* (1987).

For migration of blacks to the North, see Forette Henri, *Black Migration: Movement North, 1900–1920* (1976) for an overview. For a work based on oral histories, see Isabel Wilkerson, *The Warmth of Other Suns: the Epic Story of America's Great Migration* (2010). Similar in approach is Nicholas Lemann, *The Promised Land: The Great Black Migration and How It Changed*

America (1992). For different cities, see David Katzman, *Before the Ghetto: Black Detroit in the Nineteenth Century* (1973); Allan Spear, *Black Chicago: the Making of a Ghetto, 1890–1914* (1967); Thomas Lee Philpott, *The Slum and the Ghetto: Neighborhood Deterioration and Middle Class Reform, Chicago, 1880– 1930* (1976); James R. Grossman, *Land of Hope: Chicago, Black Southerners and the Great Migration* (1989). For the migration of blacks and whites from the South see James N. Gregory, *The Southern Diaspora: How the Great Migrations of Black and White Southerners Transformed America* (2005). For racism consult Joel Williamson, *The Crucible of Race* (1984) and George Frederickson, *The Black Image in the White Mind: The Debate on Afro-American Character and Destiny, 1817–1913* (1971).

On World War I, Fredrick Lubke, *Bonds of Loyalty: German Americans and World War I* (1974) is informative. For the home front see David Kennedy, *Over Here: The First World War and American Society* (1980). On women during the war, see Maurie W. Greenwald, *Women, War and Work: the Impact of World War I on Women Workers in the United States* (1980). See also Edward Coffman, *The War to End All Wars: The American Military Experience in the Great War* (1968). Also informative is Jeanette Keith, *Rich Man's War, Poor Man's Fight: Race, Class, and Power in the Rural South During the First World War* (2004). For ethnic groups, consult Christopher Sterbe, *Good Americans: Italian and Jewish Immigrants During the First World War* (2003).

PART II

Modern American Society
1920–Present

Chapter 8

Intolerance: A Bitter Legacy of Social Change

The Klan spreads northward. Klansmen celebrate the establishment of new headquarters in Long Branch, New Jersey, July 4, 1924.

The return of peace following World War I brought with it an era of economic boom and social change. War profits were invested in providing goods and services unavailable during wartime. The public was eager to obtain such twentieth-century products as automobiles, radios, washing machines, and refrigerators. To accommodate this demand, factories had to be built, office buildings erected to house expanding businesses and financial enterprises, and transportation facilities improved to move growing urban populations. The large influx of immigrants that had occurred during the decades before the war provided a good portion of the necessary labor pool. Though the war all but cut off the immigrant flow, a new labor supply resulted from a large migration of southern African Americans to northern cities that began during the war years and continued into the 1920s. Thus, twentieth-century America's cities changed physically and also became far more ethnically and racially diverse.

The essay that follows, from Kevin A. Boyle's book *Arc of Justice*, provides a vivid description of this postwar urban boom. However, it also relates in detail the dark side of the story, one of nativist and racist bigotry directed at the polyglot urban populations. To what does the author ascribe this backlash by native-born Americans? What were the key manifestations of the anti-black, anti-immigrant movement?

As the essay relates, one consequence of the growth of bigotry during the twenties was the revival of the Ku Klux Klan. The first document comes from a 1926 article, "The Klan's Fight for Americanism," by Klan leader Hiram Evans. Notice how Evans's message combines bigotry and an alleged adherence to traditional values. How does the document help to explain the Klan's appeal in sections of the country as different from each other in racial and ethnic makeup as Oregon, Georgia, and Massachusetts?

The Klan may be viewed as an organization run by political opportunists who gained power by appealing to the prejudices of their largely uneducated followers. But the cause of bigotry had proponents of an entirely different kind. The idea that there existed superior and inferior races and nationality groups was echoed in the halls of academia by a number of psychologists, anthropologists, and sociologists. Prominent among them was the psychologist Carl C. Bingham. In the second document, from his 1923 book *American Intelligence*, Bingham employs the results of IQ tests given to World War I soldiers to support his arguments regarding the dangers of racial mixture and the need for restricting the immigration of so-called inferior races.

As you read the Bingham piece, consider what the response to such views might be if they appeared in print today. Of course, we now recognize that the IQ tests to which he referred for support were among the earliest examples of such measurements. They were crude, and their results were largely refuted. We have also witnessed the consequence of the employment of racist policies during World War II and even in our own day. In the decade of the twenties, however, the arguments of both the Klan and Bingham had widespread political support. Evidence of this is found in the third document, an excerpt from congressional testimony in 1921 concerning U.S. immigration policy. Although those testifying do not refer to any specific countries of origin in their condemnation of immigrants, federal legislation passed in 1924 (the National Origins Act) makes it clear that legislators believed immigrants from some countries to be less desirable than those from others. The new approach, generally referred to as the national-origins system, gave preference to immigrants from northern and western Europe; it severely limited immigration from the rest of the continent and virtually barred Asians.

ESSAY

Prosperity and Prejudice in Postwar America
Kevin A. Boyle

The migrants filled the train stations of the South every day in the summer of 1925, waiting on ramshackle wooden platforms of crossroads towns such as Opelousas, Louisiana, and Andalusia, Alabama, and in cantilevered caverns such as Atlanta's Union Station. When the northbound trains pulled in, hissing and steaming, the travelers picked up cardboard suitcases bought at five-and-dimes or battered trunks carried since freedom came. Summoning up their courage, they strode past the Pullman porters—race men like themselves—making their way down the platforms to the grimy Jim Crow cars, settling into their seats for long rides north.

The landscapes rolling past the tense faces looked familiar: the seas of cotton fields that flowed from the Mississippi River to the Georgia coast; the tobacco plantations that ran from North Carolina to the outskirts of Washington, D.C.; the squalid lumber camps of East Texas; the blackened coal towns of Appalachia; and the rough mill villages of the Carolina Piedmont. Every place they passed bore the brand of segregation and the Jim Crow laws. Every station had its "whites" and "coloreds" signs hanging above separate waiting rooms. Every view had its hidden terrors.

Eight men had been lynched by white mobs in the first half of 1925, a quiet year by previous standards. Black newspapers like the *Chicago Defender* and the *Pittsburgh Courier* had given the atrocities front-page coverage. Porters had tucked the papers into their bags and carried them home to the South, to the barbershops and the roadhouses, the churches and the cafés. So the travelers had to wonder. Was that collection of sharecroppers' shacks slipping by as the train passed Greenwood, Mississippi, the place where a few months ago a posse murdered Hal Winters because he dared defend his daughter from the landlord's advances? Was that gnarled tree on the horizon just beyond Scarboro, Georgia, the site where a mob doused Robert Smith in gasoline and set him ablaze in March?

Gradually, the world outside the filthy windows became less and less familiar. At some point, the cotton fields gave way to wheat and corn; the rolling hills of Appalachia sloped into the flatlands of the Midwest. Mining camps gave way to factory towns, where the trains slowed to crawls as they passed mammoth warehouses and crossed street after nameless street.

SOURCE: *"Prosperity and Prejudice in Postwar American"* from the book *Arc of Justice: A Saga of Race, Civil Rights and Murder in the Jazz Age* by Kevin Boyle. Copyright © 2004 by Kevin Boyle. Reprinted by permission of Henry Holt and Company, LLC.

When the trains pulled into stations here, the migrants saw no signs for whites or coloreds.

In the early days of the migration, during the Great War, travelers sometimes celebrated crossing into the North by breaking into song or prayer, but so many migrants had made the trip north now—almost a million southern-born blacks since 1917—that the joy was tempered. They knew now that northern whites were as capable of brutality and murder as southern men. Rampaging whites had killed twenty-three blacks during a week of rioting in Chicago in the bitter summer of 1919.

Yet it was still hard to remain calm as the trains reached the outskirts of one of the great cities, where the industrial districts alone dwarfed anything the South could claim. Gary's vast steelworks, one of the wonders of the modern world, sprawled across the prairie south of Chicago. The streets of Trenton and Hoboken were warrens of tool shops and warehouses. On the banks of the listless Rouge River just outside Detroit, Henry Ford was building an automobile factory large enough to employ all of Nashville or Norfolk.

The migrants grew increasingly excited as the distant, hazy outlines of the downtown skylines appeared. Pillars of steel and glass gradually filled the cars' windows. Even the smallest skyscrapers—the twenty-one story Flatiron Building in lower Manhattan or the imposing Book-Cadillac Hotel in downtown Detroit—would have been landmarks almost anywhere in the South. Here they faded into the shadows of buildings that seemed to soar upward forever. Chicago's newly opened Wrigley Building stood majestically above the Loop, its brilliantly illuminated clock tower drawing all eyes, day or night. In New York, the Woolworth Building's elegant terra-cotta façade reached almost eight hundred feet into the sky, higher than any other building in the world. Behind those structures rose the skeletons of the next generation of skyscrapers, sure to be even taller, even more stunning.

The nation's cities sparkled in the summer of 1925. New York and Chicago, with more than two million residents each, were among the largest cities in the Western world, while Detroit, home to the fabulous new auto industry, was America's great boomtown, an industrial juggernaut of unprecedented power. Europe's cultural hegemony had died in the course of the Great War, its lifeblood drained away in the mud of Flanders's fields. Urban America filled the void, drowning out the ancien régime's death knell with the pounding of the jackhammer and the riotous joy of the jazz band.

New York, Chicago, and Detroit coursed with cash in the mid-1920s. The war had made the United States the world's banker. The great American investment houses—J. P. Morgan, Goldman Sachs, Lehman Brothers—managed staggering sums, pouring international wealth into the soaring stock market and swelling corporate coffers. Manufacturers pushed their companies to new heights. Backed by the investment houses, many consolidated their operations. By the summer of 1925, the economy was awash in mergers, each larger and more spectacular than the last. Sprawling factories, marvels of machinery, poured out wonderful new products as merchants battled to build the grand stores befitting them. In 1924, Macy's completed additions that brought its floor space to two million square feet. The next spring, Detroit's leading retailer, J. L. Hudson, launched construction of a store twenty-one stories high, the world's tallest, and as lavish as anything Macy's or Marshall Field's could muster. The cities literally glowed with salesmanship, the new science of the 1920s. In the spring of 1925, a giant Moses towered over Times Square, advertising Cecil B. DeMille's epic *The Ten Commandments*. Every few minutes, a flash of electric light struck the tablets he held over his head.

The cities' sparkle wasn't simply financial. It was also cultural. Massive immigration in the late nineteenth century had made the major urban centers strikingly polyglot places. By the turn of the century, the foreign-born and their children far outnumbered the native-born in almost every large city. The war slowed the mass migration from Europe, but it launched the Great Migration of Negroes from the South. There were fifty-seven hundred blacks living in Detroit in 1910, ninety-one thousand in New York. Fifteen years later, Detroit had eighty-one thousand colored citizens, New York almost three hundred thousand.

The flood of people—foreign-born and native-born, white and black—fit no single profile. Some of the newcomers were learned; others couldn't read or write. Some had spent their lives in cities; others had never been beyond the boundaries of their villages. A minority were professionals: businessmen and teachers, doctors and lawyers, priests, ministers, and rabbis. Most were working people who filled the factories, built the homes, scrubbed the floors, and nursed the babies of the well-to-do. These new residents brought more than brawn to the cities, though. They brought their religions, their politics, their institutions, and their art. They jammed the streets on the feast days of their village saints and they emptied them on the Day of Atonement. They talked of revolution in the cafés of Greenwich Village and of patronage politics in the saloons of working-class Chicago. They opened tiny storefront churches and substantial fraternal lodges. They rushed to the vaudeville theaters, where Jewish entertainers honed their craft, and to the ghetto dancehalls, where ragtime bands pushed the boundaries of American music. And they elbowed their way into the cities' public life. By the early 1900s, ethnic politicians filled city council seats and mayors' offices in city after city.

At first, native-born Americans were almost universally appalled by the world that the black and white migrants were building on the Lower East Side of New York or Chicago's Back of the Yards. In the early days of the twentieth century, though, a tiny number of sophisticates embraced immigrant working-class life as an antidote to the poisonous constraints of Victorian bourgeois culture. The first wave were artists enthralled by the color, the noise, the sheer vitality of the immigrant wards and determined to weave that life into an art that defined the modern and a politics that fostered liberation. In the 1920s, "slumming" became a mania, as urban elites sought out the exotic, the "real," wherever they could find it. They packed into the speakeasies that filled the cities after the imposition of Prohibition, where they could rub shoulders with Italian, Irish, or Jewish gangsters. They filled theaters to see ethnic entertainers such as Ragtime Jimmy Durante, late of Coney Island, or the anarchic Marx brothers. And in the most startling turn of them all, they discovered the Negroes living in their midst.

In the early 1920s, sophisticates scrambled to grab a share of the black life that the southern migration was bringing into the cities. White producers mounted all-black musicals. White couples fumbled with the Charleston. And white patrons poured into Chicago's South Side jazz joints and Harlem's nightclubs. If they were lucky, they squeezed into the Vendome, where Louis Armstrong held the floor, or Edmond's Cellar, where Ethel Waters sang the blues. The frenzy was shot through with condescension. White slummers thought black life exciting because it was "primitive" and vital. Visiting the ghetto's haunts became the era's way to snub mainstream society, to be in the avant-garde. "Jazz, the blues, Negro spirituals, all stimulate me enormously," novelist Carl Van Vechten wrote H. L. Mencken in the summer of 1924. "Doubtless, I shall discard them too in time."

When the trains pulled into their terminals, the migrants jostled against one another as they began to gather up their belongings. Finally, they filed onto platforms already mobbed with passengers and porters. Many must have paused, unsure of what to do and where to go, then simply decided to follow the flow of people up the stairs to the stations' grand concourses. There they faced for the first time the grandeur of the city. Detroit's Michigan Central Station was a Beaux Arts masterpiece, a four-story colonnade dominated by a sequence of ornate arches and glittering chandeliers. The rotunda of the Illinois Central Station, built to awe visitors to Chicago's legendary World's Fair of 1893, was swathed in a marble wainscoting fourteen feet high. But nothing surpassed the great terminals of Gotham: Penn Station, with its main concourse sheathed in soaring steel and glass, and Grand Central Station, its great hall flooded with light from three monumental arched windows, its vaulted ceiling decorated by massive murals of the constellations. "You can identify the boys and girls [from the country] if you stand in Grand Central … and watch their behavior as they step from the train," *National Geographic* reported. "They hesitate a moment, oblivious to the crowds, looking upward, gripping their bags and bundles, hearing New York, sensing it."

If they were lucky, the newcomers had friends or relatives waiting; they'd scour the crowds for familiar faces or hope to hear some voice calling their name, some voice they prayed they still might recognize. There would be the moments of reunion, hands outstretched in greeting, the sudden comforts of warm embraces. Others had no one to meet them. How terrifying it must have been to work through the waves of people alone, to step through the terminal's doors and onto the street without a guide. The Illinois Central stood at the southern end of Chicago's Grant Park, just outside the Loop. Detroit's station faced a large park ringed by hotels and boarding houses and beyond that, Michigan Avenue, the busiest thoroughfare on the city's west side. Penn Station fronted bustling Seventh Avenue, while Grand Central stood just twelve blocks away, facing elegant Park Avenue. All the streets pulsed with energy. Pedestrians, newsboys, shoeshine men, and redcaps crowded the sidewalks. Cabbies jockeyed for fares. Automobile horns blasted as drivers battled for places at the curb. Streetcars clanged by, jammed with riders. In the clamor, no one paid attention to a colored man or woman standing alone, wondering where to go and how to make his way in a new America.

American cities didn't simply sparkle in the summer of 1925. They simmered with hatred, deeply divided as always. Native-born Americans had been denouncing foreigners since the first wave of immigrants—the ragged refugees of blighted Ireland—poured into the cities in the desperate days of the 1840s. Time and again in the late nineteenth and early twentieth centuries, urban whites proved themselves capable of savagery toward their black neighbors. But no matter how deep their divisions, the cities never developed the formal systems of segregation perfected in the South. Then came the Jazz Age. And suddenly the very changes that made the cities glitter triggered a backlash so bitter that the nation's great metropolises skidded toward their own version of Jim Crow.

The backlash was fueled by a fear of moral decay. Many native-born whites were appalled by the cities' celebration of immigrant and black cultures, with its implicit condemnation of traditional standards and its unmistakable whiff of amalgamation. Political conflict and economic strain made the backlash even more incendiary. For the better part of a generation, native-born politicians had been trying to check ethnic influence in city governments. Their efforts were driven partly by self-interest, partly by their belief that politicians of immigrant stock simply weren't capable of providing disinterested public service. Calvin Coolidge, a dour Yankee from the tiny hamlet of Plymouth Notch, Vermont, had been propelled to national prominence in 1919, when as governor of Massachusetts he had broken a strike by the overwhelmingly Irish Catholic Boston police. Four years later, he became president of the United States. But his confrontation with the Boston cops still haunted him. "The unassimilated alien child menaces our children," he told the readers of *Good Housekeeping*, "as the alien industrial worker, who has destruction rather than production in mind, menaces our industry." Politicians weren't alone in sounding the alarm. From his opulent estate just outside Detroit, Henry Ford raged against Jewish bankers and their Bolshevik allies, who were conspiring to destroy all that Anglo-Saxon businessmen had built, his fury tinged with longing for those halcyon days when immigrants and Negroes knew their place.

At least Ford had his millions to console him. Many native-born whites didn't have wealth or power to buffer them from the changes sweeping over the cities. They were solid citizens—schoolteachers and shopkeepers, office workers and factory foremen, tradesmen and housewives—and they'd worked hard to build a secure and respectable life for their families. Many resented the foreigners who intruded on their world. Now the cities were filling with Negroes as well, a race many native-born whites considered even more degraded than the wretched refuse of Europe's teeming shores. Everyone knew that Negroes were a breed apart, they said, charming in their simplicity but also frightening in their volatility, their carnality, their utter incapacity to learn the lessons of civilized society. It hadn't been so bad when only a few blacks lived in the cities. But now they were everywhere, walking the streets, riding the streetcars, looking for jobs and houses that put them alongside decent white people.

In the early 1920s, native-born whites braced themselves against the threats the city posed. Shopkeepers' associations mounted boycotts against foreign-born competitors. Church groups campaigned against lewd entertainment and demanded that Prohibition be enforced. Veterans' organizations tried to purge public schools of textbooks that didn't celebrate Anglo-Saxon culture with sufficient fervor. Foremen and tradesmen used their lodge halls to prevent immigrants and Negroes from gaining access to the better-paying factory jobs. And thousands of people poured into the newest and most exciting of the cities' many fraternal clubs, the Ku Klux Klan, which had been revived by D. W. Griffith's 1915 film, *Birth of a Nation*, a paean to the Reconstruction-era KKK. The founders of the new Klan were businessmen, pure and simple, who stood for "One Hundred Percent Americanism." They protected traditional morality: they defended the virtue of white womanhood, assailed bootleggers and their besotted clients, celebrated sobriety and the triumph of a Protestant God. They made sure that all those who threatened the nation—blacks, of course, but also Catholics, Jews, and the foreign-born—were kept in their place. It was a brilliant sales job. In the early 1920s, the Klan broke out of its southern base, racing through the small towns of the Midwest and West. And it absolutely exploded in the big cities. By 1924, Detroit's Klan had thirty-five thousand members, Chicago's fifty thousand. The money rolled in, for memberships, robes, rulebooks, and the hatred spewed out from the Klan rallies and marches, protests, and political campaigns that spread across urban America.

The anger seething up from the streets blended with the fears of the well-heeled to create a fierce political movement. But the combination wasn't stable. Powerful men like Coolidge and Ford weren't always comfortable with the hoi polloi of white America; when fifty thousand Klansmen in full regalia paraded past the White House in August 1925, Coolidge

142

snubbed them. But Anglo-Saxon politicians and businessmen also found plenty of common ground with their robed brethren.

The nativists' campaign reached high tide in 1924. Anti-immigrant groups had been demanding for years that Congress restrict entry into the United States. The pressure became intense in the early 1920s. Veterans groups lobbied their representatives, the Klan launched a massive letter-writing campaign, businessmen endorsed restriction, and nativist scientists and authors appeared before congressional committees to explain the growing threat to the American racial stock. Congress finally surrendered in the spring of 1924. The National Origins Act imposed such strict limits on the number of immigrants allowed into the country that, for all intents and purposes, it ended the great era of immigration, now eight decades old. Ethnic spokesmen pleaded with the president to veto the bill. But Coolidge remained silent, as was his habit.

The nativists followed up their triumph in Congress with a raw display of political power. It was a presidential election year in 1924. When the Republicans met at their convention, a few delegates proposed that the GOP condemn Klan intolerance. But the Invisible Empire's influence was so strong that the proposal went down in flames. The Democrats' convention, held at Madison Square Garden, took an even more bitter turn. For some time, the governor of New York, Al Smith, had been positioning himself to run for the presidency. Smith was a first-rate politician. But he was also an Irish Catholic, the son of working-class parents, born in a third-floor walk-up on the Lower East Side, educated in the Fulton Street Fish Market and the smoke-filled rooms of Tammany Hall. The party's nativists were apoplectic at the thought of such a man in the White House. So they deadlocked the convention. Ballot after ballot, Smith's supporters and opponents battled over the nomination. At one point in the proceedings, William Jennings Bryan, the ancient populist turned champion of traditional values, stood up to address the convention. The Smith supporters in the gallery, New York's aspiring ethnics, showered him with catcalls. He raised his leonine head to them. "You," he shouted in the voice that had thrilled generations, "do not represent the future of our country." So it seemed. After 103 ballots, Smith—and his immigrant world—went down to defeat.

The cities' white supremacists never had such signal victories. Their campaigns were more local, their initiatives more piecemeal. But they were in their own way even more sweeping than those of the nativists. No one outside the South suggested that the flow of blacks into the cities be prohibited. Bit by bit, however, urban whites carved a color line through the city. When the migration northward began during the war, blacks had been able to find a range of factory jobs. The opportunities shrank in the early 1920s, as many employers decided that all but the most menial and dangerous work should be reserved for whites. More and more white shopkeepers banned black customers from their stores and restaurants. And, most ominously, whites decided that blacks couldn't live wherever they wanted. They were to be hidden away in a handful of neighborhoods, walled into ghettos. Businessmen infused the real estate market with racist rules and regulations. White landlords wouldn't show black tenants apartments outside the ghetto. White real estate agents wouldn't show them houses in white neighborhoods. Bankers wouldn't offer them mortgages. Insurance agents wouldn't provide them with coverage. Developers wrote legal restrictions into their deeds, barring blacks from new housing tracts.

As the structures of segregation hardened, white homeowners became more and more determined to protect their neighborhoods' racial purity. Those whites who could afford to do so left the ghetto. Those who had no black neighbors organized to keep their areas lily-white. They formed legal organizations—protective associations, they called them—to write clauses into their deeds prohibiting the sale of their homes to blacks. They monitored real estate sales to make sure no one broke the color line. And if a black family somehow managed to breech the defenses, they could always drive them out, quietly if possible, violently if necessary.

The cities weren't segregated in one quick rush. White real estate agents, bankers, and homeowners had begun shaping Chicago's ghetto in the first decade of the twentieth century; white Detroiters didn't follow their example until the late 1910s and early 1920s. What's more, no one coordinated the businessmen's practices and the homeowners' actions. They spread by quiet agreement, sealed by a handshake in the boardroom, a directive from the home office, a conversation over coffee in the neighbor's kitchen. But the forces of the marketplace have a way of imposing discipline on disparate behaviors. By the summer of 1925, racial restrictions were assuming the power of convention across the urban North. As they did, the glittering cities of the Jazz Age were inexorably being divided in two.

The migrants knew about the ghettos. Sometimes they just knew a name— Harlem, Chicago's Black Belt, Detroit's Black Bottom—sometimes even less: a direction from the train station, a stop on the streetcar line, an address committed to memory. So they set out for the subway line that ran uptown, the State Street el to South Side Chicago, or the Michigan Avenue streetcar to Detroit's east side, hoping that this was the correct place to go, that these trains were the last trains of a journey that seemed to be stretching on and on.

Racial etiquette heightened the tension. Southern whites expected blacks to be obsequious. Would northern whites expect the same? What would happen if they accidentally brushed against a white woman in the crush to board the subway train? Could they take the empty seat toward the front of the car, as they had been told they could? Or would it be better to sit in the back and avoid even the possibility of a confrontation? There was only a split second to make a decision that, if wrong, might have catastrophic consequences.

The ride across town must have seemed terribly long. The subway trains rumbled in and out of darkness; the streetcars clattered through the crowded streets. Finally, the migrants saw the stop they'd been waiting for, at 125th Street, on the rim of Harlem; at South State and 26th Street; on St. Antoine Street, in the heart of Black Bottom. As the trains rumbled away without them, the migrants turned toward the dazzling lights. The main thoroughfares were magical places. Newcomers were amazed by the sweep of black-owned businesses: "restaurants, barbershops, pool halls, cabarets, blind pigs, gamblin' joints camouflaged as 'Recreation Clubs,'" a migrant to Detroit remembered. They were awed by the street life, by the pushcart vendors hawking fresh fruits and vegetables; by the street-corner orators selling socialism, separatism, or salvation; by the jazz and blues clubs pitching their performers to the locals and the slummers. "What a city! What a world!" thrilled poet Arna Bontemps upon his arrival in Harlem in 1924.

But the migrants couldn't live in the stores and the nightclubs. No matter how entranced they might be, they eventually had to leave the gaudy brilliance of the business strips and head down the side streets in search of housing. There were a handful of attractive streets, like Harlem's 138th and 139th: Strivers' Row. For the most part, though, the glamour of the main streets gave way to poverty. Knowing that the migrants had nowhere else to go, landlords had carved Harlem's brownstones and the workmen's cottages of Black Bottom and the Black Belt into tiny apartments, which they rented at exorbitant rates. The profits rarely found their way back into the buildings. Paint peeled from the clapboards. Broken windows remained unmended, leaky roofs unrepaired. As they took in the sights, many migrants sagged with disappointment, but they knew they had few alternatives. So they simply trudged on, looking for the address they'd been given, for a rooming house where they could spend the night, for a flat they could make their own, trying to find a home better than the one they'd left behind.

DOCUMENTS

The Klan's Fight for Americanism, 1926

The real indictment against the Roman Church is that it is, fundamentally and irredeemably, in its leadership, in politics, in thought, and largely in membership, actually and actively alien, un-American and usually anti-American. The old stock Americans, with the exception of the few such of Catholic faith—who are in a class by themselves, standing tragically torn between their faith and their racial and national patriotism—see in the

SOURCE: Hiram Evans "The Klan's Fight for Americanism." The North American Review Copyright 1926 by NORTH AMERICAN REVIEW. Reproduced with permission of NORTH AMERICAN REVIEW in the format Textbook and Other book via Copyright Clearance Center.

Roman Church today the chief leader of alienism, and the most dangerous alien power with a foothold inside our boundaries. It is this and nothing else that has revived hostility to Catholicism. By no stretch of the imagination can it fairly be called religious prejudice, though, now that the hostility has become active, it does derive some strength from the religious schism.

We Americans see many evidences of Catholic alienism. We believe that its official position and its dogma, its theocratic autocracy and its claim to full authority in temporal as well as spiritual matters, all make it impossible for it as a church, or for its members if they obey it, to cooperate in a free democracy in which Church and State have been separated. It is true that in this country the Roman Church speaks very softly on these points, so that many Catholics do not know them. It is also true that the Roman priests preach Americanism, subject to their own conception of Americanism, of course. But the Roman Church itself makes a point of the divine and unalterable character of its dogma, it has never seen fit to abandon officially any of these un-American attitudes, and it still teaches them in other countries. Until it does renounce them, we cannot believe anything except that they all remain in force, ready to be called into action whenever feasible, and temporarily hushed up only for expediency.

The hierarchical government of the Roman Church is equally at odds with Americanism. The Pope and the whole hierarchy have been for centuries almost wholly Italian. It is nonsense to suppose that a man, by entering a church, loses his race or national loyalties. The Roman Church today, therefore, is just what its name says—Roman; and it is impossible for its hierarchy or the policies they dictate to be in real sympathy with Americanism. Worse, the Italians have proven to be one of the least assimilable of people. The autocratic nature of the Catholic Church organization, and its suppression of free conscience or free decision, need not be discussed; they are unquestioned. Thus it is fundamental to the Roman Church to demand a supreme loyalty, overshadowing national or race loyalty, to a power that is inevitably alien, and which at the best must inevitably inculcate ideals un-American if not actively anti-American....

The facts are that almost everywhere, and especially in the great industrial centers where the Catholics are strongest, they vote almost as a unit, under control of leaders of their own faith, always in support of the interests of the Catholic Church and of Catholic candidates without regard to other interests, and always also in support of alienism whenever there is an issue raised. They vote, in short, not as American citizens, but as aliens and Catholics! They form the biggest, strongest, most cohesive of all the alien *blocs*. On many occasions they form alliances with other alien *blocs* against American interests, as with the Jews in New York today, and with others in the case of the recent opposition to immigrant restriction....

There are three of these great racial instincts, vital elements in both the historic and the present attempts to build an America which shall fulfill the

146

aspirations and justify the heroism of the men who made the nation. These are the instincts of loyalty to the white race, to the traditions of America, and to the spirit of Protestantism, which has been an essential part of Americanism ever since the days of Roanoke and Plymouth Rock. They are condensed into the Klan slogan: "Native, white, Protestant supremacy."

First in the Klansman's mind is patriotism—America for Americans. He believes religiously that a betrayal of Americanism or the American race is treason to the most sacred of trusts, a trust from his fathers and a trust from God. He believes, too, that Americanism can only be achieved if the pioneer stock is kept pure....

Americanism, to the Klansman, is a thing of the spirit, a purpose and a point of view, that can only come through instinctive racial understanding. It has, to be sure, certain defined principles, but he does not believe that many aliens understand those principles, even when they use our words in talking about them. Democracy is one, fairdealing, impartial justice, equal opportunity, religious liberty, independence, self-reliance, courage, endurance, acceptance of individual responsibility as well as individual rewards for effort, willingness to sacrifice for the good of his family, his nation and his race before anything else but God, dependence on enlightened conscience for guidance, the right to unhampered development—these are fundamental. But within the bounds they fix there must be the utmost freedom, tolerance, liberalism. In short, the Klansman believes in the greatest possible diversity and individualism within the limits of the American spirit. But he believes also that few aliens can understand that spirit, that fewer try to, and that there must be resistance, intolerance even, toward anything that threatens it, or the fundamental national unity based upon it.

The second word in the Klansman's trilogy is "white." The white race must be supreme, not only in America but in the world. This is equally undebatable, except on the ground that the races might live together, each with full regard for the rights and interests of others, and that those rights and interests would never conflict. Such an idea, of course, is absurd; the colored races today, such as Japan, are clamoring not for equality but for their supremacy. The whole history of the world, on its broader lines, has been one of race conflicts, wars, subjugation or extinction. This is not pretty, and certainly disagrees with the maudlin theories of cosmopolitanism, but it is truth. The world has been so made that each race must fight for its life, must conquer, accept slavery or die. The Klansman believes that the whites will not become slaves, and he does not intend to die before his time.

Moreover, the future of progress and civilization depends on the continued supremacy of the white race. The forward movement of the world for centuries has come entirely from it. Other races each had its chance and either failed or stuck fast, while white civilization shows no sign of having reached its limit. Until the whites falter, or some colored civilization has a miracle of awakening, there is not a single colored stock that can claim even equality with the white; much less supremacy.

The third of the Klan principles is that Protestantism must be supreme; that Rome shall not rule America. The Klansman believes this is not merely because he is a Protestant, nor even because the Colonies that are now our nation were settled for the purpose of wresting America from the control of Rome and establishing a land of free conscience. He believes it also because Protestantism is an essential part of Americanism; without it America could never have been created and without it she cannot go forward. Roman rule would kill it.

Intelligence and Prejudice: One Professor's View, 1923

In a very definite way, the results which we obtain by interpreting the army data by means of the race hypothesis support Mr. Madison Grant's* thesis of the superiority of the Nordic type: "The Nordics are, all over the world, a race of soldiers, sailors, adventurers, and explorers, but above all, of rulers, organizers, and aristocrats in sharp contrast to the essentially peasant and democratic character of the Alpines. The Nordic race is domineering, individualistic, self-reliant, and jealous of their personal freedom both in political and religious systems, and as a result they are usually Protestants. Chivalry and knighthood and their still surviving but greatly impaired counterparts are peculiarly Nordic traits, and feudalism, class distinctions, and race pride among Europeans are traceable for the most part to the north." "The pure Nordic peoples are characterized by a greater stability and steadiness than are mixed peoples such as the Irish, the ancient Gauls, and the Athenians, among all of whom the lack of these qualities was balanced by a correspondingly greater versatility."...

We may consider that the population of the United States is made up of four racial elements, the Nordic, Alpine, and Mediterranean races of Europe, and the negro. If these four types blend in the future into one general American type, then it is a foregone conclusion that this future blended American will be less intelligent than the present native born American, for the general results of the admixture of higher and lower orders of intelligence must inevitably be a mean between the two.

If we turn to the history of races, we find that as a general rule where two races have been in contact they have intermingled, and a cross between the two has resulted. Europe shows many examples of areas where the

---

*Author of the 1916 book *The Passing of the Great Race*, in which he promulgated a belief in the superiority of the Nordic race. The work later became popular in Nazi Germany.

SOURCE: "Intelligence and Prejudice: One Professor's View," from Carl C. Brigham, *A Study of American Intelligence* (Princeton: Princeton University Press, 1923), 182–210.

anthropological characteristics of one race shade over into those of another race where the two have intermixed, and, indeed, in countries such as France and Switzerland it is only in areas that are geographically or economically isolated that one finds types that are relatively pure. The Mongol-Tatar element in Russia is an integral part of the population. The Mediterranean race throughout the area of its contact with the negro has crossed with him. Some of the Berbers in Northern Africa show negroid characteristics, and in India the Mediterranean race has crossed with the Dravidians and Pre-Dravidian negroids. The population of Sardinia shows a number of negroid characteristics. Turn where we may, history gives us no great exception to the general rule that propinquity leads to opportunity and opportunity to intermixture.

In considering racial crosses, Professor Conklin states that "It is highly probable that while some of these hybrids may show all the bad qualities of both parents, others may show the good qualities of both and indeed in this respect resemble the children in any pure-bred family. But it is practically certain that the general or average results of the crossing of a superior and an inferior race are to strike a balance somewhere between the two.... The general effect of the hybridization of races can not fail to lead to a lowering of the qualities of the higher race and a raising of the qualities of the lower one."

And as to the possibility of a cross between races in the future, Professor Conklin writes: "Even if we are horrified by the thought, we cannot hide the fact that all present signs point to an intimate commingling of all existing human types within the next five or ten thousand years at most. Unless we can re-establish geographical isolation of races, we cannot prevent their interbreeding. By rigid laws excluding immigrants of other races, such as they have in New Zealand and Australia, it may be possible for a time to maintain the purity of the white race in certain countries, but with constantly increasing intercommunications between all lands and peoples such artificial barriers will probably prove as ineffectual in the long run as the Great Wall of China. The races of the world are not drawing apart but together, and it needs only the vision that will look ahead a few thousand years to see the blending of all racial currents into a common stream."...

We must face a possibility of racial admixture here that is infinitely worse than that faced by any European country today, for we are incorporating the negro into our racial stock, while all of Europe is comparatively free from this taint....

According to all evidence available, then, American intelligence is declining, and will proceed with an accelerating rate as the racial admixture becomes more and more extensive. The decline of American intelligence will be more rapid than the decline of the intelligence of European national groups, owing to the presence here of the negro. These are the plain, if somewhat ugly, facts that our study shows. The deterioration of American intelligence is not inevitable, however, if public action can be aroused to prevent it. There is no reason why legal steps should not be taken which would insure a continuously progressive upward evolution.

The steps that should be taken to preserve or increase our present intellectual capacity must of course be dictated by science and not by political expediency. Immigration should not only be restrictive but highly selective. And the revision of the immigration and naturalization laws will only afford a slight relief from our present difficulty. The really important steps are those looking toward the prevention of the continued propagation of defective strains in the present population. If all immigration were stopped now, the decline of American intelligence would still be inevitable. This is the problem which must be met, and our manner of meeting it will determine the future course of our national life.

Congress Debates Immigration Restriction, 1921

HOUSE OF REPRESENTATIVES

Mr. [Lucian Walton] PARISH [D.-Tex.]. We should stop immigration entirely until such a time as we can amend our immigration laws and so write them that hereafter no one shall be admitted except he be in full sympathy with our Constitution and laws, willing to declare himself obedient to our flag, and willing to release himself from any obligations he may owe to the flag of the country from which he came.

It is time that we act now, because within a few short years the damage will have been done. The endless tide of immigration will have filled our country with a foreign and unsympathetic element. Those who are out of sympathy with our Constitution and the spirit of our Government will be here in large numbers, and the true spirit of Americanism left us by our fathers will gradually become poisoned by this uncertain element.

The time once was when we welcomed to our shores the oppressed and downtrodden people from all the world, but they came to us because of oppression at home and with the sincere purpose of making true and loyal American citizens, and in truth and in fact they did adapt themselves to our ways of thinking and contributed in a substantial sense to the progress and development that our civilization has made. But that time has passed now; new and strange conditions have arisen in the countries over there; new and strange doctrines are being taught. The Governments of the Orient are being overturned and destroyed, and anarchy and bolshevism are threatening the very foundation of many of them, and no one can foretell what the future will bring to many of those countries of the Old World now struggling with these problems.

Our country is a self-sustaining country. It has taught the principles of real democracy to all the nations of the earth; its flag has been the synonym

SOURCE: "Congress Debates Immigration Restriction," from *Congressional Record,* April 20, 1921, 450, December 10, 1921, 177.

of progress, prosperity, and the preservation of the rights of the individual, and there can be nothing so dangerous as for us to allow the undesirable foreign element to poison our civilization and thereby threaten the safety of the institutions that our forefathers have established for us.

Now is the time to throw about this country the most stringent immigration laws and keep from our shores forever those who are not in sympathy with the American ideals. It is the time now for us to act and act quickly, because every month's delay increases the difficulty in which we find ourselves and renders the problems of government more difficult of solution. We must protect ourselves from the poisonous influences that are threatening the very foundation of the Governments of Europe; we must see to it that those who come here are loyal and true to our Nation and impress upon them that it means something to have the privileges of American citizenship. We must hold this country true to the American thought and the American ideals....

Mr. [James V.] McClintic [D.-Okla.]. Some time ago it was my privilege to visit Ellis Island, not as a member of the committee but as a private citizen interested in obtaining information relative to the situation which exists at that place. I stood at the end of a hall with three physicians, and I saw them examine each immigrant as they came down the line, rolling back the upper eyelid in order to gain some information as to the individual's physical condition. I saw them place the chalk marks on their clothing which indicated that they were in a diseased condition, so that they could be separated when they reached the place where they were to undergo certain examinations. Afterwards I went to a large assembly hall where immigrants came before the examiners to take the literacy test, and the one fact that impressed me more than anything else was that practically every single immigrant examined that day had less than $50 to his credit....

Practically all of them were weak, small of stature, poorly clad, emaciated, and in a condition which showed that the environment surrounding them in their European homes was indeed very bad.

It is for this reason that I say the class of immigrants coming to the shores of the United States at this time are not the kind of people we want as citizens in this country. It is a well-known fact that the majority of immigrants coming to this country at the present time are going into the large industrial centers instead of the agricultural centers of the United States, and when it is taken into consideration that the large centers are already crowded to the extent that there was hardly sufficient living quarters to take care of the people, it can be readily seen that this class of people, instead of becoming of service to the communities where they go, they will become charges to be taken care of by charitable institutions. The week I visited Ellis Island I was told that 25,000 immigrants had been unloaded at that port. From their personal appearance they seemed to be the offcasts of the countries from which they came....

Chapter 9

Morals and Manners in the 1920s

No More Booze.

Following World War I, many Americans eagerly embraced what President Warren G. Harding called "a return to normalcy." The term conveyed a nostalgic vision of an America dotted with small towns and farms, with men and women pursuing traditional roles, oblivious to events in other parts of the world. But the clock could not be turned back. Indeed, this image of the "good old days" was not an accurate view of the nation even before the war. The sweeping urban-industrial revolution of post–Civil War America had stretched the social fabric and would continue to do so.

The 1920 census provided dramatic evidence of the changes, revealing that for the first time a majority of Americans lived in urban areas. More Americans than ever before, including many women, now worked in factories and offices and saw their style of living affected by the automobile, the movies, a vast array of new consumer goods, and better housing. For much of the younger generation, the good days were not to be found in some distant past; they were to be enjoyed right now. And, as this chapter's essay "Last Call" illustrates quite clearly, members of the older generation also joined in on the fun. The focus of the essay is on the powerful politicians who publicly supported and were instrumental in passing the 18th Amendment prohibiting the manufacture and sale of alcoholic beverages as well as the Volstead Act, designed to ensure the measure's enforcement. Many supporters promoted these acts as means of contributing to the moral society, first promised by the temperance movement during the reform era of the early nineteenth century. As you will discover in your reading, however, the laws governing Prohibition were flaunted not only by a sizeable portion of the public, but also by some of the leading members of the nation's government, even by those who had publicly declared their allegiance to the measures. Why did the Republicans, whose party was in the forefront of the Prohibition movement, fail to mention in their 1920 election-year platform their role in achieving a dry nation? For what acts could the 1920 Democrats be described as models of hypocrisy? Why might President Warren G. Harding also be tapped with that designation?

As noted, the twenties witnessed dramatic changes in the lives of many Americans. Women's skirts rose above the knees; radio brought local and world news and the latest jazz music into the homes of millions; going to the movies at least once a week became routine for many town and city dwellers. However, by no means did everyone applaud these and other social developments. In the first document, Senator Henry Myers of Montana singles out for criticism the movies (and the messages that they conveyed), to which millions—especially the young—flocked weekly. Could the movies have wielded as much influence as the senator claimed? What do you think his proposal of censorship would have accomplished?

Jazz music and dancing also fell victims to criticism. One example, found in the second document, is a piece by the head of the General Federation of Women's Clubs, which appeared in the August 1921 edition of the *Ladies Home Journal*. Have such terms as "evil influence," "cheap," and "immoral," applied to jazz in this article, appeared in recent depictions of hip hop, punk rock, and other forms of popular culture? If so, cite examples.

ESSAY

"Last Call: The Rise and Fall of Prohibition"
Daniel Okrent

IN THE FIRST seven months of that first dry-but-wet year, 900,000 cases of liquor found their way from Canadian distilleries to the border city of Windsor, Ontario. This worked out to roughly 215 bottles of booze for every man, woman, and child in the area. This sounds like a lot only if you don't believe the court testimony of the Windsor woman who had personally acquired nine barrels of that whiskey, plus another forty cases of it in bottles. During the late war, she told a magistrate, she had turned to the bottle to soothe her anguish about the Canadian boys at the front, in the process developing a taste for the stuff that she had not been able to shake after the armistice. Poor dear—simple math suggested she'd been drinking roughly ten bottles a day. Or perhaps she, and all the other Windsorites on the receiving end of the whiskey flood, just might have been sending it across the mile-wide Detroit River to Michigan. It was as if the whole eastern end of Ontario, and much of the north as well, had been lifted up and tilted so that every drop of liquid in the province could run downhill to Windsor.

Another conduit through Ontario—the Michigan Central tracks connecting Niagara Falls to Windsor, and thus the northeastern United States to Detroit and beyond—carried its own cargo of liquor in the summer of 1920. On June 6, an honest customs inspector boarded a train that had originated in Boston, crossed into Canada at the falls, and was now in Windsor, poised to enter the international rail tunnel to Detroit. He entered the first car and asked the occupants to hand over any liquor they were carrying. This produced twelve bottles, which the inspector placed on the floor as he entered the second car to continue his rounds. When he turned around a moment later, all twelve bottles had disappeared. Undeterred, he moved along the train, tapping the coat and pants pockets of the next car's occupants and reaping another harvest of flasks and bottles.

Inspector Graham probably didn't know that the pockets he patted belonged to two hundred Massachusetts Republicans on their way to the party's national convention in Chicago. Though the *Boston Evening Transcript* reported the misadventure, the tone of its report was conspicuously lighthearted (Graham had been "in pursuit of suspicious gurgles"), even blasé: it characterized the delegates' train trip as "politically uneventful." Beyond that, little mention of the event appeared in the newspapers.

Already, at this early moment in the evolution of prohibition, the personal habits of the men who had placed the Eighteenth Amendment in the Constitution, or who presided over its enforcement, weren't a matter of public concern.

Not even to Wayne B. Wheeler* who asked American politicians for public loyalty, not private virtue. Wheeler knew that the victories of 1919 could be undone if Congress failed to appropriate funds for enforcement, so he devoted most of 1920 to building a barrier against such an eventuality. Without continued support from both major parties, Wheeler believed, the Eighteenth Amendment could be undermined as quickly and as thoroughly as the Fifteenth. Yet as the two political parties gathered for their conventions that summer, Wheeler wanted nothing but inaction.

He was pleased that the Republicans picked the privately soaking but publicly parched (and always pliable) senator Warren G. Harding as their candidate. He was displeased that the Democrats chose Harding's fellow Ohioan, the sometimes-wet-sometimes-dry governor James M. Cox, as theirs. But Wheeler cared less about the parties' candidates than about their platforms. In that prebroadcasting era, when the only information American voters could get about national candidates came in printed form, the endlessly debated, widely circulated platforms were essential documents—and Wheeler didn't want a word about Prohibition in either one of them. "Fearing that either or both party conventions would reject" a strong dry proposal, wrote his research assistant, Justin Steuart, Wheeler chose not to risk any inference that the ASL's power and influence had waned.

The Republicans obliged; not even an allusive mention of Prohibition or the Volstead Act appeared anywhere in the 102 paragraphs of their platform, not even in the section devoted to recent GOP legislative successes. There, the party confined its self-congratulation to its efforts regarding such concerns as telegraph reform, postal pay rates, vocational education, and the future of the shipping industry. The party's controlling document boasted of its support for the pending Nineteenth Amendment—woman suffrage—but whispered not a word about what it had done for the Eighteenth.

The Democrats approached their convention a few weeks later knowing two very important things: that the other party had remained silent on Prohibition and that members of their own party wouldn't have to suffer the confiscation of hip flasks en route to San Francisco. That was because they didn't have to take any along. San Francisco had officially declared its distaste for Prohibition even before it had started. Back in 1919, the city's

---

*Wayne B. Wheeler was a leading figure of the Anti-Saloon League (ASL) and its chief Washington lobbyist. (Eds.)

considerate board of supervisors, mindful of the hardship about to be visited upon its citizens, had unanimously repealed the city ordinance banning unlicensed saloons. A judge—*a federal* judge, in fact—had declined to give a jail sentence to Louis Cordano of Mission Street, who had been convicted of a prohibition violation; among Italians, the judge said, wine "is as necessary as coffee to the average American and tea to the average Englishman." A few months before the Democratic convention got under way on June 28, an examination of a panel of fifty prospective criminal trial jurors revealed that exactly two of them identified themselves as dry.

As a result, the Democrats' sojourn by the Bay was eagerly anticipated by delegates who were, in the disapproving words of a dry delegate from Minnesota, "in communion with the spirit of John Barleycorn." Republican Mayor James Rolph Jr., who believed in accommodating his guests even if they were Democrats and even if they voted dry, provided delegates and the press corps with what a grateful H. L. Mencken characterized as "Bourbon of the very first chop, Bourbon aged in contented barrels of the finest white oak, Bourbon of really ultra and super quality." Delivered by "small committees of refined and well-dressed ladies," Mayor Rolph's bourbon was also free of charge. If you stood in a San Francisco hotel lobby and looked thirsty, wrote another journalist at the convention, "all sorts of unknown Samaritans will charitably ask you up to their room."

The Democrats who managed to drag themselves to the Cow Palace to adopt a platform and nominate a candidate seemed no more eager to address Prohibition than the Republicans had been. This was definitely true of the dry leaders who had come to the convention to loom over the proceedings like armed prison guards on a catwalk. Dry Democrats were James Cannon's responsibility, and Cannon (along with William Jennings Bryan, platform committee chairman Senator Carter Glass of Virginia, and any other dry in an influential party position) was Wayne Wheeler's responsibility. President Wilson asked his supporters to introduce a plank modifying the Volstead Act to allow the sale of beer and light wines, but Glass refused even to allow a debate on its merits. Scanning the horizon in the other direction, the ASL had to contend with a runaway train when Bryan, who did not appreciate subtlety, introduced a militantly dry floor resolution. To Cannon fell the counterintuitive task of persuading dry delegates to vote down the Bryan resolution. His private reasoning: if the Democrats had such a plank while the Republicans did not, the ASL's meticulously balanced posture of nonpartisanship would be endangered. His public position, as described by Senator Glass: Cannon nobly "shrank from the idea of having [Prohibition] made a political issue."

An ailing Bryan was devastated. The Boy Orator of the Platte was now a very old sixty, plagued by diabetes and crippled by his evident irrelevance; some called him the party's "Beerless Leader." A wisecrack published as the convention opened was not far off the mark: "There are several hundred men in this convention who would like to nail William Jennings Bryan to his cross of gold and leave him there to die of thirst." As the Democrats prepared to vote on the resolution, Wheeler encountered Bryan at the rear of the hall, prostrate on a makeshift bed fashioned from a cast-off door and two wooden supports. "I put an old coat under his head for a pillow," Wheeler would remember. "He seemed dead tired, and the expression on his face indicated that he was suffering greatly. He took me by the hand and with tears coursing down his cheeks told me he was ready to die if he could make his party take the right action as to prohibition and adopt his resolution."

Abhorred by the wets, abandoned by the drys, Bryan and his resolution were overwhelmed, losing by a vote of 929.5–155.5....

PROHIBITION WAS BETTER than no liquor at all," the saying went, and it didn't take much effort to convince the thirsty. The evidence was everywhere. In New England the liquor came from ships anchored beyond the three-mile limit and ferried to shore by an enormous fleet of sailboats, skiffs, dinghies, rowboats, and even a few seaplanes. In Philadelphia the primary source was the chemical industry of the Delaware Valley, where denatured alcohol produced under government permit for industrial uses could be diverted, renatured, diluted, flavored with a little juniper oil, and made available on Market Street within days. Chicagoans depended on the resourceful (if murderous) Genna brothers, who oversaw hundreds of home stills situated in apartments all over the Near West Side, a network so large the entire neighborhood reeked of alcohol fumes. The $15 a month the Gennas paid to each mom or pop distiller for their output added up to very little, really, if you considered that the brothers' operation grossed $350,000 a month.

Denver drinkers could look to cunning moonshiners who placed animal carcasses near their distilleries, thus disguising the telltale scent of sour mash with the more potent aroma of rotting flesh. Across the South, moonshine technology developed along local lines, Georgia contributing the Double-Stacked Mash Barrel Still, Virginia the Blackpot Still, and Alabama the Barrel-Capped Box Still, which in turn spawned a North Carolina variant fueled by propane instead of wood (no telltale plume of smoke to tip off hijackers, competitors, or lawmen).

The liquor available in Kansas—dry by state law since 1880—was largely a concoction called Deep Shaft, named for the mines in the southeast part of the state where it originated. In Detroit, so near to the bounteous output of its Canadian neighbors, subterfuge was generally unnecessary. Wrote newspaperman Malcolm Bingay, "It was absolutely impossible to get a drink in Detroit unless you walked at least ten feet and told the busy bartender what you wanted in a voice loud enough for him to hear you above the uproar."

In Washington, Warren G. Harding could get his drinks from Taylor, his manservant at the house he kept near the golf course at the Chevy

Chase Club, who kept it stocked with bourbon and Scotch; from his attorney general, Harry Daugherty, who had large quantities of seized liquor delivered by Justice Department employees to his infamous den of iniquity, the Little Green House on K Street; or from his friend Representative Nicholas Longworth of Ohio, Teddy Roosevelt's son-in-law, "who did not have the slightest intention of complying with the Eighteenth Amendment and never pretended to." That was the verdict of his wife, Alice, who believed that the family's butler made "a passable gin." The Longworth cellars also produced a homemade beer that won compliments from Arthur Balfour when the British diplomat visited Washington for the 1921 Disarmament Conference.

It was of course no surprise that Harding's Washington was awash in alcohol from the moment of his inauguration. In the Senate he'd been a dry only as a matter of convenience, doing what he felt necessary to stay on the right side of the Anti-Saloon League, which was so powerful in Ohio. Harding never really thought Prohibition would work, and his attitude toward liquor was probably best demonstrated in a sociable nature that made him, said one of his contemporaries, "not at all averse to putting a foot on the brass rail."

This was a common posture among those who frequented the private rooms at Harding's White House. The president set the tone when he arranged to have $1,800 worth of liquor that he'd purchased before January 16, 1920, transferred to the presidential living quarters from his home on Wyoming Avenue. (Going in the other direction, Woodrow Wilson had his personal supply relocated from the White House to his home on S Street.) Harding provided liquid hospitality to guests ranging from Adolph S. Ochs, publisher of the *New York Times*, to the floating cast of characters who took part in his regular poker games. Those were among the most freely lubricated nights at the White House, when Florence Harding graciously took on the responsibility of filling and refilling the glasses of her husband's Ohio cronies (including Attorney General Daugherty) and his higher-toned Washington pals. Thus could the First Lady find herself from time to time accommodating not only the nation's chief legal officer, but a future Speaker of the House (Longworth), two U.S. senators (Frank Brandegee of Connecticut and Joseph Frelinghuysen of New Jersey), the chairman of the U.S. Shipping Board (advertising pioneer Albert Lasker), and occasionally even the daunting secretary of the treasury, Andrew W. Mellon, the vastly wealthy man whose department was responsible for enforcing the Eighteenth Amendment. Florence Harding's friend Alice Longworth, who said "no rumor [about the Harding White House] could have exceeded the truth," recalled "air heavy with tobacco smoke, trays with bottles containing every imaginable brand of whisky … cards and poker chips ready at hand—a general atmosphere of the waistcoat unbuttoned, feet on the desk, and the spittoon alongside."

Because of the Teapot Dome scandal and various other outrages that brought dishonor to his administration and that for the most part became known only after what Samuel Hopkins Adams called Harding's "timely death," there's much about this least respected of presidents that has been sifted out of his historical image. He began his administration by throwing open the gates of the White House, allowing average citizens to roam the grounds of this highly symbolic piece of public property. He brought black citizens back into federal positions (Woodrow Wilson had all but purged them during his administration), implored Congress to pass an antilynching bill, and forthrightly denounced the Ku Klux Klan. On October 26, 1921, in one of the boldest speeches ever delivered by an American president, he traveled into the heart of the South to tell an enormous crowd in Birmingham, "I would say let the black man vote when he is fit to vote; prohibit the white man voting when he is unfit to vote." Wilson had refused to pardon Eugene V. Debs, who had been imprisoned on a preposterous espionage charge arising from the domestic hysteria that accompanied World War I; Harding pardoned him on Christmas Day of the first year of his presidency, with the probably unprecedented proviso that the recipient of the pardon had to come visit him in the White House.

But there was this persistent thing about Warren Harding, however enlightened (if ineffectual) some of his statements might have been: his inability to make a decision. He told one of his speechwriters, "I listen to one side and they seem right, and then—God!—I talk to the other side, and they seem just as right." He both smoked and chewed tobacco, and at times would grow so desperate to calm his raging anxiety that he'd grab a cigarette, rip it open, and stuff its contents straight into his mouth. The *New Republic* said Harding had none of "those moral or intellectual qualities which would qualify him even under ordinary circumstances for statesman-like leadership." That was accurate but not really the point. What Harding lacked was the courage of his convictions—which, practically speaking, meant he had no convictions at all.

WAYNE WHEELER HAD two primary responsibilities once the Eighteenth Amendment was ratified: keeping Congress and the president in line. This took vigilance but little heavy lifting. Congress was no problem at all; the ASL had effectively seized control of both House and Senate in the 1916 elections and had only tightened it since. The feckless Harding would have required more attention had he not been so inherently complaisant. Wheeler's grip on the short leash he allowed Harding was so firm that when he wanted something from the president, Harding would respond with the eagerness of a puppy. When Wheeler objected to the pending Supreme Court appointment of Senator John K. Shields of Tennessee, who had voted for the Eighteenth Amendment but against the Volstead Act, Harding capitulated instantly. On one occasion, hoping "to see you briefly concerning some matters of mutual interest," Wheeler heard back from Harding by return mail: "I need not tell you," the president wrote, "that I will always try to make it possible to see you when you find occasion to call." Not that it was always a pleasant prospect for Harding. When Treasury Secretary Andrew Mellon announced his permissive interpretation of a particular Volstead Act provision, Harding parried Wheeler's speedy complaint with a doleful response: "Somehow," Harding wrote, "I had rather expected your letter."

But Wheeler never complained publicly about anything Harding did; to do so, wrote his ASL colleague Justin Steuart, "might be construed as evidence that he lacked influence with the administration." If so, that would have been virtually the only such evidence extant. When the president was about to appoint a chief Prohibition enforcement officer, the Harding administration took pains to assure Wheeler that "no one would be appointed for this position who was unacceptable" to the ASL. This was how the nation won the services of Roy A. Haynes of Ohio.

If you can judge a man by his friends, then Haynes could be convicted on the basis of the wild enthusiasm in his behalf displayed by Representative W. D. Upshaw of Georgia, the driest dry in the House. Upshaw had given himself the nickname "Earnest Willie." Having lost the use of his legs in an accident, he was also billed from time to time as "the orator on crutches" or "the Rolling Chair Evangelist." Sometimes he was called "the Georgia Cyclone."* He signed his mail "Yours very dry." A religious fundamentalist and political naïf, Upshaw was an object of perpetual mirth to wets, who loved to bait him, and of substantial consternation to the ASL, which couldn't control him. Said one league official, "No one questions Mr. Upshaw's sincerity, but he is ranting and intemperate." Indiscriminate, too: Upshaw's single-minded devotion to the Prohibition cause led him to support both the Ku Klux Klan and woman suffrage, believing that both abetted the dry movement. Even more avidly, he endorsed Roy Haynes's appointment as Prohibition commissioner. Upshaw applauded Haynes's "unsullied integrity" and "amazing genius and energy," and said "the story of [his] victories reads like a revised edition of the Acts of the Apostles, with *Scottish Chiefs* and the *Arabian Nights* thrown in."

Ranting, intemperate, indiscriminate—and, judging by his appraisal of Haynes, Upshaw was also either profoundly disingenuous or just plain stupid. Roy Haynes had three characteristics ("qualifications" would be a gross overstatement) that might have led Wheeler to choose him for the job of

---

*For a man who had been severely crippled at eighteen, this particular nickname was less counterintuitive than it might have appeared. According to one contemporary account, Upshaw possessed an uncanny ability to "move about without assistance when carried away while speaking by bursts of strong emotion and temper."

supervising a national force of federal agents. He had been editor of a daily newspaper in Hillsboro, Ohio, where Mother Thompson had launched her Crusade back in 1873. He was a Harding crony. And, crucially, he was willing to be the ASL's hand puppet—or, as the head of the New York State branch of the ASL called him, "Wheeler's special pet."

A large, doughy man whose sunny nature was as expansive as his waist and as predictable as the bow tie he wore every day, Haynes was convinced that leading the federal enforcement effort was a swell assignment. He seemed equally convinced that he was good at it. The evidence? In the first full year of prohibition, he said, church membership in the United States had grown by 1.2 million, and if that wasn't a sign of the nation's turn in a moral direction, what was? And how about the wonderful "fact" he cited the following year—that 85 percent of the nation's drinkers had sworn off the stuff since the dry regime began? This was an assertion so patently at odds with reality that critics found it as humorous as the admonitory fables Haynes liked to cite. Once, warning against the perils of bootleg liquor, he told the story of "a young woman on a Hoboken ferry-boat who took a drink from a flask carried in the pocket of her escort. Almost immediately, she staggered to the stern, plunged into the Hudson and was drowned." The lesson was clear, Haynes concluded: "Who drinks bootleg drinks with Death."

This sort of thing gave Haynes a second constituency beyond Wheeler, Upshaw, and other dry consuls—namely, vaudeville comedians who could get a laugh virtually by mentioning his name. These same satirists considered Haynes's boss, Secretary of the Treasury Andrew W. Mellon, less useful, which surely disappointed any dry with a sense of humor. The drys considered Mellon their most influential enemy, the one ranking member of the Harding administration least in sympathy with the ASL's goals, its methods, and its membership.

Mellon's Treasury Department housed Haynes's Prohibition Bureau and his field agents, just as it had always been home to the federal agents in the Bureau of Internal Revenue. Frequently described as the second- or third-richest man in the United States after John D. Rockefeller and perhaps Henry Ford, except when he was described as richer than either of them, Mellon was a man of refinement (his collection would become the foundation of the National Gallery of Art) and an austere, even forbidding manner. In addition to the powerful Mellon Bank of Pittsburgh, he controlled Gulf Oil, Alcoa Aluminum, a hefty chunk of U.S. Steel, and the Republican Party of Pennsylvania. He affected no interest in how he was perceived by the public—Mellon once asked a journalist "just why should the secretary be expected to talk to the reporters?"—except when he had something to hide. About to sue his wife for divorce in 1911, he first arranged to have the tame Pennsylvania legislature pass a law allowing the trial to proceed in private, before only a judge—no public, no reporters, not even a jury.

His son referred to Mellon's "ice-water smile," but even that chilly fac-
simile of gaiety rarely appeared in public. Taut and contained, his 145
pounds stretched over a nearly six-foot frame, his white hair and gray mustache offsetting a sharply angular, even cadaverous face, Mellon looked as if
he had been carved from chalky stone. And if the personal connection with
his flabby, backslapping Prohibition commissioner was hard to discern, the
philosophical bond between Mellon and Haynes was nonexistent. In fact,
that Andrew W. Mellon was secretary of the treasury to some extent revealed
how little Harding and his inner circle must have cared about enforcing the
Volstead Act. Mellon drank and didn't apologize for it. He made no apparent
effort to hide his disapproval of the law and the amendment that had
spawned it. He loathed the income tax and believed that the best means of
supporting what he believed should be very limited government were the
sharply regressive excise taxes of the sort that had once been levied on liquor,
beer, and wine. He even owned, with his brother Richard, a company that
was the pride of Westmoreland County, Pennsylvania, where the Whiskey
Rebellion had begun in 1794: the Old Overholt rye distillery.

Mellon had purchased his original one-third interest in Old Overholt
from his friend Henry Clay Frick in 1887 (Frick's maternal grandfather
Abraham Overholt, né Overholtzer, had founded the distillery in 1810).
The transaction could only have been an act of sport or love; the $25,000
that Mellon had paid Frick for his shares was small change for the Mellon
family. To the drys, though, it was palpable evidence of Mellon's unfitness
for running the federal department responsible for implementing the Volstead Act. When Mellon's impending appointment first became known,
William H. Anderson, the ASL's New York state superintendent, sent out
alarmed notice of his involvement in Old Overholt to hundreds of daily
newspapers. Senator Matthew M. Neely of West Virginia said that "a thief
will never enforce the law against larceny; a pyromaniac will never enforce
the law against arson; a distiller will never enforce the Volstead Act." But
for once even Wheeler was unable to persuade Harding to cleave to the
ASL catechism.

ANDREW MELLON CERTAINLY didn't set out with great enthusiasm to apply the
law. Even apart from his personal distaste for Prohibition, he considered the
Volstead Act extreme, impractical, and essentially unenforceable. The odd
thing was that Roy Haynes, his unlikely lieutenant, didn't entirely disagree.
Yes, the hymns he sang about increased churchgoing and other examples of
post-Volstead moral uplift may have been filled with assertions about the
decline of drink. But how could he justify keeping a force of twenty-five
hundred men in the field if there was no booze to chase down? Nobody
may have been drinking it, Haynes seemed to say, but for some reason
there was plenty of stuff out there.

The force Haynes commanded was inept and venal. Dry politicians had all but guaranteed this when they exempted enforcement agents from the job protections provided members of the civil service, asserting that it would be all too easy for a wet applicant to pass a civil service examination and then, once hired, subvert the law. Unflinching sympathy with the Volstead Act, drys insisted, was the most important qualification, both for getting an agent's job and for keeping it. The real sine qua non for any aspiring agent was endorsement by the ASL, which had added to its other assets the ripe fruits of political patronage. In most of the country hiring power effectively belonged to the ASL, in league with its congressional allies. The more upstanding national officers and state superintendents of the ASL may have earnestly desired a skilled national police force that would enforce the law, but earnestness (compounded by naïveté) was easily snuffed out by expedience. The league used enforcement jobs to reward their faithful troops; dry politicians went along to ensure their own incumbency; and together they guaranteed the bureau's corruption and incompetence.

Some prohibitionists did keep their hands clean. Senator George Norris of Nebraska, whose dryness was a direct extension of his righteously progressive principles, recognized the perils of a politicized appointment process and refused to have anything to do with selecting agents. Andrew Volstead claimed a similar position. But when Attorney General Daugherty (who also happened to be the president's chief political operative) declared that the civil service was a "hindrance to the government," as he told Congress in 1922, the signal was unmistakable. In the increasingly corrupt Harding administration, where political exigency was holy writ, the Prohibition Bureau became, as one historian of the civil service would describe it, "a chaos of spoils."

George Norris's Senate colleague John W. Harreld of Oklahoma was typical of congressional drys. Harreld openly admitted that his reelection prospects were directly tied to his ability to appoint the enforcement agents in his state, and he acted accordingly. But this was not a moral defect that afflicted only the drys. Many wet members of Congress were just as craven, as they took their all-you-can-eat turns at what the despairing Norris called "the political pie counter." Drys charged that the very wet representative Fiorello La Guardia of New York presided over appointments in his city, and the all-wet senatorial delegations from saturated New Jersey and soaking Maryland handed out enforcement jobs to the like-minded. An officer of the National Civil Service League suggested that, at least on this issue, wet and dry could come together not as enemies but as coconspirators: "The plain fact is that the congressmen wanted this plunder," he said.

DOCUMENTS

Moving Pictures Evoke Concern, 1922

Moving pictures, their educational influence for good or for bad, their growing importance as a factor in our civilization, the announced determination of those controlling the industry boldly to enter politics, and the desirability of regulation by law through censorship constitute a subject of acknowledged importance to the American people....

The motion picture is a great invention, and it has become a powerful factor for good or bad in our civilization. It has great educational power for good or bad. It may educate young people in the ways of good citizenship or in ways of dissoluteness, extravagance, wickedness, and crime. It furnishes recreation, diversion, and amusement at a cheap price to many millions of our people—largely the young. It is the only form of amusement within the means of millions. It possesses great potential possibilities for good. It may furnish not only amusement but education of a high order.

Through motion pictures the young and the old may see depicted every good motive, laudable ambition, commendable characteristic, ennobling trait of humanity. They may be taught that honesty is the best policy; that virtue and worth are rewarded; that industry leads to success. Those who live in the country or in small interior towns, and who never visit large cities, may see pictured the skyscrapers, the crowded streets, the rush and jam of metropolitan cities. Those who live in the interior, and never see the seacoast, may see on the screen the great docks and wharves of seaports and see the loading and unloading of giant ocean steamers. Those who live in crowded cities, and never see the country or get a glimpse of country life, may have depicted to them all the beauties of rural life and scenery. All may see scenes of the luxuriant Tropics, the grandeur of Alpine Mountains, polar conditions, life in the Orient. The cities, palaces, cathedrals, ports, rural life, daily routine, scenic attractions, mode of living of every country on the globe, may be brought to our doors and eyes for a small price. The industry may be made an education to the young.

However, from all accounts, the business has been conducted, generally speaking, upon a low plane and in a decidedly sordid manner. Those who own and control the industry seem to have been of the opinion that the sensual, the sordid, the prurient, the phases of fast life, the ways of extravagance, the risqué, the paths of shady life, drew the greatest attendance and coined for them the most money, and apparently they have been out to get the coin, no matter what the effect upon the public, young or old; and when

SOURCE: A speech by Senator Henry Myers, *Congressional Record*, June 29, 1922, 9655–57.

thoughtful people have suggested or advocated official censorship, in the interest of good citizenship and wholesome morals, the owners of the industry have resented it and, in effect, declared that it was nobody's business other than theirs and concerned nobody other than them what kind of shows they produced; that if people did not like their shows they could stay away from them; that it was their business, and they would conduct it as they might please. At least they have vigorously fought all attempts at censorship and resented them....

I have no doubt young criminals got their ideas of the romance of crime from moving pictures. I believe moving pictures are doing as much harm today as saloons did in the days of the open saloon—especially to the young. They are running day and night, Sunday and every other day, the year round, and in most jurisdictions without any regulation by censorship. I would not abolish them. They can be made a great force for good. I would close them on Sunday and regulate them week days by judicious censorship. Already some dozen or more States have censorship laws, with the right of appeal to the courts, and the movement is on in many other States.

When we look to the source of the moving pictures, the material for them, the personnel of those who pose for them, we need not wonder that many of the pictures are pernicious.

The pictures are largely furnished by such characters as Fatty Arbuckle, of unsavory fame, notorious for his scandalous debauchery and drunken orgies, one of which, attended by many "stars," resulted in the death of Virginia Rappe, a star artist; William Desmond Taylor, deceased, murdered for some mysterious cause; one Valentino, now figuring as the star character in rape and divorce sensations. Many others of like character might be mentioned.

At Hollywood, Calif., is a colony of these people, where debauchery, riotous living, drunkenness, ribaldry, dissipation, free love, seem to be conspicuous. Many of these "stars," it is reported, were formerly bartenders, butcher boys, sopers, swampers, variety actors and actresses, who may have earned $10 or $20 a week, and some of whom are now paid, it is said, salaries of something like $5,000 a month or more, and they do not know what to do with their wealth, extracted from poor people, in large part, in 25 or 50 cent admission fees, except to spend it in riotous living, dissipation, and "high rolling."

These are some of the characters from whom the young people of today are deriving a large part of their education, views of life, and character forming habits. From these sources our young people gain much of their views of life, inspiration, and education. Rather a poor source is it not? Looks like there is some need for censorship, does it not? There could be some improvement, could there not?...

"Does Jazz Put the Sin in Syncopation?" 1921

We have all been taught to believe that "music soothes the savage breast," but we have never stopped to consider that an entirely different type of music might invoke savage instincts. We have been content to accept all kinds of music, and to admit music in all its phases into our homes, simply because it was music. It is true that frequently father and mother have preferred some old favorite song or dance, or some aria from opera, to the last "best seller" which has found its way into the home circle; but, after all, young people must be entertained and amused, and even if the old-fashioned parents did not enjoy the dance music of the day, they felt it could really do no harm, because it was music.

Therefore, it is somewhat of a rude awakening for many of these parents to find that America is facing a most serious situation regarding its popular music. Welfare workers tell us that never in the history of our land have there been such immoral conditions among our young people, and in the surveys made by many organizations regarding these conditions, the blame is laid on jazz music and its evil influence on the young people of to-day. Never before have such outrageous dances been permitted in private as well as public ballrooms, and never has there been used for the accompaniment of the dance such a strange combination of tone and rhythm as that produced by the dance orchestras of to-day.

Certainly, if this music is in any way responsible for the condition and for the immoral acts which can be traced to the influence of these dances, then it is high time that the question should be raised: "Can music every be an influence for evil?"

The Rebellion

In history there have been several great periods when music was declared to be an evil influence, and certain restrictions were placed upon the dance and the music which accompanied it. But all of these restrictions were made by the clergy, who have never been particularly enthusiastic about dancing anyway. Today, however, the first great rebellion against jazz music and such dances as the "toddle" and the "shimmy" comes from the dancing masters themselves. Realizing the evil influence of this type of music and dancing, the National Dancing Masters' Association, at their last session, adopted this rule: "Don't permit vulgar cheap jazz music to be played. Such music almost forces dancers to use jerky half-steps, and invites immoral variations. It is useless to expect to find refined dancing when the

SOURCE: Anne Shaw Faulkner, *"Does jazz Put the Sin in Syncopation?" Ladies Home Journal*, August 1921, pp. 16–17.

music lacks all refinement, for, after all, what is dancing but an interpretation of music?"

Several of the large dance halls in the big cities are following the lead of the proprietor of one of them in Chicago, who, when he opened his establishment a few years ago, bravely advertised that no jazz music and no immoral dances would be allowed on his floor. His announcement was met with ridicule, but his dance hall has become the most popular one in Chicago. The place is crowded every evening, and yet nothing except waltzes and two-steps are allowed on the floor and absolutely no jazz music is tolerated.

That jazz is an influence for evil is also felt by a number of the biggest country clubs, which have forbidden the corset check room, the leaving of the hall between dances and the jazz orchestras—three evils which have also been eliminated from many municipal dance halls, particularly when these have been taken under the chaperonage of the Women's Clubs.

Still another proof that jazz is recognized as producing an evil effect is the fact that in almost every big industry where music has been instituted it has been found necessary to discontinue jazz because of its demoralizing effect upon the workers. This was noticed in an unsteadiness and lack of evenness in the workmanship of the product after a period when the workmen had indulged in jazz music....

Chapter 10

The Depression Years

A line of unemployed men awaiting a free meal at a Chicago soup kitchen, a sight common throughout urban America during the Great Depression.

The crusades against changing morals and manners during the 1920s seem trivial when compared to the challenges of the Great Depression of the 1930s. Although the United States had suffered economic declines before, the Great Depression was the worst ever. Nearly a quarter of the workforce was unemployed by 1933, banks failed, the stock market crashed, businesses declared bankruptcy, and families lost their homes and farms. All sections of the nation were affected by the slide of the economy. And in the early years there were no New Deal programs to help individuals in their plight.

In the essay from Timothy Egan's book *The Worst Hard Time*, the author takes the reader to one town, Dalhart, in the Texas panhandle. Here was a community that enjoyed good times during the 1920s, years when farmers were encouraged to plant more crops in order to reap the rewards of high demand for their products. Then came the crash of 1929 and the failure of the First National Bank of Dalhart in 1931. Why was the bank crash such a disaster for the citizens of Dalhart? How did the people of Dalhart respond to the bank failure?

Another theme emerging from *The Worst Hard Time* is that of heightened prejudice. Many people looked for easy scapegoats and found them in Jews and blacks. Blacks and Jews clearly were not the cause of the hard times, but that fact was ignored by those seeking solutions to the difficulties they faced. How did market prices and nature itself add to woes of Dalhart's people?

One response to the crisis in this Texas town was to leave to find a better life elsewhere. Today we think of California as a land of sunshine and wealth. Indeed, after World War II millions of Americans, as well as many immigrants, set out for California in pursuit of the good life. Many of those heading for the Golden State during the depression years were Okies—farmers from Texas, Oklahoma, and elsewhere on the southern plains—who were driven from their homes by poverty and great clouds of dust. John Steinbeck's novel *The Grapes of Wrath* brought the plight of these dust bowl refugees to the attention of the public, as did the writings of political activist Carey McWilliams. The first document, a statement by McWilliams before a congressional committee, describes the conditions facing the Okies in California. That the Okies continued to flock to and remain in California reveals the desperate situation from which they fled. Why did they choose California as the place to rebuild their lives?

The final documents point to the hardships elsewhere. In Chicago hundreds of women became homeless when they lost their jobs. In New York the police arrested a civil engineer for vagrancy. What do these stories reveal about the scope and intensity of the Great Depression?

ESSAY

The Worst Hard Time

Timothy Egan

The First National Bank of Dalhart did not open for business on June 27, 1931. The doors were locked, the shades down. People banged on the windows and demanded answers—this was their money, not the bank's. *Open the door!* A sign said the bank was insolvent. *Thieves!* The same day, the temperature reached 112 degrees, the hottest in the short history of Dalhart. The villainous sun and the starved bank did not seem related—yet.

People slumped against the side of the building, in the oppressive shade, wondering, *What now?* Nearly two years into the Depression, the town was taking on a meaner edge, more desperate, like the rest of the country. What started on Wall Street twenty months earlier now hit the High Plains, a domino of distrust. The more things unraveled, the more it seemed like the entire boom of the previous decade had been helium.

Doc Dawson had money in the failed bank. He was approaching sixty and was worried about his future. Social Security did not yet exist. He had no pension. People owed him money from way back. Patients had offered him chickens, venison, old cars. Usually, he waved it off. The Doc looked strong, usually, but it had been a struggle to overcome his own infirmities. Bright's disease. Tuberculosis. Asthma. He didn't need much sleep, running from operation to operation, the spittoon by his side, the black Stetson atop his head. He trained himself to relax at intervals, nearly shutting his body down, and through this method he said he could go days without a normal man's sleep. It was easier to do when his labors were not so physical. Since giving up the sanitarium, he had become a full-time farmer. The work caught up with him. He felt sharp pains running up his arm, and then the lightheadedness and trouble getting his breath—a heart attack. During a month of recuperation, he took stock of his life. It boiled down to the land; he had to make the dirt work for him. But on the day the First National failed, with the temperature at 112 degrees, his fields looked dry as chalkboard.

A crowd formed outside the office of the new sheriff, Harvey Foust. They wanted him to force the bank to open. Use your power to get our money back, they said. Denrock was full of angry people, blocking the street. The fear spread with fresh rumors. Late in the day, the crowd's mood turned ugly; they went from citizens to a mob, and the heat made it like the worst kind of sweat-soaked nightmare: *Knock the bank door down! It's our money! Where did it go?* Bank accounts were not backed by anything but the good name of the people who ran the bank. And too many of them saw the personal savings of High Plains nesters as just another source of cash for the stock market or an ill-conceived business loan. No matter the exact cause: the First National was broke.

Sheriff Foust tried to calm the mob. There wasn't much he could do; it was a federal matter. But the national government could not do anything either. Deposits were uninsured. In one month alone—November 1930— 256 banks failed. The question grew louder, a demand now: *where did our money go?* The mob turned on Foust: was he afraid to do his job? They'd been robbed by the First National. *Do something!*

Foust did not seem himself of late. People saw him drinking, his words slurring, even at midday. He talked to himself, withdrew quickly, didn't look people in the eyes. Just a year earlier, Foust—then a deputy—was a hero. He was serving a warrant along with Sheriff Lon Alexander on a pair of low-level bootleggers, Spud and Ron Dellinger. At the Dellinger house, Spud fired at the sheriff, killing him with a single bullet to the brain. Foust had waited outside. When he heard gunshots, he stormed into the shack, his revolver drawn. Spud's brother lunged for the deputy. As the deputy and the bootlegger struggled, Ron's wife entered the shack with a shotgun. Foust broke away and fired at the wife, then at Ron Dellinger. He turned to a corner and got off a third shot, this one at Spud. Three shots: one killed Spud, the other killed his brother Ron, and the third wounded the wife. A week later, Foust was made sheriff. But he was a haunted man, second-guessing himself.

One block from the bank, at the DeSoto Hotel, Uncle Dick Coon tried to keep spirits up, telling the same jokes, saying failure was not going to drag Dalhart down. People thought Uncle Dick kept his dough in a mattress or a ditch out back. Big shots and paupers did the same thing. Senator "Cotton Ed" Smith of South Carolina hauled all his money around in a belt that never left his waist. Dick had his poker face on and not just for the card game. He was in trouble. The properties he had picked up after the crash were not paying rent. He knew the tenants and sympathized with their plight. Business was dead. People had stopped buying cars, clothes, hats, bicycles, even basics. Once the fear started and the wave of collapse started to spread, it was hard to let a buck go, because there might not be one to replace it. Usually, a few wildcatters could be counted on to throw money around when everyone else had closed their wallets. But oil had fallen from $1.43 a barrel to a dime. A dime! Nothing was moving. The economy was a pool of glue. The wildcatters fled as quickly as they had arrived. Dick had his hundred-dollar bill, of course. To his friends, though, he seemed worried. They could see through his poker face. The man had survived the Galveston hurricane, for Christ's sake. At Galveston, he ran a casino, and he lost it all—money, the building, all washed away. More than six thousand had died, so Uncle Dick did not mourn the paper money buried by rampaging sea and eighty-mile-an-hour winds. He knew poverty and he knew death in their worst forms. But like everyone in the summer of 1931, he had the jitters. Dalhart was sick, acting like a dog with rabies, and that mob outside the bank: what would they turn on next? Uncle Dick's namesake, the Coon Building, was empty, sitting like a hobo on the street right across the way from the DeSoto. And the hotel business had slowed to a crawl, people no longer pouring into Dalhart looking to strike oil or hit a crop.

In Dalhart's grim decline, the Number 126 house flourished. The girls were not afraid of showing it, either. The house had more girls than they could use and a fiddler, Jess Morris, who played with his band on Saturday nights until dawn. The Number 126 kept some commerce in Dalhart going: the girls getting their hair tinted and coiffed, buying new clothes, the mustard-colored house always in need of fresh blinds, new sheets, furniture. The owner, Lil Walker, drove a pink Cadillac—the nicest car in three counties.

She would pile her new girls in the car, dressed to the nines, their hair up like Mae West, and cruise past the crumbling empire of Uncle Dick. The girls waved and shouted yoo-hoo, leaving a trail of perfume.

It steamed John L. McCarty, sitting in his editor's office at the *Texan*, working to keep alive the Dalhart vision. The town had nearly eight thousand people now, almost double what it was ten years ago. In McCarty's mind, it would double again by the end of the 1930s. But Dalhart needed to be slapped to its senses time and again, and it was the job of the loudest voice in the Panhandle to do just that. McCarty could not stand that the one business still thriving in Dalhart was the whorehouse. It was time to drive Mrs. Walker and her pink Cadillac out of Dallam County, out of the Panhandle, out of Texas. McCarty prepared the front page of the *Texan* with a searing exposé, a write-up on the doings at the Number 126, and how it was a moral abomination to have these hookers parading around in a pink Caddy when Dalhart limped along, the Coon Building empty and people no longer showing up with suitcases and ambition to spare.

"SO THE PEOPLE MAY KNOW" was his headline for the next day's *Texan*. When he took the page dummy to the shop, his printer shook his head. He refused to print it. The printer had lived in Dalhart since its creation and he knew the Number 126 like people knew Rita Blanca Canyon south of town. McCarty was indignant. This whorehouse was a sore on the face of Dalhart; it had to go. It was one thing to be invisible at the edge of town but another to flash and parade painted women and their dresses and the pink Caddy. Sorry, Mr. McCarty, the printer said. Can't do it. Won't do it. We need them girls. McCarty pulled his story.

As the ranks of the jobless grew, they took to the rails, going from town to town, dodging Rock Island bulls in the south, Burlington Northern bulls in the other direction, swapping stories about places where the sun shined and a man might still get paid for a day's work. Two million Americans were living as nomads. They were not long-time drifters, most of them, according to reporters who had spent some time on the trains. They were family men, farmers and factory hands, merchants, some professionals among them, writers and bank clerks and storeowners—all broke, people who could not stand to see their kids in rags, hungry. When they arrived in Dalhart— sometimes as many as eighty people a day—at the railroad crossroads that could lead a man north to Denver, west to Santa Fe, or east to Kansas City, Sheriff Foust was supposed to put them back on the train. And if they were black, they weren't even supposed to step off the tracks, or he could arrest them for vagrancy. The penalty for "vag" was stiff: four months on a chain gang, doing hard labor. In September 1929, just over 1.5 million people were out of work; by February of the following year, the number had tripled. The economy was not fatally ill, President Hoover said; Americans had simply lost their confidence.

"All the evidences indicate that the worst effects of the crash on unemployment will have passed during the next sixty days," Hoover said on March 3, 1930.

By the end of that year, eight million people were out of work. The banking system was in chaos. The big financial institutions had once looked invincible, with the stone fronts, the copper lights, the marbled floors, run by the best people in town. Now bankers were seen as crooks, fraud artists who took people's homes, their farms, and their savings. In 1930, 1,350 banks failed, going under with $853 million in deposits. The next year, 2,294 banks went bust. At the end of 1931 came the biggest failure of all—the collapse of the Bank of the United States in New York. When the Bank of the United States folded, it had deposits of two hundred million dollars. Fittingly, the bank's biggest office was next to Union Cigar, the company whose president had committed suicide after the stock fell from $103 to $4 in a day. When the bank failed, twelve million people were without jobs—25 percent of the work force. Never before had so many people been thrown off payrolls so quickly, with no prospects and no safety net. Never before had so many people been without purpose, direction, or money.

In Dalhart, with the First National shuttered and downtown merchants unable to pay city taxes, John McCarty now worried about the survival of his paper. The *Texan* had been his before his thirtieth birthday. He had taken it from a weekly to a daily, and circulation growth had been robust. The paper would grow into a great daily only if Dalhart kept reaching for legroom. McCarty begged his advertisers to stick with him. He presented a new strategy for survival: he would emphasize good news. Good news? In the worst depression in history. Good news? When stacks of grain rotted near the railroad. Good news? When the land was starting to dry and crack with a spell of drought that had become more than a curiosity. It sounded preposterous. But from here on out, McCarty would only see the omelet in the broken eggs. A bank collapse was an opportunity. A store closing was a competitive advantage. A death was not nearly as important as a birth. As for the heat wave: it's the golden sun at its best. Other states would kill for it. He got the Mission Theater, the grocery store, a couple of lawyers, and Uncle Dick to keep advertising. And he leaned on Herzstein's, the clothing store that gave people in Dalhart something to dream about.

Some people said Jews were to blame for the bad times—that they did not belong in this country, a place where the *Texan* had boasted that its citizens were "of the highest type of Anglo-Saxon ancestry." In Nebraska, four thousand people gathered on the capitol steps, blaming the "Jewish system of banking" for the implosion of the economy. They held banners with rattlesnakes, labeled as Jews, coiled around the American farmer. Father Charles E. Coughlin, the mellow-voiced radio priest from Detroit, also blamed Jews for America's stumbles as he spoke to a weekly audience of more than a million listeners. Often, he would read the names of Hollywood movie stars and then "out" them, revealing their original Jewish names as if detailing a sinister plot.

Herzstein's filled a need in Dalhart, Boise City, and across the line at their headquarters of Clayton, New Mexico, and the fact that they were Jews in the Anglo prairie was secondary. Their customers let them be. Their sign read: "HERZSTEIN READY TO WEAR." The idea of buying a complete outfit— or even a shirt or pair of pants—that came fully stitched to size was novel. Most people bought bolts of material and sewed their own clothes. In the early years of the Depression, people made clothes from burlap potato sacks, the labels still printed on them, or tore out the seat covers from junked cars and refashioned them as something to wear. Herzstein's slashed prices below their break-even point. McCarty convinced the family to run a small ad, once a week: "new shirts, two for three dollars." But they were bleeding money like everybody else, falling further behind, looking at a growing mountain of unpaid bills. In 1931, over 28,000 businesses failed; it did not matter if they were family run institutions or big corporations, they were sucked under by the same force. Money did not circulate. Those who had jobs saw their wages collapse by a third or more. The average factory worker, lucky to be still drawing a paycheck, went from earning twenty-four dollars a week just before the collapse to sixteen dollars a week in the early thirties.

Relatives from Philadelphia would visit the Herzsteins and wonder why they held on in land so foreign, so full of cowboy twang, wildcatter bluster, and two-fisted Christianity. But the family had been in the High Plains longer than anyone in Dalhart or Boise City, and they were here to stay. As the first Jewish family in the High Plains, they had spilled blood in this land. Their struggle, their despairs and triumphs, were as tied to the hard brown flatland as anybody's. The Herzsteins had come west over the Santa Fe Trail with the first group of Jews in New Mexico—Spiegelbergs, Zeckendorfs, Floersheims, and Bibos among them—beginning in the late 1840s. In New Mexico, they found an open world: cultures of old Spain, Indians from the pueblos, and Yankee traders. The light was different. The landscape was unreal. And socially, it was unlike the layered, segregated world of the East or old Europe. One of the Jews, Solomon Bibo, married into an Indian family in Acoma, a pueblo on a high mesa that is the oldest continuously inhabited town in the United States. Bibo even became governor of Acoma, known as the Sky City, a thousand-year-old community.... Simon [Herzstein] traveled the High Plains selling fine clothes to nesters, cowpunchers, and their wives. When people would ask him what a Jew was doing peddling stiff collars in No Man's Land, he said he was doing the same as anybody else, only taking a different route. He let people buy on credit and never kept a ledger. It was all in his head. He knew they would pay. He loved baseball, poker, and bridge. He loved throwing big dinner parties, giving [his wife] Maude something to take her mind off the wind and the empty skies. And he loved the West, the freshness of it all, the Indians who came into town to trade from Navajo lands, the sons and daughters of Comancheros, who could match Simon story for story.

When the banks closed and people scrounged for food, Simon Herzstein kept up with the well-told jokes and the optimism, never letting on that he had his own troubles. As businesses folded in Dalhart, Clayton, and Boise City, the triangle of towns at the center of the High Plains, the Herzsteins fell further behind. The town of Dalhart went after Simon Herzstein, claiming in foreclosure papers that he had not paid his taxes in more than a year. Dick Coon owned the property, and he now consulted his lawyer about what to do about the only man on the High Plains trying to keep people dressed to match their lost dignity.

As Dalhart collapsed, people in other parts of the Panhandle kept their faith, looking to the upcoming harvest of 1931 to rescue them. Sure, the First National was gone, all that money vaporized in the prairie heat, but these folks had something more lasting: they had land, and from this land came food. People *were* starving now in parts of the United States, despite what Hoover had said and despite the song that played in the background, Rudy Vallee's "Life Is Just a Bowl of Cherries." American families were reduced to eating dandelions and foraging for blackberries in Arkansas, where the drought was going on two years. And over in the mountains of the Carolinas and West Virginia, a boy told the papers his family members took turns eating, each kid getting a shot at dinner every fourth night. In New York, nearly half a million people were on city relief, getting up to eight dollars a month to live on.

But here on the High Plains—look at this wheat in the early summer of 1931: it was pouring out of threshers, piling high once again, gold and fat, and so much of it that it formed hillocks bigger than any tuft of land in Dallam County, Texas. On the Texas Panhandle, two million acres of sod had been turned now—a 300 percent increase over ten years ago. Up in Baca County, two hundred thousand acres. In Cimarron County, Oklahoma, another quarter million acres. The wheat came in just as the government had predicted—a record, in excess of 250 million bushels nationwide. The greatest agricultural accomplishment in the history of tilling the land, some called it. The tractors had done what no hailstorm, no blizzard, no tornado, no drought, no epic siege of frost, no prairie fire, nothing in the natural history of the southern plains had ever done. They had removed the native prairie grass, a web of perennial species evolved over twenty thousand years or more, so completely that by the end of 1931 it was a different land—thirty-three million acres stripped bare in the southern plains.

And what came from that transformed land—the biggest crop of all time— was shunned, met with the lowest price ever. The market held at nearly 50 percent below the amount it cost farmers to grow the grain. By the measure of money—which was how most people viewed success or failure on the land—the whole experiment of trying to trick a part of the country into being something it was never meant to be was a colossal failure. Every five bushels of wheat brought in from the fields was another dollar taken out of a farmer's pocket.

The grain toasted under the hot sun. With the winds, the heat gathered strength; it chased people into their cellars all day, and it made them mean. Their throats hurt. Their skin cracked. Their eyes itched. The blast furnace was a fact of summer life, as the Great Plains historian Walter Prescott Webb said, causing rail lines to expand and warp. "A more common effect is that these hot winds render people irritable and incite nervousness," he wrote. The land hardened. Rivers that had been full in spring trickled down to a string line of water and then disappeared. That September was the warmest yet in the still-young century. Bam White scanned the sky for a "sun dog," his term for a halo that foretold of rain; he saw nothing through the heat of July, August, and September. He noticed how the horses were lethargic, trying to conserve energy. Usually, when the animals bucked or stirred, it meant a storm on the way. They had been passive for some time now, in a summer when the rains left and did not come back for nearly eight years....

Drifters, lunatics, and bankrupt shopkeepers filled the courtrooms in Dalhart. On many days, the slow grinding of the law against people who could no longer stay afloat was the only business in town. Uncle Dick Coon took title to a pool hall that was one of the oldest hangouts in town, foreclosing on a debt of $612. The court awarded Coon four pool tables, four domino tables, twelve chairs, five cue racks, four sets of dominoes, and two cigar cases. Banks foreclosed on red bulls and black steers, on tractors, combines, water tanks, windmills, light fixtures. Simon Herzstein tried but could not find a way to reopen his store in town. By 1935, Herzstein was three years behind on city taxes. He had stayed open through days when not a single shirt sold before finally calling it quits. After Herzstein was foreclosed on $242 in back taxes, the City of Dalhart had title to a piece of space long occupied by the leading clothier on the southern plains. It became another empty hole in a sagging town.

The sign at the edge of Dalhart—"BLACK MAN DON'T LET THE SUN GO DOWN ON YOU HERE"—was strictly enforced. In February, a norther came through the High Plains, sending the mercury plummeting to seven degrees. The hazy, arctic air hung on for a week. When two black men got off the train in Dalhart, hungry and nearly hypothermic, they looked around for something to eat and a place to get warm. They found a door open in a shed at the train depot. Inside was some food and shelter from a cold so painful it burned their hands and feet like a blowtorch.

"TWO NEGROES ARRESTED:" the *Dalhart Texan* reported how the men, aged nineteen and twenty-three, had sniffed around the train station, looking for food. They were cuffed, locked up in the county jail, and after a week brought out for arraignment before a justice of the peace, Hugh Edwards. The judge ordered the men to dance. The men hesitated; this was supposed to be a bond hearing. The railroad agent said these men were good for nothing but Negro toe-tapping. The judge smiled; he said he wanted to see it.

"Tap dance," Edwards told the men.

"Here?"

"Yes. Before the court."

The men started to dance, forced silly grins on their faces, reluctant. After the tap dance, the judge banged his gavel and ordered the men back to jail for another two months.

As the ground took flight through the middle years of the Dirty Thirties, the courts had to contend with a new type of mental illness—the person driven mad by dust. Texas, like most states, had a civil procedure for committing people to involuntary confinement in a state institution. County courts had jurisdiction. A young judge, Wilson Cowen, impaneled a jury of six to hear a story that was common on the High Plains: a young woman found wandering the streets, muttering incoherent pleas. Cowen was deeply troubled by these insanity trials. He had been elected in the summer of 1934, despite his youth (he had just turned thirty) and his inexperience (he had been in Dalhart for only five years). While running for judge, Cowen roamed all over Dallam County and saw firsthand how the dirt-packed winds were taking the life out of the place. He drove for days without seeing a single green thing. He saw farmhouses without a chicken or cow. He saw children in rags, their parents too frightened of dust pneumonia to send them to school, huddling in shacks shaped into wavy formations on the prairie, almost indistinguishable from the dunes....

DOCUMENTS

The Okies in California, 1939

The most characteristic of all housing in California in which migrants reside at the moment is the shacktown or cheap subdivision. Most of these settlements have come into existence since 1933 and the pattern which obtains is somewhat similar throughout the State. Finding it impossible to rent housing in incorporated communities on their meager incomes, migrants

SOURCE: Carey McWilliams, testimony from U.S. Congress, House Select Committee to Investigate the Interstate Migration of Destitute Citizens, *Hearings*, 76th Cong., 3d sess., 1941, 2543–44.

have created a market for a very cheap type of subdivision of which the following may be taken as being representative:

In Monterey County, according to a report of Dr. D. M. Bissell, county health officer, under date of November 28, 1939, there are approximately three well-established migrant settlements. One of these, the development around the environs of Salinas, is perhaps the oldest migrant settlement of its type in California. In connection with this development I quote a paragraph of the report of Dr. Bissell:

"This area is composed of all manners and forms of housing without a public sewer system. Roughly, 10,000 persons are renting or have established homes there. A chief element in this area is that of refugees from the Dust Bowl who inhabit a part of Alisal called Little Oklahoma. Work in lettuce harvesting and packing and sugar beet processing have attracted these people who, seeking homes in Salinas without success because they aren't available, have resorted to makeshift adobes outside the city limits. Complicating the picture is the impermeable substrata which makes septic tanks with leaching fields impractical. Sewer wells have resulted with the corresponding danger to adjacent water wells and to the water wells serving the Salinas public. Certain districts, for example, the Airport Tract and parts of Alisal, have grown into communities with quite satisfactory housing, but others as exemplified by the Graves district are characterized by shacks and lean-tos which are unfit for human habitation."…

Typical of the shacktown problem are two such areas near the city limits of Sacramento, one on the east side of B Street, extending from Twelfth Street to the Sacramento city dump and incinerator; and the other so-called Hoovertown, adjacent to the Sacramento River and the city filtration plant. In these two areas there were on September 17, 1939, approximately 650 inhabitants living in structures that, with scarcely a single exception, were rated by the inspectors of this division as "unfit for human occupancy." The majority of the inhabitants were white Americans, with the exception of 50 or 60 Mexican families, a few single Mexican men, and a sprinkling of Negroes. For the most part they are seasonally employed in the canneries, the fruit ranches, and the hop fields of Sacramento County. Most of the occupants are at one time or another upon relief, and there are a large number of occupants in these shacktowns from the Dust Bowl area. Describing the housing, an inspector of this division reports:

"The dwellings are built of brush, rags, sacks, boxboard, odd bits of tin and galvanized iron, pieces of canvas and whatever other material was at hand at the time of construction."

Wood floors, where they exist, are placed directly upon the ground, which because of the location of the camps with respect to the Sacramento River, is damp most of the time. To quote again from the report:

"Entire families, men, women, and children, are crowed into hovels, cooking and eating in the same room. The majority of the shacks have no sinks or cesspools for the disposal of kitchen drainage, and this, together with garbage and other refuse, is thrown on the surface of the ground."

Because of the high-water table, cesspools, where they exist, do not function properly; there is a large overflow of drainage and sewage to the surface of the ground. Many filthy shack latrines are located within a few feet of living quarters. Rents of the houses in these shacktowns range from $3 to $20 a month. In one instance a landlord rents ground space for $1.50 to $5 a month, on which tenants are permitted to erect their own dugouts. The Hooverville section is composed primarily of tents and trailers, there being approximately 125 tent structures in this area on September 17, 1939. Both areas are located in unincorporated territory. They are not subject at the present time to any State or county building regulation. In Hooverville, at the date of the inspection, many families were found that did not have even a semblance of tents or shelters. They were cooking and sleeping on the ground in the open and one water tap at an adjoining industrial plant was found to be the source of the domestic water supply for the camp....

Homeless Women Sleep in Chicago Parks, 1931

CHICAGO, SEPT. 19 (AP).—Several hundred homeless unemployed women sleep nightly in Chicago's parks, Mrs. Elizabeth A. Conkey, Commissioner of Public Welfare, reported today.

She learned of the situation, she said, when women of good character appealed for shelter and protection, having nowhere to sleep but in the parks, where they feared that they would be molested.

"We are informed that no fewer than 200 women are sleeping in Grant and Lincoln Parks, on the lake front, to say nothing of those in the other parks," said Mrs. Conkey. "I made a personal investigation, driving from park to park, at night, and verified the reports."

The commissioner said the approach of Winter made the problem more serious, with only one free women's lodging house existing, accommodating 100.

A Vagrant Civil Engineer, 1932

A heavily bearded man in a faded brown suit, who said he was a graduate of the University of Colorado and had held responsible positions as a civil engineer in this country, China, Panama and the jungles of Venezuela, was arraigned yesterday on a charge of vagrancy in Flatbush Court, where he

SOURCE: *The New York Times*, September 20, 1931.

SOURCE: "A Vagrant Civil Engineer," from *The New York Times*, May 4, 1932. Copyright © 1932 by The New York Times. All rights reserved. Used by permission and protected by the copyright laws of the United States. The printing, copyright, redistribution, or retransmission of the Content without express written permission is prohibited.

told such a dramatic and straightforward story of his experiences that he held the attention of the crowded courtroom for nearly an hour. Magistrate Eilperin adjourned the case until Friday so that a thorough investigation could be made.

The defendant said he was Langlan Heinz, 44 years old. He was arrested at 4 A.M. by a policeman who found him sleeping on an improvised cot in a vacant lot near Flatbush Avenue, between Fillmore Avenue and Avenue R, Brooklyn. Heinz said he had made this lot his home for forty-six days.

In a well-modulated voice, Heinz began the recital of his experiences by saying that he was born in Dodge City, Kan., had received his early schooling there and then had entered the University of Colorado from which he was graduated with a Bachelor of Science degree in 1911. He worked in various parts of the country as a civil engineer until 1921, when he came to New York City and worked for the city for seven years as a structural draftsman....

Chapter 11

World War II

Homefront workers, both men and women, contribute to the war effort.

The New Deal exerted an enormous impact on American society. For the embattled farmers and workers and their families described in the previous chapter, the federal government offered relief, mortgage aid, crop payments, and even employment—programs that helped to restore the nation's flagging morale and maintain the people's faith in their government and economic system.

Yet as dramatic and innovative as the New Deal was, World War II brought even more upheavals in the lives of Americans. Nearly 15 million men and women found themselves serving in the armed forces, and the government intervened in an unprecedented way in the economy. Rationing of such products as butter, meat, sugar, and gasoline was introduced, and war contracts, initiated as early as 1939, stimulated the manufacture of millions of uniforms and the production of hundreds of thousands of ships, airplanes, tanks, and pieces of military equipment. While millions served in the army, navy, air corps, and marines, many civilians flocked to urban centers to work in the booming military economy.

William O'Neill's essay "The People Are Willing" describes numerous changes unfolding during this period, changes that enabled the United States to outproduce its enemies and win the war. But as O'Neill notes, innovations did not always come easily. What does he identify as the major challenges in uniting the American people and its economic system behind the war effort? How does he account for the many difficulties and government "bungling," especially in the early days of the war? Finally, how did the nation eventually achieve both full production and unity of purpose?

The first document, an excerpt from the U.S. Department of Labor's Women's Bureau, gives one reason for America's huge wartime production: during the war, women worked in many job formerly barred to them. Thus the labor shortage created by the induction of millions of men (and some women) into the armed services was relieved by women who entered the labor force. The economy could therefore produce both war goods and consumer items.

In spite of dislocations on the homefront, most Americans found that their standard of living improved during the war years. For Japanese Americans on the West Coast, however, this was not the case. Native-born American citizens of Japanese ancestry as well as Japanese immigrants were interned in virtual concentration camps, an imprisonment ordered by President Franklin Roosevelt and sanctioned by the United States Supreme Court on the ground of national security. The second document, a government report issued in 1984 about the wartime internment of civilians, describes some of the conditions encountered by these unfortunate Americans. In 1942, Earl Warren, then attorney general of California, responded to questions regarding the civil rights of Japanese Americans by stating, "I believe, sir, that in time of war every citizen must give up some of his normal rights." Even accepting this premise, does it justify the treatment that Japanese Americans received, as described in the document?

Your answer to the above question may be affected by reading the final document, extracted from the obituary of Barney Hajiro, who served with the 442nd Regimental Combat Team during World War II. What does the document reveal about the consequences of the hysteria that often accompanies the outbreak of war? Given their treatment by the national and state governments, how do you account for the patriotism and courage displayed by the Japanese American soldiers?

ESSAY

⸺•◆•⸺

The People Are Willing

William O'Neill

After Pearl Harbor a flood of volunteers overwhelmed recruiting offices, especially in the South. When the entire Lepanto, Arkansas, football team joined the Navy, one member attempted suicide after failing to pass his physical. "I was afraid folks would think I was yellow because I didn't get into the service," he explained. Millions who were ineligible to serve wished to know what civilians could do to further the war effort....

Most Americans believed that government did not need to be overly effective because the people themselves could manage. While they overstated its benefits, voluntarism was a fact of life, and Americans were capable— within limits—of doing what elsewhere were functions of government. This attribute manifested itself immediately after Pearl Harbor. Agencies like the Red Cross and local civilian defense offices were overwhelmed with offers to help. Because many commodities would soon be scarce, scrap drives were organized that collected not only rubber items but paper, fats, bones, a wide variety of metal goods, and other essential materials.

Towns convened meetings to discuss ways of aiding the war effort. Citizens' committees sprang up. Neighborhoods organized. When a Milwaukee air-raid warden could not afford a telephone, the other families on his block agreed to donate 10 cents a month apiece so he could subscribe to the service. In Chicago, 23,000 block captains were sworn in at a mass ceremony by the head of the Office of Civilian Defense. West Coast hospitals reeled before waves of enthusiastic blood donors. The hottest literary property of 1942 was the Red Cross first aid manual, which, though not considered a book and therefore omitted from best seller lists, sold 8 million copies. Farmers began plowing at night in order to put their spring crops in early. Shipyard employees in San Francisco offered to work Sundays for free. That summer an event called The National Salvage Fair was held in New York as part of a campaign to establish Salvage Sewing Workrooms in which volunteers could use mill ends and scraps of cloth to make garments for the needy and establish a clothing reserve.

Though very much in the American grain, efforts such as these suffered from the limitations intrinsic to thousands of uncoordinated local schemes, often inspired by an excess of willing hands rather than any clear sense of

SOURCE: From DEMOCRACY AT WAR: America's Fight at Home and Abroad in World War II by William O'Neill. Copyright © 1992 by William O'Neill. Reprinted with the permission of Free Press, a Division of Simon & Schuster, Inc. All rights reserved.

183

purpose. By summer *Life* was overflowing with complaints. Congress was not doing a good job. Neither were the people. All the powerful interest groups continued to pursue their own agendas. Every scrap campaign had failed, the rubber drive most of all. People were still motoring frivolously. Washington was asking too little, and getting what it asked for. Everyone was living their dream of a "Hollywood war," instead of facing up to the real one in which sacrifices would have to be made.

These complaints were well founded. In 1941 when aluminum was in short supply, the call went out for housewives to turn in their pots and pans. Ten thousand tons of aluminum would build 4,000 fighter planes was what they were told. Obedient to duty's call, women stripped their kitchens and donated 70,000 tons of aluminum, apparently solving the problem. It transpired that only virgin aluminum was suitable for aircraft, so the donated cookware gathered dust until it was finally sold to scrap dealers. Then the stuff was turned into new pots and pans, women buying back what they had previously given.

More serious than bungling was government's reluctance to take full advantage of civilian support for the war effort, especially that of women. The public was encouraged to buy war bonds and practice conservation. Otherwise, it often seemed as if Washington did not want public participation in national defense, which had been the case before Pearl Harbor. In January 1941 one of Dr. Gallup's polls had revealed that 67 percent of those questioned were willing "to spend one hour each day training for home guard, nursing, first aid work, ambulance driving," and similar activities.

Though officials frequently remarked on the gravity of the world situation and the need to prepare for hardships, they seldom took their own advice. When asked what people could do, Frank Bane, Chief of the National Defense Advisory Commission's Division on State and Local Cooperation, suggested that it might be nice if women living near Army posts would help entertain the troops. They could also work as volunteers in the overburdened health and welfare programs of "war boom" towns, laudable suggestions, to be sure, but hardly a call to action.

In August the president of the General Federation of Women's Clubs— an old, large, and conservative body—complained that women were being discriminated against "intolerably" in the civil-defense program. The Office of Civilian Defense did not even have a women's division. There were only seven women in the entire federal government at the policymaking level. Women were excluded from serving in Civil Aeronautics Authority programs for training student pilots. The female Assistant National Civilian Defense Director had just resigned because Director Fiorello La Guardia disapproved of her effort to have the WPA survey and catalogue volunteer associations around the country, many of them women's groups, as possible contributors to civil defense.

Women were joining the Red Cross and other emergency related bodies in large numbers, but not because government was encouraging them to, or promising that if war came it would utilize their services. This lack of interest would not change very much after Pearl Harbor. In the age of total war the United States would make a semitotal effort, a limitation that was prefigured by government's earlier policy on civilian defense. This prejudice against women would seriously weaken the war effort.

It was obvious that vast numbers of men in uniform would be performing clerical tasks and other duties that were not gender-specific. Yet military leaders were slow to admit that women could do these jobs as well, if not better than, men, thereby freeing able-bodied males for combat. Early in 1942 the Army agreed to accept 10,000 volunteers for a Women's Army Auxiliary Corps only because a bill introduced in Congress by Representative Edith Nourse Rogers (R, MA) forced its hand. The Navy went on refusing to accept women in any capacity. There were plenty of men as yet undrafted, the military's reasoning went—which was true at the time, but this surplus did not last, forcing a change of heart....

Lacking official outlets, women formed numerous paramilitary groups of their own, including the Powder Puff Platoon of Joplin, Missouri, the Green Guards of Washington, and the Women's Defense School of Boston, which taught a course in field cooking modeled on that of the Army. Some 25,000 women volunteered for the Women's Ambulance and Defense Corps of America, whose slogan was "The Hell We Can't." Its more than 50 chapters trained women to serve as air-raid wardens, security guards, and couriers for the armed forces. However, most who wished to contribute joined the Red Cross, which, with 3.5 million female volunteers, was by far the most important outlet for patriotic womanhood.

Some government agencies actually recognized opportunity when they saw it. The Office of Civilian Defense employed a number of female volunteers. The Office of Price Administration used 50,000 women in five states to conduct a three-day canvas in July 1942, during which they briefed 450,000 retailers on the new price regulations. For the most part, though, except for defense contractors who gradually warmed to the idea of hiring women workers, volunteer organizations remained the main outlets.

Of these latter groups, the most controversial was the American Women's Voluntary Services, founded by a group of Anglophile socialites in 1940 to prepare women for emergency work in a London-style blitz. It soon enrolled 350,000 members in almost every state. To refute mockers who accused them of being social butterflies out on a lark, AWVS cast a remarkably broad net for the times, organizing several units in Harlem, at least one Chinese chapter, a number of Hispanic units, and one affiliate consisting entirely of Taos tribeswomen. Defying local taboos, the New Orleans chapter bravely included Negro women. When it became evident that America was not going to be attacked by German bombers, the AWVS took on new assignments. In New

York members sold $5 million worth of war bonds. In California there were AWVS "chuckwagons" that delivered food, including late-night snacks, to Coast Guard stations and remote military sites. In San Francisco AWVS women taught Braille to blinded veterans. Others organized agricultural work camps in California and Colorado. Some New York suburbs had ambulances staffed entirely by AWVS members.

Though it was the biggest, AWVS was by no means the only volunteer women's organization that made a place for itself in the war effort. At least three other women's groups provided land and air ambulance services. There were also volunteer groups of working women, such as WIRES (Women in Radio and Electric Service), WAMS (Women Aircraft Mechanics), and WOWS (Women Ordinance Workers)—the latter of whom by 1943 had a membership of 33,000 in dozens of munitions plants. As part of an elaborate recruiting campaign, Oldsmobile created WINGS (also known as the "Keep 'Em Winning Girls"), workers who were given uniforms with a torch-and-wing insignia on the front pocket. So that housewives should not feel excluded, the *Ladies Home Journal* organized WINS (Women in National Service), saying that housewives were "the largest army in the nation fighting on the home front." The outpouring of female volunteers in a host of organizations enabled women to accomplish much, and suggested how much more they might have done had there been a system in place to take full advantage of their enthusiasm. Even as it was, when in April 1942 ten thousand women volunteers marched down Fifth Avenue in New York there were so many different uniforms that no one could identify them all....

While the numerous complaints about government's incompetence and neglect were fully justified, it was important to keep in mind that the mills of American democracy were supposed to grind slowly. Though this was not apparent at first, the mess in Washington would improve. Private initiatives too would become more fruitful. Scrap drives got better, the rule seeming to be that behind every successful local drive there was one especially determined person. In Seattle, which had a very big one, that man was a local jeweler by the name of Leo Weisfield.

A landmark effort was the great Nebraska scrap drive of 1942, inspired by Henry Doorly, publisher of the state's biggest newspaper, the Omaha *World-Herald*. A unique feature of his plan was that prizes worth up to $2,000 in war bonds would be given to individuals and organizations who collected the most scrap, regardless of whether it was sold to dealers or donated gratis. This was a significant feature, not just because it meant that donors could mingle patriotism with profit, but because scrap dealers had the heavy equipment required to salvage large metal structures.

The drive collected 135 million tons of scrap, the equivalent of 103 pounds for every person in Nebraska. By comparison, the previous national scrap campaign collected only 213 million tons in its first two weeks, an average of barely more than a pound and a half for each American. Many

Nebraska companies donated trucks, 40 a day on average, which were employed to transport scrap. The *World-Herald* itself contributed nine tons of old press parts which a frugal foreman had been stockpiling for 30 years. In the town of Oldrege a local department-store owner and a farm-implement dealer set up a nonprofit corporation that paid $10 a ton for salvage, a dollar and a half above the going rate. To finance it they borrowed money from the local bank, and with the aid of hundreds of volunteers ended up breaking even—a feat they accomplished by sorting the scrap, which enabled them to resell it to dealers for a premium that covered their overpayments.

Rural salvage was the most rewarding because of its scale. While townspeople were turning in old appliances, the countryside yielded up treasures in the form of disused iron bridges, farm machinery, and 537 tons of abandoned track donated by the Burlington Railroad. When the prizes were given out, the individual winner was a section hand for the Burlington who brought in 97,000 pounds of scrap. The winning business was a dinette in Norfolk whose owner hired two women to run the place while he collected 81,000 pounds of salvage. The junior prize went to the Omaha Future Farmers of America, who took time out from agricultural pursuits to amass a staggering 445,000 pounds.

The most successful state drive yet, the Nebraska model was widely copied, demonstrating that the will was there and could be mobilized with inventive planning. If the weakness of democracy was inefficient government, the strength was volunteerism, especially when it exploited the national love of competition.

An example of what could be done with official support was gasoline rationing, which went into effect on December 1, 1942—tardily, of course, but as so often happened, delay was needed to convince people that the rubber crisis really existed. Americans who hated rationing, complied with the rules as a whole, despite the inevitable chiseling and the rise of black marketeers and forgers of gas-ration permits. It helped that most people walked to work (40 percent) or took public transportation (23 percent). Even the 36 percent who commuted by car ultimately accepted gasoline rationing. Though only 49 percent of all Americans saw a need for it when first proposed, by the end of 1942 the great majority of motorists (73 percent) supported gasoline rationing. The 35 mph speed limit won almost universal approval, with 89 percent of car owners backing it. Fortunately, though the black market in gasoline eventually became a big business, it never grew so large as to jeopardize the war effort.

Rationing, an inconvenience to some, meant real sacrifice for others—such as small businesses that depended on the drive-in trade. Nine hundred restaurants in Los Angeles alone closed within the first two weeks after rationing took effect. Labor and other kinds of shortages would also devastate small businessmen and farmers. In Arkansas, 6,000 small businesses would fail by 1943 for lack of workers, while the state's farm population declined from 667,000 in 1940 to 292,000 by the spring of 1944.

In January 1943 pleasure driving was banned completely on the East Coast, where a genuine gasoline shortage existed, virtually emptying the streets of major cities. Compliance was encouraged by police officers, who confiscated the gas-ration books of offending drivers. If after a court hearing the accused were found guilty of frivolous motoring, the fine was in gasoline coupons rather than cash—a powerful and effective deterrent. More important than stiff fines was patriotism, since experience would demonstrate that programs with which most Americans did not agree were ultimately unenforceable.

Conversely, programs that Americans believed in could not be stopped. Victory gardens were a case in point. Food production and conservation had been strongly encouraged in the First World War, and many families that did not ordinarily grow their own produce established kitchen gardens in response. People took it for granted that food would be short this time as well. They began planting vegetables in the spring, despite the Department of Agriculture, which initially dragged its feet. By April 1942, at least 6 million gardens were being cultivated, inspiring Secretary of Agriculture Claude Wickard to call for 18 million victory gardens—a goal that was easily reached. In 1943, more than 8 million tons of produce was grown on 20 million individual plots, many of them very small. In cities with populations above 100,000, victory gardens averaged only 500 square feet in size—that is, about 20 by 25 feet—but nevertheless amounted collectively to 7 million acres, an area the size of Rhode Island.

Victory gardens appeared everywhere, not only on private lots but in parks, before the San Francisco City Hall, in the yards of schools and prisons, wherever there was arable soil, and hands to do the tilling. The Agriculture Department reported that the amount of vegetables grown in victory gardens exceeded "the total commercial production for fresh sale for civilian and non-civilian use." This was all the more impressive because, after being grown, much of this produce had to be canned—hence the slogan, "Eat what you can and can what you can't," no small thing, as a mistake could result in glass canisters exploding, or even bacterial growths that were potentially lethal.

Most of the conservation burden fell on women—and children, too, who were good collectors of scrap. In the fully mobilized household there were separate holders for tins, rags, bottles, paper, and bones. Tin cans were washed and flattened. Tinfoil and rubber bands were collected in balls. Bottle caps, chewing gum wrappers, and flashlight batteries were saved for later recycling. Because it was used to make munitions, schools had "Fat Parades," enabling children to make ceremonial deposits of accumulated kitchen grease. In rural areas they collected milkweeds, whose silken fibers would be stuffed into life jackets....

Secretary of the Treasury Henry Morgenthau ... wanted bonds sold widely and in such a way as to make Americans "war-minded." He believed this was even more important than helping finance defense purchases. To sell bonds was to sell the war, so bond drives were aimed at the average American rather than at wealthy investors—which meant, in turn, drawing heavily on the popular culture. Movie stars played important parts, with Hollywood organizing seven tours that played in 300 communities. Dorothy Lamour alone, the star of a series of "Road" pictures with Bob Hope and Bing Crosby, was credited with selling $350 million worth of bonds. Carole Lombard, a popular movie actress, gave her life to the cause, dying in a plane crash on her way home from a bond tour. In addition to bonds, "war stamps" costing only pennies were sold—mainly to children, though sometimes to adults, as when scantily-clad showgirls covered their flesh with 10¢ savings stamps for happy businessmen to peel off and purchase. Every form of hucksterism was employed in this cause, few managing to escape it....

Despite occasional lapses, [President] Roosevelt did not truly believe in propaganda. In 1917, precisely because opinion was divided on the merits of intervention, Washington had cranked up a vast publicity machine to bolster the war effort. A Committee on Public Information was created to that end, which distributed 75 million pamphlets, issued 6,000 press releases, placed ads in leading magazines, enlisted a corps of "Four-Minute Men" who gave short, canned talks emphasizing German atrocities, and in other ways sought to promote war fever. The intellectual content of most of this is suggested by some of the war films endorsed by CPI, such as "The Prussian Cur" and "The Kaiser, the Beast of Berlin." ...

After World War I many felt that the mixture of propaganda and intimidation had encouraged the violation of basic American rights, inflamed passions, contributed to vigilante action, stimulated xenophobia, oversimplified the issues, and aroused unrealistic expectations. FDR was not going to repeat the mistake. Public relations was one thing, a ministry of domestic propaganda another. Congress seconded his motion, conservatives fearing that government propaganda campaigns would glorify Roosevelt, the New Deal, and liberal internationalism—what Congresswoman Clare Boothe Luce referred to as "globaloney." ...

Given Washington's lack of interest in propaganda, writers eager to aid the war effort were inspired to create their own. West Coast patriots formed the Hollywood Writer's Mobilization. Its counterpart on the East Coast was organized by Rex Stout, author of the popular Nero Wolfe detective novels, who launched the Writer's War Board two days after Pearl Harbor. Initially it helped sell war bonds, but soon grew "into a liaison office between writers and government departments, a kind of unpaid extension of the Office of War Information." Looking back, a former member described its purpose thusly. "The government was slow; we were fast. They were timid; we were bold. They used official gobbledygook; we had some wit. World War II was strangely unemotional and needed a WWB to stir things up." As this suggests, the mobilized wordsmiths put a high premium on ardor.

Members not only wrote advertising copy for war bonds, but used every known outlet to reach the public. The WWB itself might instigate a campaign; other times it responded to official requests. An example of the latter case occurred when the Air Force wanted to promote the enlistment of flight crew other than pilots. WWB's contribution included 12 short stories, 24 syndicated columns, three radio broadcasts, one novel, one handbook, and two popular songs—one of them entitled "I Wanna Marry a Bombardier." The campaign had to be terminated after it produced a surplus of volunteers....

These were America's strengths, a lack of regimentation, the refusal to indoctrinate; and most of all the initiative of ordinary people organizing, conserving, collecting, recycling, buying war bonds—or if, like writers and entertainers, they had special skills, devoting them to public service. That government never found a way of fully exploiting their eagerness to help was its biggest wartime failure, and a curious one in light of the opinion polls showing a willingness to give beyond what was ever asked of civilians....

Civilians contributed more to the winning of World War II than to any previous American conflict—on the homefront, but directly too in the battle against the U-boats. In this campaign the front lines were manned not just by sailors and fliers, but by civilian seamen of the U.S. merchant fleet, thousands of whom lost their lives to keep Britain and Russia going. Many more would have died had it not been for a handful of men in government and business who played key roles at critical points that were to make a tremendous difference....

The war changed everything except human needs and desires. Many once ordinary tasks became fiendishly difficult to perform. Numerous goods previously taken for granted all but disappeared, and were replaced by inferior substitutes, or disappeared altogether. People got by as best they could and some discovered in the war a welcome degree of excitement. Most found it possible, despite shortages and censorship, to amuse themselves, taking their pleasure in ways that tell us much about the American people and what they considered important.

It seems fair to say that life on the homefront was most difficult for married women. A 48-hour week and long commutes were the rule for all workers, regardless of gender. Because so many goods and services—including household appliances and supplies, certain foodstuffs, domestic help, and medical care—were in short supply, wives and mothers, whether employed or not, had to devote more time to such activities as housework and getting their children to doctors. Shopping was further complicated by ration books and the need to go from store to store looking for scarce products.

Like their husbands, service wives could "take it" and did not let fear for their absent loved ones keep them from shouldering what often were heavy burdens. One Illinois mother was left to care for three small boys when her husband went overseas. She worked eight hours a day in a local canning factory, yet managed to run a Cub Scout troop, keep a victory garden, and put a hot meal on the table every night—if only tunafish casserole. When the fare prompted complaints she serenely replied, as every mother did in those years, "Think of the poor, starving children in Europe."

Consumers had to return used toothpaste tubes in order to buy new ones, while tinfoil and cellophane simply disappeared—as did bobby pins, which were replaced by wooden toothpicks and thread. Mostly a drain, shopping could be adventuresome if you had the right kind of luck. In April 1945, Audrey Davis triumphantly wrote to her husband at sea:

> Honey, I'm a success. I got sheets! Such a time—went to four of the biggest stores first and was turned down cold. Finally ended up in the basement of J. C. Penney's ... and saw some bedding so on the off-chance, I asked. The girl said, shhh, and sneaked into a back room and brought out some carefully wrapped—didn't even know what I had bought, until I got home. I felt like someone buying hooch during Prohibition.

New clothes were devoid of elastic thread and webbing, metal buttons, zippers, hooks and eyes, silk, nylon, canvas, duck, and sometimes leather. Coats could not have pleats, gussets, bellows, yokes. A "victory suit," which carried economy to the point of eliminating lapels, was ruled out. To save wool, double-breasted suits could not be vested, and no suit could come with more than one pair of pants. Cloth could not go over cloth, eliminating trouser cuffs and patch pockets. Women's skirts were limited in length and circumference and certain dyes, especially greens and browns, were sometimes unavailable. Girdles, still everyday wear for women, had to be made of bone or piano wire instead of rubber. Shoes, when you could get them, came in six colors only, three of them shades of brown. Almost anything from coffee to canned goods, half the 1943 production went overseas, could run out without notice, cigarette shortages being a particular trial for a nation of smokers.

Irritation over rationing was continuous and so sharp that in 1943 Leon Henderson, one of the most brilliant New Dealers, had to resign as head of the Office of Price Administration even though he was, according to economist Kenneth Galbraith (who worked for him), one of the "unsung heroes of World War II".... Urban Americans grew used to queuing up. Not only were food and clothing rationed, but the number of ration "points" required for specific items fluctuated, obliging every housewife to update her calculations on a weekly, or even daily, basis. Black-marketeering, especially in meat, aggravated shortages. For some, getting meat was a major preoccupation. One mother seems never to have written her son abroad without addressing the problem, although in the mandatory positive voice, as when she told him of her discovery that "Spam fried in butter makes a very tasty Easter dinner."

A striking feature of the war effort, and a source of many problems, was the enormous increase in physical mobility. Including service personnel, 27.3 million people moved from their original county of residence. In the period 1935–40, an unusually active one, total civilian mobility had amounted to 2.8 million persons a year, but during each of the peak war years it averaged 4.7 million. With automobile use restricted, most long-distance travel was by train, putting enormous stress on the rail system and also the passengers—jammed into overcrowded and poorly maintained cars which were slow and often late due to breakdowns or from having been sidetracked for high-priority troop trains.

Difficult as travel became, starting over in strange places was worse. Adolescents were particularly affected, not only because relocation is emotionally most difficult at that age, but also because so many were going to work full-time or entering the services. In 1940 the number of employed persons between the ages of 14 and 17 was 1.7 million, whereas in 1944 it came to 4.61 million, of whom 1.43 million were part-time students. During World War II the decline in child labor was temporarily reversed, as also the trend toward longer periods of education. Total school attendance for the 14–19 age group in 1940 came to 9.159 million persons, whereas by 1944 it had fallen to 7.93 million. The number of boys and girls aged 14 to 18 who were employed rose from 1 million in 1940 to 2.9 million—the number of mill girls alone rising from 271,000 to 950,000.

By May 1943 some 1.8 million boys and girls under the age of 18 were employed by farms and factories. One Lockheed plant had 1,500 boys laboring as riveters and electricians and in metal fabrication and assembly work. According to the firm, two boys in four hours could accomplish more than an adult worker during a regular eight-hour shift. For those children who remained in school full-time, life was harder, too, as teacher quality declined and class sizes went up. In Arkansas by the 1945–46 school year half the prewar teachers were gone and 72 percent of their replacements had completed less than a semester of college. During 1942–43, out of 170,000 Arkansas youngsters between the ages of 13 and 18 about 100,000 failed to attend school, some taking jobs but many because teachers were not available.

As might be expected, crime rates were strongly influenced by the physical and social changes affecting such a large number of people. Since so many young males, the principal crime-committing group, were in uniform, most crimes declined—except possibly rapes, though as they were seldom reported, the statistics are not very useful. But the number of murders, a more reliable figure, fell from 8,329 in 1940 to a low of 6,675 in 1944. Auto thefts went up in 1942 when new cars became unavailable, but the total number of reported crimes followed the same curve as murders, falling after 1940 and rising again only in 1945 when veterans began reentering civilian life. Suicides declined by a third, from about 19,000 in 1940 to some 13,000 four years later. It is an all too human irony that life seemed more worth living in wartime, the suicide rate showing this even more than the rising birthrate.

All these figures are evidence that—not to make light of its hardships—the war was more interesting than the peace had been. The war put an end to Depression America and gave meaning to ordinary lives, since all citizens were to some degree participants in the national effort. Everything changed, not always for the better, to be sure, but change of itself was often welcome after the monotonous years of austerity that followed the stock market crash of 1929. Many people were given jobs they never expected to get, saw places they would otherwise not have known, and lived richer lives....

DOCUMENTS

The Woman Worker, 1942

Half a million women were estimated early this year [1942] to be serving their country in war industries. The number of these increases day by day. In some 30 plants making small-arms and artillery ammunition, where 40,000 women were employed in the last quarter of 1941, over 70,000 are expected to be at work by late summer. In some of these the woman labor force will be doubled, in others trebled, and some will employ 10 times as many women as before. These are chiefly new jobs, not those vacated by men. Before 1941 almost no women were in aircraft.

Women in Jobs Vacated by Men

Many reports from all parts of the country show that men called to war service actually have been replaced by women in types of work formerly not done, or done only very rarely, by women, though of course there is no way to discover the full number of these. They include clerks, cashiers, and pharmacists in drug stores, theater ushers, hotel elevator operators, taxi drivers, bank tellers, electricians, acetylene welders, milling-machine operators, riveters, tool-keepers, gage checkers, gear cutters, turret and

SOURCE: U.S. Department of Labor, Women's Bureau, *The Woman Worker* (Washington, D. C.: Government Printing Office, May 1942), 3–4.

engine lathe operators. Women are operating service stations. They are replacing men as finger-print classifiers. A southern city reports a woman manager of a parking lot.

One of the country's major airfields has women on maintenance work, engaging them chiefly in cleaning spark plugs and painting luminous dials. One woman hired as a secretary now directs landings and take-offs by radio. In another city a woman has entered for the first time an airfield office as a meteorologist. Both an eastern and a southern airport have definite plans to place women in their reservations departments, and in flight watch or in the traffic operations departments, and the Civil Aeronautics Administration is considering training women as radio operators.

Women telegraph messengers now number 325 in New York City alone, and in the country as a whole 3,000 women are expected to do such work this year. In New York, they must be at least 21 years of age. Girls also are performing other messenger service, formerly done by boys, in many plants and offices. A major chemical company is now training a few women as its chemists.

Labor Shortages Open Jobs to Women

There are many types of work long done by women but in which women now are being taken on in large numbers, because of plant expansion as well as declining supply of male labor. For example, as armature winders, inspectors, power-press and drill-press operators, assemblers. Shortages of workers are reported in many places in fields usual for women; for example, in hotel and restaurant work, as retail clerks, stenographers, and as sewing-machine operators in certain great clothing centers. Shortages of school teachers are growing, because of better-paid jobs in industry as well as the drafting of men, and the National Education Association reports that the enrollment in teachers' colleges and normal schools has declined by 11 per cent. Certain of the army camps already have employed considerable numbers of women in their offices and laundries, jobs formerly done by men but of a type frequently performed by women. A woman's job at present done by men in camps is canteen work, but serious consideration is being given to employing women in this.

Unemployment of Women

Contrary to the movement of women into the manufacture of war products, and into jobs being vacated by men, runs that opposite line of women losing jobs due to curtailment of civilian goods and of critical materials. Such "priorities unemployment" became acute at certain points in the second half of 1941. Plants making many of the products curtailed employed large numbers of women-as on aluminum kitchenware, refrigerators, silk hosiery, washing machines, radios, typewriters, photographic supplies, metal toys, costume jewelry, slide and snap fasteners, and so forth. Others depend on equipment now curtailed, as for example the apparel industry threatened with shortages of steel needles and consequent danger of unemployment. In many cases it takes longer to place women than men in new jobs, since their industrial experience is less similar to the new types of work required. Moreover, some of these products are made in localities that offer women little chance of other plant jobs.

Conditions in the Camps (1942–1945), 1948

A visiting reporter from *The San Francisco Chronicle* described quarters at Tule Lake:

> Room size—about 15 by 25, considered too big for two reporters.
> Condition—dirty.
> Contents—two Army cots, each with two Army blankets, one pillow, some sheets and pillow cases (these came as a courtesy from the management), and a coal-burning stove (no coal). There were no dishes, rugs, curtains, or housekeeping equipment of any kind. (We had in addition one sawhorse and three pieces of wood, which the management did not explain.)

The furnishings at other camps were similar. At Minidoka, arriving evacuees found two stacked canvas cots, a pot-bellied stove and a light bulb hanging from the ceiling; at Topaz, cots, two blankets, a pot-bellied stove and some cotton mattresses. Rooms had no running water, which had to be carried from community facilities. Running back and forth from the laundry room to rinse and launder soiled diapers was a particular inconvenience....

Others, however, found not even the minimal comforts that had been planned for them. An unrealistic schedule combined with wartime shortages of labor and materials meant that the WRA* had difficulty meeting its construction schedule. In most cases, the barracks were completed, but at some centers evacuees lived without electric light, adequate toilets or laundry facilities....

Mess Halls planned for about 300 people had to handle 600 or 900 for short periods. Three months after the project opened, Manzanar still lacked equipment for 16 of 36 mess halls. At Gila:

> There were 7,700 people crowded into space designed for 5,000.
> They were housed in messhalls, recreation halls, and even latrines.
> As many as 25 persons lived in a space intended for four.

*Wartime Relocation Administration. (Eds.)

SOURCE: Commission on Wartime Relocation and Internment of Civilians, *Personal Justice Denied* (Washington, D.C: Government Printing Office, 1984), 159–161.

As at the assembly centers, one result was that evacuees were often denied privacy in even the most intimate aspects of their lives.... Even when families had separate quarters, the partitions between rooms failed to give much privacy. Gladys Bell described the situation at Topaz:

> [T]he evacuees ... had only one room, unless there were around ten in the family. Their rooms had a pot-bellied stove, a single electric light hanging from the ceiling, an Army cot for each person and a blanket for the bed. Each barrack had six rooms with only three flues. This meant that a hole had to be cut through the wall of one room for the stovepipe to join the chimney of the next room. The hole was large so that the wall would not burn. As a result, everything said and some things whispered were easily heard by people living in the next room. Sometimes the family would be a couple with four children living next to an older couple, perhaps of a different religion, older ideas and with a difference in all ways of life—such as music.

Despite these wretched conditions the evacuees again began to rebuild their lives. Several evacuees recall "foraging for bits of wallboard and wood" and dodging guards to get materials from the scrap lumber piles to build shelves and furniture.... Eventually, rooms were partitioned and shelves, tables, chairs and other furniture appeared. Paint and cloth for curtains and spreads came from mail order houses at evacuee expense. Flowers bloomed and rock gardens emerged; trees and shrubs were planted. Many evacuees grew victory gardens. One described the change:

> [W]hen we entered camp, it was a barren desert. When we left camp, it was a garden that had been built up without tools, it was green around the camp with vegetation, flowers, and also with artificial lakes, and that's how we left it.

The success of evacuees' efforts to improve their surroundings, however, was always tempered by the harsh climate. In the western camps, particularly Heart Mountain, Poston, Topaz and Minidoka, dust was a principal problem. Monica Sone described her first day at Minidoka:

> [W]e were given a rousing welcome by a dust storm.... We felt as if we were standing in a gigantic sand-mixing machine as the sixty-mile gale lifted the loose earth up into the sky, obliterating everything. Sand filled our mouths and nostrils and stung our faces and hands like a thousand darting needles. Henry and Father pushed on ahead while Mother, Sumi and I followed, hanging onto their jackets, banging suitcases into each other. At last we staggered into our room, gasping and blinded. We sat on our suitcases to rest, peeling off our jackets and scarves. The window panels rattled madly, and the dust poured through the cracks like smoke. Now and then when the wind

subsided, I saw other evacuees, hanging on to their suitcases, heads bent against the stinging dust. The wind whipped their scarves and towels from their heads and zipped them out of sight.

In desert camps, the evacuees met severe extremes of temperature as well. In winter it reached 35 degrees below zero and summers brought temperature as high as 115°. Because the desert did not cool off at night, evacuees would splash water on their cots to be cool enough to sleep. Rattlesnakes and desert wildlife added danger to discomfort.

The Arkansas camps had equally unpleasant weather. Winters were cold and snowy while summers were unbearably hot and humid, heavy with chiggers and clouds of mosquitos....

The WRA walked a fine line in providing for evacuees' basic needs. On the one hand was their genuine sympathy for the excluded people. On the other was a well-founded apprehension that the press and the politicians would seek out and denounce any evidence that evacuees were being treated generously. WRA's compromise was to strive for a system that would provide a healthy but Spartan environment. They did not always succeed, and it was usually the evacuees who suffered when they failed.

Japanese American Servicemen (1942–1945), 2011

After Barney Hajiro, an Army private, single-handedly wiped out two German machine gun nests and killed two snipers in a gallant charge in World War II, his superiors recommended him for the Medal of Honor.

As part of a regiment composed entirely of Japanese-Americans below the officers' ranks, Private Hajiro epitomized the unit's brash motto, "Go for Broke!" His commanding officer's report said that in October 1944 in eastern France, he had run 100 yards through a stream of bullets, walked through a booby-trapped area and led the charge up "Suicide Hill" screaming "Banzai!" before taking out the machine gun nests.

He was shot four times—then insisted that 40 other wounded men be evacuated first.

But he, like Senator Daniel K. Inouye of Hawaii, who was also a member of the regiment, did not initially receive the Medal of Honor for which he was recommended. Only in 2000, after 56 years and a belated Pentagon review, did President Bill Clinton present the medal, the nation's top military honor, to Mr. Hajiro, Senator Inouye and 20 other Asian-American soldiers. Racial prejudice, Mr. Clinton said, had prevented such a ceremony after the war.

"I nearly gave up hope," Mr. Hajiro said at the time.

"Barney was a good man," Senator Inouye said in an interview on Wednesday. "He didn't go around blowing his own horn. He would just say he was doing something he was supposed to do."

Mr. Hajiro, who had battled cancer, died on Jan. 21 in Honolulu at 94, his family said. He had been the nation's oldest Medal of Honor recipient. His background was modest: born in Hawaii, he dropped out of school in the eighth grade to work for 10 hours a day, at 10 cents an hour, on a sugar plantation. He was a dockworker when he was drafted into the Army in 1942 and assigned to dig ditches. He resented not being allowed to carry arms.

"I didn't bomb Pearl Harbor," Mr. Hajiro said in an interview in 1999. "Why did they blame us?"

As angry about Pearl Harbor as anybody, many Japanese-Hawaiians were eager to fight. Mr. Hajiro was one of the first to volunteer, in March 1943.

The 442nd Regimental Combat Team, a newly formed unit, would go on to be called the most decorated regiment for its size and length of service: its 14,000 men earned 9,486 Purple Hearts, 8 Presidential Unit Citations and 52 Distinguished Service Crosses, the second-highest individual honor in the Army. Mr. Hajiro received three of those.

He and many of his comrades were decorated for the regiment's most celebrated operation, known as "the rescue of the Lost Battalion," in which they saved 211 fellow soldiers trapped in southern France while suffering more than 800 casualties.

One regiment member, Pfc. Sadao S. Munemori, actually did receive a Medal of Honor, posthumously, in 1945, after the Japanese American Citizens League persuaded a Utah senator to take up the soldier's cause. A Filipino-American also won the medal in World War II. But they were the rare exceptions for Asian-Americans.

The battlefield exploits of Asian-Americans came under review by the Pentagon beginning in 1996, after a similar examination, prompted by the Congressional Black Caucus, had begun looking into why no blacks had been awarded the Medal of Honor in World War II. Senator Daniel K. Akaka, Democrat of Hawaii, had sought the review of Asian-Americans.

(In the review of African-Americans, seven were awarded the medal in 1997, six posthumously. The seventh, Vernon Baker, died last July.)

Some criticized the reviews of both blacks and Asian-Americans as political pandering, noting that similarly qualified whites were not part of the review. But President Clinton said that facing racial slurs and forced internment, Japanese-Americans had not gotten a fair deal.

James C. McNaughton, the Defense Department historian who led the Asian-American review, said in 2000 that the very fact that the 442nd was segregated amounted to "institutional discrimination." But he said he could find no instance of white officers deliberately ignoring the valor of Asian-American troops.

Of the 22 Asian-Americans whose decorations were upgraded to the Medal of Honor, all but two were Japanese-Americans and members of either the 442nd or the 100th infantry Battalion, which the 442nd absorbed in 1944. (Of the two others, one was of Filipino heritage and one of Chinese heritage.)

Senator Inouye, who lost his right arm in fierce fighting in Italy, said he and his former comrades had been modest about finally receiving the medal. "Why did we get recognized when there are hundreds of others who did the same thing?" he asked.

Barney Fushimi Hajiro, the oldest of nine children, was born on Sept. 16, 1916, in Puunene, on the island of Maui, where his parents had immigrated from Hiroshima during World War I. The family was so poor that the children were given a bottle of soda only on New Year's Day. Barney left school as a teenager and would later say his biggest regret was not pursuing his dream of running track.

He fought in Italy, then moved with his unit to eastern France, where he was cited for bravery on Oct. 19 and Oct. 22, 1944, in battles in mountainous terrain.

On Oct. 29, in the fighting that brought him the Medal of Honor, the 442nd was pinned down, its soldiers picked off one by one by Germans on higher ground. Private Hajiro suffered wounds in his face, shoulder and wrist in leading the counterattack.

"I couldn't run backward," he said. "I had to run forward. That's the job of a soldier."

Chapter 12

Americans on the Move: Suburbs and the Sunbelt

A postwar family views its dream house.

World War II set off an economic boom marked by the steady growth of family and individual incomes that lasted, with few interruptions, until 1973. Never before had the nation experienced such prosperity. Never before had material products that Americans associated with "the good life"—automobiles, dishwashers, stereos, televisions, and more—become so readily available to large segments of the population.

The keystone of the middle-class dream was home ownership. During the 1930s and 1940s, the lyrics of popular ballads like "My Blue Heaven" had expressed the desire for a bungalow in the suburbs, in which husband, wife, and children would live an idyllic life. But wartime demands for the construction of military bases and for defense industries had brought private home building, already slowed by the Depression, to a virtual halt. Within a few years of the war's end, however, the building boom was under way. Kenneth Jackson's essay "The Baby Boom and the Age of the Subdivision" describes how the postwar demand for suburban housing, fueled by veterans and their growing families, was served by government assistance and enterprising builders. Among the latter, William Levitt was possibly the most ingenious; the housing tracts that he built, called Levit towns, came to symbolize post–World War II construction.

Jackson's study was finished in the early 1980s, before other movements of the American people were pronounced. One major change in suburban life in the last twenty years has been the new immigrants' (especially those who were well off) pattern of avoiding cities and settling directly in the suburbs. The first document discusses this new movement. What does it tell us about the lack of diversity of the suburbs described by Jackson? The second document points to another major movement, the rise of the Sunbelt, from the South to the Southwest and especially new areas of development in states such as Arizona and Nevada. Why has the Sunbelt become so attractive?

ESSAY

The Baby Boom and the Age of the Subdivision
Kenneth Jackson

What the Blandings wanted ... was simple enough: a two-story house in quiet, modern good taste, ... a good-sized living room with a fire place, a dining room, pantry, and kitchen, a small lavatory, four bedrooms and accompanying baths, ... a roomy cellar ... plenty of closets.

—ERIC HODGINS,
Mr. Blandings Builds His Dream House (1939)

No man who owns his own house and lot can be a Communist. He has too much to do.

—WILLIAM J. LEVITT, *1948*

At 7 P.M. (Eastern time) on August 14, 1945, radio stations across the nation interrupted normal programming for President Harry S Truman's announcement of the surrender of Japan. It was a moment in time that those who experienced it will never forget. World War II was over. Across the nation, Americans gathered to celebrate their victory. In New York City two million people converged on Times Square as though it were New Year's Eve. In smaller cities and towns, the response was no less tumultuous, as spontaneous cheers, horns, sirens, and church bells telegraphed the news to every household and hamlet, convincing even small children that it

SOURCE: The Baby Boom and the Age of the Subdivision," from Crabgrass Frontier: The Suburbanization of the United States by Kenneth T. Jackson. Copyright © 1985 by Oxford University Press. Used by permission of Oxford University Press.

was a very special day. To the average person, the most important consequence of victory was not the end of shortages, not the restructuring of international boundaries or reparations payments or big power politics, but the survival of husbands and sons. Some women regretted that their first decent-paying, responsible jobs would be taken away by returning veterans. Most, however, felt a collective sigh of relief. Normal family life could resume. The long vigil was over. Their men would be coming home.

In truth, the United States was no better prepared for peace than it had been for war when the German *Wehrmacht* crossed the Polish frontier in the predawn hours of September 1, 1939. For more than five years military necessity had taken priority over consumer goods, and by 1945 almost everyone had a long list of unfilled material wants.

Housing was the area of most pressing need. Through sixteen years of depression and war, the residential construction industry had been dormant, with new home starts averaging less than 100,000 per year. Almost one million people had migrated to defense areas in the early 1940s, but new housing for them was designated as "temporary," in part as an economy move and in part because the real-estate lobby did not want emergency housing converted to permanent use after the war. Meanwhile, the marriage rate, after a decade of decline, had begun a steep rise in 1940, as war became increasingly likely and the possibility of separation added a spur to decision making. In addition, married servicemen received an additional fifty dollars per month allotment, which went directly to the wives. Soon thereafter, the birth rate began to climb, reaching 22 per 1,000 in 1943, the highest in two decades. Many of the newcomers were "good-bye babies," conceived just before the husbands shipped out, partly because of an absence of birth control, partly because the wife's allotment check would be increased with each child, and partly as a tangible reminder of a father who could not know when, or if, he would return. During the war, government and industry both played up the suburban house to the families of absent servicemen, and between 1941 and 1946 some of the nation's most promising architects published their "dream houses" in a series in the *Ladies' Home Journal*.

After the war, both the marriage and the birth rates continued at a high level. In individual terms, this rise in family formation coupled with the decline in housing starts meant that there were virtually no homes for sale or apartments for rent at war's end. Continuing a trend begun during the Great Depression, six million families were doubling up with relatives or friends by 1947, and another 500,000 were occupying quonset huts or temporary quarters. Neither figure included families living in substandard dwellings or those in desperate need of more room. In Chicago, 250 former trolley cars were sold as homes. In New York City a newly wed couple set up housekeeping for two days in a department store window in hopes that the publicity would help them find an apartment. In Omaha a newspaper advertisement proposed: "Big Ice Box, 7 × 17 feet, could be fixed up to live in." In Atlanta the city bought 100 trailers for veterans. In North Dakota surplus grain bins were turned into apartments. In brief, the demand for housing was unprecedented.

The federal government responded to an immediate need for five million new homes by underwriting a vast new construction program. In the decade after the war, Congress regularly approved billions of dollars worth of additional mortgage insurance for the Federal Housing Administration. Even more important was the Servicemen's Readjustment Act of 1944, which created a Veterans Administration mortgage program similar to that of FHA. This law gave official endorsement and support to the view that the 16 million GI's of World War II should return to civilian life with a home of their own. Also, it accepted the builders' contention that they needed an end to government controls but not to government insurance on their investments in residential construction. According to novelist John Keats, "The real estate boys read the Bill, looked at one another in happy amazement, and the dry, rasping noise they made rubbing their hands together could have been heard as far away as Tawi Tawi."

It is not recorded how far the noise carried, but anyone in the residential construction business had ample reason to rub their hands. The assurance of federal mortgage guarantees—at whatever price the builder set—stimulated an unprecedented building boom. Single-family housing starts spurted from only 114,000 in 1944, to 937,000 in 1946, to 1,183,000 in 1948, and to 1,692,000 in 1950, an all-time high. However, ... what distinguished the period was an increase in the number, importance, and size of large builders. Residential construction in the United States had always been highly fragmented in comparison with other industries and dominated by small and poorly organized house builders who had to subcontract much of the work because their low volume did not justify the hiring of all the craftsmen needed to put up a dwelling. In housing, as in other areas of the economy, World War II was beneficial to large businesses. Whereas before 1945, the typical contractor had put up fewer than five houses per year, by 1959, the median single-family builder put up twenty-two structures. As early as 1949 fully 70 percent of new homes were constructed by only 10 percent of the firms (a percentage that would remain roughly stable for the next three decades), and by 1955 subdivisions accounted for more than three-quarters of all new housing in metropolitan areas.

Viewed from an international perspective, however, the building of homes in the United States remained a small-scale enterprise. In 1969, for example, the percentage of all new units built by builders of more than 500 units per year was only 8.1 percent in the United States, compared with 24 percent in Great Britain and 33 percent in France. World War II, therefore, did not transform the American housing industry as radically as it did that of Europe.

The family that had the greatest impact on postwar housing in the United States was Abraham Levitt and his sons, William and Alfred, who ultimately built more than 140,000 houses and turned a cottage industry into a major manufacturing process. They began on a small scale on Long Island in 1929 and concentrated for years on substantial houses in Rockville Center. Increasing their pace in 1934 with a 200-unit subdivision called "Strathmore" in Manhasset, the Levitts continued to focus on the upper-middle class and marketed their tudor-style houses at between $9,100 and $18,500. Private commissions and smaller subdivisions carried the firm through the remainder of the prewar period.

In 1941 Levitt and Sons received a government contract for 1,600 (later increased to 2,350) war workers' homes in Norfolk, Virginia. The effort was a nightmare, but the brothers learned how to lay dozens of concrete foundations in a single day and to preassemble uniform walls and roofs. Additional contracts for more federal housing in Portsmouth, Virginia, and for barracks for shipyard workers at Pearl Harbor provided supplemental experience, as did William's service with the Navy Seabees from 1943 to 1945. Thus, the Levitts were among the nation's largest home builders even before construction of the first Levittown.

Returning to Long Island after the war, the Levitts built 2,250 houses in Roslyn in 1946 in the $17,500 to $23,500 price range, well beyond the means of the average veteran. In that same year, however, they began the acquisition of 4,000 acres of potato farms in the Town of Hempstead, where they planned the biggest private housing project in American history.

The formula for Island Trees, soon renamed Levittown, was simple. After bulldozing the land and removing the trees, trucks carefully dropped off building materials at precise 60-foot intervals. Each house was built on a concrete slab (no cellar); the floors were of asphalt and the walls of composition rock-board. Plywood replaced ¾-inch strip lap, ¾-inch double lap was changed to ⅜-inch for roofing, and the horse and scoop were replaced by the bulldozer. New power hand tools like saws, routers, and nailers helped increase worker productivity. Freight cars loaded with lumber went directly into a cutting yard where one man cut parts for ten houses in one day.

The construction process itself was divided into twenty-seven distinct steps—beginning with laying the foundation and ending with a clean sweep of the new home. Crews were trained to do one job—one day the white-paint men, then the red-paint men, then the tile layers. Every possible part, and especially the most difficult ones, were preassembled in central shops, whereas most builders did it on site. Thus, the Levitts reduced the skilled component to 20–40 percent. The five-day work week was standard, but they were the five days during which building was possible; Saturday and Sunday were considered to be the days when it rained. In the process, the Levitts defied unions and union work rules (against spray painting, for example) and insisted that subcontractors work only for them. Vertical integration also meant that the firm made its own concrete, grew its own timber, and cut its own lumber. It also bought all appliances from wholly owned subsidiaries. More than thirty houses went up each day at the peak of production.

Initially limited to veterans, this first "Levittown" was twenty-five miles east of Manhattan and particularly attractive to new families that had been formed during and just after the war. Squashed in with their in-laws or in tiny apartments where landlords frowned on children, the GI's looked upon Levittown as the answer to their most pressing need. Months before the first three hundred Levitt houses were occupied in October 1947, customers stood in line for the four-room Cape Cod box renting at sixty dollars per month. The first eighteen hundred houses were initially available only for rental, with an option to buy after a year's residence. Because the total for mortgage, interest, principal, and taxes was *less* than the rent, almost everyone bought; after 1949 all units were for sale only. So many of the purchasers were young families that the first issue of *Island Trees*, the community newspaper, opined that "our lives are held closely together because most of us are within the same age bracket, in similar income groups, live in almost identical houses and have common problems." And so many babies were born to them that the suburb came to be known as "Fertility Valley" and "The Rabbit Hutch."

Ultimately encompassing more than 17,400 separate houses and 82,000 residents, Levittown was the largest housing development ever put up by a single builder, and it served the American dream-house market at close to the lowest prices the industry could attain. The typical Cape Cod was down-to-earth and unpretentious; the intention was not to stir the imagination, but to provide the best shelter at the least price. Each dwelling included a twelve-by-sixteen-foot living-room with a fireplace, one bath, and two bedrooms (about 750 square feet), with easy expansion possibilities upstairs in the unfinished attic or outward into the yard. Most importantly, the floor plan was practical and well-designed, with the kitchen moved to the front of the house near the entrance so that mothers could watch their children from kitchen windows and do their washing and cooking with a minimum of movement. Similarly, the living room was placed in the rear and given a picture window overlooking the back yard. This early Levitt house was as basic to post–World War II suburban development as the Model T had been to the automobile. In each case, the actual design features were less important than the fact that they were mass-produced and thus priced within the reach of the middle class.

William Jaird Levitt, who assumed primary operating responsibility for the firm soon after the war, disposed of houses as quickly as other men disposed of cars. Pricing his Cape Cods at $7,990 (the earliest models went for $6,990) and his ranches at $9,500, he promised no down payment, no closing costs, and "no hidden extras." With FHA and VA "production advances," Levitt boasted the largest line of credit ever offered a private home builder. He simplified the paperwork required for purchase and reduced the entire financing and titling transaction to two half-hour steps. His full-page advertisements offered a sweetener to eliminate lingering resistance—a Bendix washer was included in the purchase price. Other inducements included an eight-inch television set (for which the family would pay for the next thirty years). So efficient was the operation that *Harper's Magazine* reported in 1948 that Levitt undersold his nearest competition by $1,500 and still made a $1,000 profit on each house. As *New York Times* architecture critic Paul Goldberger has noted, "Levittown houses were social creations more than architectural ones—they turned the detached, single-family house from a distant dream to a real possibility for thousands of middle-class American families."

Buyers received more than shelter for their money. When the initial families arrived with their baby strollers and play pens, there were no trees, schools, churches, or private telephones. Grocery shopping was a planned adventure, and picking up the mail required sloshing through the mud to Hicksville. The Levitts planted apple, cherry, and evergreen trees on each plot, however, and the development ultimately assumed a more park-like appearance. To facilitate development as a garden community, streets were curvilinear (and invariably called "roads" or "lanes"), and through traffic was shunted to peripheral thoroughfares. Nine swimming pools, sixty playgrounds, ten baseball diamonds, and seven "village greens" provided open space and recreational opportunities. The Levitts forbade fences (a practice later ignored) and permitted outdoor clothes drying only on specially designed, collapsible racks. They even supervised lawn-cutting for the first few years—doing the jobs themselves if necessary and sending the laggard families the bill.

Architectural critics, many of whom were unaccustomed to the tastes or resources of moderate-income people, were generally unimpressed by the repetitious houses on 60-by-100-foot "cookie cutter lots" and referred to Levittown as "degraded in conception and impoverished in form." From the Wantagh Parkway, the town stretched away to the east as far as the eye could see, house after identical house, a horizon broken only by telephone poles. Paul Goldberger, who admired the individual designs, thought that the whole was "an urban planning disaster," while [social critic] Lewis Mumford complained that Levittown's narrow range of house type and income range resulted in a one-class community and a backward design. He noted that the Levitts used "new-fashioned methods to compound old-fashioned mistakes."

But Levittown was a huge popular success where it counted—in the marketplace. On a single day in March 1949, fourteen hundred contracts were drawn, some with families that had been in line for four days.

"I truly loved it," recalled one early resident. "When they built the Village Green, our big event was walking down there for ice cream."

In the 1950s the Levitts shifted their attention from Long Island to an equally large project near Philadelphia. Located on former broccoli and spinach farms in lower Bucks County, Pennsylvania, this new Levittown was built within a few miles of the new Fairless Works of the United States Steel Corporation, where the largest percentage of the community's residents were employed. It was composed on eight master blocks, each of about one square mile and focusing on its own recreational facilities. Totaling about 16,000 homes when completed late in the decade, the town included light industry and a big, 55-acre shopping center. According to Levitt, "We planned every foot of it—every store, filling station, school, house, apartment, church, color, tree, and shrub."

In the 1960s, the Levitt forces shifted once again, this time to Willingboro, New Jersey, where a third Levittown was constructed within distant commuting range of Philadelphia. This last town was the focus of Herbert Gans's well-known account of *The Levittowners*. The Cape Cod remained the basic style, but Levitt improved the older models to resemble more closely the pseudo-colonial design that was so popular in the Northeast.

If imitation is the sincerest form of flattery, then William Levitt has been much honored in the past forty years. His replacement of basement foundations with the radiantly heated concrete slab was being widely copied as early as 1950. Levitt did not actually pioneer many of the mass-production techniques—the use of plywood, particle board, and gypsum board, as well as power hand tools like saws, routers, and nailers, for example—but his developments were so widely publicized that in every large metropolitan area, large builders appeared who adopted similar methods....

FHA and VA programs made possible the financing of their immense developments. Title VI of the National Housing Act of 1934 allowed a builder to insure 90 percent of the mortgage of a house costing up to nine thousand dollars. Most importantly, an ambitious entrepreneur could get an FHA "commitment" to insure the mortgage, and then use that "commitment" to sign himself up as a temporary mortgagor. The mortgage lender (a bank or savings and loan institution) would then make "production advances" to the contractor as the work progressed, so that the builder needed to invest very little of his own hard cash. Previously, even the largest builders could not bring together the capital to undertake thousand-house developments. FHA alone insured three thousand houses in Henry J. Kaiser's Panorama City, California; five thousand in Frank Sharp's Oak Forest; and eight thousand in Klutznick's Park Forest project.

However financed and by whomever built, the new subdivisions that were typical of American urban development between 1945 and 1973 tended to share five common characteristics. The first was peripheral location. A Bureau of Labor Statistics survey of home building in 1946–1947 in six metropolitan regions determined that the suburbs accounted for at least 62 percent of construction. By 1950 the national suburban growth rate was ten times that of central cities, and in 1954 the editors of *Fortune* estimated that 9 million people had moved to the suburbs in the previous decade. The inner cities did have some empty lots—serviced by sewers, electrical connections, gas lines, and streets—available for development. But the filling-in process was not amenable to mass production techniques, and it satisfied neither the economic nor the psychological temper of the times.

The few new neighborhoods that were located within the boundaries of major cities tended also to be on the open land at the edges of the built-up sections. In New York City, the only area in the 1946–1947 study where city construction was greater than that of the suburbs, the big growth was on the outer edges of Queens, a borough that had been largely undeveloped in 1945. In Memphis new development moved east out Summer, Poplar, Walnut Grove, and Park Avenues, where FHA and VA subdivisions advertised "No Down Payment" or "One Dollar Down" on giant billboards. In Los Angeles, the fastest-growing American city in the immediate postwar period, the area of rapid building focused on the San Fernando Valley, a vast space that had remained largely vacant since its annexation to the city in 1915. In Philadelphia thousands of new houses were put up in farming areas that had legally been part of the city since 1854, but which in fact had functioned as agricultural settlements for generations.

The second major characteristic of the postwar suburbs was their relatively low density. In all except the most isolated instances, the row house completely lost favor; between 1946 and 1956, about 97 percent of all new single-family dwellings were completely detached, surrounded on every side by their own plots. Typical lot sizes were relatively uniform around the country, averaging between 1/5 (80 by 100 feet) and 1/10 (40 by 100 feet) of an acre and varying more with distance from the center than by region. Moreover, the new subdivisions allotted a higher proportion of their land area to streets and open spaces. Levittown, Long Island, for example, was settled at a density of 10,500 per square mile, which was about average for postwar suburbs but less than half as dense as the streetcar suburbs of a half-century earlier. This design of new neighborhoods on the assumption that residents would have automobiles meant that those without cars faced severe handicaps in access to jobs and shopping facilities.

This low-density pattern was in marked contrast with Europe. In war-ravaged countries east of the Rhine River, the concentration upon apartment buildings can be explained by the overriding necessity to provide shelter quickly for masses of displaced and homeless people. But in comparatively unscathed France, Denmark, and Spain, the single-family house was also a rarity. In Sweden, Stockholm committed itself to a suburban pattern along subway lines, a decision that implied a high-density residential pattern. Nowhere in Europe was there the land, the money, or the tradition for single-family home construction.

The third major characteristic of the postwar suburbs was their architectural similarity. A few custom homes were built for the rich, and mobile homes gained popularity with the poor and the transient, but for most American families in search of a new place to live some form of tract house was the most likely option. In order to simplify their production methods and reduce design fees, most of the larger developers offered no more than a half-dozen basic house plans, and some offered half that number. The result was a monotony and repetition that was especially stark in the early years of the subdivision, before the individual owners had transformed their homes and yards according to personal taste.

But the architectural similarity extended beyond the particular tract to the nation as a whole. Historically, each region of the country had developed an indigenous residential style—the colonial-style homes of New England, the row houses of Atlantic coastal cities, the famous Charleston town houses with their ends to the street, the raised plantation homes of the damp bayou country of Louisiana, and the encircled patios and massive walls of the Southwest. This regionalism of design extended to relatively small areas; early in the twentieth century a house on the South Carolina coast looked quite different from a house in the Piedmont a few hundred miles away.

This tradition began eroding after World War I, when the American dream house became … the Cape Cod cottage, a quaint one-and-a-half-story dwelling. This design remained popular into the post–World War II years, when Levittown featured it as a bargain for veterans. In subsequent years, one fad after another became the rage. First, it was the split-level, then the ranch, then the modified colonial. In each case, the style tended to find support throughout the continent, so that by the 1960s the casual suburban visitor would have a difficult time deciphering whether she was in the environs of Boston or Dallas.

The ranch style, in particular, was evocative of the expansive mood of the post–World War II suburbs and of the disappearing regionality of style. It was almost as popular in Westchester County as in Los Angeles County. Remotely derived from the adobe dwellings of the Spanish colonial tradition and more directly derived from the famed prairie houses of [architect] Frank Lloyd Wright, with their low-pitched roofs, deep eaves, and pronounced horizontal lines, the typical ranch style houses of the 1950s were no larger than the average home a generation earlier. But the one-level ranch house suggested spacious living and an easy relationship with the outdoors. Mothers with small children did not have to contend with stairs. Most importantly, the postwar ranch home represented newness. In 1945 the publisher of the *Saturday Evening Post* reported that only 14 percent of the population wanted to live in an apartment or a "used" house. Whatever the style, the post–World War II house, in contrast to its turn-of-the-century predecessor, had no hall, no parlor, no stairs, and no porch. And the portion of the structure that projected farthest toward the street was the garage.

The fourth characteristic of post–World War II housing was its easy availability and thus its reduced suggestion of wealth. To be sure, upper-income suburbs and developments sprouted across the land, and some set high standards of style and design. Typically, they offered expansive lots, spacious and individualized designs, and affluent neighbors. But the most important income development of the period was the lowering of the threshold of purchase. At every previous time in American history, and indeed for the 1980s as well, the successful acquisition of a family home required savings and effort of a major order. After World War II, however, because of mass-production techniques, government financing, high wages, and low interest rates, it was quite simply cheaper to buy new housing in the suburbs than it was to reinvest in central city properties or to rent at the market price.

The fifth and perhaps most important characteristic of the postwar suburb was economic and racial homogeneity. The sorting out of families by income and color began even before the Civil War and was stimulated by the growth of the factory system. This pattern was noticeable in both the exclusive Main Line suburbs of Philadelphia and New York and in the more bourgeois streetcar developments which were part of every city. The automobile accentuated this discriminatory "Jim Crow" pattern. In Atlanta, where large numbers of whites flocked to the fast-growing and wealthy suburbs north of the city in the 1920s, [it was] reported that: "By 1930, if racism could be measured in miles and minutes, blacks and whites were more segregated in the city of Atlanta than ever before." But many pre-1930 suburbs—places like Greenwich, Connecticut; Englewood, New Jersey; Evanston, Illinois; and Chestnut Hill, Massachusetts—maintained an exclusive image despite the presence of low-income or minority groups living in slums near or within the community.

The post-1945 developments took place against a background of the decline of factory-dominated cities. What was unusual in the new circumstances was not the presence of discrimination—Jews and Catholics as well as blacks had been excluded from certain neighborhoods for generations—but the thoroughness of the physical separation which it entailed. The Levitt organization, which was no more culpable in this regard than any other urban or suburban firm, publicly and officially refused to sell to blacks for two decades after the war. Nor did resellers deal with minorities. As William Levitt explained, "We can solve a housing problem, or we can try to solve a racial problem. But we cannot combine the two." Not surprisingly, in 1960 not a single one of the Long Island Levittown's 82,000 residents was black.

The economic and age homogeneity of large subdivisions and sometimes entire suburbs was almost as complete as the racial distinction. Although this tendency had been present even in the nineteenth century, the introduction of zoning—beginning with a New York City ordinance in 1916—served the general purpose of preserving residential class segregation and property values. In theory zoning was designed to protect the interests of all citizens by limiting land speculation and congestion. And it was popular. Although it represented an extraordinary growth of municipal power, nearly everyone supported zoning. By 1926 seventy-six cities had adopted ordinances similar to that of New York. By 1936, 1,322 cities (85 percent of the total) had them, and zoning laws were affecting more property than all national laws relating to business.

In actuality zoning was a device to keep poor people and obnoxious industries out of affluent areas. And in time, it also became a cudgel used by suburban areas to whack the central city. Advocates of land-use restrictions in overwhelming proportion were residents of the fringe. They sought through minimum lot and set-back requirements to insure that only members of acceptable social classes could settle in their privileged sanctuaries. Southern cities even used zoning to enforce racial segregation. And in suburbs everywhere, North and South, zoning was used by the people who already lived within the arbitrary boundaries of a community as a method of keeping everyone else out. Apartments, factories, and "blight," euphemisms for blacks and people of limited means, were rigidly excluded.

While zoning provided a way for suburban areas to become secure enclaves for the well-to-do, it forced the city to provide economic facilities for the whole area and homes for people the suburbs refused to admit. Simply put, land-use restrictions tended to protect residential interests in the suburbs and commercial interests in the cities because the residents of the core usually lived on land owned by absentee landlords who were more interested in financial returns than neighborhood preferences. For the man who owned land but did not live on it, the ideal situation was to have his parcel of earth zoned for commercial or industrial use. With more options, the property often gained in value. In Chicago, for example, three times as much land was zoned for commercial use as could ever have been profitably employed for such purposes. This overzoning prevented inner-city residents from receiving the same protection from commercial incursions as was afforded suburbanites. Instead of becoming a useful tool for the rational ordering of land in metropolitan areas, zoning became a way for suburbs to pirate from the city only its desirable functions and residents. Suburban governments became like so many residential hotels, fighting for the upper-income trade while trying to force the deadbeats to go elsewhere.

Because zoning restrictions typically excluded all apartments and houses and lots of less than a certain number of square feet, new home purchasers were often from a similar income and social group. In this regard, the postwar suburbs were no different from many nineteenth-century neighbor-hoods when they were first built. Moreover, Levittown was originally a mix of young professionals and lower-middle-class blue-collar workers.

As the aspiring professionals moved out, however, Levittown became a community of the most class-stratifying sort possible. This phenomenon was the subject of one of the most important books of the 1950s. Focusing on a 2,400-acre project put up by the former Public Housing Administrator Phillip Klutznick, William H. Whyte's *The Organization Man* sent shudders through armchair sociologists. Although Whyte found that Park Forest, Illinois, offered its residents "leadership training" and an "ability to chew on real problems," the basic portrait was unflattering. Reporting excessive conformity and a mindless conservatism, he showed Park Foresters to be almost interchangeable as they fought their way up the corporate ladder, and his "organization man" stereotype unfortunately became the norm for judging similar communities throughout the nation.

By 1961, when President John F. Kennedy proclaimed his New Frontier and challenged Americans to send a man to the moon within the decade, his countrymen had already remade the nation's metropolitan areas in the short space of sixteen years. From Boston to Los Angeles, vast new subdivi-sions and virtually new towns sprawled where a generation earlier nature had held sway. In an era of low inflation, plentiful energy, federal subsidies, and expansive optimism, Americans showed the way to a more abundant and more perfect lifestyle. Almost every contractor-built, post–World War II home had central heating, indoor plumbing, telephones, automatic stoves, refrigerators, and washing machines.

There was a darker side to the outward movement. By making it possi-ble for young couples to have separate households of their own, abundance further weakened the extended family in America and ordained that most children would grow up in intimate contact only with their parents and siblings. The housing arrangements of the new prosperity were evident as early as 1950. In that year there were 45,983,000 dwelling units to accom-modate the 38,310,000 families in the United States, and 84 percent of American households reported less than one person per room.

Critics regarded the peripheral environment as devastating particularly to women and children. The suburban world was a female world, especially during the day. Betty Friedan's 1963 classic *The Feminine Mystique* chal-lenged the notion that the American dream home was emotionally fulfilling for women. As Gwendolyn Wright has observed, their isolation from work opportunities and from contact with employed adults led to stifled frustration and deep psychological problems. Similarly, Sidonie M. Gruen-berg warned in the *New York Times Magazine* that "mass produced, stan-dardized housing breeds standardized individuals, too—especially among youngsters." Offering neither the urbanity and sophistication of the city nor the tranquility and repose of the farm, the suburb came to be regarded less as an intelligent compromise than a cultural, economic, and emotional wasteland. No observer was more critical than Lewis Mumford, however. In his 1961 analysis of *The City in History*, which covered the entire sweep of civilization, the famed author reiterated sentiments he had first expressed more than four decades earlier and scorned the new developments which were surrounding every American city:

> In the mass movement into suburban areas a new kind of community was produced, which caricatured both the historic city and the archetypal suburban refuge: a multitude of uniform, unidentifiable houses, lined up inflexibly, at uniform distances, on uniform roads, in a treeless communal waste, inhabited by people of the same class, the same income, the same age group, witnessing the same television performances, eating the same tasteless prefabricated foods, from the same freezers, conforming in every outward and inward respect to a common mold, manufactured in the central metropolis. Thus, the ultimate effect of the suburban escape in our own time is, ironically, a low-grade uniform environment from which escape is impossible.

Secondly, because the federally supported home-building boom was of such enormous proportions, the new houses of the suburbs were a major cause of the decline of central cities. Because FHA and VA terms for new construction were so favorable as to make the suburbs accessible to almost all white, middle-income families, the inner-city housing market was deprived of the purchasers who could perhaps have supplied an appropriate demand for the evacuated neighborhoods.

The young families who joyously moved into the new homes of the suburbs were not terribly concerned about the problems of the inner-city housing market or the snobbish views of Lewis Mumford and other social critics. They were concerned about their hopes and their dreams. They were looking for good schools, private space, and personal safety, and places like Levittown could provide those amenities on a scale and at a price that crowded city neighborhoods, both in the Old World and in the New, could not match. The single-family tract house—post–World War II style—whatever its aesthetic failings, offered growing families a private haven in a heartless world. If the dream did not include minorities or the elderly, if it was accompanied by the isolation of nuclear families, by the decline of public transportation, and by the deterioration of urban neighborhoods, the creation of good, inexpensive suburban housing on an unprecedented scale was a unique achievement in the world.

DOCUMENTS

The Melting Pot Goes Suburban, 2002

MAYNARD [MA]—Fist-sized chunks of lamb and pork turned slowly over a crackling barbecue as Dennis Lima, co-owner of the new Rio Cafe on Main Street, patiently explained why thousands of Brazilian immigrants are bypassing Boston and heading straight to the suburbs of Middlesex County.

"Parking tickets. Cockroaches. People sleeping on the steps of the building. And expensive—very expensive," he said of his short time living in Boston, where immigrants have historically settled.

When he moved to Acton and later Boxborough, he said, "We could park. We have a pool. We have everything here."

Down the street in downtown Maynard, where Portuguese is heard more than English along Railroad Street and Florida Road, Americano Borges said Brazilian transplants snap up the Brazilian CDs, soaps, and food products he sells.

"I don't think people go to Boston," he said. "It's too far."

Whether Brazilians in Maynard, Turks in Methuen, Koreans in Newton, or Indians in Shrewsbury, the melting pot is increasingly a suburban phenomenon.

Across the country, immigrants are joining singles and the elderly in a continuing dispersal from cities, according to researchers at the Brookings Institution in Washington, D.C.—fueling a massive change in the demographics of areas long associated with subdivisions and country clubs.

The trend, supported by preliminary Census figures—with more detailed data set to be released by early summer—is so pronounced that immigrants in the suburbs are changing the terms of the debate on sprawl.

Free-market conservatives applaud how immigrants are reviving older suburban communities and cite it as evidence that cities are no longer preferable, even among those who have traditionally settled there. But in another example of the shifting alliances in the politics of sprawl, those who want to slow immigration are trying to align themselves with environmentalists and smart-growth advocates—identifying immigrant-laden population growth as the most powerful force driving sprawl.

The increase of immigrants in the suburbs is leading to conflicted feelings among environmentalists and planners, similar to the discussion about the link between sprawl and housing for low-income families.

The source of that angst, say observers and immigrants who have settled in the Maynard–Acton–Hudson area, lies with two economic truths: the suburbs are where the jobs are; the more development is spread, the more opportunities there are to find affordable housing.

"The rents are low" compared with Allston–Brighton, Cambridge, or Somerville, said Lima, who opened Cafe Rio in December with Jonathan Wise, who he met while working at a Dunkin' Donuts in Acton.

The trade-off, Lima said, is that immigrants must buy a car, because there is virtually no public transportation.

But a 10-year-old car can be had for $500 down, through a network of car dealers that have sprung up in the area that specialize in helping Portuguese-speaking immigrants, Lima said. Many immigrants then car-pool to get to jobs in maintenance or groundskeeping for high-tech firms along I-495, as cooks or waiters at suburban restaurants, as cleaners in suburban homes, or as employees of major retailers. "To start with, it's a matter of learning the English skills to work at the drive-through window," said Karen Pervier, coordinator of the Maynard Adult Learning Center, which includes instruction in English and has a waiting list of 300.

The process of finding those kinds of classes, a home, and a job is repeated over and over as friends and relatives join those who have established themselves. Yet today's suburban-oriented immigrants are less apt to confine themselves to one area, said Isabel Skoog, who assists immigrants as part of the South Middlesex Opportunity Council, a human services organization.

"They have a very good network, and information is passed on—they know where the services are and where their dollar will go the furthest," she said.

Accordingly, Portuguese-speaking immigrants have spilled from Hudson to adjoining towns, and from Framingham to Marlborough, where officials estimate there are 6,000 Brazilians and at least as many people from Russia, Southeast Asia, Mexico, the Caribbean, Peru, Ecuador, and Chile.

Marlborough, Chicopee, and Maynard are the melting-pot hot spots with the most rapidly diversifying populations, said Fatinha Kerr, executive director of Marlborough Community Services Inc.

In the area defined by the US Census Bureau as essentially Eastern Massachusetts, the foreign-born population grew by almost 300,000 from 1990 to 2000. Roughly 85 percent of that growth occurred in the areas around Boston, according to an analysis of the 1990 Census and the Census 2000 Supplemental Survey.

In a study of the Washington, D.C., metropolitan area, Audrey Singer, a researcher at the Brookings Institution's Center for Urban and Metropolitan Policy, found that nearly 90 percent of recent immigrants headed straight for suburban communities. Immigrants are either settling in first- or second-ring suburbs surrounding cities in the Northeast, Singer said, or going to high-growth, low-density areas in the Southwest or West, such as Atlanta or Las Vegas.

Combined with other demographic changes—a Brookings study released last month found that singles and seniors outnumber traditional married couples in the suburbs—the choices being made by immigrants will radically change perceptions of suburbia, she said.

"There are huge implications, for schools, for housing, the labor market. There are some areas that aren't used to receiving immigrants. There can be conflict within neighborhoods," she said.

For Maynard, with a population of about 10,000, the influx of Brazilians is being viewed as a more positive development for a community with a history of economic ups and downs—as the latest phase of a continuing reinvention. The computer company Digital used the original woolen mill for its headquarters but then went out of business; the offices around the Clock Tower are just filling back to capacity with smaller firms. "Obviously there must be jobs around," said Maynard resident Roy Helander, a member of the Maynard Historical Society.

Maynard High School recently had all of its students research their family histories and then displayed the flags of their countries of origin in the school cafeteria. There were nearly 100.

Selectwoman Anne Marie Desmarais, who has lived in Maynard for 22 years, said she worries that "we're a bit thin on support services. We can't reach out like a big city can." She also believes that the traditionally quiet area can be "culturally and emotionally isolating," especially for women without job skills.

But, she said, the fact that immigrants would come to Maynard is heartening to many residents, and testament to how the community is more affordable than its neighbors Sudbury, Wayland, and Concord: "They wouldn't come here unless they felt welcome."

Big Apple, Southern Cities Tops in Growth, 2011

The century-long quest of Americans to live in perpetual sunshine and far from snow shows no sings of letting up as surging growth infuses Sun Belt cities with new residents.

The Census Bureau reports today that seven of the 10 most populous U.S. cities are within 500 miles of Mexico. In 1910, all 10 of the biggest cities were within 500 miles of the Canadian border. The once-dominant industrial cities of Cleveland, Pittsburgh and Buffalo find themselves smaller than Mesa, Ariz, and Fresno.

The big exception to the smaller gains outside the Sun Belt is the Big Apple. New York City ranks No. 1 in attracting new residents since 2000,

SOURCE: "Big Apple, Southern Cities Top in Growth," from Dennis Cauchon and Paul Overberg, USA Today, Feb. 7, 2011. From *USA Today*, a division of Gannett Co., Inc. Reprinted with Permission.

adding nearly 206,000 people. That's more than Phoenix, Houston or Los Angeles gained. Of the 35 cities that added the most population, New York is the only one not located in the South or West.

Economic prosperity and the arrival of new immigrants, who have higher birth rates than the overall population, are driving the city's growth. "It's written into the DNA of New York that immigrants are welcome," says Warren Brown of the Cornell Institute for Social and Economic Research.

In a change more symbolic of national population trends, Phoenix has supplanted Philadelphia as the nation's fifth-largest city, according to Census estimates for July 1, 2006.

"It's hard to think of the cradle of liberty being overtaken by a rough-and-tumble, independent Western town, but that tells you something about the nature of our country," says Brookings Institution demographer William Frey. "We're a country that's always seeking new horizons."

The explosive growth in parts of the South and West has created boom cities that many people have never heard of Gilbert, Arlz, a Phoenix suburb, has been adding more than 1,000 people a month for five years and had a population of 191,517 last year.

"It's fun. It's exciting to be growing this fast," says Gilbert Mayor Steve Berman, who moved to town in 1981 when the population was 4,000. "We're creating the coolest place to live."

By contrast, Green Bay, Wis., (100,353) has been losing population.

"We don't want to fall below 100,000," says Green Bay City Council President Chad Fradette. "That has a little prestige with it."

Chapter 13

Minorities' Struggles for Equality

Integrating Little Rock's Central High School, October 3, 1957.

Southern white educators, relying on the "separate but equal" doctrine announced in the 1896 *Plessy v. Ferguson* Supreme Court decision, insisted that their states could operate dual racial school systems. Consequently, segregated public education was the norm throughout the South. In the late 1930s, the National Association for the Advancement of Colored People (NAACP) began to attack racial inequality in American schools, at first suing communities that ran inferior schools for African-American children and students. The NAACP pointed out that schools for black children received far less funding than was allocated to white schools and were housed in inferior facilities. Feeling the pressure, some communities did begin to spend more for black education. Gradually, some southern state universities also began to admit limited numbers of African Americans to their graduate-level programs. But primary and secondary schools continued to be racially segregated into the early 1950s, and southern communities continued to spend considerably more for white schools than for blacks.

Finally, the NAACP assailed the "separate but equal" doctrine itself, claiming that racially segregated schools were inherently unconstitutional. In 1954 the Supreme Court, in a unanimous decision (*Brown v. Board of Education*) written by Chief Justice Earl Warren, agreed and overturned the *Plessy v. Ferguson* decision as it applied to education. But as William Doyle points out in his essay "Crisis in Little Rock," it was one thing to hand down a court decision and another for the states and local communities to enforce it. In 1957, a modest plan to introduce desegregation in Little Rock, Arkansas's Central High School led to a major crisis that engulfed a handful of black children, angry white mobs, Governor Orval Faubus, and the National Guard. Eventually the crisis forced a reluctant President Dwight Eisenhower to intervene on the side of desegregation and federal authority. The Little Rock conflict received major coverage in the nation's media, became the subject of a famous painting by Norman Rockwell, and helped win increased support for black civil rights outside the South. What do you think there was about this event that so stirred emotions throughout the nation? Based on what you have read in this essay, how would you evaluate Dwight Eisenhower's record on civil rights?

The first document, an account of growing up in the racially segregated South, is by African-American civil rights leader Hosea Williams. How do his experiences help explain why so many young African-American youth, like those in Little Rock, were willing to subject themselves to physical danger in order to achieve their full and equal rights as citizens?

As the second document illustrates, opposition to desegregation was by no means limited to street mobs. It is an excerpt from "The Southern Manifesto," signed by most southern members of Congress in 1956. Based upon what you have read, what is your opinion of the Manifesto's view of the "relations between the white and Negro races" during the ninety years prior to *Brown v. Board of Education?*

The third document, from a 2005 report by the National Urban League, reveals the status of wealth and income among blacks compared to that of whites. While acknowledging progress in many areas since the civil rights movement of the 1960s, the study provides statistical evidence that blacks remain victims of a considerable "racial wealth gap." What does the author identify as the chief factors that place African Americans in this position?

African Americans were not alone in their protest against injustice. The last document relates to American Indians. In 1969 a group of fourteen Native Americans seized Alcatraz Island in San Francisco Bay, demanding that the U.S. government make amends for centuries of ill treatment of their people. As you read, be aware of the note of irony as the protests purposely turn the history of Indian-white relations upside down before presenting a list of current grievances.

ESSAY

Crisis in Little Rock

William Doyle

We could have another Civil War on our hands.

—President Dwight D. Eisenhower, cabinet meeting, March 1956

Little Rock, Arkansas, September 8, 1957, 8:50 A.M.

A shy 15-year-old girl wearing bobby sox, ballet slippers, and a crisp black-and-white cotton dress stepped off a bus and walked toward Central High School, carrying a set of school books.

Elizabeth Eckford and nine other black students hoped to enter the all-white school today as part of a desegregation plan ordered by a federal judge. Because Eckford's family did not have a phone, she had missed the instructions to join the other students this morning, so she was walking toward the school completely alone.

Until today, Arkansas was making slow, peaceful progress toward integration. The state university was quietly desegregated in 1948, the state bus system had been integrated, and black patrolmen were on the Little Rock police force. Several school districts were planning to accept black students this semester. In the wake of a lawsuit by the NAACP (National Association for the Advancement of Colored People), the Little Rock school board had approved a plan to gradually desegregate Central High, and 10 volunteer students were selected to go in.

Through her sunglasses Eckford could see the school up ahead, and she was amazed at how big it was. She was so nervous, she hadn't slept at all the night before, so to pass the time she had read her Bible. She dwelled on the opening passage of the Twenty-seventh Psalm: "The Lord is my light and my salvation; whom shall I fear? the Lord is the strength of my life; of whom shall I be afraid?"

As she neared the school, the girl became vaguely aware of a crowd of white people swarming around her. Somewhere a voice called out, "Here she comes, get ready!" People started shouting insults. "Then my knees started to shake all of a sudden," Eckford later explained privately to Little Rock NAACP leader Daisy Bates, "and I wondered whether I could make it to the center entrance a block away. It was the longest block I ever walked in my whole life."

Eckford could see uniformed soldiers ringing the entrance and letting white students into the school, and she assumed they were supposed to protect her. But when she approached the entrance, one soldier waved her away. When she tried to move past another soldier, he and his comrades lifted their bayonet-tipped M-1 rifles and surged toward her to block her path.

The soldiers were Arkansas National Guardsmen, and their commander in chief was Democratic governor Orval Eugene Faubus, who had ordered the troops to block the black students at gunpoint. Faubus was a hound dog–faced populist who was born in a plank cabin in a remote Ozark forest near a place called Greasy Creek, and grew up trapping skunks to help his family scrape out a living. Until today, he was considered something of a moderate on racial issues. But Faubus was up for reelection, and sensing a rising white backlash to integration, he decided to become its champion.

When she faced the solid wall of soldiers, Elizabeth Eckford wasn't sure what to do, so she retreated back across the street and into the white mob. Voices called out, "Lynch her! Lynch her!" and "Go home, you burr-head!" She scanned the mob for someone who might help her and spotted an old woman who seemed to have a kind face. The woman spat on her. A voice from the mob announced, "No nigger bitch is going to get in our school. Get out of here!"

The chanting mob swelled toward five hundred. Behind Eckford, someone said, "Push her!" Eckford later explained that she was afraid she would "bust out crying," and she "didn't want to in front of all that crowd." Ahead of her, news photographers snapped photos of a young white student named Hazel Bryan screaming at Eckford behind her back, a searing image that would soon be flashed around the world. "I looked down the block and saw a bench at the bus stop," recalled Eckford. "I thought, 'If only I can get there I will be safe.' I don't know why the bench seemed a safe place to me but I started walking toward it."

Eckford made it to the bus stop and sat down with her head bowed, tightly gripping her books as news cameras whirred and snapped. Someone in the crowd said, "Get a rope and drag her over to this tree." Benjamin Fine, an education reporter from the *New York Times* who had been scribbling notes in his steno pad, sat down next to Eckford, wrapped his arm around her shoulder, and whispered, "Don't let them see you cry."

A furious white woman named Grace Lorch fought her way through the mob, and screamed, "Leave this child alone! Why are you tormenting her? Six months from now, you will hang your heads in shame." Lorch tried to enter a drugstore to call a taxi for Eckford, but the door was slammed in her face.

"She's just a little girl," Lorch declared to the mob as she moved next to Eckford to defend her. "I'm just waiting for one of you to dare touch me! I'm just aching to punch somebody in the nose!"

Eventually a bus came, Mrs. Lorch helped Eckford up the stairs, and the bus pulled away. Eckford got off at the school for the blind, where her mother taught, and ran to her classroom. "Mother was standing at the window with her head bowed," Eckford recalled, "but she must have sensed I was there because she turned around. She looked as if she had been crying, and I wanted to tell her I was all right. But I couldn't speak. She put her arms around me and I cried."

Minutes after Eckford was turned away, her colleagues, who with her would soon become world famous as the "Little Rock Nine," were refused admission as well: Melba Pattillo, Gloria Ray, Carlotta Walls, Minnijean Brown, Thelma Mothershed, Ernest Green, Jefferson Thomas, and Terrence Roberts. A tenth black student who was turned back, Jane Hill, chose to return to all-black Horace Mann High School.

Over the next two weeks, frantic negotiations resulted in a summit conference between President Dwight D. Eisenhower and Governor Faubus at Ike's vacation retreat in Newport, Rhode Island, during which the president thought he'd made a deal with Faubus to deploy Arkansas National Guardsmen to protect the black students as they entered Central High. But on September 23, when the Little Rock Nine tried again to enter the school, Faubus ordered the National Guard instead to abandon the premises.

Escorted by Little Rock police, the Nine briefly made it inside the school and started their classes. But outside the building, a furious mob of more than one thousand white civilians was surging against barricades, threatening to overwhelm the police trying to hold them in check. A white woman cried out hysterically to the police, "They've got the doors locked. They won't let the white kids out. My daughter's in there with those niggers. Oh, my God, oh God!" Policemen lashed out with their billy clubs, knocking down two men in the mob. "Come out!" adults yelled to the white students. "Don't stay in there with those niggers!"

A pack of fifty white men peeled off down a side street to chase a tall black journalist named Alex Wilson, civil rights reporter for Defender Publications, a national chain of black newspapers. A voice warned, "Run, nigger, run!" The mob caught up with Wilson and attacked him from behind with their fists. A brick slammed point-blank into the back of his head, and he tumbled to the ground like a mighty tree. Wilson raised himself to a kneeling position, was kicked and punched, but still he rose, grasping his hat in his hand. He brushed off his fedora, recreased it, and resumed walking.

"Strangely, the vision of Elizabeth Eckford flashed before me," Wilson recalled soon after the attack. "I decided not to run. If I were to be beaten, I'd take it walking if I could—not running." He told his wife, Emogene, "They would have had to kill me before I would have run." Another brick scored a direct hit on the back of Wilson's head, but he kept walking. "I looked into the tear-filled eyes of a white woman. Although there was sorrow in her eyes, I knew there would not be any help."

222

In a frantic effort to take Wilson down again, a crazed-looking, stocky white man in coveralls jumped clear up onto Wilson's back and wrapped his arm around his neck in a choke hold, but the ex-marine Wilson shook him off. "Don't kill him," a voice in the crowd cautioned the mob. Finally Wilson reached his car and escaped.

In front of Central High, a white policeman named Thomas Dunaway suddenly flung his billy club to the street, threw down his badge, and walked away from the barricade. The crowd cheered him, and a young man yelled, "He's the only white man on the force!"A hat was passed around the crowd, and it soon filled up with two hundred dollars in donations for the officer.

Inside Central High School, police and school officials gathered the nine black students. Word was relayed from the mob that they would not storm the building if one black pupil was turned over to them, presumably to be torn to pieces or hung from a tree. Instead, the Little Rock police chief evacuated the Nine out a side door into police cars that blasted away from the school.

At 12:14 P.M., police lieutenant Carl Jackson faced the mob and announced through a loudspeaker, "The Negroes have been withdrawn from the school." Someone in the crowd replied, "That's just a pack of lies!" Then another shouted, "We don't believe you!" A Mrs. Allen Thevenet stepped out from the mob and offered to verify the claim. After a full tour of the building, Mrs. Thevenet marched to the loudspeaker, and proclaimed, "We went through every room in the school and there was no niggers there."

White supremacists across the South rejoiced. Integration at Central High had been defeated in barely half a day.

The next day, September 24, President Eisenhower was back at the White House, and he was furious. He was supposed to still be on vacation. Instead, the old general was sitting at his desk in the Oval Office, dripping with rage over the treachery of Orval Faubus. "He double-crossed me," fumed the president.

On the wall of the elliptical presidential office were two small paintings, one of Union general and U.S. president Ulysses S. Grant, the other of Confederate general and Southern demigod Robert E. Lee. They captured the paradox at the heart of the America Eisenhower led. Nearly a century after the Civil War, as the nation asserted global moral leadership and reached out to explore the heavens, millions of black Americans were effectively not citizens of the country in which they were born.

That morning, the mayor of Little Rock had sent a desperate telegram to the president, who had been still savoring his relaxing vacation in Newport, Rhode Island. "The immediate need for federal troops is urgent," the mayor pleaded. "Situation is out of control and police cannot disperse the mob." Ike now feared a full-blown insurrection in the city.

The battle Eisenhower never wanted was hurtling toward him, and he was afraid it could tear the country apart. As his officials debated civil rights at a March 1956 Cabinet meeting, Eisenhower confessed, "I'm at sea on all this." He added, "Not enough people know how deep this emotion is in the South. Unless you've lived there you can't know…. We could have another Civil War on our hands."

On May 17, 1954, in its decision on *Brown v. the Board of Education of Topeka, Kansas*, the United States Supreme Court outlawed government-imposed segregation in public schools, but a year later the Court ruled that the order should be implemented not immediately, but "with all deliberate speed." This ambiguous phrase gave federal judges leeway to impose integration on varying timetables in different school districts, which delayed progress in some places well into the next decade.

Privately, Eisenhower disagreed with the *Brown* decision, and believed it could only be implemented slowly. "When emotions are deeply stirred," he wrote in July 1957 to his childhood friend Swede Hazlett, "logic and reason must operate gradually and with consideration for human feelings or we will have a resultant disaster rather than human advancement."

"School segregation itself," Ike pointed out, "was, according to the Supreme Court decision of 1896 [the *Plessy v. Ferguson* case], completely Constitutional until the reversal of that decision was accomplished in 1954. The decision of 1896 gave a cloak of legality to segregation in all its forms." People couldn't change overnight, Ike believed.

Dwight Eisenhower was a creature of forty years in the hermetically segregated U.S. military, and he personally had no quarrel with separation of the races. Although as president he quietly completed Harry S. Truman's 1948 order desegregating the armed forces and ordered the integration of public facilities in the nation's capital, not once in eight years in office did Ike publicly endorse the concept of integration. In that time he met with civil rights leaders on a grand total of one occasion—in a meeting that took less than an hour.

On the rare occasions he met with other black audiences, Eisenhower would sternly say, "Now, you people have to be patient." His attitude toward the black White House servants was "definitely not friendly" in the words of one of them, "the President hardly knew we were there." In private, he traded "nigger jokes" with his tycoon cronies.

Eisenhower appointed only one black person to his staff, and E. Frederic Morrow's experience as the first black White House official in history was pathetic. Promised a job during the 1952 campaign, Morrow showed up in Washington only to find the offer was withdrawn because White House employees threatened to boycott their jobs if he entered the building. The White House wouldn't return his calls.

Seventeen months later, an unemployed Morrow was offered temporary work in the Commerce Department. After he was finally moved to the White House two years later to work on miscellaneous "special projects," he was ignored by Eisenhower and humiliated by most everybody else. He couldn't find anyone to be his secretary. Women entered his office only in pairs to avoid talk of sexual misconduct. Morrow was not formally appointed and sworn in until 1959, and he spent much of his time feeling heartsick and ridiculous as he traveled the country defending Ike's indifferent civil rights stand to black audiences.

At the final White House Christmas party, Eisenhower pulled Morrow aside to say he had called all his friends but no one would hire a Negro. "Literally, out on my ear," Morrow reported. "I was the only member of the staff for whom the president could not find a job." It took him three years to find one.

In the days after the *Brown* decision, the man who defeated Hitler was too timid to lift a finger as black Americans and federal courts launched probing assaults on segregation, and white supremacists counterattacked with speed, imagination, brutality, and a strategy of "massive resistance" to integration.

In 1955, when fourteen-year-old black Chicago boy Emmett Till was tortured and executed by a gang of Mississippi whites for allegedly whistling at a white woman, Ike ignored his mother's telegrams pleading for justice.

During the epic bus boycott triggered in 1955 by Rosa Parks to protest segregation in public transportation in Montgomery, Alabama, Eisenhower stubbornly sat on his hands. He even refused to oppose the state's plan to arrest the Reverend Martin Luther King, Jr., for leading the peaceful, entirely legal campaign. In February 1956 Eisenhower did nothing when white mobs went on a rampage at the University of Alabama and chased black applicant Autherine Lucy out of town.

On March 12, 1956, nearly one hundred senators and congressmen introduced a "Southern Manifesto," which rejected *Brown* and pledged "to use all lawful means to bring about a reversal of this decision which is contrary to the Constitution and to prevent the use of force in its implementation." Eisenhower had virtually no comment. Later that year, Texas governor Allan Shivers deployed Texas Rangers to block the federal court-ordered integration of Mansfield High School and Texarkana Junior College. Again Ike did nothing. The armies of white "massive resistance" grew stronger.

Even Dwight Eisenhower had his limits, though. He supported blacks' right to vote and was disgusted by Southern Democratic attempts to block it. On September 9, 1957, he signed the Civil Rights Act of 1957, the first federal civil rights legislation since Reconstruction.

The law empowered the federal government to enforce voting rights, but congressional Democrats, including Lyndon Johnson, John F. Kennedy, and the Southern bloc, gutted the act by requiring that voting-rights offenses be prosecuted before jury trials, which guaranteed acquittals in the South. Eisenhower issued a rare public statement on civil rights, saying that the jury-trial requirement of the Civil Rights Act would be "bitterly disappointing" to many millions of Americans who "will continue to be disenfranchised."

Eisenhower also took his constitutional obligations to uphold the laws very seriously, and the mob violence in Little Rock was giving them their first battlefield test.

On the flight from Newport back to Washington, he scribbled angrily on a notepad, "Troops—*not* to enforce integration but to prevent opposition by violence to orders of a court." Whatever his feelings on *Brown*, he felt, "there must be respect for the Constitution—which means the Supreme Court's interpretation of the Constitution—or we shall have chaos.

Now, at the White House, at 12:15 P.M. on September 24, Eisenhower called the Pentagon and ordered U.S. Army paratroopers of the 101st Airborne Division "Screaming Eagles" to seize Little Rock. "If you have to use force," Ike believed, "use overwhelming force and save lives thereby." Within hours, fifty-two planeloads of airborne infantry troops were racing westward from Fort Campbell, Kentucky.

Eisenhower was disgusted that he had to order troops into action on American soil, but he felt secure in his authority to do so. In his proclamation, which committed the troops, he invoked provisions of the U.S. Code, including Chapter 15 of Title 10, Section 332, which specified that "if rebellion against the authority of the United States" made it impossible to enforce the law, the president "may call into Federal service such of the militia of any state, and use such of the armed forces, as he considers necessary to enforce those laws or to suppress the rebellion." When the Supreme Court reviewed the principle in 1879, it ruled as follows: "We hold it to be an incontrovertible principle, that the Government of the United States may by means of physical force, exercised through its official agents, execute on every foot of American soil the powers and functions that belong to it."

Accompanied by wailing sirens and flashing headlights, federal paratroopers in sharply pressed olive-green battle fatigues jumped out of trucks and half-tracks and assumed dress formation around the Central High School perimeter, M-1 rifles slung on their shoulders and entrenching tools stuffed in their belts. One thousand soldiers were in place by nightfall.

On the morning of September 25, Major General Edwin Walker, in dress uniform, sped up to the school and took command. He was a general's general, a tall, lean Texan who had served under Eisenhower as a commando in Europe during World War II, fighting in the Anzio invasion and in the conquest of southern France. Walker flatly disagreed with this operation, believing that American troops had no business getting involved in domestic peacekeeping; that was the job of civilian police only. Privately, Walker offered his resignation, but Ike refused to accept it.

General Walker and his officers huddled over a battle map and aerial photos of the assault zone, reviewing the tactical plan: paratroopers lining the street at intervals of three yards ... a detachment, with rifles, in the hallway outside every classroom ... troops not to enter the classroom unless a teacher calls for help ... all Negro troops to be kept out of sight at the Little Rock University Armory until further notice ... any group of more than three adults within a mile of the school to be dispersed ... civilians to be treated politely and addressed as "sir" and "ma'am" at all times.

At 8:00 A.M., pockets of sullen white onlookers gathered around the school. An otherworldly silence prevailed, soon pierced by bursts of radio traffic on the troops' walkie-talkies. An army helicopter appeared low in the sky, buzzing the area in search of trouble. A pink-shirted boy jeered at the troops. "Why don't you tin soldiers go home?"

Coy Vance, a white seventeen-year-old student planning to study medicine, declared, "I'm not going to school with niggers, because they are inferior to us." The boy vowed, "If I catch one, I'll chase him out of the school." Bonnie Vance, his sixteen-year-old sister, chimed in, "If they didn't have soldiers in the halls the niggers would get murdered." Senior Tommy Dunn speculated: "I think that if they get chased in the halls enough they will leave by themselves. Don't they know we don't want them?"

Major James Meyers called up an army mobile public-address system and announced, "You are instructed to go to your homes peacefully. Disperse and return to your homes." The crowd wouldn't budge. Soon two platoons of infantrymen dog-trotted in formation toward the two biggest crowd concentrations. "Back!" a soldier yelled. "Back on the sidewalk!"

A sergeant barked the command, "Bayonets at the back of their heads, move 'em fast!" The paratroopers advanced, bayonets pointed out, and began pushing the crowds down the side streets. Forty-seven-year-old railroad worker C. E. Blake stood his ground and tried to grab a paratrooper's rifle. The trooper quickly flipped his rifle around and punched Blake over the eye with the rifle butt, knocking him to the ground. Nearby, Paul Downs of Springfield, Arkansas, got jabbed in the arm with a bayonet when he didn't move fast enough.

General Walker dispatched army station wagons, jeeps with mounted turret guns, and trucks packed with bayonet-wielding troops to pick up the black teenagers at a designated group-pickup spot and drive to the school at high speed to avoid possible snipers, under the watchful gaze of an escort helicopter. Then he ordered the white students of Central High to an assembly. The astonished teenagers passed bayonet-wielding Airborne troops and filed into the auditorium for an address by General Walker. There was dead silence as Walker took the stage.

"As an officer of the United States Army," General Walker announced to the wide-eyed students, "I have been chosen to command these forces and to execute the President's orders.... We are all subject to all the laws whether we approve of them or not, and as law-abiding citizens, we have an obligation in conscience to obey them. There can be no exceptions; if it were otherwise, we would not be a strong nation but a mere unruly mob.

"You have nothing to fear from my soldiers, and no one will interfere with your coming, going or your peaceful pursuit of your studies," the general concluded. "They are seasoned, well-trained soldiers, many of them combat veterans. Being soldiers, they are as determined as I to carry out their orders." Walker strode out of the hall.

At 9:20 A.M., shouts erupted outside the school, "There they come!" A U.S. Army station wagon raced through a security barricade up to the front entrance of Central High, flanked by two jeeps stuffed with helmeted troops. The black students got out of the wagon, six girls in brightly colored dresses and with books under their arms, and three boys in sport shirts, one swinging his books on a strap. The windows of the school were packed with white students quietly peering down at the historic tableau.

Thirty paratroopers formed a protective bubble around the black children as 350 soldiers stood at attention around the school. "Forward march," an officer called out. "We began moving forward," wrote Melba Pattillo. "The eerie silence of that moment would forever be etched in my memory. All I could hear was my own heartbeat and the sound of boots clicking on the stone. Everything seemed to be moving in slow motion as I peered past the raised bayonets of the 101st soldiers." That morning, Pattillo heard her colleague Minnijean Brown say, "For the first time in my life, I feel like an American citizen."

Many white Southerners reacted with horror at the spectacle, and Southern newspapers launched a chorus of outrage. Governor Faubus, now riding a wave of popular support in Arkansas for his defiance, said in a TV speech, "We are now an occupied territory." "In the name of God," he implored, "what's happening in America?"

In Marshall, Texas, a speaker at a Kiwanis meeting proclaimed the Little Rock event "the darkest day in Southern history since Reconstruction." The Kiwanians then refused to pledge allegiance to the American flag. Georgia's senator Herman Talmadge thundered, "The South is threatened by the President of the U.S. using tanks and troops in the streets of Little Rock. I wish I could cast one vote for impeachment right now." South Carolina's senator Olin Johnston proposed an even more radical step: "If I were Governor Faubus, I'd proclaim a state of insurrection down there, and I'd call out the National Guard and I'd then find out who's going to run things in my state."

President Eisenhower himself was defensive, knowing that while 75 percent of Northerners in a Gallup Poll thought his Little Rock operation was right, only 36 percent of Southerners did. "No one can deplore more than I do the sending of federal troops anywhere," he told a press conference after the deployment. At the same time, he pointed out, "the courts must be sustained or it's not America."

Inside Central High School, however, there were some hopeful signs. Melba Pattillo recalled entering her first class: "My heart skipped a beat as the classroom door closed behind me." Then she looked back and saw her bodyguard, a helmeted young soldier of the 101st Airborne, gazing through the door window, keeping watch over her. "Sunlight flooded into the room through a full bank of windows along the far wall," she wrote. "It was a beautiful morning."

During lunch, one of the black male students sat alone in the cafeteria with a glass of milk and a sandwich. Some white students nearby asked him, "Won't you join us?" The boy broke into an enthusiastic smile. "Gee, thanks," he replied. "I'd love to." They finished their meals together, eating and chatting.

The "Battle of Little Rock" was over nearly as soon as it started, without a single serious injury and without a shot fired.

DOCUMENTS

Growing Up Black in the South: A Remembrance, 1977

I was born in poverty. My mother was never married to my father, which was a stigma in the American society…. I was reared up in Decatur County, Georgia … that's southwest Georgia, and the racism of segregation was so prevalent until it was something that you had to notice, like black farmers couldn't plant tobacco. They didn't allow black men to plant tobacco, 'cause there's a lot of money in it. White people virtually owned black people … they'd concoct debts, like you get in jail, all the white man had to do, to come there, and the sheriff would let you out, and the white man tell the sheriff to tell you he paid a hundred dollars for you, but you didn't have to worry 'bout that hundred dollars long as you stay on his farm and work. If you ever left to go to Florida, he'd come get you, arrest you and bring you back…. There's a white man down there named Wonnie Miller. On the Wonnie Miller farm, all the blacks were born and worked and lived and died in poverty, and they worked like slaves from "cain't to cain't"— say, "Ya cain't see your hand before your face when you go out in the field, and ya cain't see your hand when you come in from the field," because it was dark each time. And Mr. Wonnie used to ride a big horse and never really worked, and he died a millionaire. All his children are rich….

We used to walk two and a half miles to school … the white kids always had a bus. No black kids were allowed to ride the bus, and I guess every day of my life—it looked like to me every day, probably just my

SOURCE: From *My Soul Is Rested*, by Howell Raines. Copyright © 1977 by Howell Raines. Used by permission of G. P. Putnam's Sons, a division of Penguin Group (USA).

imagination—those white kids would spit on us or throw rocks at us, holler, and call us "niggers." *Every* day. Pick at us, and I just knew that was not right.

In my early life once whites tried to lynch me about a little white girl that was from a very poor family that lived up there. Her father was a bum, wouldn't work; all he did was fish and hunt all the time, just like some of the black families. The word got around that I was havin' affair with the girl. This was a rumor, and they came to the house to lynch me ... and my grandfather stood 'em off with a gun. We went over to white man's house, Mr. Wonnie Miller, who took the thing up and stopped the whites....

The vast majority of blacks was reared in the same circumstances I was reared in. It's just hard for me to see how they can go along and take it. Then I educated myself and became a professional person. I thought you could escape black America by being educated and professional and being rich, and you just cain't do it.* ...

I was paid well. I went right up, straight up the ladder. I was accepted, *I thought*, but what I really finally decided, I had hit that "nigger ceiling." They wasn't gonna let me go no higher.... I had more publication than all the white guys put together, except an old Ph.D. who had thirty years in the lab. So the assistant chief's job became open, and I thought sure they'd make me the assistant chief, because I thought they had accepted me as a scientist. And they gave the job to a white girl who knew very little chemistry, and that was a very hard pill for me to swallow. But you know the old thing 'bout how Jackie Robinson made it in baseball, the old poem, "Life Ain't Been No Christmas Day," and all this jazz, so I bought it and buckled my bed up: "After all, I'm black and she's white. My day comin'."

I remember one time after I bought this new home and new car.... You know, I was a social climbin', middle-class Negro. I guess I was the first black person in Savannah to have a zoysia lawn. I remember buying this grass from Sears and Roebuck, and had sodded my lawn, and I was out there one day tryin' to water it, and my hose would not stretch to sprinkle across the whole lawn. I had a big lot there. And I went back up to this new drugstore ... gonna buy some hose connectors, an extension to a hose.... And I carried my two sons with me. They wasn't but about six and seven, six and eight years old then, and as we walked into this drugstore, it had a long lunch counter and these white kids were sittin' on these stools, spinnin' around, eatin' hot dogs and drinkin' Co-cola.

And my boys started askin' me, "Daddy, let's get a sandwich and a Coke." But I always will believe what they wanted to do was play on those stools, and I said, "Naw, you cain't have a Coke and sandwich."

---

*Williams became a chemist with the U.S. Department of Agriculture Bureau of Entomology in Savannah.

And one of 'em started cryin'. And I said, "Well, you know, I'm gonna take you back home and Momma'll fix you a hot dog and give you a Coke," and then both of 'em started cryin'. And both of them just fell out in the floor, which was very unusual for my kids to do me like that. And I remember stoopin' down and I started cryin', because I realized I couldn't tell 'em the truth. The truth was they was black and they didn't 'low black people to use them lunch counters. So I picked the two kids up and went back to the car and I guess I made 'em a promise that I'd bring 'em back someday. So that really got me involved.

The Southern Manifesto, 1956

The unwarranted decision of the Supreme Court in the public school cases is now bearing the fruit always produced when men substitute naked power for established law.

The Founding Fathers gave us a Constitution of checks and balances because they realized the inescapable lesson of history that no man or group of men can be safely entrusted with unlimited power. They framed this Constitution with its provisions for change by amendment in order to secure the fundamentals of government against the dangers of temporary popular passion or the personal predilections of public officeholders.

We regard the decision of the Supreme Court in the school cases as a clear abuse of judicial power. It climaxes a trend in the Federal Judiciary undertaking to legislate, in derogation of the authority of Congress, and to encroach upon the reserved rights of the States and the people.

The original Constitution does not mention education. Neither does the 14th amendment nor any other amendment. The debates preceding the submission of the 14th amendment clearly show that there was no intent that it should affect the system of education maintained by the States.

The very Congress which proposed the amendment subsequently provided for segregated schools in the District of Columbia.

When the amendment was adopted in 1868, there were 37 States of the Union. Every one of the 26 States that had any substantial racial differences among its people, either approved the operation of segregated schools already in existence or subsequently established such schools by action of the same law-making body which considered the 14th amendment.

As admitted by the Supreme Court in the public school case (*Brown* v. *Board of Education*), the doctrine of separate but equal schools "apparently originated in *Roberts* v. *City of Boston* (1849), upholding school segregation against attack as being violative of a State constitutional guarantee of

SOURCE: Declaration of Constitutional Principles," *Congressional Record*, 84th Cong., 2d sess., March 12, 1956, 4460–61.

equality." This constitutional doctrine began in the North, not in the South, and it was followed not only in Massachusetts, but in Connecticut, New York, Illinois, Indiana, Michigan, Minnesota, New Jersey, Ohio, Pennsylvania and other northern States until they, exercising their rights as States through the constitutional processes of local self-government, changed their school systems.

In the case of *Plessy* v. *Ferguson* in 1896 the Supreme Court expressly declared that under the 14th amendment no person was denied any of his rights if the States provided separate but equal public facilities. This decision has been followed in many other cases. It is notable that the Supreme Court, speaking through Chief Justice Taft, a former President of the United States, unanimously declared in 1927 in *Lum* v. *Rice* that the "separate but equal" principle is "within the discretion of the State in regulating its public schools and does not conflict with the 14th amendment."

This interpretation, restated time and again, became a part of the life of the people of many of the States and confirmed their habits, customs, traditions, and way of life. It is founded on elemental humanity and common-sense, for parents should not be deprived by Government of the right to direct the lives and education of their own children.

Though there has been no constitutional amendment or act of Congress changing this established legal principle almost a century old, the Supreme Court of the United States, with no legal basis for such action, undertook to exercise their naked judicial power and substituted their personal political and social ideas for the established law of the land.

This unwarranted exercise of power by the Court, contrary to the Constitution, is creating chaos and confusion in the States principally affected. It is destroying the amicable relations between the white and Negro races that have been created through 90 years of patient effort by the good people of both races. It has planted hatred and suspicion where there has been heretofore friendship and understanding.

Without regard to the consent of the governed, outside agitators are threatening immediate and revolutionary changes in our public-school systems. If done, this is certain to destroy the system of public education in some of the States....

Wealth and Income Inequality, 2005

Race and Wealth

Racial inequality remains a festering public and private issue in American society. Because we have dismantled the most oppressive racist policies

SOURCE: National Urban League, *The State of Black Americans: The Equality Index*, 2005, 41–45.

and practices of our past, many have come to believe that the United States has moved beyond race and that we should center now on race-neutrality and color blindness. Proclaiming the successes of the civil rights agenda and the dawning of a postracial age in America, books by Shelby Steele, Abigail and Stephan Thernstrom, and others influenced not only the academic debates but elite, media, and popular opinion as well. Indeed, a review of the record shows impressive gains since the mid-1960s, most particularly in the areas of law, education, jobs, and earnings. During the 2004 Presidential election, for instance, and into the second term of the Bush Administration, politicians and the media treat racial inequality as a non-issue, or as if it no longer existed. Even though progress is real, this new political sensibility about racial progress and equality incorporates illusions that mask an enduring and robust racial hierarchy and continue to hinder efforts to achieve our ideals of democracy and justice.

In fact, we can consider seriously the declining economic significance of race because the measures we have traditionally used to gauge racial inequality focus almost exclusively on salaries and jobs. The black-white earning gap narrowed considerably throughout the 1960s and 1970s. The earnings gap has remained relatively stable since then, with inequality rising again in the 1980s and closing once more during tight labor markets in the 1990s. The average black family earned 55 cents for every dollar earned by the average white family in 1989; by 2000, it reached an all-time high of 64 cents on the dollar. For black men working full-time, the gains are more impressive, as their wages reached 67 percent of those of fully employed white men, up from 62 percent in 1980 and only 50 percent in 1960. How much the racial wage gap has closed, why it has closed, and what it means are the subjects of academic and political debate. One study, for example, argues that the racial wage gap is really 23 percent higher than the official figures because incarceration rates hide low wages and joblessness among blacks. In any case, it takes more African-American family members to work to earn the same money as white families. For example, middle-income black families worked the equivalent of 12 more weeks than white families to earn the same family income in 2000.

The tremendous growth of the black middle class often is cited as the triumphant sign of progress toward racial equality. The raw numbers appear to justify celebration: In 1960, a little more than three-quarters of a million black men and women worked in middle-class occupations. By 1980, the number increased to nearly three and a half million and nearly seven million African Americans worked in middle-class jobs in 1995. This impressive growth in achieving middle-class status, however, does not tell the whole story, as one can point out that stagnating economic conditions and blacks' lower middle-class occupational profile have stalled the march into the great American middle class since the mid-1970s.

The classic argument is that racial inequality in significant areas like family wealth represents huge disparities in education, jobs, and income. Once these disparities are alleviated, our traditional understanding and theory leads to an expectation that racial inequality will be diminished to a great extent. Confounding this traditional understanding, and demonstrating the need for new thinking about civil rights in the twenty-first century, examining middle-class families demonstrate that even black and white families with equal accomplishments are separated by a dramatic wealth gap. Defining middle-class by income, we see a reduction in the baseline racial wealth gap to $44,500 for whites and $17,000 for blacks. Clearly, income is important to wealth accumulation. At the same time, however, middle-class black families with similar incomes to whites own only 26 cents of wealth for every dollar owned by whites. Defining middle class by occupation changes the ratio to 22 cents on the dollar. And, using a college education as a hallmark of middle-class status moves the wealth ratio to 27 cents on the dollar. One needs to be asking how it is that blacks with equal accomplishments in income, jobs, and degrees possess only about a quarter of the wealth of their white counterparts.

A Native American Protest, 1969

We, the native Americans, re-claim the land known as Alcatraz Island in the name of all American Indians by right of discovery.

We wish to be fair and honorable in our dealings with the Caucasian inhabitants of this land, and hereby offer the following treaty:

We will purchase said Alcatraz Island for twenty-four dollars (24) in glass beads and red cloth, a precedent set by the white man's purchase of a similar island about 300 years ago. We know that $24 in trade goods for these 16 acres is more than was paid when Manhattan Island was sold, but we know that land values have risen over the years. Our offer of $1.24 per acre is greater than the 47 cents per acre the white men are now paying the California Indians for their land.

We will give to the inhabitants of this island a portion of the land for their own to be held in trust by the American Indian Affairs and by the bureau of Caucasian Affairs to hold in perpetuity—for as long as the sun shall rise and the rivers go down to the sea. We will further guide the inhabitants in the proper way of living. We will offer them our religion, our education, our life-ways, in order to help them achieve our level of civilization and thus raise them and all their white brothers up from their savage and unhappy state. We offer this treaty in good faith and wish to be fair and honorable in our dealings with all white men.

SOURCE: American Indian Center, 1969, cited in *Digital History*, June 28, 2006.

We feel that the so-called Alcatraz Island is more than suitable for an Indian Reservation, as determined by the white man's own standards. By this we mean that this place resembles most Indian reservations in that:

1. It is isolated from modern facilities, and without adequate means of transporation.
2. It has no fresh running water.
3. It has inadequate sanitation facilities.
4. There are no oil or mineral rights.
5. There is no industry and so unemployment is very great.
6. There are no health care facilities.
7. The soil is rocky and non-productive; and the land does not support game.
8. There are no educational facilities.
9. The population has always exceeded the land base.
10. The population has always been held as prisoners and kept dependent upon others.

Further, it would be fitting and symbolic that ships from all over the world, entering the Golden Gate, would first see Indian land, and thus be reminded of the true history of this nation. This tiny nation would be a symbol of the great lands once ruled by free and noble Indians.

Chapter 14

The Sixties and Beyond: Times of Protest

Bettmann/Corbis

Anti-Vietnam War protesters taunting military police, 1967.

The civil rights revolution that began in the 1950s erupted into a full-scale protest movement during the 1960s and eventually led to the enactment of the Civil Rights Act of 1964 and the Voting Rights Act of 1965, both of which greatly expanded the rights of African Americans. Largely rooted in the churches of the southern black community and appealing to black youth, the movement also attracted a substantial following among white students in the north. In the early 1960s, young men and women of both races headed south to aid in voter registration and to test segregation. They also joined protest marches to support African Americans' aspirations for equality.

The experiences of the students heightened their awareness of injustice in America and led them to question institutions on a broad scale. In addition to those institutions supporting racial discrimination and segregation, students closely scrutinized their own colleges and universities. The University of California became a center of turmoil as students protested against the numerous restrictions on political debate and student activism imposed by the administration at that campus. In the essay from Terry Anderson's *The*

Movement and the Sixties, Berkeley student leader Mario Savio states that he had gone to Mississippi to struggle for civil rights and was now engaged in "another phase of the same struggle." How would you characterize this new phase, and what do you think prompted it? Anderson also describes the free speech movement at Berkeley during the 1960s and how it escalated into a major confrontation between students and the university administration. What does Anderson consider to be the key issues during those hectic times? Anderson acknowledges that on many campuses dissatisfaction was strangely absent, that students were often "optimistic and comfortable." How was it possible for both student satisfaction and protest to exist in the same decade?

Some students were not content to limit their protests to racial discrimination and restrictions on speech on their campuses; they also objected to university rules and regulations on social behavior, such as drinking and sexual activity. Still others saw the university as only one institution in need of fundamental change. In 1962 Students for a Democratic Society (SDS) was formed. From an organizational meeting at the United Auto Workers's Port Huron center in Michigan, SDS issued the Port Huron agenda, calling for radical solutions to what they believed to be injustice in America.

Terry Anderson notes at the end of his essay that unhappiness with the Vietnam War was a major factor in explaining the upheavals of the sixties, and that without the war the "sixties generation" might have taken a different shape. It is understandable why male students especially objected to the war, for they were faced with the draft and the possibility of being sent to fight thousands of miles across the Pacific in a war in which they did not believe. But students were by no means the only Americans to oppose what many termed "Lyndon Johnson's war." Returning veterans organized Vietnam Veterans Against the War. The first document, a statement by veteran John Kerry who would become a U.S. senator from Massachusetts, speaks for these veterans. What was there about this war that led to such widespread disillusionment?

The second document comes from a more recent era. Gay men and women who served in the military and whose sexual orientation became known were often given discharges that did not entitle them to veterans benefits. Under President Bill Clinton the military branches put into a place a "don't ask, don't tell" policy. However, several thousand gays in the services continued to be harassed and ultimately discharged. In 2010, Congress and President Barack Obama set into motion the repeal of that policy. President Obama's statement on the new policy is indicated in a White House blog.

ESSAY

The Movement and the Sixties Generation
Terry Anderson

"Last summer I went to Mississippi to join the struggle there for civil rights," said Berkeley student Mario Savio in 1964. "This fall I am engaged in another phase of the same struggle, this time in Berkeley. In Mississippi an autocratic and powerful minority rules, through organized violence, to suppress the vast, virtually powerless majority. In California, the privileged minority manipulates the university bureaucracy to suppress the students' political expression."

That expression had been curtailed by the University of California as students arrived on the Berkeley campus for fall semester in September. As was typical for university officials during the cold war era, a dean simply informed all student organizations that from now on they were no longer permitted to set up tables on campus to promote "off-campus" causes such as civil rights, and this ban applied to the traditional area for such endeavors, a small strip of property at the campus's main entrance where Telegraph Avenue met Bancroft Way.

Activism had long since arrived in Berkeley. In 1958 students organized Towards an Active Student Community, which later became SLATE, and a few dozen began discussing civil rights, capital punishment, and nuclear disarmament. "For us," student Michael Rossman later wrote, "the discovery was of each other. We began to realize we were not alone."

In spring 1960 they acted, holding silent vigils at San Quentin to protest the execution of Caryl Chessman and picketing the House Un-American Activities Committee investigation of Communist activities in the Bay Area, a demonstration that led to Black Friday.* Activism increased, and by the 1963–64 academic year hundreds of students had become involved in civil rights demonstrations, picketing hotels, automobile dealerships, restaurants, and other businesses that had discriminatory employment practices. At Lucky food stores, activists held "shop-ins," filling grocery carts with food, and after going through the checkout line, saying, "Sorry, I forgot my money. If you would hire some Negroes I would remember it next time." They picketed the Oakland *Tribune,* whose conservative owner was

---

*In May 1960 a student protest against the House Un-American Activities Committee in San Francisco resulted in a violent confrontation between the police and the demonstrators. (Eds.)

on the university's board of regents, and in March the local campaign reached a crescendo when 2,000 violated a court order restricting the number of protesters in front of the Sheraton Palace Hotel; police arrested 800.

Political debate also was mounting. The Republican convention was held during June 1964 in San Francisco, and the candidacy of conservative Barry Goldwater inspired discussion as he faced Lyndon Johnson in the upcoming elections. Then, in August, just weeks before students returned to classes, President Johnson declared that North Vietnam had attacked U.S. ships in the Gulf of Tonkin. He asked for and received from Congress the Gulf of Tonkin Resolution, which stimulated more student debate about America's role in South Vietnam. And as fall semester began in September approximately fifty students returned from volunteer work during Mississippi Summer.* At Berkeley and at other universities many of these students were welcomed back to campus as "civil rights heroes."

The university administration apparently was under pressure by conservatives in the state, community, and on the board of regents to curb activism when they issued the political ban. The students' response was dramatic. On September 21 campus organizations of all political persuasions united—from the Young Socialist Alliance to Youth for Goldwater— and they violated the ban. Two hundred students picketed on campus with signs such as "UC Manufactures Safe Minds," "Ban Political Birth Control," and "Bomb the Ban." To most, the issue was freedom of speech. "We're allowed to say why we think something is good or bad," said activist Jackie Goldberg, "but we're not allowed to distribute information as to what to do about it. Inaction is the rule, rather than the exception, in our society and on this campus." The movement gained support, and a week later some students set up political tables. Administrators took down names, and ordered civil rights veteran Jack Weinberg to appear in front of a dean. He did the next day, but he was followed by 500 supporters who packed into the administration building, Sproul Hall, and stayed until early the next morning. University of California president Clark Kerr suspended eight activists, but that did not stifle dissent as it would have in the 1950s. It only increased ill will and resulted in more protest. "A student who has been chased by the KKK in Mississippi," said student Roger Sandall, "is not easily scared by academic bureaucrats."

The Free Speech Movement it was called, and along with the civil rights protests the previous spring it demonstrated the emergence of a new generation. "How proud I felt," wrote Berkeley student Sara Davidson. "I belonged to a great new body of students who cared about the problems of the world. No longer would youth be apathetic. That was the fifties. We were *committed*." ...

---

*A campaign to encourage voter registration among blacks. (Eds.)

The role of the university in the first half of the 1960s ... was not only to train students but to tame them to be conventional adults. To fit in, to become their parents. Students who did not play the game often were expelled or left in disgust; professors who did not teach the game usually were fired. Journalism major Phil Ochs at Ohio State was slated to become editor of the school paper, *The Lantern,* but faculty advisers rejected him because his views were "too controversial." He quit in his last year and became a folksinger. Illinois professor Leo Koch wrote in the *Daily Illini* that in his opinion premarital sex was all right for mature unmarried college students. The university president found the views "offensive and repugnant ... contrary to the accepted standards of morality," and he fired Koch. For similar reasons St. John's University fired two dozen faculty members in 1966—none even received a hearing, for according to university rules the board of trustees could give or take away tenure at any time without explanation. *Newsweek* editorialized that "college must not abdicate its role in conserving, transmitting, and helping to mold both moral and intellectual values" of its students.

Yet many students by the mid-1960s had little desire to "be molded." This generation was different from older brothers and sisters who had been cowed by McCarthyism. That campaign was ancient history to them, hardly remembered and not taken seriously. Furthermore, these students had learned from the struggle. "If there is any one reason for increased student protest," a University of Utah journalist wrote, "it would probably be the civil rights movement. The movement ... convinced many of them that non-violent demonstrations could be an effective device on the campus. It also served to make them more sensitive of their own civil rights." Problems in society had to be confronted and resolved, not blamed on imaginary subversives or outside agitators, and that called for student activism.

The reasons for student power were stated by the activists themselves in their campus papers and in new student undergrounds. This generation felt *in loco parentis* rules were absurd. Texas student Jeff Shero complained that campus regulations were "aimed at maintaining a 'proper image' for the University, rather than protecting girls." The young editor of *The Paper* declared "Michigan State is the Mississippi of American universities," protesting the administration's "closed-mindedness, intolerance and backwoods McCarthyism." The *New Orleans Freedom Press* proclaimed that student discontent resulted from "administrative restrictions on student autonomy," while University of Florida activists were blunt in their campus underground, *Freedom Forum:* "The American university campus has become a ghetto. Like all ghettoes, it has its managers (the administration), its Uncle Toms (the intimidated, status-berserk faculty), its raw natural resources processed for outside exploitation and consumption (the students)." Their demand highlighted the reasons for student power: "NO RESTRICTIONS MAY BE PLACED ON STUDENT DRINKING,

GAMBLING, SEXUAL ACTIVITY, OR ANY SUCH PRIVATE MORAL DECISION."

The sixties generation began to confront its university administrations in 1964, politely demanding to be heard. During spring semester the administration at Brandeis consulted no one and then instituted new, stricter dorm visitation rules. That prompted several hundred students to stage a two-day demonstration, and the campus newspaper declared that such regulations "makes impossible any meaningful relationship between boy and girl." That fall semester, Syracuse University students approached their administrators with a simple request—they felt that holiday break, which began on December 23, was too close to Christmas. A few dozen students asked for more travel time to get home by Christmas Eve. After officials turned down all petitions, the students called a rally in December, and they were surprised when 2,000 appeared. They demanded a speech from the chancellor, and he gave a short address, again saying no. As he ended his talk, some students jeered and booed, which shocked elders. "The students were supposed to show proper respect," a journalist wrote, "to know their place and keep it." Student activists, however, had a different interpretation. They wanted some role in the university. "If today's demonstration proves nothing else," the student paper editorialized, "we are not ones to be ignored or taken lightly."

Students at Berkeley certainly were not going to be taken lightly—they again challenged the ban on disseminating literature. On October 1, Jack Weinberg and others set up a few tables outside the administration building on Sproul Plaza and began passing out civil rights and political flyers. Before noon two university deans and a policeman approached Weinberg. "Are you prepared to remove yourself and the table from university property?" asked the dean. "I am not," replied Weinberg. After a brief discussion the official informed Weinberg of his arrest, and at this point several hundred students who were gathering for a free speech rally startled the officials by shouting, "Take us all, take us all!" Policemen drove a car onto the plaza and placed Weinberg inside, but suddenly someone shouted, "Sit down!" "I'm around the police car," recalled Michael Rossman. "I'm the first person to sit down. You will hear five hundred others who say that, and everyone is telling the truth." Students either laid or sat down around the car. They refused to move. The police could not drive their prisoner to jail as the crowd swelled to 3,000. Mario Savio and many others climbed on top of the car and gave speeches, and later the crowd sang civil rights songs. They remained on the plaza all night. The next morning the area looked like a campsite, filled with sleeping bags, blankets, and even a pup tent. The crowd increased to 4,000 that afternoon, and President Kerr realized that the free speech issue was not going to disappear. After a thirty-hour sit-in, university administrators finally agreed to meet the activists.

To university officials, and to most citizens after the law and order 1950s, Berkeley had been reduced to chaos. Although campus rebellion would become common later in the decade, this was the first major eruption, and administrators responded forcefully. Under pressure from conservatives in the community and state government, they allowed 500 police officers to appear on campus minutes before they met activists. The police were armed with nightsticks, and the sight shocked students who never could remember a police army on campus and who felt that the incident was novel in American educational history. As police stood by, civil rights veterans taught non-violent arrest tactics and urged those with police records or children to leave. Administrators had the support of California Governor Edmund G. Brown, a Democrat who stated that the demonstration was "not a matter of freedom of speech" but was an attempt by the students to use the campus illegally. "This will not be tolerated." He continued, "We must have—and will continue to have—law and order on our campuses."

Negotiations with Kerr continued for two hours, and then Savio and other students emerged from Sproul Hall. Savio climbed on the police car and announced that an agreement had been reached. A student–faculty committee would examine the free speech issue and make recommendations to the president. The university would not press charges against Weinberg or FSM leaders, and the eight students suspended earlier would have their case reviewed. Kerr seemed to support establishing a small free speech area at the campus's main entrance where Telegraph Avenue met Bancroft Way.

The October 2 agreement collapsed by November. The administration filled the committee with their own supporters, and then stalled for weeks. Meanwhile, Kerr took the issue to the press. Under pressure from conservative regents and politicians, the president attacked activists by raising the old bugaboos: "Reds on Campus," Kerr told the *San Francisco Examiner*. The article reported that the president "declared flatly that a hard core of 'Castro–Mao-Tse-tung line' Communists were in the crowd of demonstrators." The president then rejected political activity, provoking students to petition the regents and to set up tables on Sproul Plaza. The regents refused to hear the case, and on November 29 Kerr surprised students by announcing that the university was going to press new charges against FSM leaders Art Goldberg and Savio for their actions during the October 1 demonstrations. Charges included "entrapping a police car," "packing in" Sproul Hall, and, against Savio alone, biting a policeman "on the left thigh, breaking the skin and causing bruises."

The administration's behavior only alienated more students, irritated many professors, and fueled more protest as students and faculty began to feel that the university all along had been negotiating in bad faith. "The Administration sees the free speech protest as a simple problem of disobedience," proclaimed an FSM steering committee statement. "By again arbitrarily singling out students for punishment, the Administration avoids facing the real issues.... We demand that these new charges be dropped." Thousands of activists took those demands to Sproul Plaza on December 2, and Savio voiced the students' frustration by telling the crowd: "There is a time when the operation of the machine becomes so odious, makes you so sick at heart, that you can't take part; you can't even tacitly take part, and you've got to put your bodies upon the gears and upon the wheels, upon the levers, upon all the apparatus and you've got to make it stop."

"We Shall Overcome," sang Joan Baez, and others joined in as they moved toward Sproul Hall. "We'll walk hand in hand," for "the truth will make us free." The activists shut down the university administration—again they confronted the establishment.

Governor Brown responded immediately: "We're not going to have anarchy in California." He informed Kerr that force must be used to oust the students and ordered police to arrest activists who refused to leave the administration building. At about 4 a.m. some 600 policemen entered Sproul Hall and began arresting students, eventually about 770, in the largest mass arrest in California history. Some 7,000 students remained on the plaza, and that morning they began picketing all entrances to the campus, handing out flyers:

IT IS HAPPENING NOW!

In the middle of the night, the police began dragging 800 of your fellow students from Sproul Hall. Sproul Hall was turned into a booking station; the University has become an armed camp—armed against its own students! ...

Now the police take over.

Instead of recognizing the legitimacy of the students' demands, the administration is attempting to destroy the FSM.... The administration position is clear. It is saying "We decide what is acceptable freedom of speech on this campus. Those who disagree will be ignored; when they can no longer be ignored, they will be destroyed."

We have not been defeated by the University's troops! Our protest will continue until the justice of our cause is acknowledged. You must take a stand now! No longer can the faculty attempt to mediate from the outskirts of the crowd. No longer can students on this campus afford to accept humbly administrative fiat. Raise your voice now!

WE SHALL OVERCOME

The faculty met, and after a long and heated discussion in their senate, they declared their position: professors overwhelmingly voted to condemn the use of police on campus and to support the FSM. As faculty left the meeting, students cheered, and on December 4 both students and faculty held a huge rally on Sproul Plaza. Arrested activists had been released on bail, many wore a large white "V" on black shirts, and they and several professors criticized Governor Brown, the regents, and President Kerr. Students declared a strike, and that week half the classes were canceled.

With business as usual disrupted, Kerr called a special meeting for December 7 at the Greek Theater. About 16,000 students, faculty, and staff gathered, and the president condemned the sit-in but offered clemency for all acts of civil disobedience before December 2 and stated that the university would abide by "new and liberalized political action rules" then being developed by the faculty senate. The speech sounded conciliatory, and as the president left the podium Savio began walking across the stage apparently to make an announcement. Before he reached the microphone, campus police astonished the crowd by grabbing the activist and dragging him backstage. When other activists attempted to help, the police wrestled them off the stage.

"The crowd was stunned," wrote participant Bettina Aptheker, "then there was pandemonium." Students cried out "We Want Mario! We Want Mario!" Kerr, realizing that the police were ruining his efforts to reach an understanding, quickly agreed to let Savio make his announcement—a rally would be held at noon. Nevertheless, most spectators remembered the incident and its inescapable symbolism: authorities physically preventing a student committed to free speech from speaking on his own campus. As Aptheker later wrote: "That episode more than any other single event revolutionized the *thinking* of many thousands of students."

The next day the faculty met and overwhelmingly passed a motion affirming that "speech or advocacy should not be restricted by the university." While the administration and regents discussed the motion during the next two weeks, the FSM invited CORE national director James Farmer to address a rally on December 15. The administration was conciliatory, informing students that Farmer could talk on campus, but FSM activists decided to hold a legal rally off campus as a token of good faith. Farmer told the crowd that the "battle for free speech" could not be lost, for that would "turn off the faucet of the civil rights movement." When someone charged that he was an "outside agitator," he replied, "Every housewife knows the value of an agitator. It's the instrument inside the washing machine that bangs around and gets out all the dirt."

The administration eventually decided to accept the faculty's liberalized political rules. On January 4, 1965, the Free Speech Movement held its first legal rally on Sproul Plaza. The FSM was a success, Savio told the crowd, because "it was so obvious to everybody that it was right."

The FSM raised a philosophical debate that divided many students and administrators: What is the nature of a public university? While Kerr thought of himself as a liberal and had been praised for his stand favoring academic freedom, he stated the usual reasoning of cold war culture. The "university is an educational institution that has been given to the regents as a trust to administer for educational reasons, and not to be used for direct political actions." FSM advocates and many professors disagreed, arguing that the mission of higher education was much broader. "The university is the place where people begin seriously to question the conditions of their existence and raise the issue of whether they can be committed to the society they have been born into," wrote Savio. At a public institution supported by all tax-payers, activists felt that discussion should not be reserved only for campus issues but should be open to all concerns of the Republic. Art Goldberg advo-cated making Berkeley "a marketplace of ideas" where citizens would be exposed to "new and creative solutions to the problems that every American realizes are facing this society in the mid-60s."

That idea was not original in 1964, for actually students had initiated free speech movements earlier at a few other campuses, including Ohio State and Indiana University. In March 1963 three students at Indiana, offi-cers of the Young Socialist Alliance, sponsored a speech by a black socialist on the civil rights movement. In May, the county prosecuting attorney charged the students with violating the Indiana Anti-Communist Act, meet-ing with the purpose of "advocating the violent overthrow" of the govern-ments of Indiana and the United States. The prosecutor also demanded that the university drop its recognition of YSA. "We may all be ten years away from Senator McCarthy," wrote one professor, "but I am ten blocks away from the office of the Prosecuting Attorney." Supporters of the three estab-lished the Committee to Aid the Bloomington Students, which eventually received assistance from 50 colleges in 15 states. Over 140 faculty members signed a statement that the indictment was not "motivated by zeal for law enforcement, but by a desire to dictate to Indiana University that it shall not permit the use of University facilities for the expression of ideas repugnant to the Prosecutor." The university president agreed, and state courts found the law unconstitutional: The faculty continued supporting the students and broadly defined the university as a community where "debate, disagree-ment and the sharp confrontation of opposing ideas is a vital part of the attempt to come closer to the truth."

The free speech episode at Indiana differed from that at Berkeley. The Indiana administration viewed the conservative attack as a threat to the institution, and eventually the president supported the First Amendment. If Berkeley administrators had subscribed to such views, the sit-in of Sproul Hall probably would have been avoided. Flexible officials could avoid most confrontations on campus—a point remembered by hundreds of successful university presidents throughout the 1960s.

Kerr and the regents could not overcome their authoritarian 1950s men-tality. They treated the students like subordinates, gave orders to tuition-payers, which only increased resentment toward authority. Activists felt that "liberal" administrators, the "power elites" who ran the university in Berkeley, seemed more interested in maintaining the status quo than changing rules, even if those regulations denied rights guaranteed by the First Amendment of the U.S. Constitution. Looking back, Kerr's position was indefensible. During the 1950s he had supported academic freedom for professors, yet in 1964 his administration curtailed freedom of speech for students. Many students wondered, if they could not hand out political statements, if freedom of speech did not exist on a public campus, then where did it exist in the land of the free?

The administration brought on the crisis, handled it poorly, and lost to students. As in the civil rights struggle, the FSM students put another dent in the idea that those in charge should be in charge, that the older generation had some monopoly on determining the proper path for the present and future in America. "Don't trust anyone over thirty," said Jack Weinberg and others, meaning that the generation who grew up in the 1950s had a different view of the world than their parents. During cold war culture the older generation "told the truth" to students, but in the 1960s students were "discovering the truth" for themselves, and their younger siblings would continue the process throughout the decade. At Berkeley, the young began to realize that the older generation had no monopoly on truth or on virtue. Once students began to raise their voices and question policy, Michael Rossman wrote, then "the emperor had no clothes." President Kerr's decision to uphold an untenable regulation at Berkeley could be just as wrong as Chief of Police Bull Connor's enforcement of segregation rules in Birmingham.

The FSM was significant for many other reasons. Activists adopted a political style that reflected the ideas of the new left and some of the practices of SNCC.* Unlike traditional organizations or political parties, Berkeley students "worked through direct personal involvement in small autonomous interest groups. Our groups were ad hoc," Rossman recalled, "problem-orientated, flexible. They strove to govern themselves by participatory democracy, and to come to consensus on decisions." They also were pragmatic. "We were experimental social scientists, placing practice before theory.... . We also were cheerful and funny, and made art as we went.

[B]y the end of spring semester 1965 the climate on campus had shifted dramatically from the 1950s and early 1960s. "An End to Panty Raids," wrote a student at Kansas. The most important issues were civil and student rights; another continued that his generation was "fed up with their elders over such things as mass faceless education .... Students want to feel a sense of participation." With successes in the South and on their campuses, many students were optimistic about change, and as they became

---

*At this stage in its history, the Student Nonviolent Coordinating Committee (SNCC) employed peaceful demonstrations to achieve civil rights goals. (Eds.)

involved many began to think of themselves as part of a movement. "The thing for me right now is the movement," said Steven Block, an activist at Williams College. "That's an interesting word, if you think about it—movement. Because it is people in motion. It's not an end; it's not static. That's a very apt word for what we are doing."

The silent generation was history. *College Press Service* in December declared, "1964 Is Year of Protest on Nation's Campuses," and Professor Andrew Hacker called 1964–65 the "Year of the Demonstration." It was when compared with any time in memory.

But, more important, Hacker then placed the activists in context of the larger sixties generation. "Certainly, this year's protesters and demonstrators were not representative of their classmates, and it is instructive how quickly their ranks have tended to dwindle away after the first flamboyant outbursts. So long as a school will give an undergraduate his passport into the upper-middle-class without demanding more than ... 15 weekly hours of studying, few are going to complain." Few indeed. Two years later, in 1967, professors Seymour Lipset and Philip Altbach flatly declared that it "should be made clear that ... the scope of the American student 'revolution' has been greatly exaggerated by the mass media."

Newsweek confirmed such sentiments during spring 1965 when it conducted interviews and a poll of over 800 students at numerous universities. Over 90 percent expressed confidence in higher education, big corporations, and the federal government, while over 80 percent were satisfied with college and had positive views about the armed forces, organized religion, and the United Nations. When asked what students thought their lives would be like in fifteen years, most of them mimicked their older brothers: "I'll be secure, financially, married, have children, at least three," said one. Another aimed to be "upper middle class," and a third predicted, "I'll be living in a Long Island suburb." A journalist labeled the students "Flaming Moderates."

In mid-decade only a few students were activists while the larger sixties generation was comfortably moderate. A conservative student at the University of Miami wrote about the "deadly infection called student apathy" and referred to his campus as a "hotbed of apathy." Fraternities and sororities still dominated campus life, and a coed at Kansas as late as 1967 admitted that the biggest craze on her campus was "to get your boyfriend's fraternity sweater." Most college papers were similar to the *Daily Illini*, printing regular features like "The Party Line" which announced lavalierings, pinnings, engagements, and marriages. "I have respect for the ones who went to Mississippi or joined the Peace Corps, who committed themselves," said an English professor at Illinois in 1965, "but there are very, very few of them. Very few on this campus."

While some students had been provoked out of apathy by campus issues and civil rights, most of the sixties generation sitting in crowded classes during spring semester of 1965 were optimistic and comfortable—still best defined as the cool generation—mildly alienated from their parents' values and eager to sing along and "let the good times roll." *Time* surveyed the generation then and reported conformity: "Almost everywhere boys dress in madras shirts and chinos, or perhaps green Levis, all trim and neat. The standard for girls is sweaters and skirts dyed to match, or shirt-waists and jumpers plus blazers, Weejun loafers, and knee socks or stockings." At that time no one would have predicted that just two years away were the Summer of Love and the March on the Pentagon. Campus life that spring semester was cool, the good life. As the student body president of University of Texas said, "We haven't really been tested by war or depression. We live very much in the present because we don't have to be overly concerned about the future."

"There was that little conflict in Vietnam," Bob Calvert remembered, "but most of us in the movement felt optimistic during the summer of 1965." Indeed, most Americans felt that the nation was moving forward, and that mood was glowing in August when LBJ signed the Voting Rights Act. The president asked civil rights leaders to be present, and the signing ceremony included Bayard Rustin, Roy Wilkins, A. Philip Randolph, and Martin Luther King, Jr. LBJ had met with King the previous day and they discussed the remarkable advances during 1964 and 1965, not only in civil rights but also in the War on Poverty and Great Society programs—massive federal aid to education and job training, Headstart, Medicare, and Medicaid. King spoke of the president's amazing sensitivity to the difficult problems that Negro Americans face in the stride toward freedom," and at the signing celebration the president declared, "Today is a triumph for freedom as huge as any victory that's ever been won on any battlefield." The civil rights leaders proclaimed LBJ the "greatest President" for blacks, even surpassing Abraham Lincoln.

"There was a religiosity about the meeting," recalled a presidential aide, "which was warm with emotion—a final celebration of an act so long desired and so long in achieving." Now liberals could sit back in their easy chairs and relax. In spring 1964 a new president had made his pledge, had declared his vision of the future. "This nation, this people, this generation, has man's first chance to create a Great Society: a society of success without squalor, beauty without barrenness, works of genius without the wretchedness of poverty. We can open the doors of learning. We can open the doors of fruitful labor and rewarding leisure, of open opportunity and close community—not just to the privileged few, but, thank God, we can open those doors to *everyone*." Now, just fifteen months later, it seemed that the liberals were delivering. The civil and voting rights acts had outlawed racial discrimination in public accommodations, employment, and the vote, and social programs were beginning to help the poor—white and black—to share the American Dream. On that day in August, liberalism reached its zenith in the 1960s.

Then, during the next two years, President Johnson gave the sixties generation a reason to be concerned about the future—he massively escalated America's role in the Vietnam War. The cool generation became history.

What would have happened to the sixties generation without the experience of Vietnam? Certainly, many would have continued to support and some would have demonstrated for civil rights. Five years of the struggle meant that it had become part of the generation's consciousness, and students began demanding classes on black literature and history at universities such as Stanford, Cornell, and San Francisco State. The "movement" would have been remembered as the civil rights struggle and the rise of student power. Increasing enrollments meant that the university was going to continue evolving in size and in substance, and that students would continue demanding and supporting change. In spring 1966 Stanford activist David Harris won election as student body president by calling for student control of regulations, equal policies for men and women, option of pass-fail grades, legalization of marijuana, elimination of the board of trustees, and the end of all university cooperation with the Vietnam War. The next year students challenged campus rules and regulations at Brown, Cornell, Oregon, Washington, and administrators at the best institutions were moving toward adopting the suggestion of a committee at Wisconsin that advocated "withdrawal by the University from its *in loco parentis* activities." By mid-decade it also was clear that 1950s morality was cracking and that the younger generation was revolting against the values of Ma and Pa. Most of this quest would be superficial, beer bashes and bundling at the beach as the sixties became a party decade. But for a few others, the questioning of morals would lead them to substantial changes as they became part of an emerging counterculture. Finally, the massive size of the generation alone meant that it would have modified society, and thus would have made an impact.

What would have been remembered as the "sixties" without Vietnam? The Johnson administration would have continued civil rights legislation and Great Society programs, and along with the significant rulings of the Supreme Court of Chief Justice Earl Warren, the decade would have been taught today as another major reform era in American history.

Without the war, however, one wonders if the decade would have been as dramatic—would have been remembered as "the sixties." The decade had been a turning point for blacks since Greensboro in 1960.* For white students and their parents the decade began to take shape in 1964 and 1965 as the young began to exhibit their new values and make demands on their campus administrators. Then, between autumn 1965 and the end

---

*It was in Greensboro, North Carolina, that black college students began the nonviolent sit-in movement to desegregate eating facilities in southern stores and restaurants. (Eds.)

of 1967, the Johnson administration escalated American involvement in Vietnam—and for the entire nation the decade became "the sixties."

DOCUMENTS

Vietnam Veterans Against the War, 1971

[S]everal months ago in Detroit we had an investigation at which over 150 honorably discharged and many very highly decorated veterans testified to war crimes committed in Southeast Asia, not isolated incidents but crimes committed on a day-to-day basis with the full awareness of officers at all levels of command.

It is impossible to describe to you exactly what did happen in Detroit, the emotions in the room, the feelings of the men who were reliving their experiences in Vietnam, but they did. They relived the absolute horror of what this country, in a sense, made them do.

They told the stories [of] times they had personally raped, cut off ears, cut off heads, taped wires from portable telephones to human genitals and turned up the power, cut off limbs, blown up bodies, randomly shot at civilians, razed villages in fashion reminiscent of Genghis Khan, shot cattle and dogs for fun, poisoned food stocks, and generally ravaged the countryside of South Vietnam in addition to the normal ravage of war, and the normal and very particular ravaging which is done by the applied bombing power of this country....

We who have come here to Washington have come here because we feel we have to be winter soldiers now. We could come back to this country; we could be quiet; we could hold our silence; we could not tell what went on in Vietnam, but we feel because of what threatens this country, the fact that the crimes threaten it, not reds, and not redcoats but the crimes which we are committing that threaten it, that we have to speak out....

I would like to talk to you a little bit about what the result is of the feelings these men carry with them after coming back from Vietnam. The country doesn't know it yet, but it has created a monster, a monster in the form of millions of men who have been taught to deal and to trade in violence, and who are given the chance to die for the biggest nothing in history; men who have returned with a sense of anger and a sense of betrayal which no one has yet grasped....

In our opinion, and from our experience, there is nothing in South Vietnam, nothing which could happen that realistically threatens the United States of America. And to attempt to justify the loss of one American life

SOURCE: Hearings Before the Committee on Foreign Relations, U.S. Senate, 92nd Cong., 1st sess., 1971.

in Vietnam, Cambodia, or Laos by linking such loss to the preservation of freedom, which those misfits supposedly abuse, is to us the height of criminal hypocrisy, and it is that kind of hypocrisy which we feel has torn this country apart....

We found that not only was it a civil war, an effort by a people who had for years been seeking their liberation from any colonial influence whatsoever, but also we found that the Vietnamese whom we had enthusiastically molded after our own image were hard put to take up the fight against the threat we were supposedly saving them from.

We found most people didn't even know the difference between communism and democracy. They only wanted to work in rice paddies without helicopters strafing them and bombs with napalm burning their villages and tearing their country apart....

We rationalized destroying villages in order to save them. We saw America lose her sense of morality as she accepted very coolly a My Lai* and refused to give up the image of American soldiers who hand out chocolate bars and chewing gum....

Now we are told that the men who fought there must watch quietly while American lives are lost so that we can exercise the incredible arrogance of Vietnamizing the Vietnamese....

... Each day to facilitate the process by which the United States washes her hands of Vietnam someone has to give up his life so that the United States doesn't have to admit something that the entire world already knows, so that we can't say that we have made a mistake. Someone has to die so that President Nixon won't be, and these are his words, "the first President to lose a war."

We are asking Americans to think about that because how do you ask a man to be the last man to die in Vietnam? How do you ask a man to be the last man to die for a mistake? ...

We wish that a merciful God could wipe away our own memories of that service as easily as this administration has wiped their memories of us. But all that they have done and all that they can do by this denial is to make more clear than ever our own determination to undertake one last mission, to search out and destroy the last vestige of this barbaric war, to pacify our own hearts, to conquer the hate and the fear that have driven this country these last 10 years and more, and so when, in 30 years from now, our brothers go down the street without a leg, without an arm, or a face, and small boys ask why, we will be able to say "Vietnam" and not mean a desert, not a filthy obscene memory but mean instead the place where America finally turned and where soldiers like us helped it in the turning....

---

*My Lai refers to the village in which American soldiers killed many innocent Vietnamese civilians. (Eds.)

Gays in the Military: President Barack Obama Notes the New Policy, 2010

Today, President Obama released a statement on the Don't Ask, Don't Tell Repeal Act of 2010. Today's historic vote would not have happened without the tireless efforts of many, including leaders in Congress, advocates, and the clear leadership provided by the President. As recently as this morning, the President has been reaching out to Senators from both sides of the aisle to help secure votes. It was only 11 months ago that the President called for the repeal in his first State of the Union and then laid out the plan, including the Pentagon's Comprehensive Review for the Repeal of Don't Ask Don't Tell, that has taken us to where we are today.

Here's the President's full statement:

> Today, the Senate has taken an historic step toward ending a policy that undermines our national security while violating the very ideals that our brave men and women in uniform risk their lives to defend. By ending "Don't Ask, Don't Tell," no longer will our nation be denied the service of thousands of patriotic Americans forced to leave the military, despite years of exemplary performance, because they happen to be gay. And no longer will many thousands more be asked to live a lie in order to serve the country they love.
>
> As Commander-in-Chief, I am also absolutely convinced that making this change will only underscore the professionalism of our troops as the best led and best trained fighting force the world has ever known. And I join the Secretary of Defense and the Chairman of the Joint Chiefs of Staff, as well as the overwhelming majority of service members asked by the Pentagon, in knowing that we can responsibly transition to a new policy while ensuring our military strength and readiness.
>
> I want to thank Majority Leader Reid, Senators Lieberman and Collins and the countless others who have worked so hard to get this done. It is time to close this chapter in our history. It is time to recognize that sacrifice, valor and integrity are no more defined by sexual orientation than they are by race or gender, religion or creed. It is time to allow gay and lesbian Americans to serve their country openly. I urge the Senate to send this bill to my desk so that I can sign it into law.

SOURCE: http://www.whitehouse.gov/blog/2010/12/18/president-dont-ask-dont-tell.

Chapter 15

The Revival of Feminism

A march in support of the Equal Rights Amendment, Washington DC, August 26, 1977.

When women gained the vote in 1920, the women's movement that had long sought this goal—dating back to the mid-nineteenth century—became dormant for several decades. Yet that victory by no means marked the end of the struggle for equality of opportunity and treatment for women. The franchise gained women entry to the voting booth, but few won elective office. Women still found most of their employment opportunities in the traditional, low-paying, "feminine" occupations, and their wages typically ranged lower than those of men with similar experience, education, skill, and responsibility. Moreover, during the Great Depression married women discovered that many employers hesitated to hire them, insisting that men be given preference for available jobs.

Economic discrimination had much to do with the emergence of a new wave of feminism beginning in the 1960s, but there were other factors as well. In the essay "Feminism's Second Wave: The Opening Salvos," author Flora Davis points to wide-ranging discontent among airline stewardesses during the 1950s and early 1960s. *Stewardess,* rather than today's term, *flight attendant,* was the designation of the then almost totally feminine occupation. What were the major issues in the women's struggle with their airline employers? What tactics proved most significant in determining the final outcome? Can you think of other occupations, usually low-paid, that are dominated by women?

In 1923, a group of women led by Alice Paul had proposed an equal rights amendment (ERA) to the Constitution designed to ensure sexual equality. The idea lay quiescent for nearly half a century until the resurgence of the women's movement in the 1960s. By 1970, the ERA had again become a live issue.

In 1972 Congress approved the ERA by the necessary two-thirds margin, and opinion polls indicated support for the amendment by a vast majority of the American public. Nevertheless, the amendment failed to receive ratification by the required three-quarters of the states. Opposition centered in the South, several western states, Missouri, and Illinois.

The defeat of the ERA, although a major setback, did not fatally injure the women's movement. A growing number of women ran for and were elected to office. In 1976, 21 women held seats in the United States Congress. Twenty years later, 55 women were in Congress, and both United States senators from California were women. In 1984, for the first time, a woman, Geraldine Ferraro, was selected as a vice-presidential candidate.

Encouraged by the spirit of feminism and aided by civil rights legislation, favorable court decisions, and government-directed affirmative action programs, increasing numbers of women entered traditionally male occupations. Since 1980 women have outnumbered men in undergraduate colleges and universities, and they have been increasing their presence in graduate schools. Women received 14.3 percent of the Ph.D.s granted in 1970, but by 1994 the figure had reached 38.5 percent. In 1960, only 6.8 percent of physicians were women, but in the academic year 2004–2005, 48.6 percent of medical students were women, thus assuring that they would be a strong presence in the practice of medicine in the twenty-first century. The change among lawyers has been even more startling. In 1960, women won only 2.5 percent of the law degrees granted that year, but today their numbers have risen to 50 percent. Men continue to earn more than women, however, and the plight of mothers in single-parent households remains difficult, with many living in poverty.

In addition to the ERA, abortion became a highly controversial issue after 1973. The Supreme Court in *Roe v. Wade* (1973), parts of which are included in the first document, paved the way for the legalization of abortion in many states that had formerly imposed severe limits on the procedure. What did the justices say about the right to privacy and how it affected abortion? Did the court suggest that abortion was an absolute right? The second document is a statement by President George W. Bush to a group of pro-life (anti-abortion) marchers in the nation's capital. What possibilities for compromise, if any, do you see in this issue?

Many observers believed that the feminist movement had come to an end by the 1990s, and they alleged that many highly educated women did not pursue careers, opting instead to choose family life and the rearing of their children. The last document, by Harvard economist Claudia Golden, casts doubt on this assumption. What does Golden see as the pattern of work and family of highly educated women?

ESSAY

Feminism's Second Wave: The Opening Salvos
Flora Davis

The women's movement, as reincarnated in the 1960s, is often called the "second wave" of feminism, to distinguish it from the "first wave," which arose during the nineteenth century and won the vote for women in 1920. The wave analogy is helpful because it underscores the fact that the women's movement didn't die after 1920, though it did lose much of its momentum. The analogy also reminds us that major social changes tend to happen in waves. First, there's a lot of intense activity and some aspects of life are transformed; then, when the public has absorbed as much as it can stand, reaction sets in. Stability reigns for a while, and if there's a strong backlash, some of the changes may be undone. Eventually, if vital issues remain unresolved, another wave of activism arises....

The turbulent, affluent, optimistic 1960s provided an unusually hospitable climate for feminism. The civil rights movement had broken new ground and a number of related social movements sprang up in its wake. One of them was the women's movement. Like a brush fire in a dry season, it ignited simultaneously in two different places: among older, liberal women and among the young radicals of the New Left.

Throughout the sixties, the women's movement grew steadily, but most Americans were barely aware of what was happening. Then in the early 1970s, feminism exploded across the national scene as groups of activists cropped up almost everywhere. Often, women coalesced around a single issue, pouring their efforts into a rape hotline, a battered women's shelter, or some other highly focused project.

At the same time, a broad-based right-wing backlash began to build, fueled by white male resentment at the challenges from feminists and from the civil rights movement. When conservatives won the White House in 1980, feminists were thrown on the defensive; for the next decade, they had to fight to hang onto the ground they'd already gained. They lost some battles and won others, and overall, progress for women stalled.

SOURCE: *"Feminism's Second Wave: The Opening Salvos,"* from *Moving the Mountain: The Women's Movement in America Since 1960* by Flora Davis, pp. 11, 15–25. Copyright © 1991 by Flora Davis. First Published by Simon & Schuster. Reprinted by permission of Curtis Brown, Ltd.

Nevertheless, new feminist groups kept emerging, many of them now being formed by women of color. Going into the 1990s, the women's movement was bigger, stronger, and more diverse than ever.

Between 1960 and 1990, feminists achieved half a revolution. Laws were passed, court decisions were handed down, and sex discrimination was officially prohibited; women were elected to office, grudgingly accepted into male occupations, and promoted to positions that women had never held before. New terms entered the nation's vocabulary: People spoke of "sexism" and "male chauvinism." Probably, the movement's single greatest achievement was that it transformed most people's assumptions about what women were capable of and had a right to expect from life.

The Battle with the Airlines

The story of how airline stewardesses forced American airlines to change unfair work rules is the perfect introduction to the second wave. By throwing into sharp relief the old attitudes to women and the impact those attitudes had on people's lives, it shows just how far women have come. The activists involved were few in number, and they challenged just one aspect of the pervasive problem of sex discrimination. That was typical of the second wave and illustrates the point that social transformations, like jigsaw puzzles, are put together one piece at a time.

The battle with the airlines spanned a crucial period in the history of the women's movement. Stewardesses fought to be treated as workers, rather than as sex objects, at a time when the term "sex object" hadn't yet been invented. The work rules they challenged decreed that to keep their jobs they must remain single, and they were fired the minute they married. Many airlines fired them, in any case, as soon as they turned thirty-two, while others set the limit at thirty-five. Women much over the age of thirty were no longer considered attractive enough to fly for an airline. It hadn't even occurred to most Americans that the system was unfair, and that made changing the rules an uphill fight in a way it wouldn't have been a few years later.

The stewardess unions actually began their campaign before the second wave, at a time when few people had any interest in women's rights. When the women's movement caught up with them, union leaders used its impetus, and as they did, they quickly came to identify themselves as feminists fighting sex discrimination, not just as unionists confronting management.

At one time or another, stewardess unions at most of the major airlines joined the struggle to change the work rules. There was some communication between union leaders, but they never really made a coordinated effort. Instead, the battle was fought simultaneously on many different fronts by different groups. The women who worked for American Airlines belonged to a union called ALSSA—the Air Line Stewards and Stewardesses Association— and their campaign was typical.

The Age and Marriage Issues

In the hierarchy of "glamour" jobs open to white women in the early sixties, stewardesses ranked right after movie stars and models.* In fact, for every woman hired as a stewardess, more than a hundred applicants were turned away. Those who were chosen embodied the American image of the wholesome girl-next-door.

As the airlines saw it, these "girls" would fly for a few years, then leave the job to marry and settle down. In the midsixties, stewardesses lasted 32.4 months, on the average, less than three years. "If that figure ever got up to thirty-five months, I'd know we're getting the wrong kind of girl. She's not getting married," a personnel manager for United Airlines said solemnly in 1965.

In the early 1960s, the social pressure to marry was relentless. The average woman became a wife at age twenty, younger than in any generation since the turn of the century. Seventy percent of American women made it safely to the altar before they were twenty-four, and a woman still unmarried at the advanced age of twenty-five was considered an "old maid." She was pitied, and people wondered what was wrong with her that no man had asked her to be his wife. Most stewardesses themselves assumed when they were hired that they'd marry within a few years. In fact, at American Airlines the gold wings presented to a woman after five years of flying were known as "your failure pin," because they signified that she had so far failed to marry.

By becoming a stewardess, an adventurous young woman had a chance to travel and meet interesting people in the time warp between the end of her schooling and the beginning of marriage. And the job was said to be good experience for marriage. At the airline training schools the women learned safety procedures, but also took classes in make-up, grooming, and social skills, "the perfect course for being a perfect hostess at home," according to one stewardess. (At American, the school was known irreverently as "the charm farm.")

Although most stewardesses seemed to love their jobs, they lived with more restrictions than the most overprotected teenager. They were told how long to wear their skirts and their hair and how high their heels could be. They could be fired for gaining too much weight. Girdles were generally required and supervisors did "touch checks" to make sure employees were wearing them. In addition, the women were paid so little that home was often a small apartment shared with as many as half a dozen other stewardesses.

Almost from the beginning, most airlines expected their stewardesses to resign when they married. Age didn't become an issue until the early 1950s,

---

*Stewardesses (also called air hostesses) became known as flight attendants during the 1970s, as men began to be hired for the job.

when American Airlines became the first company to retire the women as soon as they reached their midthirties. To get the union to agree to the age limit, management negotiators exempted those already working for the company. They stipulated that only women hired after November 1, 1953, would be forced to retire at thirty-two.

Dusty Roads got in under the wire. So did Nancy Collins, who would become the union's master executive chairman (equivalent to being its president) in the early sixties. They led the long struggle to get the airline to lift the age restriction, because both felt a moral issue was involved.

As the 1950s wore on, more and more airlines routinely dismissed stewardesses for growing too old. By 1965, fifteen of the thirty-eight U.S. airlines were doing it. "I was twenty-eight when we fought the age issue, and I was absolutely hysterical," said Lynda Oswald, who was with American Airlines. "I was trying to prepare myself for another job, but when I tried to get into a university, they wouldn't accept me as a part-time student. The whole climate was catch-22."

Yet many stewardesses saw nothing wrong with the airlines' regulations, and union leaders found it hard to marshall support. Roads recalled that "some of our own flight attendants would say, 'I don't think you should fly when you're fat or old.'" Younger women weren't interested in the age issue. "When you're twenty, you don't believe you're ever going to be thirty-two," Roads observed drily. Older women, as their thirty-second birthday approached, often cast about desperately for a ground job with the company. Reluctant to antagonize management, most "retired" from flying without a protest. As for the marriage regulation, many women did marry and kept their marriage a secret. At one point, airline officials estimated that 30 to 40 percent of stewardesses were secretly married.

In short, the battle with the airlines was fought by a minority of activists who were willing to take risks. Most of the women who ultimately benefited from their efforts were initially too timid or indifferent to take part, or actually opposed any change in the status quo. That was the case with the first challenges to sex discrimination in many occupations.

In defending their regulations, the airlines talked a lot about the image of a stewardess as a young, single woman, and the importance of maintaining that image. However, the union's leaders were well aware that, as Collins put it, "Ninety percent of this had to do with economics." Money was usually the bottom line when employers discriminated against women. In their stewardesses, the airlines had the ideal work force. Few stayed long enough to earn more than beginners' wages, and the savings on fringe benefits must have been considerable. What other company could guarantee health insurers a group of insurees who would never be older than 32?

In the beginning, ALSSA's leaders believed their problem was unique; they didn't see it as part of a pattern of discrimination against women.

Dusty Roads's eyes were opened in the late fifties. She had a good friend, Ann Cooper Penning, who was administrative assistant to Congresswoman Martha Griffiths, a Michigan Democrat. Roads recalled that "I was telling Annie about things the airlines did, and she said, 'You've got to be kidding me. I can't wait to tell this to Martha.' Eventually, I met Martha." Before that, Roads had more or less accepted the way stewardesses were treated. "But Martha was so upset about it," she said. From conversations with Griffiths, Roads came to realize that sex discrimination was widespread.

"The Old Broads' Bill"

At that point, there seemed to be two possible strategies open to the stewardesses. They could try to persuade the airlines at the bargaining table to drop the age and marriage regulations, or they could push for legislation.

Stewardess leaders tried bargaining first. However, they got minimal support from male union colleagues. All the stewardess unions were actually subunits of huge, male-dominated unions, and the union men were mostly blue-collar males who had come up the hard way. In dealing with the stewardesses, they were protective but autocratic. They had traditional ideas about a woman's role and little sympathy for women's issues.

Without the support of male unionists, the stewardesses were unable to get rid of the age and marriage restrictions. It was also clear that no airline was likely to give up these money-saving measures as long as other airlines were still taking advantage of them. Thus, in the early sixties, Collins and Roads tried to solve the problem by getting Congress to pass a law.

By that time, Roads was ALSSA's official, if unpaid, lobbyist. She was chosen for the job in 1958 because she was flying in and out of Washington, D.C., regularly, was dating a congressman, and could count Congresswoman Griffiths as a friend. Roads did her lobbying on her own time between flights. She had no trouble getting appointments with male members of Congress; she was a stewardess, and the men simply assumed that she would be young and attractive. Once through the door, she could often interest them in her union's case against the airlines.

Roads's efforts resulted in one early attempt to pass a law against the airlines' restrictions, but it was a piece of legislation few were comfortable with. Was it fair for Congress to target one industry and forbid one or two specific practices? "They didn't know how to go about this," said Roads. "To introduce a bill that would keep a company from firing anybody at the age of thirty-two was kind of preposterous. It was a very narrow attack on a very broad issue, which was age discrimination or discrimination against women. Eventually, the bill became a joke—they called it 'the old broads' bill.'"

In 1963, Collins and Roads decided to go public with their problem. They held a press conference at the Commodore Hotel in New York City.

Collins wanted stewardesses there in significant numbers, to prove a lot of them cared about the age issue, but it wasn't easy to find women who were willing to take a public stand and risk their jobs.

Once again, the aura of glamour that came with the stewardess job paid off. Many newspapers sent reporters and photographers, and after Roads pointed out that four of the stewardesses in the room were actually over thirty-two—hired before November 1953, they couldn't be fired—one photographer seized the chance to set up a picture that ultimately appeared in papers across the country. It showed nearly a dozen uniformed women, shoulder to shoulder and displaying quite a lot of leg, over a caption that in many cases invited readers to guess which of the women were over thirty-two. Columnist Art Buchwald maintained that older stewardesses were better cooks and were just as attractive—missing the point, that the women had a right not to be fired arbitrarily. Collins and Roads were willing to be patronized as long as they got the story out. The press conference produced sheaves of clippings, but there was still no progress on the age issue.

In 1964, stewardess unions filed a complaint against American and TWA with the New York State Commission for Human Rights. New York and some other states had laws against discrimination because of age, but had nothing on the books as yet about sex discrimination.

Congress, too, was concerned about just treatment for older workers. On September 2, 1965, women from several airlines appeared before a House Labor subcommittee to talk about the age issue; other stewardesses, many in uniform, were in the audience to show support. One of the congressmen on the committee seemed to think it funny that attractive women in their thirties were talking of discrimination because of age. Representative James H. Scheuer, a Democrat from New York, turned to the stewardesses and asked them to "stand up, so we can see the dimensions of the problem."

Colleen Boland, then head of ALSSA, testified that an airlines executive had explained the age regulation this way: "It's the sex thing. Put a dog on an airplane and twenty businessmen are sore for a month." Representative Scheuer gallantly replied, "I would oppose with my dying breath the notion that a woman is less beautiful, less appealing, less sensitive after thirty...." Nancy Collins said, "In those days, we felt we were being patted on our little heads about 90 percent of the time."

The congressional hearing brought no visible progress, and in New York the age discrimination case dragged on through hearings and appeals. It wasn't until early 1968 that the state's five-man Appellate Court ruled unanimously against the stewardesses on the grounds that the age law was intended to apply only to those between forty and sixty-five.

Though the stewardesses' glamour image gave them advantages in pressing their case, they were very much aware of the way society devalued older women. Once a woman was no longer young and sexually appealing to men, she had lost whatever leverage she originally had.

The EEOC: Reluctant Enforcer

In 1964, as part of a landmark civil rights bill, Congress banned sex discrimination by employers and created a new federal agency, the Equal Employment Opportunity Commission (EEOC), to enforce the law. The stewardess unions were quick to seize the chance it offered them, and when the EEOC officially opened its doors in the summer of 1965, two American Airlines stewardesses were among the first people through them.

"We got there so early, we had to help unpack the typewriters; they were still in boxes," said Dusty Roads.

With Roads that day, ready to sign a sex discrimination complaint, was Jean Montague, who was due to be fired by American because she would soon turn 32. The women assumed that, thanks to the section of the new civil rights law known as Title VII, the airlines would have to mend their ways. "We were naive," Roads admitted later.

The EEOC staffer who handled their complaint that day was an African-American woman. At first she couldn't see how young, educated, white women could possibly be victims of discrimination, but she soon got into the spirit of the thing. "Do they fire pilots at thirty-two?" she asked Roads. "Do they fire flight engineers?" When Roads assured her the airlines didn't, she said with relish, "Go get 'em." That's just what Roads and her union did.

However, it took almost a year before the EEOC finally held a hearing on the women's charges in May 1966. Afterward, Roads couldn't be certain how the session had gone, but it was clear that at least one of the five commissioners, Aileen Hernandez, was sympathetic. In an unexpected way, Hernandez played a key role in the stewardess story. She resigned from the EEOC in October that year, disillusioned because the Commission was so reluctant to act on women's issues. Later, she recalled that "Commission meetings produced a sea of male faces, nearly all of which reflected attitudes that ranged from boredom to virulent hostility whenever the issue of sex discrimination was raised." Hernandez noted that the EEOC's priority was race discrimination—but apparently only as it affected black *men*. She was particularly frustrated by the long delay in ruling on complaints brought by stewardesses. At the time she resigned, there were ninety-two such cases pending, and some were more than a year old.

Hernandez resigned on October 10, giving a month's notice. On the last weekend in October, a brand-new feminist organization, NOW (the National Organization for Women), held its founding conference. Afterward, the women issued a press release. Among other things, it backed the stewardesses; it also announced that Hernandez had been elected executive vice-president of NOW, subject to her consent. According to Hernandez, her election was "a charitable, but unauthorized gesture," apparently intended to express support for her decision to resign from the EEOC.*

On November 9, the day before Hernandez's resignation was to take effect, the Commission finally ruled that company policies setting age limits for stewardesses amounted to sex discrimination. Just two weeks later, the airlines won a temporary court order which blocked the ruling on the grounds that Hernandez had a conflict of interests, because presumably she was a member of NOW. In an effort to prove she was, they had a federal court subpoena Betty Friedan, NOW's newly elected president, and Muriel Fox, who was in charge of public relations, and dragged them into court in New York City on Christmas Eve, while on the West Coast Hernandez was subpoenaed in the same way. A lawyer for the airlines demanded that Friedan produce a list of NOW's members; she declined. "We had all agreed to keep the membership list of NOW secret," Friedan wrote later, "for in those early days no one was sure she wouldn't be fired or otherwise excommunicated for belonging to an organization to overthrow sex discrimination."

In February 1967, a federal district court judge issued an injunction that, in effect, erased the EEOC decision on the age question because of Hernandez's supposed conflict of interests. The Commission and the stewardesses had to begin all over again with hearings.**

Meanwhile, the unions were trying to end the marriage restriction, working on it as a separate issue from the age limit. The airlines resisted, maintaining that married women would miss work too often and would gain weight. (Some supervisors apparently believed that with marriage a woman inevitably became plump and docile.) Eventually, the unions brought marriage-regulation complaints, too, to the EEOC. In June 1968, the agency finally announced in a case involving an American Airlines stewardess that the marriage restriction violated Title VII. In the meantime, unions at other airlines had been able to resolve the marriage issue at the bargaining table.

There was still no word from the EEOC about the age restriction, and ALSSA was soon deep in contract negotiations with American with the age limit a key issue. "We were ready to roll on a strike then," said Roads. "I called Martha and said, 'If you know anyone on the Commission, call them and tell them that if they would just make a decision, there wouldn't have to be a strike.'"

Griffiths made the phone call, and on August 10, 1968, the EEOC finally released new guidelines that barred the airlines from dismissing stewardesses

*In 1970, Hernandez succeeded Betty Friedan as president of NOW.
**NOW ultimately did help the stewardess unions a great deal by persistently lobbying the EEOC on their behalf.

for being overage. The following day, ALSSA reached agreement with American on a new contract, and, as Nancy Collins put it, "The age and marriage issues just faded into the woodwork."

From the time the women filed their complaint with the EEOC in July 1965, more than three years had passed; it had been five years since Roads and Collins staged their press conference. However, the struggle wasn't over yet. Some stewardesses took the airlines to court, because they not only wanted to return to their jobs but they wanted back pay and accumulated seniority. There were many individual suits as well as class-action suits. The stewardess unions also challenged the airlines successfully on the question of whether a woman should be allowed to return to her job after having a baby.

Throughout the sixties, class and race were invisible elements in the struggle between women and the airlines, for the unions never addressed the fact that women of color and white women from working-class backgrounds were seldom hired as stewardesses. At the time, most white feminists saw "women's issues" solely in terms of white women's issues—and were unaware that that was what they were doing. The second wave's size and scope were limited as a result.

The Aftereffects

In tackling the age and marriage restrictions, stewardesses assaulted some of society's ingrained assumptions: that marriage was all women really wanted; that it was perfectly natural to judge a woman solely on her looks; and that men somehow had a right to the services of women—and if it could be arranged that the women doing the serving were young, single, and attractive, so much the better.

Lynda Oswald said, "I think many of us who were stewardesses during the 1960s suffered deep psychological scars. We still have a terror of age and of being discarded because our skin isn't quite smooth enough any more."

Roads, Collins, and other activists improved the lot of most women and men who were subsequently hired as (gender-neutral) "cabin crew." In 1985, flight attendants kept their job, on the average, for ten years; they were now required to retire at age seventy; and some long-term employees were making more than $40,000 a year.

There were other, less tangible gains as well. As they stood up for their rights, the stewardesses found that their image of women and of themselves changed profoundly. A story Roads liked to tell summed up the difference. A male passenger once complained to her, "I don't know why you girls should object to being called 'girls.'"

"That's because you don't know the difference between a girl and a woman," she told him. "A 'girl' is somebody who rents an apartment. A 'woman' owns a house."

In 1991, Dusty Roads and Nancy Collins were still flying. Their names weren't likely to be the first to pop into anyone's mind during a discussion of the women's movement, but their victory was typical of the second wave. American women owed the progress they made largely to thousands of unknown activists like Roads and Collins, who tackled a small piece of the overall problem of sex discrimination. Social change advanced like an incoming tide at many different points simultaneously.

DOCUMENTS

A Woman's Right to Abortion, 1973

We forthwith acknowledge our awareness of the sensitive and emotional nature of the abortion controversy, of the vigorous opposing views, even among physicians, and of the deep and seemingly absolute convictions that the subject inspires. One's philosophy, one's experiences, one's exposure to the raw edges of human existence, one's religious training, one's attitudes toward life and family and their values, and the moral standards one establishes and seeks to observe, are all likely to influence and to color one's thinking and conclusions about abortion.

In addition, population growth, pollution, poverty, and racial overtones tend to complicate and not to simplify the problem.

Our task, of course, is to resolve the issue by constitutional measurement, free of emotion and of predilection. We seek earnestly to do this, and, because we do, we have inquired into, and in this opinion place some emphasis upon, medical and medical-legal history and what that history reveals about man's attitudes toward the abortion procedure over the centuries....

It perhaps is not generally appreciated that the restrictive criminal abortion laws in effect in a majority of States today are of relatively recent vintage. Those laws, generally proscribing abortion or its attempt at any time during pregnancy except when necessary to preserve the pregnant woman's life, are not ancient or even of common-law origin. Instead, they derive from statutory changes effected, for the most part, in the latter half of the nineteenth century....

The Constitution does not explicitly mention any right of privacy. In a line of decisions, however, the Court has recognized that a right of personal privacy, or a guarantee of certain areas or zones of privacy, does exist under the Constitution....*

*In 1970, many colleges were centers of the struggle for civil rights for women and minorities and the anti–Vietnam War movement. (Eds.)

SOURCE: *Roe v. Wade* (1973).

This right of privacy, whether it be founded in the Fourteenth Amendment's concept of personal liberty and restrictions upon state action, as we feel it is, or, as the District Court determined, in the Ninth Amendment's reservation of rights to the people, is broad enough to encompass a woman's decision whether or not to terminate her pregnancy. The detriment that the State would impose upon the pregnant woman by denying this choice altogether is apparent. Specific and direct harm medically diagnosable even in early pregnancy may be involved. Maternity, or additional offspring, may force upon the woman a distressful life and future. Psychological harm may be imminent. Mental and physical health may be taxed by child care. There is also the distress, for all concerned, associated with the unwanted child, and there is the problem of bringing a child into a family already unable, psychologically and otherwise, to care for it. In other cases, as in this one, the additional difficulties and continuing stigma of unwed motherhood may be involved. All these are factors the woman and her responsible physician necessarily will consider in consultation.

On the basis of elements such as these, appellant and some amici argue that the woman's right is absolute and that she is entitled to terminate her pregnancy at whatever time, in whatever way, and for whatever reason she alone chooses. With this we do not agree. Appellant's arguments that Texas either has no valid interest at all in regulating the abortion decision, or no interest strong enough to support any limitation upon the woman's sole determination, is unpersuasive. The Court's decisions recognizing a right of privacy also acknowledge that some state regulation in areas protected by that right is appropriate. [A] State may properly assert important interests in safeguarding health, in maintaining medical standards, and in protecting potential life. At some point in pregnancy, these respective interests become sufficiently compelling to sustain regulation of the factors that govern the abortion decision. The privacy right involved, therefore, cannot be said to be absolute....

We, therefore, conclude that the right of personal privacy includes the abortion decision, but that this right is not unqualified and must be considered against important state interests in regulation....

The appellee and certain amici argue that the fetus is a "person" within the language and meaning of the Fourteenth Amendment. In support of this, they outline at length and in detail the well-known facts of fetal development. If this suggestion of personhood is established, the appellant's case, of course, collapses, for the fetus's right to life is then guaranteed specifically by the Amendment. The appellant conceded as much on reargument. On the other hand, the appellee conceded on reargument that no case could be cited that holds that a fetus is a person within the meaning of the Fourteenth Amendment.

The Constitution does not define "person" in so many words. Section 1 of the Fourteenth Amendment contains three references to "person." The first, in defining "citizens," speaks of "persons born or naturalized in the United States." The word also appears both in the Due Process Clause and in the Equal Protection Clause. "Person" is used in other places in the Constitution.... But in nearly all these instances, the use of the word is such that it has application only postnatally. None indicates, with any assurance, that it has any possible prenatal application.

All this, together with our observation, supra, that throughout the major portion of the nineteenth century prevailing legal abortion practices were far freer than they are today, persuades us that the word "person," as used in the Fourteenth Amendment, does not include the unborn....

President George W. Bush Opposes Abortion, 2002

For almost 30 years, Americans from every State in the Union have gathered on the Washington Mall in order to march for life. This march is an example of an inspiring commitment and of deep human compassion.

Everyone there believes, as I do, that every life is valuable, that our society has a responsibility to defend the vulnerable and weak, the imperfect, and even the unwanted, and that our Nation should set a great goal that unborn children should be welcomed in life and protected in law.

Abortion is an issue that deeply divides our country, and we need to treat those with whom we disagree with respect and civility. We must overcome bitterness and rancor where we find it and seek common ground where we can. But we will continue to speak out on behalf of the most vulnerable members of our society.

We do so because we believe the promises of the Declaration of Independence are the common code of American life. They should apply to everyone, not just the healthy or the strong or the powerful. A generous society values all human life. A merciful society values all human life. A merciful society seeks to expand legal protection to every life, including early life, and a compassionate society will defend a simple, moral proposition: Life should never be used as a tool or a means to an end.

These are bedrock principles, and that is why my administration opposes partial-birth abortion and public funding for abortion, why we support teen abstinence and crisis pregnancy programs, adoption and parental notification laws, and why we are against all forms of human cloning.

And that is why I urge the United States Senate to support a comprehensive and effective ban on human cloning, a ban that was passed by an overwhelming and bipartisan vote of the House of Representatives last July.

We are a society with enough compassion and wealth and love to care for both mothers and their children and to seek the promise and potential of

SOURCE: *Weekly Compilation of Presidential Documents: George W. Bush,* January 22, 2002.

266

every single life. You're working and marching on behalf of a noble cause and affirming a culture of life. Thank you for your persistence, for defending human dignity, and for caring for every member of the human family.

May God continue to bless America. Thank you very much.

Working It Out, 2006

Highly educated women are getting a bum rap from the press. There has recently been a spate of news and opinion articles telling us that these women, especially graduates of the best universities and professional schools, are "opting out" in record numbers, choosing the comforts of home and family over careers.

And because there are now 1.33 women graduating from college for every man, the best and brightest women will either have to "marry down" or, more likely, we are told, remain single. Taken together, highly educated women will have either family or career. Half of it all, rather than "having it all."

But the facts speak loudly and clearly against such suppositions. Women who graduated 25 years ago from the nation's top colleges did not "opt out" in large numbers, and today's graduates aren't likely to do so, either.

To know whether a woman sacrificed career for her family, we need to know her employment status over many years. The Mellon Foundation did just that in the mid-1990's, collecting information on more than 10,000 women (and 10,000 men) who entered one of 34 highly selective colleges and universities in 1976 and graduated by 1981. We thus have detailed data about their educational, family and work histories when they were in their late 30's. That gives us enough information to figure out whether many women who graduated from top-ranked schools have left the work force.

Among these women fully 58 percent were never out of the job market for more than six months total in the 15 or so years that followed college or more advanced schooling. On average, the women in the survey spent a total of just 1.6 years out of the labor force, or 11 percent of their potential working years. Just 7 percent spent more than half of their available time away from employment.

These women were, moreover, committed not just to their careers. They were also wives and mothers—87 percent of the sample had been married, 79 percent were still married 15 years after graduation and 69 percent had at least one child (statistics that are similar to national ones for this demographic group from the Census Bureau's Current Population Survey). Women with at least one child spent a total of 2.1 years on average out of the labor force, or 14 percent of their potential time. Fifty percent of those with children never had a non-employment (non-educational) spell lasting more than 6 months.

You could argue that they opted out of their careers in more subtle ways, say, by choosing less demanding careers than those for which they had trained. But the occupation data for these women suggest otherwise. Women in these graduating classes stuck with their specialties to about the same-degree as did comparable men. The vast majority of women who went to medical school were employed as doctors when in their late 30's; similarly, women who received law degrees were practicing lawyers.

What about more recent graduates, those who finished school 10 years ago and are, today, in their early 30's? It is too early to tell for sure, but there are strong hints that little has changed on the opt-out front. Statistics from the National Vital Statistics System show that highly educated women today are having babies even later in life on average than did the entering class of 1976 (and are having more of them). The Current Population Survey tells us that the percentage of college-educated women in their 30's who work has been high (in the 80 percent range) and fairly constant since the early 1990's, although the percentage dropped a bit—along with that of their male counterparts in the recent economic slump.

The fraction in their late 30's who are married, moreover, is around 75 percent and has not budged in the last 25 years. Taken together, the facts—later babies, more babies, high and fairly constant employment rates, stable marriage rates—don't spell big opt-out to me. And they don't spell big opt-out change either.

I'm not saying that all is rosy. These hard-working women still earn less than their male counterparts and they work more around the house. Given their lower earnings, it isn't surprising that some do opt out. But for the most part, female college graduates—especially those from top-notch schools—who are in their 30's are career women who care for their children if they have them and work hard for their families.

These are the opt-out facts. So why is there so much focus on women leaving the work force instead? My friend Ellen, a Ph.D. economist with two young children who teaches in a top-ranked medical school, recently noted with frustration that many people have difficulty believing that "women can actually contribute professionally and participate meaningfully in the raising of a family." But the truth is that a greater fraction of college women today are mixing family life and career than ever before. Denying that fact is ignoring the facts.

Chapter 16

The New Immigration

May, 1, 2006, Detroit, Michigan. Mexican-Americans rally in support of immigrant rights.

Following the end of World War II, Congress began to pass new laws that opened immigration once again. Whereas only 700,000 newcomers arrived between 1930 and 1945, from 1990 to 2010 nearly 20 million immigrants arrived. That number was the highest in any two-decade period in American history. Congress abolished the nation origin quotas that limited migration from southern and eastern Europe; the Hart-Celler Act of 1965 gave all nations in the Eastern Hemisphere an equal quota of 20,000. In 1986 legislators gave amnesty to nearly 3 million people who entered without proper immigration papers. Four years later Congress passed the Immigration Act of 1990 that increased immigration by 35 percent. It was not simply the numbers that impressed Americans, but also the shifting source of immigration. Europeans still arrived, but in the late twentieth century immigrants came from all over the world—from Asia, Latin America, and Africa as well as Europe. In 2009 more people arrived from Africa than from Europe.

In spite of the increases voted by Congress and the President's admission of large numbers of refugees, more people wanted to come than the law permitted. The essay "Why Immigrants Come to America" concentrates on Mexicans, the nation that contributed the largest number of immigrants after

1970. In some cases the wait to immigrate to the United States stretched into years. The essay tells the story of Mexicans who were willing to take chances in crossing the border rather than waiting in a long line. What can you learn from the essay about conditions in Mexico that prompted so many to cross the border without legal permits?

Next to Latin American immigration in numbers were Asian countries. Many Asians, especially Indians, arrived with impressive credentials. They often found well-paying employment. Today many hospitals rely upon Asian Indian physicians and Filipino nurses. Asians with technical abilities also found the adjustment to the New World relatively easy. Yet it is a mistake to see only the successful newcomers. The first document illustrates the difficulties of many immigrants, including refugees. As the first document, the story of a Vietnamese fisherman, shows, life was very hard indeed. Besides the issues of language and education, what else did Tuan Tran encounter in his efforts to build a new life in the United States as the child of Americans that was difficult?

The second document was written by Florita Williams, who was originally from the Philippines. Does her story indicate why she sought a better life in America? Why did she place such importance on obtaining an American high school diploma?

ESSAY

―•◦•―

Why Immigrants Come to America
Robert Joe Stout

Between 1965 and 1977 more than 4 million Mexican citizens entered the United States. Six hundred thousand entered legally—that statistic can be verified. The estimates for illegal entries and the statistics for deportations don't take into account multiple actions by the same individual. As Felix Maytorena bragged during one of our conversations, "Look at me! You see just one man but I am fifty!" He was exaggerating but by his own count, he had gone back and forth between California and Mexico six to eight times a year each year during the early 1970s. During one three-week span he was deported twice, reentered three times, worked five different jobs and got drunk "well, *really drunk*, just once."

Even for non-agricultural workers, crossing to *The Other Side* was temporary and seasonal. Layoffs were frequent, particularly in the food service and construction industries. Canneries, packing plants, beet sugar factories,

SOURCE: *Why Immigrants come to America: Braceros, Indocumentados, and the Migra* by STOUT, ROBERT Copyright 2008 Reproduced with permission of ABC-CLIO INC. in the format Textbook and Other Book via Copyright Clearance Center.

and lumber mills hired only when they were in full production. In addition, particularly during the 1960s and 1970s, many single men headed for the United States to fulfill specific financial needs. Antonio Valencia wanted to further his education.

Although Valencia grew up in the northeastern part of the country he had been living in Mexico City since he was 17. He had a scholarship to the national Politécnico university but couldn't afford housing or books after moving out of his brother-in-law's apartment to make room for his sister's new baby. He spent a week or two visiting a schoolmate in Guadalajara and the two of them decided to head for Tijuana to earn enough money to return to school. At the last minute his schoolmate reneged but Valencia, finding Guadalajara no more lucrative than Mexico City, boarded a bus for the border city.

As he stepped off in Tijuana he was besieged by brutal voices shouting, *"Va para Los Angeles, compadre?" "A Los Angeles?" "Va para la pasada?"* He pushed past, brushing off the hawkers but several of them followed him, repeating offers to take him to Los Angeles. A young woman blocked his exit. "Come with us ... Los Angeles ..." he heard her say as he ducked away to escape the confusion and noise.

The street in front of the station was almost as hectic. Taxi drivers whistled to get his attention. A frenetic young man not much older than Valencia grabbed his shirtsleeve. "Safe ... easy ..." he intimated" ... Los Angeles ... not expensive ..." An older man in a ratty sweater leaning against the door of a grimy barbershop urged, *"Go, chavito,* go. Better now than later. Better you get out of this place."

Unlike most young jobseekers arriving in Tijuana, Valencia was not naïve to city ways. He threaded his way through the commotion, bought a couple of tacos and a few chunks of spiced fresh coconut and went to look for a place to stay on the fringe of Tijuana's Zona Norte—the red-light district. Through a temporary job cutting and loading rebar for a construction site he met a sailor who'd become stranded in Tijuana and who had decided to cross the border. He had crossed once before with a *pollero* and felt that he could duplicate the trip on his own. He persuaded Valencia and one other man to go with him.

Their few clothes and personal items crammed into backpacks they rode together as far as a local bus would take them. Squatter villages—jammed together shelters of lamina and cardboard, car parts, and stacks of ripped up tires—marked their advance along the barbed wire barrier that separated Mexico from the United States. For more than an hour as the sun was setting they trudged along the International High-way as though they were hitchhiking or headed for some distant rancho, then the ex-sailor led Valencia to the battered remains of an old delivery van turned on its side. It reeked of defecation and urine: Countless emigrants before them had huddled there waiting for an opportunity to cross.

Twice as they made their four a.m. dash across the highway and along the fence to a place where they could squeeze through, the three men flung themselves face forward on the ground to avoid being seen by the drivers of cars flitting along the highway. The trio scoured through thorny dry growth and thick sand, holding onto each other as they waded into the murky water of a canal that separated them from a highway visible half-a-mile away. Clouds of mosquitoes hovered above them, the attacks so pervasive the three men could hardly resist flailing their arms and cursing.

For most of the following day they huddled out of sight, sleeping fitfully and wishing they had brought more with them to eat, then they hiked all night through the darkness, paralleling the road at a safe distance so as not to be seen by passing cars. Just at dusk they caught a ride in an old truck driven by a *compa*—a Chicano who laughed at their appearance but said he'd gone through worse tribulations ten years before. Not until months later did Valencia make it to Los Angeles, enriched, he claimed, by his experiences but scarred by them as well.

Estimates vary widely on the percentages of crossers apprehended compared to those who slipped through. Border patrol officials in Tijuana suggested that they apprehended one out of three in 1979 but other researchers guess that four out of five crossed successfully for every one that was caught. Even border patrol veterans admitted that trying to catch illegal entrants was "a cat and mouse game" and, as one reassigned *migra* confided to me, "I was always glad to be the cat."

Although many *indocumentados* like Valencia were able to cross without assistance, most arrived at the border knowing they'd need help to get past the *migra*. Felix Maytorena claimed never to have recruited *amigos* to leave Mexico but he admitted that several of his compatriots became solicitors for *contrabandistas*. These solicitors would exaggerate what great opportunities existed in the United States, explain how much it would cost to arrive safely and put the recruits, with their money, on the bus to Tijuana with instructions about how to contact the person who would then contact the person who would take them across the border. Often these rural recruiters would make the bus trip north with their *pollitos* to protect them from criminal gangs who would waylay travelers or pick up unsuspecting emigrants in Tijuana or other border cities and rob them, for it was common knowledge that many of those heading for the border were carrying substantial amounts of cash.

Getting that money before the *coyotes* could get it competed with car theft and drug smuggling as a criminal activity. The *coyotes* themselves could become victims. Their cash-only business made them vulnerable if they were unprepared to defend themselves. Some carried pistols and most of them set up networks of contacts to decrease their exposure and to conceal their identities. A prospective client had to go through several intermediaries before he could meet the person who actually would conduct him across the border.

Herman Baca, in 1981 the president of the Commission for Chicano Rights, noted that the Border Patrol's hard-nosed policies prompted more immigrants to seek help from smugglers and brokers in cities south of the border. The Mexico City daily, *Excelsior*, reported that these *polleros* earned more than $22 million dollars in 1978. According to *Excelsior* approximately 100 separate bands, some of them with gangland connections, were overseeing nearly 20,000 guides, each of whom earned hundreds of thousands of dollars a year.

"Transporting people," a Calexico border official admitted, "has replaced the drug traffic as a profitable enterprise. Not only is it safer, but few guides go to jail, even when they do get caught."

The *coyote*, of course, divvied part of his earnings with the feeders who brought him clients and often had employer contacts in the United States for whom he supplied workers. For that reason few *coyotes* would make excursions with fewer than five or six *pollos*, and usually they preferred between eight and twelve. A Chula Vista, California, woman, now a legal resident in California, told me about crossing Otay Mesa, east of Tijuana, at night with another woman who suffered an asthma attack just as Border Patrol agents were approaching with flashlights.

"There were eight of us," she described the scene, "and our guide told us to spread out in different directions. My husband and I managed to dive into a culvert and we lay there shivering and trying not to cry for what seemed like hours until the *migra* finally went away. I think they apprehended all of the rest except the guide, who like us escaped."

As noted in the introduction, most Spanish-speaking immigrants did not regard *coyotes* as criminals but as necessary intermediaries whose business was to get them safely across the border. Many immigrant communities in the United States maintained close contact with communities in Mexico, and the two shared their knowledge of who could best facilitate crossing. Escobar Latapf, et al., refer to these interconnections as "microstructures of migration"—persons from the same communities or same trades who grouped together to help each other and to help others with similar backgrounds to migrate. Once established in the United States these interconnected groups maintained contact with *coyotes* they could trust. And the *coyotes*, for their part, took special care to accommodate groups they had worked with before and from whom they could expect prompt and accurate payment.

These *coyotes* "do not just feed off or prey upon the migrant stream," insists David Spener. "Rather, they themselves are an integrated part of it. These enterprises are structured around tightly bound, transborder networks of trust that link Mexican immigrants in the U.S. interior to friends and kin in ... the migrant sending regions in Mexico's interior."

A baby crying, a sneeze, a panic attack, a dropped backpack, a displaced boulder could lead to discovery and deportation. Some *polleros* wouldn't accept women with children because they felt children were too difficult to keep quiet. Others charged higher prices to take women across because women slowed a group down when it became necessary to run for cover. Once inside San Diego or Los Angeles the new arrivals became parts of the Hispanic communities there and risked deportation only if they were apprehended for some misdemeanor or infraction.

Crossing the Rio Grande into Texas presented different problems. The river was shallow enough in some places that *indocumentados* could wade across, or swim, and paddle from one shore to the other on inner-tube rafts. Even so the waters could be very deceptive. The first time that a would be emigrant named Abraham Aguilar made his attempt he tied his clothes, water, and some food in a plastic garbage bag and with it fastened to one wrist, he edged into the water. The current was stronger than he'd expected and the water colder. He paused to catch his breath, then he pushed forward, slipping and sliding as he tried to keep his footing and not be forced downstream by the current.

As he twisted around to make sure he was following a route directly across the river, he stepped into a hole and lost his balance. He was able to push himself erect but halfway across the river, already exhausted and not sure how far downstream he'd detoured, he fell again and panicked because he could not touch the bottom. He tried to swim but the plastic bag attached to his wrist impeded him. Blubbering and plunging again beneath the surface, he managed to release the bag and, half-swimming and half-crawling, make his way back to the Mexican shore.

Wrapped only in a couple of half-rotten gunnysacks that he scrounged along the bank, shivering and coughing the dank water he'd swallowed, Aguilar followed the river until he came to a little cluster of cement-block houses. The residents of one of them laughed at his condition, gave him some raggedy old clothes and commented that he was lucky not to have washed up on the "Playa de Muertos," where the bodies of unsuccessful *espaldas mojadas* sometimes were found.

Twelve weeks later Aguilar tried again, this time in the company of six others. One of them, an experienced ranch hand and horseman, showed them how to tie themselves together with knots they could yank loose if they were being pulled under the current. They fastened plastic bags holding their possessions to the rope in order to have their hands free. Two of those crossing wore old life jackets they'd acquired in a Reynosa *segunda* and all of them went naked into the water.

Fighting the current, as Aguilar had done on his previous attempt, they forged across slowly. To Aguilar's surprise the water in the middle of the river seemed shallower than it had closer to the bank. But just before they reached the U.S. side they slid into water above their heads, where the force of the current had gouged a channel. Swimming and tugging each other they groped along the washed-out bank trying to find a place to pull themselves out. Aguilar managed to grab a clump of mesquite and cling to it while one of his companions looped the rope around a knobby stump beside it. They dried themselves off as best they could, tugged on clothes, and stumbled through coarse mesquite and chaparral until they were far enough from the river not to be detected by any passing border patrol vehicles.

Even having crossed the river they still had a long way to go. Traveling only at night and diving out of sight when they saw approaching head-lights, the seven *indocumentados* skirted the border patrol checkpoint outside Falfurrias, over hundred miles north of Reynosa, and finally made it to San Antonio. The several among them who'd crossed the Rio Grande before jested to Aguilar," It's the first time that's the hardest. It gets easier after this," a concept that he found it very hard to believe.

Some farm labor contractors recruited workers for cotton, citrus, and grain plantings and harvests, and transported them to the areas where they'd be working. Other independent "contractors" solicited clients by arranging safe transportation for them to areas where they would be likely to find work. The *transportista* would cram between eight to 20—sometimes more—men, women, and children into a windowless van or delivery truck. José Cortés, a government health worker for the state of Tamaulipas in Mexico, described one group who traveled over 300 miles in a truck com-partment which the driver covered with manure.

"The manure was damp," he told a Reynosa newspaper reporter," and soon permeated the compartment. Over half of those being transported got sick and vomited the food they'd brought for their lunches."

Other migrants jammed into pickup camper shells, converted school buses, trailers, and rental moving vans. The trips became longer as more and more jobs became available in construction industry and food service in other parts of the country. Instead of a twelve-hour ride to Dallas or Houston, trucks and vans filled with migrants stayed on the road, often without stopping, for twenty to thirty hours before unloading their human cargo in Milwaukee, in Chicago, in Minneapolis, or in Washington D.C. By the mid-1970s transporting *indocumentados* had become big business. So had hiring them for half of what non-*indocumentados* could be paid.

LAND OF OPPORTUNITY

According to official INS statistics, U.S. authorities deported 952,200 Mexican *indocumentados* in 1978. That statistic is inflated because it does not include multiple deportations of the same individual. It does, however, reflect stepped up law enforcement action on the part of U.S. authorities who had been under increasing pressure from politicians, labor unions, and various citizen groups to effectively close the frontier. The U.S. Congress poured money into border control personnel recruitment through-out President Jimmy Carter's administration (1976–1980) in what they announced was a "get tough" policy against undocumented aliens.

Construction crews erected barbed wire-topped walls on the U.S. side of the border to make Tijuana crossings more difficult. Helicopter patrols and electronic surveillance devices alerted border patrol units to possible infiltrations. INS (Immigration and Naturalization Service) spokespersons asserted that entering the United States illegally was a federal offense and that agents no longer would mollycoddle those they apprehended. A border patrol agent shot and killed two men while they were handcuffed together a few hundred feet from the border near Tijuana. Several other would be immigrants died of gunshot wounds and countless others, including an ill-fated group of Salvadorans whose bodies were recovered from Organ Pipe Cactus National Park in July 1980, perished from thirst, starvation, and exposure.

Despite the increased ratio of migration throughout the 1970s the rate of employment remained relatively high within Mexico. Oil prices were up and the federally owned monopoly, Pemex, had extended its capacity by constructing "floating city" platforms to pump crude from beneath the waters of the Gulf. Most workers and business and industry owners and investors were unprepared for the financial collapse that occurred at the end of President Jose López Portillo's administration. The "Crash of 1981" and consequent floating of the peso against the dollar triggered soaring inflation and thrust the median incomes of hundreds of thousands of Mexicans well below the poverty level.

Factories and businesses laid off employees they no longer could afford to pay or they simply closed their doors, leaving hundreds of thousands out of work. Even those who managed to maintain some kind of employment or business incomes saw their savings depleted by as much as 1,000 percent and small business owners, farmers, and the employees of companies that had been dealing in dollars collapsed into bankruptcy. The tightened anti-immigrant policies instituted by the Carter administration and expanded by President Ronald Reagan's first years in office made it harder for *aspirantes* to slip into the United States but did nothing to discourage those affected by the Crash from trying to get across the border. Crossing attempts increased rather than decreased despite the "get tough" program.

The Crash also lowered the cost of labor for firms doing business on the U.S.-Mexican frontier. The number of *maquiladoras* operating in Tijuana, Mexicali, and Ciudad Juarez quadrupled as Korean and Japanese companies set up new assembly plants, many of them associated with the electronics industry. Most of them, like the U.S.- and Mexican-owned establishments, hired only young single women and set stiff production quotas for them.

That *indocumentados* would work for less than minimum wage, and were less likely to complain about either how little they earned or working conditions, encouraged more and more marginal enterprises to rely on them. The majority of places that offered new employment were in the northern Midwest (particularly Chicago) and the East and Northeast. Few emigrants could get there on their own; almost all of them needed help. Supply and demand elevated those who could import and transport immigrants to elite status. Few earned as much money—or ran continual risks—as the *coyotes* did.

By 1970, according to Cerrutti and Massey, over 60 percent of first-time *aspirants* contracted *coyotes* to get them into the United States. The percentage rose to nearly 80 percent by 1986 when the Simpson-Rodino Act went into effect. It has remained that high—or higher—since. As border enforcement has stiffened and become more sophisticated, the prices *coyotes* charge have risen from $150 for a simple Tijuana to San Diego jaunt forty years ago to as much as $2,000 for Mexico-to-Chicago or other U.S. city delivery in 2005.

Benign LaBouyer told me that he paid $800 for the trip from Brownsville, Texas, to Washington, D.C. with eighteen other immigrants in the back of a U-Haul truck in 1979. The descendant, he claimed, of a French soldier who'd come to Mexico in the mid-1860s with Emperor Maximilian, Le Bouyer had lost his position as a primary school music teacher and couldn't pay off what he'd borrowed to finalize the purchase of the house he'd acquired in Tampico. He resisted "may be a dozen" job broker offers before accepting one that gave him names and contacts in Washington, D.C. that he could telephone to verify that he would arrive safely and have a job waiting when he arrived.

"We had nothing to eat but some vegetables that the driver bought us. For a toilet, we had a bucket that we emptied at night. Two brothers with us on the trip—they were youngsters, maybe fifteen, sixteen—got very scared and we had to put gags in their mouths and hold them against the floor whenever we slowed down, or stopped to get gas."

LeBouyer stayed in the District of Columbia only six months. After he returned to Matamoros, he learned that the *coyote* who had transported him across the United States had been arrested. Although persons convicted of bringing illegal immigrants into the United States faced up to five years in prison for each person they imported, convictions before 1986 were rare. LeBouyer said his *coyote* was "back at work" within six months. The *Atlas World Press Review* quoted Alfonso Fuentes Ruiz, the Mexican consul in San Isidro, California, as saying in 1978 that 15,000 "guides" were arrested but barely 1 percent were punished, and all of those convicted were freed on bail.

Many immigrant brokers capitalized on the publicity given to the arrests and deportations to discourage would be emigrants from attempting to cross on their own. Their contact people exaggerated horror stories about *migra* violence and unjust detention to enlist recruits. They also described the risks non-escorted *aspirants* faced from being shaken-down for payoffs or bribes by Mexican police and the dangers to which they would be exposed if gangster bands detected them trying to cross the border on their own. They pointed out that getting to the border was as dangerous as trying to get across it.

Some of these gangster bands were well organized and included members of municipal police forces but most were wildcat gangs of young delinquents who'd given up trying to get into the Unites States and/or who had criminal records on one or both sides of the border. Some had their own informants (or the same informants, or "heels," who directed newcomers to the *coyotes*). They learned which *coyotes* chose which routes, what vehicles they used, how they operated. Sometimes the members of these bands would intercept emigrant groups and extort money from them; others chose more violent methods, particularly when they came across emigrants in isolated areas.

Just as a nineteen-year-old migrant named Luis Pulido and the group of eight other men and three women left the van that had taken them to a deserted spot east of Tecate, they heard a series of loud whistles.

"Back! Back to the van!" their guide shouted, but before they could turn and strumble through the loose sandy soil four men dressed in black jeans and black sweatshirts cut them off. Two of them flashed knives and another pulled a gun from his belt. They ordered the men to step forward one at a time. While the one holding the pistol watched, the others frisked and stripped each of the migrants of money and valuables. They then forced them to get back into the van but wouldn't let the three women accompany them. One of women's husbands twisted away and lunged at the pistol carrier but the other assailants threw him against the back of the van and kicked and beat him. They slashed the van's tires and three of them forced the women to go off with them while the other stood guard with the pistol. Pulido and the other migrants could hear the women screaming and crying as the assailants raped them, then the four attackers fled, leaving the group to get back to Tijuana, moneyless and devastated, as best they could.

Despite that experience, Pulido later made it across the border after borrowing money from his relatives and paying a different *coyote*. Between those two crossings, he made two other attempts and was caught both times. The first time he and several dozen men and women decided to cross Otay Mesa, east of the San Diego suburb of Chula Vista, during the night. Knowing that it would be almost impossible to make it all the way into and out of the canyons and barrancas lining the mesa without being detected by the border service helicopters that patrolled the area, they agreed that as soon as they were spotted three or four of the men would break out of concealment and split in different directions while the others threaded their way upward, trying to stay hidden as best they could.

They were nearly halfway across the mesa when the helicopter appeared, its huge floodlight blanching the hillside and its rotary blades flinging dust, brush, and debris in murky swirls beneath it. Sighting the men dashing ahead of the other aspirants, the helicopter veered sharply above two of them, a loudspeaker giving staticky warnings that were impossible to understand. Headlights appeared on the hilltop as first one, then another Border Patrol all-terrain vehicle bumped along a makeshift road toward two of the men who has stopped running. Pulido rolled beneath a patch of dense brush as the helicopter swerved back and forth overhead.

One border agent came so close to the place Pulido was hiding he could hear commands being issued on the *migra's* walkie-talkie but the officer's attention was diverted and he rushed away without seeing Pulido. Hours later the young migrant made it to a highway that he thought would take him into Chula Vista, but he'd lost his sense of north and south and headed in the wrong direction. A passing truck driver radioed the Border Patrol; two officers picked Pulido up and, after ascertaining that he didn't have identification papers, drove him back to Tijuana and released him to the Mexican side of the border without booking or fingerprinting him.

A few weeks later, when Pulido was apprehended trying to cross again, the arresting officers took him to a detention center, fingerprinted him and told him he would face criminal charges if he made another attempt to illegally enter the United States. For that reason, he explained, he chose to borrow money and make his next attempt with a "professional." This time he was successful, although the trip turned out to be nearly as hazardous as his previous efforts.

The *coyote*, a tall fidgety man who kept looking at a huge watch strapped to his wrist, crammed his charge into the back of a minivan and drove slowly out of Tijuana. He pulled onto a rutted unpaved path and turned off his headlights as the vehicle bumped toward the border. It was so dark that Pulido, on his knees on the floorboard between the driver and front seat passengers, couldn't see either the road or anything on either side. Now and then he heard the van slap against some kind of brush and was aware, from the driver's muttered grunts, that other vehicles were in the vicinity but, like the van, were driving without lights. The tightly packed passengers groaned as the van lurched into depression or banged over rocks. The driver sat rigidly hunched over the steering wheel, twisting it this way and that as he maneuvered past what to Pulido were unseen obstacles.

Flashing lights to their right splayed the mesa with patches of red and blue as the driver accelerated and the van careened forward, almost tipping over twice. Pulido could hear sirens and, behind them, the roar of an approaching helicopter as the van vaulted onto a graveled straight-away, barely missing another car, and sped forward. Twenty minutes later the driver swerved into what appeared to be an abandoned barnyard and shoved his charges into the camper shell of a pickup that would take them into Chula Vista. To the thanks they offered he responded only, "Bah! Like shooting cats in barrel."

Photographer Ken Light spent time on the border in the mid-1980s and reported, "On some nights there were so many people coming across that the patrol was overrun." He witnessed a single *migra* arrest forty-eight *indocumentados* at one time. "Those forty-eight could have jumped him but the didn't." Although desperate, they weren't violent; they merely wanted to get through to places that they could find jobs.[12]

Estimates made in 1982 indicated that one out of every twenty-five *indocumentados* living in the United States had entered legally but no longer had legal documentation.[13] Some were *ex-braceros* who'd never returned to Mexico after the program was disbanded. Others had been granted work permits or student visas and had let them expire. Still others had come legally as tourists and never returned to Mexico.

Many residents of Mexican border cities work in U.S. cities and even more residents of Mexican border cities purchase clothes, small appliances, and other items north of the border. Many *indocumentados* like Maribel Diaz simply "went shopping" and never returned. "As long as you didn't look like a farm worker they [the Border Patrol], didn't bother you," along-time *indocumentado* who later acquired legal residency through the amnesty provisions of the Simpson-Rodino Act told me in 1989.

Southern California, in particular, hosted hundreds of thousands of residents who had been issued short-term passes to visit family members, shop, or participate in business dealings. These permits, called "white cards" or Forms 1-186, enable Mexican border residents to spend a maximum of seventy-two hours in the United States. When they first were authorized for issue in 1952, they restricted the bearer from traveling more than 150 miles from the border. That limitation was lowered in 1969 to a maximum of twenty-five miles, which allows those crossing from Tijuana to go as far as San Diego, but not legally to Los Angeles. Throughout the 1970s and early 1980s, white card holders frequently shrugged aside this restriction, however, despite Border Patrol checkpoints set up at San Clement and Temecula, they seldom were hassled and often, if questioned, were told simply to return to within twenty-five miles of the border.

Those possessing white cards cannot work in the United States but "green card" holders can. Green cards were and are highly prized possessions. Rumors circulating during the mid and late 1970s hinted that there were three times as many cards in circulation as had actually been issued. Probably that is exaggeration, but they often were loaned, sold, copied and counterfeited. Jorge A. Bustamante, the former president of the Colegio de la Frontera Norte in Tijuana, asserted, after a detailed investigation that only 10–15 percent of green card holders actually used them to regularly cross the border to work.

With *braceros* no longer available after 1965 many U.S. agriculturalists petitioned the U.S. government for help and thousands of "Form H-II" admissions were authorized. From H-II workers could be hired only if they didn't displace jobs that could be held by U.S. citizens. More than 12,000 of them were rushed across the border to salvage citrus, sugar beet, olive, and onion harvests in each of the years 1965, 1966, and 1967. The admissions declined after that; between 1,000 and 2,000 entered the United States each year during the 1970s and early 1980s.

Few Mexican emigrants seeking work in the United States knew anything about the H-II program. Most of those who participated lived close to the border and referred friends, relatives, and acquaintances to whoever was accepting applications. After the desperation harvests of the mid 1960s most U.S. farmers were able to contract enough workers on their own rather than go through the Department of Labor for H-II help. A northern California olive grower told me in 1980 that "illegals" were easier to hire and manage than H-II employees because "you can just write their names down and send 'em out to the tress" instead of "filling out paperwork up the bazoo."

White cardholders, green cardholders, H-II importees, tourists, and immigrants possessing fake or counterfeit documents swelled the ranks of those who had become permanent or semi-permanent U.S. residents. For many entrants having a legal document—any kind of legal document, visa, social security card, driver's license, work permit—made both employment and residency easier. In some cases these legal documents were shared by more than one person. An immigrant I met through friends while I was in Los Angeles in the early 1980s jokingly passed off references to a "double identity," then explained that he was one of four or five—or perhaps twenty or thirty—legally admitted "Jorge Loredos." A dark, squat porcine fellow, he'd grown a thick mustache and plastered his hair straight back from his forehead to resemble the Mexican passport and U.S. visa photos the real Jorge Loredo had let him use for what, he said, was a "hefty" price.

"We fat Mexicans all look alike to you gringos," he laughed, defining his entrance through immigration as "casual and cursory" although, he admitted, customs inspectors had made him disrobe "checking to see if all my fat was really me." Using the acquired documents as verification, he'd obtained a California driver's license and a social security number. He said he carried a photocopy of the visa in his wallet, confident that he could explain that the original document was at his work place, in a safety deposit box, or had been lost if he was called upon to prove his legality.

Counterfeit documents of all kinds could be purchased in Tijuana or across the border in Chula Vista, San Diego, and Los Angeles. Some of these fakes were better than others but most served as "legal" identification for an agricultural or sweatshop employer who only needed to see a photocopy in order to hire the bearer. Beneath the inscription *Resident Alien* across the top of the card, the 1-151 bears a photo, fingerprint, birthdate, card number and expiration date. To produce fake cards the counterfeiter only needed the basic equipment that any fast-photo or Kinko's-type copy shop would use.

Social security cards were equally easy to duplicate. Those printing fake cards usually took the pains to make sure that the numbers they put on them corresponded to numbers being issued to people about the same age as the recipient. Periodic raids closed some shops but invariable others popped up and the crackdowns north of the border only stimulated business on the Mexican side. Police raids there netted similar results the counterfeiters were arrested and the equipment confiscated but there were few convictions and fewer prison sentences meted out. The pseudo Jorge Loredo that I met in Los Angeles insisted that the Tijuana raids were shakedowns to force the operators to pay bigger bribes. He compared them to drug busts, where the authorities only muscled the little and mid-level dealers, not the "big guys" who could pay huge *mordidas* for protection from police commissioners, mayors, governors, and Army generals.

Despite the ease with which some *indocumentados* crossed the border with white cards or tourist documents, 70 percent of those surveyed in 1999 and 2000 claimed they'd gone through experiences that put their lives in danger while trying to enter the United States, either from extreme heat or cold or the lack of water, food, and exertion that caused insurmountable fatigue.

DOCUMENTS

Struggling to Get Ahead: The Life of a Vietnamese Fisherman, 2010

NEW ORLEANS—On a normal night, Hong Le, a deckhand on a fishing boat, would be miles out on the water laying nets and lines to catch tuna. Instead, he lies awake in his rented room agonizing over the money he is not sending to his wife and children in Vietnam and the delay in his longtime dream of bringing them here, ...

Officials with the Louisiana Department of Health and Hospitals said staff members had counseled 749 people in the last week of May and the first week of June to "mitigate" symptoms that could lead to destructive behavior.

"Most people are in disbelief," said Dr. Tony Speier, deputy assistant secretary of the department's office of mental health. "There's fear not just for economic survival, but for a way of life."

While state officials have emphasized the resiliency of Gulf Coast residents, who suffered through Hurricane Katrina and other major storms like Hurricanes Gustav and Ike in 2008, experts say the region should brace for long-term psychological strain....

At each day passes, Mr. Le, 58, says he feels more hopeless. "I just wait at home," he said hollowly through an interpreter.

Beyond the environmental and economic damage, the toll of the mammoth spill in the Gulf of Mexico is being measured in hopelessness, anxiety, stress, anger, depression and even suicidal thoughts among those most affected, social workers say.

Mindful of the surge in psychological ailments after Hurricane Katrina hit the Gulf Coast in 2005, community groups are trying to tend to the collective psyche of fishermen like Mr. Le even as they address more immediate needs like financial aid.

When fishermen arrive to pick up emergency aid checks at the Mary Queen of Vietnam Community Development Corporation, a nonprofit group in this city's Vietnamese-American enclave, crisis counselors from Catholic Charities are on hand to screen for signs of emotional distress and to offer help.

"Are you having trouble sleeping?" the counselors ask through interpreters. "Do you feel out of energy?" Do you have thoughts that you would be better off dead?"

He arrived in the United States in 1979. Nine years ago, he married on a visit home to Phan Thiet in southeastern Vietnam, assuring his wife that one day she would join him here.

Mr. Le said he used to send up to $5,000 a year to his wife and their 8-year-old son and 6-year-old daughter. As his family turns to other relatives for support, he is living on an initial payment of $1,200 from BP and whatever aid comes his way.

In phone conversations, his wife urges him to find a job outside the fishing industry. He applied at two Vietnamese restaurants, but neither would hire him for even the most menial work, Mr. Le said.

"I don't know what's going to happen," he murmured. "Any opportunity for work, I'll do it."

Story of an Immigrant from the Philippines, 2008

I'm Florita Williams, originally from the Phillipines. My life in the Phillipines was hard. I worked in the sugar cane fields from the ages of 10 to 12. After that I worked as a housekeeper between the ages of 12 and 16. Then I worked in a factory from the time I was 16 to 29 years old.

The conditions in the factory included working long hours, eating poor food, drinking coffee to stay awake until morning, on into the next day. I was always rushed and pushed by my boss and paid a very small amount of money for my work—about $40 per week. Normal working hours were

SOURCE: "Story of an Immigrant from the Philippines," from *The Green Mountain Eagle*, Published by Vermont Adult Learning in Middlebury, Feb 2008. Reprinted by permission of the author.

from 8 am to 10 pm. When there was a rush, especially just before shipping, we would be made to work 24 hours straight. We would then sleep for 2 or 4 hours and be woken up again to work more until the shipment was done. I managed working there for 13 years.

In 1992, I was married to a co-worker in the factory. He later died of lung cancer. We had a son together. I was widowed for six years, and it was hard being a single mother. I was forced to work far from my son Ian so I could support him. I went back to work in the factory as a high-speed sewer, and later became head of the department of linking machines.

I began thinking about my life and how I could change it. I met a person while riding the ferryboat. The woman gave me a form and said to fill it out and send it to the address above. I filled out the form and sent it. While I was waiting for the response to the form I sent, I started reading books in English, reading the dictionary, watching movies in English, and writing the words that I didn't know, and understanding them by looking in the dictionary. I was having trouble learning English because I had no teacher. The first time I communicated with someone I was nervous because I didn't have enough knowledge of English. I was concerned that maybe he wouldn't understand me. I thank God for him. His name is Horace.

Horace petioned for me to come to the United States, starting the process on June 29, 1999. He miraculously had me on U.S. soil by August 27, 1999. He is a very strong-hearted person, taking the risk of getting me out of there, and he managed it. It took him only two months instead of the usual 8 to 9 months. The reason it was quick was because of the conditions I was working in at the factory.

Horace and I went back to the Phillipines to get my son. Horace is such a good father to him. He treats him like his own biological child. We have been married for almost 9 years, and we have a daughter named Maricel. We live together as happy as can be.

Now my life is different than before. I live in a nice home, and wake up in the morning without feeling pressure. I'm very happy because I can be with my kids. When the kids come home from school, we're there for them. I can do the work that I like to do, or not do anything at all. I'm my own boss, not like before when everything worried me. I can sew whenever I want as I now have my own small business, Flori's Sewing Service. Now I'm pursuing and earning my high school diploma and hoping to graduate soon. I'm hoping to expand my own business.

I am very strong-hearted and determined. Without these qualities, I would not be where I am now. I'm very hard-working and enjoy my simple life. I keep the experiences of my life with my parents as a treasure. It is meaningful and valuable being poor. I would rather live and begin with a hard life, rather than having everything come easily. Being poor, I learned a lot about how to value small things. That is why I care about the poor people I see anywhere, especially those with no houses of their own.

I'm very honest about how I feel and what I think. I manage my time well. I never waste time. I don't spend lots of time wishing I was doing something else. I am in complete control of my time.

I learn better in a one-to-one situation. I do better alone than in a class or group. My other learning styles are verbal, aural, and social. I learn well when talking and listening. My experience with Mary has been a good fit, working one-on-one with her as my teacher. I'm also the kind of person who learns best by seeing and doing.

At this point of my life, I have a chance to address my education. I have learned a lot, reading and understanding words more. I'm now able to add, subtract, multiply, divide, do decimals and percents. It was a good feeling to understand all of this, because I had never learned it before. I only learned by going back to school in this kind of program.

I want to focus on one thing first and that is achieving my high school diploma. After that I will move on to the next steps and challenges ahead. I would like to learn more about bookkeeping, so I can help my husband take care of his business, doing taxes every year. I would like to learn about health, so I can be a caregiver. I like human resources, something I can use to help people. I also want to help my husband expand his business in Canada, and to be able to communicate with people properly. I want to volunteer to be a helper in my children's school.

There are lots of dreams to think about, but achieving my diploma first will help me with any of them.

FLORITA WILLIAMS

Starksboro

Suggestions For Further Reading

On prohibition, see Andrew Sinclair, *Era of Excess: A Social History of the Prohibition Movement* (1964) and Daniel Okrent, *Last Call: The Rise and Fall of Prohibition* (2010). On the Klan, see Kenneth Jackson, *The Ku Klux Klan in the Cities, 1915–1930* (1965) and David Chalmers, *Hooded Americanism: The First Century of the Ku Klux Klan* (1956). For gay history, see George Chauncey, *Gay New York: Gender, Urban Culture, and the Making of the Gay Male World, 1890–1940* (1994) and Lillian Faderman, *Odd Girls and Twilight Lovers: A History of Lesbian Life in Twentieth-Century America* (1991).

On the Great Depression, a good introduction is Robert S. McElvane, *The Great Depression: America, 1929–1945* (1984) and David Kennedy, *Freedom from Fear: The American People in Depression and War, 1929–1945* (1999). See also William Leuchtenburg, *Franklin Roosevelt and the New Deal* (1963). For women during the 1930s, see Susan Ware, *Holding Their Own: American Women in the 1930s* (1982). On blacks, read Nancy Weiss, *Farewell to the Party of Lincoln: Black Politics in the Age of FDR* (1983) and Ira Katznelson, *When Affirmative Action Was White: An Untold History of Racial Inequality in Twentieth Century America* (2005). Especially good are Lizabeth Cohen, *Making a New Deal: Industrial Workers in Chicago, 1919–1939* (1990) and Neil Foley, *The White Scourge: Mexicans, Blacks and Poor Whites in Texas Cotton Culture* (1997).

America during World War II has received increasing attention. For introductions, see William O'Neill, *A Democracy at War* (1993) and Peter Lingerman, *Don't You Know There Is a War On?* (1970). Also see the above mentioned book by David Kennedy. On Japanese Americans, see Peter Irons, *Justice at War* (1983) and Roger Daniels, *Prisoners Without Trial: Japanese Americans in World War II* (1993). On women, see D'Ann Campbell, *Women at War with America: Private Lives in a Patriotic Cause* (1984) and Maureen Honey, *Creating Rosie the Riveter: Class, Gender and Propaganda During World War II* (1984). The experience of gay men and women is told in Allan Berube, *Coming Out Under Fire: The History of Gay Men and Women in World War II* (1997). A revisionist account of the war is provided in Michael Adams, *The Best War Ever: America and World War II* (1994). Two studies of ethnicity during World War II are Deborah Moore, *GI Jews: How World War II Changed a Generation* (2004) and K. Scott Wong, *Americans First: Chinese Americans and the Second World War* (2005). For an overall view, consult Ronald Takaki, *Double Victory: A Multicultural History of America in World War II* (2000).

For the postwar era, see Kenneth Jackson, *Crabgrass Frontier: The Suburbanization of the United States* (1985) and Gavin Wright, *Old South, New South: Revolutions in the Southern Economy Since the Civil War* (1986). Also on the South is James Cobb, *The South Since 1945* (2010) and Glenda Elizabeth Gilmore, *Defying Dixie: The Radical Roots of Civil Rights, 1919–1950* (2002). Suburban developments are covered in Herbert J. Gans, *Levittowners: Ways of Life and Politics in a New Suburban Community* (1982). See also Thomas J. Sugrue, *The Origins of the Urban Crisis: Race and Inequality in Postwar Detroit* (1997). For marriage trends, see Kristin Celello, *Making Marriage Work: A History of Marriage and Divorce in Twentieth Century America* (2009).

The suburbs and consumerism are treated in Lizabeth Cohen, *A Consumer's Republic: The Politics of Mass Consumerism in Postwar America* (2003). On civil rights and the suburbs, see Matthew D. Lassiter, *The Silent Majority: Suburban Politics in the Sunbelt South* (2006). On housing, see Charles M. Lamb, *Housing Segregation in Suburban America Since 1960* (2005).

The civil rights movement has received a great deal of attention. For an overview, see Harvard Sitkoff, *The Struggle for Black Equality, 1954–1992* (1993). For the North, see Thomas J. Surgue, *Sweet Land of Liberty: The Forgotten Civil Rights in the North* (2008). On racism, read Peggy Pascoe, *Doing What Comes Naturally: Miscegenation, Law, and the Making of Race in America* (2009). Richard Kruger, *Simple Justice: The History of* Brown v. Board of Education: *Black America's Struggle for Equality* (1976) is useful. Taylor Branch has written several books on Martin Luther King, Jr.; see his *Parting the Waters: America in the King Years, 1954–1963* (1988). On women in the movement see Blinda Robnet, *How Long? African American Women in the Struggle for Civil Rights* (1997). For the progress of African Americans, see Adam Fairclough, *Better Day Coming: Blacks and Equality, 1890–2000* (2001). See also Terry H. Anderson, *The Pursuit of Fairness: A History of Affirmative Action* (2004). Especially worthwhile is Nancy McLean, *Freedom Is Not Enough: The Opening of the American Workplace* (2006). On the freedom rides, see Raymond Aarsenault, *Freedom Riders: 1961 and the Struggle for Racial Justice* (2006). Another book worth reading is Philip A. Klinder with Rogers Smith, *The Unsteady March: The Rise and Decline of Racial Equality in America* (1999).

For women one might begin with Gail Collins, *When Everything Changed: The Amazing Journey of American Women from 1960 to the Present* (2009). See also Elaine May, *The Pill* (2010) and Alice Harris, *In Pursuit of Equity: Women, Men and the Quest for Economic Citizenship in 20th Century America* (2001); and Stephanie Coontz, *A Strange Stirring: The Feminine Mystique and American Women at the Dawn of the 1960s* (2011). Also helpful on women and the New Left is Sara Evans, *Personal Politics: The Roots of Women's Liberation in the Civil Rights Movement and the New Left* (1979).

On the 1960s the standard treatment of the Vietnam War is George Herring, *America's Longest War: The United States and Vietnam, 1959–1975* (1996). See also *They Marched into the Sun Light: War and Peace, Vietnam and America, October 1967* (2003); and David Burner, *Making Peace with the 60s* (1996).

On recent immigration, consult Ronald Takaki, *Strangers from a Different Shore: A History of Asian Americans* (1989); Roger Daniels, *Guarding the Golden Door: American Immigrant Policy and Immigrants Since 1882* (2004); and Mary C. Waters and Reed Ueda (eds.), *The New Americans: A Guide to Immigration Since 1965* (2007). Another sourcebook is Elliott Robert Barkan (ed.), *A Nation of Peoples; A Sourcebook on America's Multicultural Heritage* (1999). Also worth reading is David Roediger, *Working Toward Whiteness: How America's Immigrants Became White: The Strange Journey from Ellis Island to the Suburbs* (2005) and Frank D. Bean and Gillan Stevens, *America's Newcomers and the Dynamics of Diversity* (2003). On Latinos, consult Roberto Suro, *Strangers Among Us: How Latino Immigration Is Transforming America* (1991) and Gregory B. Weeks and John R. Weeks, *Irresistible Forces: Latin American Migration to the United States and Its Effects on the South* (2011). See also Elliott Robert Barkan, *And Still They Come: Immigrants and American Society, 1920s–1990s* (1996). An interesting book about war brides is Susan Geiger, *Entangling Alliances; Foreign War Brides and American Soldiers in the Twentieth Century* (2010). For the United States-Mexico border, see Kelly Lytle Hernandez, *Migra: A History of the U.S. Border Patrol* (2010).